FROM LEENANE TO L.A.

To Marian – Again and Always

From Leennane to L.A.: The Theatre and Cinema of Martin McDonagh by Eamonn Jordan receives financial assistance from The Arts Council.

FROM LEENANE TO L.A.

THE THEATRE AND CINEMA OF MARTIN McDONAGH

EAMONN JORDAN

IRISH ACADEMIC PRESS

First published in 2014 by Irish Academic Press
8 Chapel Lane
Sallins
Co. Kildare, Ireland

British Library Cataloguing in Publication Data
An entry can be found on request

ISBN: 978 0 7165 3216 3 (cloth)
ISBN: 978 0 7165 3217 0 (paper)
ISBN: 978 0 7165 3227 9 (ebook)

Library of Congress Cataloging–in–Publication Data
An entry can be found on request

Printed in Ireland by
SPRINT–print Ltd.

Table of contents

Acknowledgements

First of all, I would like to thank all the staff at Irish Academic Press who have helped make this book possible. Lisa Hyde's patience, encouragement, advice and guidance have proved exceptionally helpful. I gratefully acknowledge Knight Hall Agency Limited for permission to quote from the work of Martin McDonagh.

There are numerous commentators writing about Martin McDonagh's work and many of them are cited in this book, but in particular, I wish to single out Fintan O'Toole, Catherine Rees, Ondřej Pilný and Patrick Lonergan, who have been most instrumental in the field of McDonagh scholarship. My work in Drama Studies, UCD School of English, Drama and Film (1994–99 and 2006–) has benefited from some inspiring colleagues over the years: Dan Farrelly, Hilary Gow, Kellie Hughes, Karen Jackman, Joseph Long, Frank McGuinness, Conor McPherson, Emilie Pine, Sara Keating, Marie Kelly, Christopher Murray, Redmond O'Hanlon, Carmen Szabó, Kevin Wallace, Eric Weitz, Marilena Zarouilla and most especially, Enrica Cerquoni, Finola Cronin, Cathy Leeney, Anthony Roche and Ian Walsh.

In UCD School of English, Drama and Film, to my many colleagues, I would like to say thank you, and particular thanks to Heads of School, Andrew Carpenter, Nicholas Daly and Anne Fogarty, along with the Principal of the College, Maeve Conrick. Research leave in 2011 helped give this project great initiative.

Over the last number of years I have been lucky to teach a full undergraduate module dedicated to Martin McDonagh's work. Secondly, I have supervised many undergraduate and graduate theses on McDonagh's writing. To all of these students I express my gratitude. Thanks also to Anne O'Reilly, Susanne Colleary, Finola Cronin, Michael Maguire, Audrey McNamara, Iris Park, Noelia Ruiz and Eva Urban, whose PhD work I have had the privilege of supervising.

For many years I have taught Contemporary Irish Theatre modules for the Institute of the International Education of Students (IES) Dublin and Tisch School of Arts (NYU), Dublin. It was a pleasure to work with such dedicated students. Seminar conversations on McDonagh's work in particular benefitted me in a variety of ways.

I have presented a number of papers on McDonagh's work, one, organised by Robert Gordon, in Goldsmiths College, University of London (2010) on the Transformations of Narrative in the Postcolonial Era and another at an International Association for the Study of Irish Literature (IASIL) conference in Maynooth in 2010. I shared that panel with Christopher Morash and Shaun Richards, who gave me valuable feedback on my draft paper. Further, at a number of conferences organised by the Irish Society for Theatre Research (ISTR) I have presented papers on McDonagh's work, Trinity College Dublin (2009), University of Pecs (2011), National University of Ireland, Galway (2012).

I appreciate ISTR members and their commitments more generally to scholarship and performance. I was pleased to receive recent invitations to give papers at Charles University, Prague, Scottish Summer School, Edinburgh University and the School of Drama, Trinity College Dublin, where some of these ideas were first aired.

In addition, I would like to thank those who have asked me to contribute book chapters and journal articles on McDonagh. Many editors of journals and books have fed into the process of revising my thoughts over the years. Versions of these chapters have appeared in an array of publications and the work has been revised and shaped now for another purpose.

Part 1 includes or makes reference to previously published work including: 'The Native Quarter: The Hyphenated-Real: The Drama of Martin McDonagh' in *Sub-Versions, Trans-National Readings of Modern Irish Literature,* Ciaran Ross (*ed.*) (Amsterdam: Rodopi, 2010), 'Performing Postmodern Whiteness in the West of Ireland Plays of Martin McDonagh' in Marianna Gula, Maria Kurdi, Istvan D. Racz (eds), *The Binding Strength of Irish Studies: Festschrift in Honour of Csilla Bertha and Donald E. Morse* (Debrecen: Debrecen University Press 2011) and 'Heterotopic and Funerary Spaces: Martin McDonagh's *A Skull in Connemara*,' *Focus: Papers in English Literary and Cultural Studies*, 2012.

Part 2 draws on some arguments made in the following: 'Martin McDonagh and postcolonial theory: practices, perpetuations, divisions and legacies' in *The Theatre and Films of Martin McDonagh* by Patrick Lonergan (London: Methuen, 2012) and 'Martin McDonagh's *The Lieutenant of Inishmore*: Commemoration and Dismemberment through Farce', *Hungarian Journal of English and American Studies*, 15.2, 2009, 'A Grand Guignol Legacy: Martin McDonagh's *A Behanding in Spokane*', *Irish Studies Review*, 24, Winter 2012, and in '"The Kings of Odd": Farce and Depleted Masculinities in Martin McDonagh's *The Lonesome West*' in Catherine Rees (ed.) *Changes in Contemporary Ireland: Texts and Contexts* (Newcastle: Cambridge Scholars Publishing).

Part 3 makes use of work published in 'The Fallacy of Agency in Arthur Miller's *Death of a Salesman* and Martin McDonagh's *The Pillowman*', *Hungarian Journal of English and American Studies*: (2005), on 'War on Narrative: Martin McDonagh's *The Pillowman*' in *The Theatre of Martin McDonagh: A World of Savage Stories* (Dublin: Carysfort Press, 2006), which also formed part of a chapter in my book *Dissident Dramaturgies* and on 'Playwrights and Gangland,' (working title) in Eric Weitz (ed.), *Dublin City Comedy: Doing things with laughter in Irish society* (Carysfort Press, 2013, forthcoming).

Parts of this book were read by Marian, Ian and Róisín Jordan and by Rhona Trench, and I thank them for their invaluable advice and guidance. I alone am responsible for any errors.

Thanks to the literary departments and archive staff at Druid Theatre Company, National Theatre, London, Victoria and Albert Museum and New York Public Library for giving me access to recorded materials. I am very appreciative of funding support from the Arts Council of Ireland and the National University of Ireland. (Thanks to Maria Kurdi and Lisa Fitzpatrick for letters of support for the NUI application.)

Thanks to theatre companies, directors, designers and administrators, and to the actors, many of whom, I will discuss in this book, for their energy and commitment to their craft and whose work shaped the nature of my project. Finally thanks to Martin McDonagh for such a body of accomplished and challenging work.

Eamonn Jordan, August 2013

Introduction

INITIATIONS

Since the premiere of his first play *The Beauty Queen of Leenane* in February 1996, Martin McDonagh's work has been widely performed throughout the world.[1] Born in London on 26 March 1970, McDonagh was reared initially in Elephant and Castle, amongst a significant Irish immigrant community and later in Camberwell. His two-and-a-half years older brother, John Michael, is a respected screenwriter and film director.[2] McDonagh's father, Michael, grew up in Lettermullan in County Galway and his mother, Mary (*neé* Harte) hails from Killeenduff, Easkey in County Sligo. According to Fintan O'Toole, 'McDonagh's father, a construction worker, and his mother, a cleaner and part-time housekeeper, met and married in the 1960s, in London, where they had moved from Ireland in search of better wages.'[3] The McDonagh family regularly holidayed in both Sligo and in Connemara in the west of Ireland during the summer period. However, any suggestion that these holidays were McDonagh's only substantial contact with Ireland is to underplay, even misrepresent, the complex nature of any diasporic community's relationship with the country of familial origins, either first generation or further back, particularly in metropolitan environments as vast, complex and distinct as London.[4]

According to most reports, McDonagh's first time attending theatre was in 1984, as a fourteen year-old, when he went to see Al Pacino in a production of David Mamet's *American Buffalo*. In 1986 McDonagh saw Martin Sheen, 'whom he had loved in *Badlands*',[5] playing the lead role in a London production of Larry Kramer's *The Normal Heart*. Although his attendance at theatre was not substantial, this was counter-balanced by what he read, his experiences of film, and by what he saw on television, especially television plays.

McDonagh was an early school leaver and spent some time on welfare, then got employment in a supermarket.[6] His parents returned to Ireland in 1992, with Martin and John remaining in London where both brothers set about pursuing writing careers. In an interview with Donald Clarke McDonagh states '"I never wanted to have a proper job," he says. "I had a love of film and a developing love of books. And I hoped that would go somewhere. Studying seemed to be 'studying for work' and there was no job I wanted. I'm sure I read more when I was on the unemployment than I would ever have done if I was studying the classics."'[7]

According to Rick Lyman, 'McDonagh started writing plays, he says, only when he had failed at scripts for film, television shows and radio dramas. He had been working his way through a writer's handbook and theater just happened to be the chapter after radio. "If this hadn't worked, I'd have gone on to the next chapter," he says. "I think it was painting, actually, so I'd have had to beg some brushes somewhere."'[8] Martin's initial flurry of work includes short stories and numerous radio plays. His radio play *The Tale of Wolf and the Woodcutter* was chosen as one of the five winners of the London Radio Playwrights' Festival during late 1994 or early 1995.

O'Toole claims that McDonagh 'had written [only] about 150 of his grotesque tales' during this early part of his career.[9] (Patrick Pacheco's estimate is 200 stories.[10]) And it has been claimed that the BBC rejected 22 or 24 of his radio plays,[11] depending on the source consulted.[12] Factual inconsistency is part and parcel of the mythology surrounding McDonagh's work and the absence of an archive to date to either confirm or disregard such accounts is indeed, on some levels problematic. Pacheco reports McDonagh as saying: '"I was interested in doing something new, vital and fun," he says, "and their rejection was that class thing": "We know what is good and artistic and you're not part of it." "So there's a lot of anger, I guess, in the stories and in the plays."'[13] Dominic Dromgoole notes of the very early plays submitted to the Bush Theatre that: 'the evidence of the talent was clear, but he had nowhere to put it [....] There was nothing remotely Irish about them, nor was there anything particular to say. There was just talent.'[14]

Between 1994 and 1996 McDonagh claims to have drafted most of his plays.[15] In the spring of 1995, Garry Hynes, the artistic director of the Druid Theatre Company in Galway, read a draft of *A Skull in Connemara* and she remembers: 'As soon as I read the dialogue, I wanted to hear it, to the degree that I started reading it aloud to myself. I very clearly remember reading it aloud and throwing myself on the floor in paroxysms of laughter.'[16] Hynes phoned McDonagh and asked to see his other plays. In response, he sent her

The Beauty Queen of Leenane and *The Lonesome West* and Hynes took a huge risk by taking options on three plays by an unknown writer. There was no definite plan to do all three dramas. All the plays are set in Leenane in the early, but not accurately specified, 1990s.

McDonagh was also, it must be noted, developing a relationship with the National Theatre in London. In his programme note to the first production of *The Cripple of Inishmaan*, Jack Bradley, the then literary manager at the National Theatre, tells of McDonagh's eight-week studio residency in the spring of 1995 which produced a draft of *The Lieutenant of Inishmore*. In May 1996, as resident playwright at the National under the Pearson Television Writer's Scheme, McDonagh worked on two more scripts, *The Cripple of Inishmaan* and *Dead Day at Coney*, Bradley confirms.

The Beauty Queen of Leenane premiered on 1 February 1996, *A Skull in Connemara* on 3 June 1997 and *The Lonesome West* on 10 June 1997, all at the Town Hall Theatre Galway. *Beauty Queen* had its London opening at the Royal Court's Theatre Upstairs on 5 March 1996, *Connemara* opened in London's Royal Court Theatre Downstairs on 11 July 1997 and *Lonesome* at the same venue on 19 July 1997. Though initially known as *The Connemara Trilogy*,[17] these three plays later became known as *The Leenane Trilogy*.[18] All three were directed by Hynes, co-produced by Druid Theatre Company, Galway and the Royal Court, London (where Hynes was an Associate Director) and all were designed by Francis O'Connor, lit by Ben Ormerod and performed by Irish actors. In 1997 The Royal Court did *The Leenane Trilogy* from 17 July to 13 September. *The Cripple of Inishmaan*, which is set in 1934 on the Aran Island of Inishmaan, opened on 7 January 1997 at the National Theatre's Cottesloe auditorium in London and later transferred to the larger Lyttleton Theatre on 30 April 1997.[19]

Going from having very little success as a writer to having four plays in the one year playing on London stages in 1997 is a very obvious landmark achievement. These plays were followed by the premiere of *The Lieutenant of Inishmore* at the Royal Shakespeare Company's Other Place, Stratford-upon-Avon on 11 April 2001, and this play is set on the Aran Island of Inishmore circa 1993.[20] *The Pillowman*,[21] which premiered at the National Theatre's Cottesloe auditorium on 13 November 2003, is set in an imagined and unspecified eastern European totalitarian state, and is published without any clear-cut indication as to what time period in which it is set. His most recent play *A Behanding in Spokane* premiered on 4 March 2010 at the Gerald Schoenfeld Theatre, New York and this play is set in contemporary America, in the imaginary town of Turlington.[22]

The Oscar-winning live action short film *Six Shooter* (2005) is set in Ireland, but again has no named locale.[23] *In Bruges* (2008), McDonagh's first full-length feature film, while set in the Belgium city of Bruges, is based mainly around two London-based Irish criminals.[24] Finally, *Seven Psychopaths* (2012) is set in Los Angeles, and its main character is an Irish screenwriter named Marty who is struggling with writer's block.[25] So given his diasporic status and given that most of the locations and the majority of the main characters are Irish in both the films and plays, there is a tendency, often in a general way, to place McDonagh loosely within an Irish writing tradition.[26] His background suggests that McDonagh could be regarded equally as English-Irish, Anglo-Irish or neither of these.[27] In an interview with Alex Godfrey he states: '"If you're a working-class kid and you end up working in British theatre, especially with an Irish background, you feel like you're not welcome," he says. "So that kind of stuck. And if you've got that kind of punk rock spirit in you too, you say, 'I don't give a fuck', and you try to shake it up a little bit. I guess I don't have that as much anymore. But the punk rock thing is always gonna be there. You've always got Joe Strummer in your head whenever you're doing anything. I don't have to be outrageous, but the punk sensibility's still there. You still always wanna be honest."'[28] Apart from being a global citizen, I prefer to see McDonagh tagged as a cosmopolitan, diasporic writer and complex 'post-colonial subject', with a very strong awareness of class dynamics.[29]

FAIRYTALES OF GALWAY, LONDON AND NEW YORK

Early in his career, McDonagh was all too willing to give press interviews to help promote the work.[30] However, some of the ill-considered and not critically measured statements that McDonagh expressed with regard to his playwriting peers, and comments on the merits of his own work, left him seeming to be especially arrogant. That said, closer inspection of some of these early interviews reveal that McDonagh is clearly being flippant and intentionally provocative, knowing that by courting controversy, greater attention is drawn towards productions of the work. Going from anonymity to almost celebrity stardom brought many challenges, opportunities and pressures, some of which account for some of McDonagh's occasionally anomalous behavior which at times even drew the attention of the tabloid press.[31] And as Patrick Lonergan has correctly noted, 'In Britain, McDonagh was presented as the "bad boy" of British theatre', whereas 'American journalists celebrated him as an example of the American "rags to riches" narrative.'[32]

McDonagh admits that the swiftness of his early successes meant that 'his hubris nearly devoured him'.[33] And he continues, "I didn't even have the social skills that a normal person would have, having gone to college or university, so it was just being in the deep end, with meeting people and girls and all that stuff, finding just having people wanting to talk to you was very strange."' [34] 'Growing up I never would have thought I'd have three plays on Broadway,' adding, 'I thought my life was going to be working in supermarkets or offices,'[35] he maintains. In an interview with Donald Clarke McDonagh states: 'Seeing all this stuff rejected when I knew it was good actually bred that arrogance. So, success didn't change me. I had already become a knobhead. But having that arrogance allows you to defend your work. In the early days you get so much rejection and you meet all these people who have an opinion about changing the work. Frankly, if you didn't have that arrogance to stop it being changed then you would be screwed.'[36]

When the Royal Shakespeare Company produced *The Lieutenant of Inishmore* in 2001, he again courted controversy when he was reported in the media as saying that the play was rejected by the National Theatre, the Royal Court and by Druid Theatre Company for the wrong reasons; indeed, he went so far as to say that the play went un-produced because people saw it as a threat to the Peace Process in Northern Ireland. (Graham Whybrow, then literary manager of the Royal Court, publically rejected McDonagh's account.[37])[38]

Equally, McDonagh has been at times a little less than tactful in his comments about theatre audiences, especially wealthier audience members that can afford the hundred dollar plus tickets on Broadway. However, the appeal of the plays in many developing countries and the general draw of the work across genders and social classes complicate his comments on audiences for his work. Yet, such comments do reflect his healthy ambivalence about theatre more generally and its status within cultures and societies. In terms of film, it is the industry and the actions of studios that attract his wrath.

McDonagh finds working in film difficult, despite his successes. In an interview with Alex Godfrey McDonagh notes: 'Don't work with c**** would be my mantra,' he says. 'But then any money person who thinks their opinion is more valid than the film-maker's, I just won't go there. You just don't write a $100m script. If you get hassle from a $15m film, which is what *Bruges* was, that's hard enough to deal with, he says, referring to a war of attrition he had with *In Bruges* producers Focus Features. I'm pretty strong-minded and tough, and even that grinds you down. And I'm tough as fuck about principles and integrity.'[39] McDonagh also notes: 'We structured *Seven Psychopaths* so that nobody in the money field had a final voice. You have to – there was too much of that shit on the last one. They never won, but you don't want to constantly fight a war.'[40]

In many ways, film is McDonagh's first love. While McDonagh has not directed any of his plays, he did take directorial responsibility for all three of his films. *Six Shooter* displays many apprentice errors, but *In Bruges* and *Seven Psychopaths* are clearly very well directed. (He was also a producer of his brother's film, *The Guard* and the earlier short film *The Second Death* (2000).) It would be simply ridiculous to ignore the fact that theatre and film are not only cultural activities, but are also businesses, and it is fair to say in terms of theatre that not many are as creatively and financially astute as Druid Theatre Company, under Hynes's stewardship. Nick Curtis notes that McDonagh 'is a hugely vital and popular talent and remains one of the few people (Stephen Daldry is another) to have made serious money in theatre.'[41] All three films to date have been very successful both critically and commercially.

HAVEN'T WE BEEN HERE BEFORE?

The sheer mainstream box-office draw and award-winning successes of McDonagh's early work encouraged many swift responses to the writing and performances, with some commentators singing its praises, while others were more suspicious of it, or at least had questions about it, and others again were openly and trenchantly hostile to the work. Some accused the writing of being dramaturgically derivative and formulaic; others took grave offence at the regurgitation of what appeared to be the classic and non-evolved stereotypes of Irishness and others again were outraged by how the west of Ireland was conceptually misrepresented. The generally more measured responses one might expect from academic commentators were notable, in many instances by their absence, as assertiveness appeared to make way for unyielding convictions and circumspection for definitive pronouncements.

First and foremost, many early critics identified the influence on McDonagh's work of both screenwriters and film directors, along with the inspiration of television and popular culture more generally The movies of Quentin Tarantino, especially *Reservoir Dogs* (1992) and *Pulp Fiction* (1994) were regularly mentioned as influences, as was Terrence Malick's *Badlands* (1973). The wider cinematic impact of Billy Wilder, Orson Welles, David Lynch, Ingmar Bergman, Frank Capra, Sam Peckinpah, John Woo and especially Martin Scorsese cannot be underestimated.

Cartoons and animations like *Tom and Jerry* and *Beavis and Butt-head* were also referenced as informing the work, as were television series such as *I Love Lucy*, *Steptoe and Son* and *Father Ted*. Australian and British soap operas, like *Home and Away* and *Brookside* and the slasher/horror genre were also mentioned. Novelists like Vladimir

Nabokov and Jorge Luis Borges were also signalled as being influential. Following on from these there are also the musical influences of bands like The Clash, The Sex Pistols and Nirvana, with a special place being given to The Pogues, a band whose members emerged from a somewhat similar diasporic background to that of McDonagh and whose music, he said, 'helped him define what it was to be a second-generation Irish Londoner'.[42] The list of influences appears substantial, sometimes endless and tracking them often can be a futile activity, especially if one is looking for direct links.

From a theatrical point of view, there were also connections suggested between McDonagh's work and that of an older generation of American writers like David Mamet and Sam Shepard, along with British playwrights such as Joe Orton and Harold Pinter. In addition, more obvious influences include the work of contemporary British peers like Mark Ravenhill and Sarah Kane and the American playwright Tracy Letts and his play *Killer Joe* (1991), which was first performed in London at the Bush Theatre in 1995, directed by Wilson Milam, who would go on to direct the premier of *Inishmore*. The work of these peers form part of the *In-Yer-Face* movement that Aleks Sierz has identified – playwrights whose style included a plenitude of violence and taboo violation, people who were comfortable in unnerving, shocking and offending audiences by being controversial and provocative.[43] Here was a London-Irish playwright, writing plays that appeared to be set in a traditional, old-fashioned Ireland yet is linked with a series of writers whose work was mainly urban and contemporary. McDonagh was proving difficult to place.

Comments by the theatre critic Paul Taylor, while not exemplary, offer serious insight into the thinking behind the negative criticism: 'There's something creepy about the Martin McDonagh phenomenon. If you didn't know that he enjoys a genuine existence as an award-winning 27-year-old dramatist who was reared and still resides in London yet churns out plays set in a half-invented rural Ireland, you'd be tempted to think that he was a clever hoax dreamt up by a committee of postmodernist pranksters.'[44] To this Taylor adds, 'Prolonged exposure to his work [...] intensifies this weird feeling of some central absence. Is McDonagh, for all his prodigious gifts for zany "Oirish" pastiche and intertextual Synge-song tricks, several sandwiches short of the full emotional lunch box?'[45] Taylor's comments illustrate again how the work was overly personalised by many. Such negative criticisms, it must be added, were balanced by glowingly positive reviews and favourable analysis, the multiple prestigious awards that came to the work internationally, and last but not least, by substantially positive audience reception.

However, give the Irish locations of most of the plays, and given the predominance of Irish characters, there were also strenuous attempts to align the work firmly with the Irish tradition of John Millington Synge, Lady Augusta Gregory, Samuel Beckett[46] and Tom Murphy, in particular many noted the similarities between Murphy's *Bailegangaire* (1985) and *The Beauty Queen of Leenane*. The setting of the early work in a nominal Ireland is the most strategic and fundamental dramaturgical decision that McDonagh happened upon. McDonagh himself has admitted that the need to escape the influences of David Mamet and Harold Pinter to be one of the key motivations in setting his work in the west of Ireland, a move which allowed him to appropriate, embrace and re-construct rhythms, inflections and patterns of speech that he heard used by his extended family.[47] In an interview with Donald Clarke McDonagh states '"I think writing the Irish plays was the first time I felt properly free."[....] "Until then, they were like imitations of Pinter or Mamet. There is still something of those writers in the plays, but the Irish plays freed me up and I felt I wasn't imitating them so much anymore. Ireland is slightly removed from where I was. That allowed the stories to go anywhere they needed to go. I couldn't have done that writing about London."'[48]

Graham Whybrow, the Royal Court's literary manager, during the period that McDonagh's work was first performed, suggests that 'McDonagh writes both within a tradition and against a mythology'.[49] For Christopher Morash, *The Leenane Trilogy* is a series of 'copies that have forgotten their originals'.[50] Dominic Dromgoole's perspective is slightly different again, arguing that McDonagh's flaw as a writer is 'too much quotation, it is too directly from other fiction'. And he continues: 'McDonagh's greatest talent is as a pasticheur, he is able to produce perfect forgeries of any of these writers at will [namely Tom Murphy, Billy Roche, Beckett, Synge, O'Casey, even Wilde].'[51] (The extent of these named influences remains to be well documented.) But Dromgoole adds:

> The rub and resistance of life is absent here. The slow comedy of the world is not reflected in its manic hysteria, nor is the deep pain reflected in its titillating sadomasochistic narrative structures. As pot-boilers they are masterful, but they are not yet a lot more. Using his great narrative skill and a strong imaginative grasp of theatrical plasticity, he has come up with a unique voice. It's a pastiche soup, a blend of Irish greats, with a pinch of sick punk humour thrown in. Its greatest achievement is that it is entertaining. It asks the audience to live on the edge of its wits, and at the end of its nerves. Thrills, spill and laughs, served up

> giddily on the surface of a violent, cruel, chthonic world. This is increasingly what a late twentieth-century audience wants.[52]

I cite Dromgoole at length here, because I see the same strengths as Dromgoole does, but I would not consider what he sees as negative or weaknesses at all. Firstly, I think it is simplistic to think that McDonagh only gives audiences what they want. Secondly, the patterns, the rubs and resistances of life are very evident in the work and while there is often 'manic hysteria,' it is wonderfully controlled and regulated. Thirdly, both the fast and the 'slow comedy of the world' are evident always and clearly one of the functions of theatre is not simply to reflect the deep pain of living; more it is about finding ways of contesting, challenging and accommodating both the pleasures and pains, the joys, uncertainties, transitions and transgressions of living. Finally, the 'titillating sadomasochistic narrative structures' are but one aspect of a dramaturgical instinct that is always inclusive of other more positive forces, and the heartening perspectives evident in either *The Pillowman* or *Seven Psychopaths* challenge this overview.[53] Admittedly these comments were not written with the benefits of seeing the later work.

All three perspectives by Dromgoole, Morash and Whybrow are focusing on McDonagh's writing as something that derives while not exclusively, but primarily from an Irish tradition, but I would argue that it is less important to place his lineage simply within this tradition, as it is more substantial to see him as someone who has utilised many aspects of this tradition for his own purposes, not simply parasitically, but synergistically, through a connection based on his readings and responses, both conscious and unconscious, to an Irish tradition of writing but also to a culture. McDonagh's connection to this tradition is palimpsest-like, intertextual and dialogical, also partially shaped by diasporic and cultural osmosis, as one absorbs language, tones and sensibilities growing up, without ever knowing from where they originate.

GUARANTEED IRISH

Since the 1980s, and especially throughout the 1990s, there seems to have been an additional surge in interest in Irish theatre internationally. The increasing awarenesses of London and New York theatre companies and producers of Irish-themed plays and the profitability that might ensue is not only indicative of the increasing Hibernophilia of British and American societies at that time, but also of the increasing successes of Irish cultural output more generally across the globe.[54] For example, Brian Friel's *Translations* (1980) and *Dancing at Lughnasa* (1990), Sebastian Barry's *The Steward of Christendom* (1995) and Conor McPherson's *The Weir* (1997) were all exceptionally successful internationally. These works can be benchmarked against the highest international standards of excellence in their own rights and deserved all the plaudits that they garnered. While these plays might appear on the surface to be relatively conservative dramaturgically, they are in fact far more complex.

Almost each of them places major emphasis on tradition, on rural spaces, on a quality of homeliness, dealing with complex family or communal bonds where subsistence living is almost a prerequisite.[55] Most of these works share, with a few exceptions, a basic heteronormativity and display a fixation on alcohol and celibacy. The characters have little sense of their own agency, that the forces of history or industrialisation or wider circumstances overtake them, but that these negative experiences of loss, inequality and subsistence living are tempered by defiance and dignity, by a shared sense of core values and by the consolation of supportive communities. Almost all of the plays gave great significance to loss, death and grieving, with a survival impulse to the fore, which is based more in language rather than actions and the comforts of memory.

Terry Gifford has written impressively about the pastoral and he addresses Roger Sales's idea that the pastoral represents 'refuge, reflection, rescue, requiem and reconstruction.' According to Gifford, Sales's view is that the pastoral 'is essentially escapist in seeking refuge in the country and often also in the past: that it is a selective "reflection" on past country life in which old settled values are "rescued" by the text, and that all this functions as a simplified "reconstruction" of what is, in fact, a more complex reality.'[56]

While McDonagh is not in this same territory, there remains a need to rationalise his formations of Irishness, which does not equate to a representational model whereby his plays are simply about Ireland. They use Ireland and Irishness for dramaturgical rather than emblematic or figurative purposes. And within that it is important to keep in mind Moynagh O'Sullivan's remarks that in relation to Irish studies generally, 'the category of Irishness (Irish subjectivity) is repeatedly deconstructed, questioned, recontextualised and interrogated, but masculinity remains an unquestioned, presumptively static, template for such identity politics'.[57] This comment applies to most but not all literary work and secondly, there are categorisations within masculinity, as Brian Singleton demonstrates in work discussed later, such as 'subordinate masculinities' (R.W. Connell's term), that can also be accounted for in terms of class and sexual orientation and as I do here also, in terms of whiteness.

So, it could be argued that the traditional conceptions of Irishness have always been in process, diversifying and sometimes even mutating, even if restrained or prompted by dominant ideologies. Others suggest that

Irishness has evolved very little if at all, that old prejudices and alignments have simply been refined, tempered by sentiment, re-framed thanks to the increasing currency and circulation of Irishness globally and re-phrased due to the impact of politically correct thinking around issues of ethnicity.

Both historically and contemporaneously, many of the negative stereotypes towards the Irish are seen in the commentaries of many, including economists, sociologists, politicians, historians, philosophers and in work by journalists, musicians, artists, storytellers, writers, performers, critics and social commentators. These expressions were and are generated as much from within Ireland as from without. Northern Irishness is attributed with many of the same characteristics and qualities, with 'The Troubles', sectarianism, militarism, paramilitarism and impressions of the Peace Process from 1994 forward, adding different and additional variables to the mix.

Irishness is informed by references to behaviours, attitudes and beliefs, by skin tone and hair shade, clothing, sports, rituals and customs.[58] On the one hand characterisations of Irishness remain frequently equated with violence, drunkenness, waywardness, religious superstitious, slovenliness and fecklessness, but also, on the other hand, with a warmth towards others, generosity and pleasant humour.[59] There is also the potential of Irishness to suggest more problematically perhaps, authenticity, humanity, sociability and an inclination to contest injustice, inequalities and rebelliousness. Additionally, and at its most naive and simplistic, Irishness is also in line with the sentiments provided by the flat-packed Irish theme pub experience, as a kitsch, whimsical, attributional fantasy. In a way this concept is so open and porous that it can be manipulated to signify almost anything one might want it to mean.

What might be said of the successes of McDonagh's early work, covered in Part One of this book, in America, Britain and in other developed cultures becomes more difficult to summarise or to generalise, when the work is performed, translated or transposed into emerging and developing countries, or ex-communist countries where the relationships between urban and rural, first and developing world, wealth and subsistence are especially complicated. In this instance, it is more likely that Irishness is aligned more with dissent and with blatant hostility or irreverence towards power and authority.

While one can be relatively clear as to the significance of Irishness from textual evidence, it is impossible to be in any way definitive as to how it is vectorised in performances. And with the performances I discuss, Irishness is regularly and successfully tabulated in very complex ways. I prefer to address this type of accomplished work rather than simply chide the ineptness of weaker productions. Throughout the three parts of this book, I demonstrate that it is more important to see the interconnections between Irishness, violence and morality, than simply to isolate any of these variables.

In Part 1, scholarly writing by Declan Kiberd, Ania Loomba and Paul Murphy on the roles of colonisation and ideology in the circulation of Irish stereotypes are meshed with critiques surrounding issues of whiteness as raised by the works of Richard Dyer and Diane Negra. In *Inishmaan*, the appropriation and subversion of Robert Flaherty's documentary-film *Man of Aran* (1934), is part of McDonagh's interrogation, deconstruction and marking of Irishness. The repressive essentialisation of the Irish historically led to forms of 'strategic essentialism', to use Gayatri Spivak's phrase, but equally it promoted an awareness of the importance of a subversive relationship with performativity, in terms of mimicry,[60] mask (white face/ whiter mask) and duplicity, which Helen Gilbert and Joanne Tompkins identify in their book on post-colonial drama.[61] Such an inclusion of a framework of postcolonialism is not without its complications.

Moreover, whiteness as a framing mechanism raises complicated issues in terms of the production and reception of McDonagh's work globally, where the Irishness of his characters serves as a variation on whiteness, whether it is subordinate or 'enriched,'[62] invisible or 'recoverable,'[63] legible or illegible, surface or palimpsest, depleted or transgressive, or legitimately or illegitimately performative. *Inishmaan* is a far more complex play than many acknowledge. Space is an essential aspect of this work, as it is for the other plays featured in this first part.

Una Chaudhuri argues that in Henrik Ibsen's realist works domestic spaces are particularly problematic, as they establish 'both the *condition for* and the *obstacle to* psychological coherence.'[64] Many of McDonagh's domestic cottage spaces are the locations for destructive acts, and a number of murders or attempted murders, where killing brings no 'psychological coherence.'[65] The traditional domestic space is not safe, and is also the location for major transgressions and taboo violations. A few examples will suffice: domestic items transform into objects of torture in *Beauty Queen*, in *Connemara* the kitchen table serves as a workbench for the smashing up of skeletal remains, in *Lonesome*, out of despair, Fr Welsh plunges his hands into molten fibreglass, and in *Inishmore*, two characters are tasked with the hacking up of body parts of three dead paramilitaries in a blood-soaked cottage. There is little or nothing traditional or redemptive about these spaces, as they offer anything but the sentiment, nostalgia and romantic connotations of a pastoral west of Ireland way of life.

Playwright Declan Hughes has been one of the most trenchant critics of plays set in rural Ireland, suggesting that he 'could live a long and happy life without seeing another play set in a Connemara kitchen, or a country pub'. Hughes goes so far as to suggest that the village 'no longer signifies, doesn't resonate any more' on a mythological level. I will agree with Hughes on that point, but while rural Ireland is less likely to 'resonate' mythologically, it does resonate in a different fashion.[66] As McDonagh's west of Ireland locations are not pastoral, romantic or utopian,[67] one must ask also about their relationship with the real. So in order to address issues of domestic spaces and how they might 'resonate' in a way different to Hughes's conception of it, in *Connemara* I bring together Michel Foucault's thinking on heterotopic spaces alongside Nina Witoszek's and Pat Sheeran's reflections on the destructive hold of a funerary consciousness on much of Irish writing.

When it comes to the playtexts of Martin McDonagh's writing for theatre, to the variety of *mise-en-scène* that these inspire, and to audiences' expectations of and encounters with the work, one of the initial and probably most significant challenges facing a theatre director is how to accommodate and give coherence to the basic fact that these scripts initially appear to be tentatively aligned with realism or naturalism, terms often but not usefully deployed as interchangeable. Instead, these texts seem to be infused with a variety of different, sometimes almost discordant tones, idioms and sensibilities, and what can appear as inconsistencies, even incompatibilities, may too easily, because of the contradictory genre signals, confuse or antagonise a spectator's experience of the work. This is something which has huge implications for the reception of the work.

For example, Michael Billington's review of the first production of *Beauty Queen* at the Royal Court notes that 'down to the illuminated crucifix', the hilltop cottage of Francis O'Connor's set is a 'model of rustic realism'.[68] Apart from the performance sensibility, which I will discuss later, Billington ignores the implications of O'Connor's expressionistic use of colour and lighting.[69] In contrast Ben Brantley in his 1998 review of the New York premiere of the same play notes not only the 'merciless detail by Francis O'Connor', but he also highlights both the psychological and physical entrapments of the characters and reads the performance more on the level of fairytale rather than the real.[70] Brian Richardson argues that it must be remembered that:

> there is no comparable, unmediated slice of reality to which any fictional narrative can be juxtaposed. There is at best a more or less contradictory set of texts and fragments that may be repeated or altered. A realistic novel or play never reflects but instead

> reconstitutes its object; no text or performance can ever attain the status of a definitive reproduction of the real.[71]

In my discussions in Part 1 of Hynes's premiere of *Beauty Queen* I follow through on Richardson's argument. I note that the actors created characters that were notionally real, but also artificial, playful and sinister, vulnerable and destructive, inhibited and licensed, repressed and mischievous, thereby achieving a simultaneity that is often lacking or cannot be sustained in realistically motivated performances.[72]

Context is equally a challenge across this body of work, even if the plays are not particularly realistic. However, I am not in full agreement with Fintan O'Toole when he suggests 'as descriptions of sociological reality, these [the plays] are, of course, dramatic exaggerations. But they are not pure inventions. McDonagh makes sure that the action is continually brushing up against verifiable actuality.'[73] Instead I argue slightly differently that there is ample evidence of the ideological circulation of social, material, sexual and familial values, expectations and repressions, the evident pressures of subsistence living, the pains, traumas, pleasures, delights and duties of collective bonds, but that such a circulation is not there to affirm the work's relationship with 'verifiable actuality,' because what McDonagh seems to do is sensationalise and eradicate particular patterns of expectation – the casual links and proportionality of what we might regard as the real.[74]

I deploy William W. Demastes and Michael Vanden Heuvel's reflections on 'unpredictable determinism' in order to illustrate how the plays, and in particular *Beauty Queen*, contest a simplistic understanding of verisimilitude and character motivations.[75] I will further demonstrate in Part 1 how *Inishmaan* affirms that identity is not fixed but dependent on narratives that are never affirmed by either the character themselves or another, and are mediated by various forms of fiction from gossip to film scripts, and obscured and rehashed by a perverse performance of history in the Ireland/England game as devised by Helen McCormick.

Secondly, *Connemara* confirms that the characters are frequently utterly inconsistent in many ways, irresponsible, anarchic, perverse, rude, crude and licensed to misbehave. There is no coherence to the detective work or to any moral framework, as Tom Hanlon's policing methods are based more on the instinctive hunches of television detectives rather than being grounded in any reality. Character motivation is not clarified and not grounded. The illusions of 'total visibility' and total coherence or rationality, make way for impulse, randomness, incoherence and the absence of justification, as this work moves from a performative, unsettling reality into fantasy, as reality and madness almost coalesce. Part 1 demonstrates that expectations of a certain orderliness, of certain etiquette and of relating, and of a certain value placed on life associated with traditional Irish spaces do not hold. Instead, these are disorderly environments, where chaotic behaviours are normalised and morality is tokenistic. Destructive and self-destructive violence, morality and empathy are aspects of this governing incoherence and I start accounting for violence in Part 2.

HOME RUN

McDonagh suggests that he likes 'to write sinister but quite funny guys, who can combine a sense of menace and danger but also real loss'.[76] In relation to *Spokane* he adds, 'Carmichael is all of that, but he's also someone who is very, very honorable in his own crazy way, with a moral code that gets crossed by people.'[77] Crucial to these comments is not only a sense of honour but also an acknowledgement of how individualist moral codes may not chime with governing metanarratives, as these moral codes seem almost unique, like fingerprints, and tend not to be ones consistent with the governing ideologies of first world cultures or significant, traditional religions.

Across the plays there are various forms of violence and destructiveness, ranging from physical intimidation to depriving others of comforts, from obstructing the opportunities of others to the harming of animals, and from incidental verbal slights or psychological put-downs and racial, gender and sexual orientation stereotyping, discriminations towards disability, to the killing of family members, strangers or children. These acts of violence are sometimes narrated as formative identity experiences by many characters and recalled and reported in gruesome detail. But more frequently violent acts are transacted between characters on stage or re-enacted, as in *The Pillowman*, in an alternative, imaginative, performance space.

The violence can be seen to be destructive, revengeful or pathological, also as anarchic, surreal, symbolic, mythic and sometimes as merely wanton. Seldom is the violence justified. It can be heavily motivated and almost unmotivated, premeditated and reflexive. Violence is more problematic as either self-defence or in the protection of others. Part 2 deploys the theories of Slavoj Žižek and Steven Pinker on violence, scholars who take two very different approaches, the former a neo-Marxist one, the latter based on a combination of evolutionary and cognitive psychology with neuroscience. In *The Better Angels of Our Nature: A History of Violence and Humanity*, Pinker traces the fundamental decline in rates of violent death and puts these down to a series of transitions, first a pacification process as humankind shifted from hunter gathering to agricultural-based civilisations with the associated developments of cities and centralised governance, a civilising process from the late middle ages to the early twentieth century, based on 'centralized authority and the infrastructure of commerce', and a humanitarian revolution, from the 'time of the Age of Reason and the European Enlightenment'.

After that there is what he calls the Long Peace, the post Second World War era of relative stability, followed by the New Peace, the time since the end of the cold war and the collapse of the Berlin wall, and finally, a rights revolution, which he delineates from the late 1940s forward.[78] Pinker argues that violence changes primarily due to exogenous forces, but that there is also the question whether through natural selection, 'violence is heritable'.[79] Pinker rejects that hypothesis; while genetics may offer plausible explanations, cultural and social inputs are even more substantial.

Pinker's theory of mind 'is a synthesis of cognitive science, affective and cognitive neuroscience, social and evolutionary psychology and other sciences of human nature'. [80] For Pinker: 'the mind is a complex system of cognitive and emotional faculties implemented in the brain which owe their basic design to the processes of evolution', whereby some of the faculties are linked to various forms of violence, and other parts are inclined towards 'co-operation and peace' and changes in culture and material conditions have increasingly given 'our peaceable motives the upper hand'.[81]

From the Age of Reason and the Enlightenment, one can track the move from torture, burning at the stake, public executions, the harming of animals as spectator sport, the elimination of slavery and debt bondage to something a bit more humane, more democratic, as a more universalist notion of human nature is formulated in rights-based societies. It is legislation which outlawed much of the cruelty and some governments policed this, leading to a humanitarian revolution of sorts, Pinker argues. The (liberal) rights revolution saw the rights of animals, women, gay people, children and racial minorities alter significantly. Pinker accounts for these in terms of enhanced democracies and greater access to justice, increased prosperity, better education, but most of all to the mobility of people and ideas thanks to new technologies, and cosmopolitanism. Such an attitude to change places McDonagh's work in an interesting place by way of contrast.

For Pinker, 'whatever causes violence, it is not a perennial urge like huger, sex, or the need to sleep'.[82] So, he rejects the 'hydraulic theory of violence: that humans harbour an inner drive toward aggression (a death instinct or thirst for blood), which builds up inside us and must be periodically discharged'.[83] Pinker argues: 'aggression is not a single motive, let alone a mounting urge. It is the output of several psychological systems that differ in their environmental triggers, their internal logic, their neurobiological basis and their social distribution.'[84] He categorises these as predatory or instrumental violence – as a practical means to an end; the violence of dominance – in terms of power, prestige, authority posturing or contests; the violence of revenge, driven by a need for retribution, punishment and justice; the violence of sadism in the taking of pleasure from another's pain; and finally, the violence of 'ideology', which justifies 'unlimited violence in the pursuit of unlimited good'.[85] Each of these categories identified by Pinker I will use in different ways across Parts 2 and 3.

In his book *Violence*, Žižek distinguishes between two types of violence. The first type of violence, the far more visible one, he identifies as 'subjective violence', 'violence performed by a clearly identifiable agent'. For Žižek, this 'subjective' violence is measured against a norm of non-violence; it is seen as a 'perturbation of the "normal" peaceful state of things.' Thus 'we need to perceive the contours of the background which generates such outbursts. A step back enables us to identify a violence that sustains our very efforts to fight violence and to promote tolerance.' [86] As he sees it, 'objective' violence is precisely the violence inherent in the 'normal' state of things. Žižek continues: 'Objective violence is invisible since it sustains the very zero-level standard against which we perceive something as subjectively violent.'[87]

While Pinker sees changes in attitudes and behaviours towards violence as being exogenous and setting civilisation on a positive trajectory, and sees society moving towards liberalism as an expanding freedom, Žižek regards objective violence as a systematic and fundamental oppression designed to maintain the inequalities of liberal capitalism. In McDonagh's work, evidence of the exogenous forces acting on his characters, and the dark matter of broader injustices are very evident. Yet, audiences and the producers of cultural content can get so obsessed with violence in a general way, they cannot see how it is normalised and accommodated all around them in their own lives, through injustice, repression, poverty, gender discrimination and racism.

The violence in McDonagh's work is not simply an action or a mindset; it is framed within generic sensibilities which complicate its relationship with the larger world and even sometimes deems that external world as irrelevant. Essential thus are Eric Bentley's and Jessica Milner Davis's work on Farce, and the writing of Richard J. Hand and Michael Wilson on Théâtre du Grand-Guignol (hereafter Grand-Guignol). Both farce and Grand-Guignol combined help articulate more clearly the relationship between violence, terror, horror, gore and sensation in *Lonesome, Spokane* and *Inishmore*. In Farce generally, exorbitant energies are almost always committed to the pursuit of petty or venial desires, resulting in threats to inflict violence on others and are expressed with a degree of casualness and instinctive calculation that frequently unnerves. And when actions displace words, mayhem often follows. McDonagh's two clear-cut farces, *Lonesome* and *Inishmore*, are populated by murderous sons, crazed paramilitaries, teenagers, young adults, middle-aged and mature-aged misfits. My discussions of Hynes's production of *Lonesome* and Wilson Milam's of *Inishmore* will outline how McDonagh deploys farce in a way that is informed by Joe Orton's anarchic dramaturgy and how it moves away from classical farce. Farce is also associated with much of the other work as well.[88]

Grand-Guignol, which was established in Paris in 1897 by Oscar Metenier, is a theatrical style that some critics and commentators have mentioned in passing in relation to McDonagh's work, without offering substantial deliberations on the nature of this connection.[89] For Hand and Wilson, Grand-Guignol 'is a kind of carnival ride belonging to the tradition of popular entertainment, a Big Puppet Show or a Puppet Show for Grown-Ups as a literal translation of the theatre's name suggests'.[90] Hand and Wilson identify 'madness, claustrophobia, infection, technophobia, exoticism, eroticism, infidelity, mutilation,' and 'revenge' as some of the defining features of the style.[91] The impulses of this dramatic style is to sensationalise, much like melodrama, as it includes amputations, disembowelments, crucifixions, flaying, murders, strangulations and voyeurism, while relying on easy and highly sophisticated stagings to achieve its stage illusions. Yet regardless of Grand-Guignol's association with blood and gore it was not always very blatant in its staging strategies.

And despite its avoidance of the supernatural, Grand-Guignol 'pushed the human subject into monstrosity, extrapolating, as it were, *la bête humaine* into *le monster humain*', as Hand and Wilson note.[92] This style is substantially influential in relation to *Spokane*, to some of the narratives in *Seven Psychopaths*, but equally to the productions of *The Pillowman* in London and New York both directed by John Crowley and designed by Scott Pask, in which they deployed a bizarre, expressionistic, fairytale, cartoon-like narrative or re-enactment space for Katurian's grotesque stories that include child torture, electrocution, crucifixion and burial alive.

The interface between Farce and Grand-Guignol helps establish the predominant comic sensibility of McDonagh's work. The production that caused most problems in terms of violence, farce and contextualisation was the Royal Shakespeare Company's production of *Inishmore*. While the production emphasised the play's farcical dramaturgy, its *mise-en-scène* had a complicated relationship with context, as the work was effectively written as a direct response to the Provisional Irish Republican Army's (PIRA) bomb in Warrington in 1993, which led to the deaths of two young children, Jonathan Ball (aged 3) and Tim Parry (aged 12).

McDonagh challenges the ways that non-constitutional republicans (hereafter republicans), in this instance Irish National Liberation Army (INLA) paramilitaries rather that PIRA, legitimise 'freedom fighting' or 'armed struggle', by querying simplistic narratives of historical oppression and injustice and by disputing the rhetoric of blood sacrifice. He poses fundamental questions about the acceptability of the collateral damage of the innocent and the links between republican paramilitarism, criminality and vigilantism. He asks indirectly if there were options such as constitutional politics, or forms of resistance that are equivalent to personal self-defence and nothing more than that.

McDonagh's exceptionally negative approach to republican paramilitarism left him open to a whole range of accusations, which at best saw his actions as a misguided betrayal of sorts, and at their worst he was viewed as collaborative in the obliteration of historic injustices, in his perpetuation of stereotypes of the simian, barbarian terrorist that have long been part of a colonial strategy against any kind of resistance, peaceful or otherwise. For some, the grand narratives of republicanism were seen to be savagely and unfairly deconstructed, while the metanarratives and logical justifications for imperialism and state militarism got away scot free.

Overall, the violence of this Farce/Grand-Guignol style is driven by a strange de-contextualising disposition, as it appears not to be grounded necessarily in anything that could be again aligned with authentic psychological motives or serve as simply being indicative of broader social or conflictual dynamics. However, it is reductive, even inappropriate, if one simply identifies the violence as cartoon-like or as a form of inadequate postmodern violence, because there are sensibilities and other awarenesses intermingling and co-habiting, which are plucked from archetype, from the unconscious formulations of fairy tales as I will argue later in Part 3. The deeds of violence are often associated with a failure to discriminate between the incidental and the significant, in terms of what prompts the actions, thus keeping in mind the lack of causal determinism I will raise in Part 1.

PLAYING WITH FIRE

In dealing with characters who struggle with morality, violence and justice, McDonagh is prompted to express the following:

> Well, we're all cruel, aren't we? We're all extreme in one way or another at times, and that's what drama, since the Greeks, has dealt with. I hope the overall view isn't just that, though, or I've failed in my writing. There have to be moments when you glimpse something decent, something life-affirming even in the most twisted character. That's where the real art lies. See, I always suspect characters who are painted as lovely, decent human beings. I would always question where the darkness lies.[93]

Shaun Richards maintains that 'what is most striking about *The Leenane Trilogy* is the absence of any informing moral structure on which authority itself rests'.[94] The lack of an authoritative 'moral structure' is something that clearly irks many others as well. However, Fintan O'Toole's position on this is different, claiming that the world of *The Leenane Trilogy* is:

> ... a version of one of the great mythic landscapes – the world before morality. It is the ancient Greece of *The Oresteia* – a cycle of death and revenge before the invention of justice. It is, perhaps more to the point, the Wild West of John Ford's westerns or Cormac McCarthy's novels, a raw frontier beyond civilization.[95]

While the dramatic universe might be regarded by O'Toole as 'before morality', equally it could be seen as being after very narrow forms of morality or between moralities. Either way, the morality of the work seems, on the one hand, postmodern in its parodic consistency with the sentiments of and morally motivated punishments of characters in soap opera, detective series, films and popular narratives, and on the other, an apparently older worldly and curious engagement with the moral tenets of Catholicism in particular, despite the ongoing sidelining or rejection of its teachings. *In Bruges* is a particularly good example.

In *Lonesome*, attitudes to life can be seen as much in the responses of Coleman and Valene to the death of their father as in their investment in the attainments of the local under-12's girl's gaelic football team, a team that can do no wrong even as they cause mayhem whenever they play. In *Lonesome*, Valene surrounds himself with religious icons, but for him nothing appears earthed. The guides and markers to their worlds are provided in the main, not so much by the moral framework of religion for which the characters have a surface affection and little understanding, but more by the values of popular culture, television series, women's magazines and comics – *Hill Street Blues*, *Alias Smith and Jones*, *Woman's Way*, *Take a Break*, *Bella* and *Spider Man*.

In addition, one can recognise how popular culture can be self-validating in terms of personal values, as it regularly distinguishes between what is normal and abnormal. However, in the world of the brothers, and with almost all of the characters in the plays and the films, dysfunctionality remains the norm, different to most narratives of supportive families and sacrifices made for friends or neighbours found in many women's magazines for instance, to which they are addicted.

The Connor brothers have great difficulty in having a basic sympathy for a woman like Maryjohnny, who is suffering with Alzheimer's disease, no concern for what drove Tom Hanlon to commit suicide or for the trauma of the near demented Fr Welsh, in the aftermath of Tom's suicide. At best, Valene can feign to 'bat a big eye'. (p.150) Later, on the discovery that they have been mocking a priest, who has just killed himself, Coleman is prompted to reconsider his behaviour a little; 'I suppose he must've been upset o'er something,' is all that he can muster. (p. 178) (Kid says a similar thing about Mrs Dooley's suicide in *Six Shooter*.) The information and consumerist agenda that guides much of popular culture in *Lonesome* ensures the ideological dissemination of conservative values, which are humane and empathetic in identification and sentiment only, and not with the ability to complete the empathy cycle.

While in this part I utilise the work of a a range of theorists to discuss issues of fairytales, morality, psychopathology, empathy and non-reciprocated altruism, it is never done with the idea that the characters are in any way akin to human figures – rather they are defined by actions and language, character type and dramaturgical function. While I am talking about drama and characters, I believe that the studies of humankind can inform our thinking and understanding of McDonagh's characters. Morality, empathy, self-control and reason are the 'Better Angels' according to Pinker. Here 'the parts of the brain that restrain our darker impulses were also standard equipment in our ancestors who kept slaves, burned witches and beat children, so they clearly don't make people good by default.'[96]

Alongside Pinker's taxonomy of moral sense, I utilise Bruno Bettelheim's classic book *The Uses of Enchantment: The Meaning and Importance of Fairy Tales* along with Simon Baron-Cohen's *Zero Degrees of Empathy: A New Theory of Human Cruelty*, which examines the social, environmental, biological and neurological variables that provide individuals with an empathy. Bettelheim's book is great at teasing out in relation to fairy tales the mechanisms of a child's mind, in terms of childish need, maturation and choices and decisions made. For Bettelheim, 'Action takes the place of understanding for a child, and this becomes increasingly true the more strongly he feels [....] the child does not experience anger as anger, but only as an impulse to hit, to destroy, to keep silent. Not before puberty do we begin to recognise our emotions for what they are without immediately acting on them, or wishing to do so.'[97]

Many of McDonagh's characters are locked into patterns of impulsive, destructive confrontations, of instant retorts and reactions and seem incapable of either seeing danger or the consequences to their actions. Bettelheim claims that for most individuals, a 'growth process begins with the resistance to the parents and fear of growing up, and ends when youth has truly found itself, achieved psychological independence and moral maturity'.[98] While there may not be absolute clarity between a beginning resistance and some sort of end point to the processes that Bettelheim articulates, most of the characters in the plays have not advanced much beyond resistance and defiance, as infatuation and sensation rather than 'independence and moral maturity' drive these characters forward.

As is the case with the fairytale characters Hansel and Gretel, there is as Bettelheim notes, 'the need to transcend a primitive orality, symbolized by the children's infatuation with the gingerbread house'.[99] In the fixation on sweets in *The Cripple of Inishmaan* and on food in both *Beauty Queen* and *Lonesome*, it seems as if that 'primitive orality' phase has not been transcended. Thus psychoanalytically, Bettelheim continues that the challenge of living ultimately is to whether to be governed by the pleasure or reality principles, the former 'drives us to gain immediate satisfaction of our wants or seek violent revenge for our frustrations, even on those who have nothing to do with them' and the latter, 'to which we must be willing to accept many frustrations in order to gain lasting rewards'.[100] The Connor brothers, for example, cannot let go of the pleasure principle in that sense, but are additionally denied a range of pleasures by means of how they are incited to live, making this interplay between pleasure and reality principles especially complex. Empathy can be regarded as one of the fundamental indicators of maturation and evidence of a looking beyond the self.[101]

More than most commentators Pinker is tougher on empathy: for him, empathy is 'a sentimental ideal', extolled in catchphrases (what makes the world go round, what the world needs now, all you need) but overrated as a reducer of violence, as 'prudence, reason, fairness, self-control, norms and taboos and conceptions of human rights' are just as important.[102] For Pinker, 'Today's empathy craze has been set off by scrambling the various senses of the word *empathy*. The confusion is crystallized in the meme that uses *mirror neurons* as a synonym for *sympathy*, in the sense of compassion.'[103] Pinker disassociates empathy from the notion of an 'altruistic concern for others', the kind of 'pretending to be them, feeling what they are feeling, walking a mile in their moccasins, taking their vantage point'.[104] However, Baron-Cohen's definition of empathy is different to Pinker's, but it has the same emphasis on 'altruistic concerns', noting that for individuals 'Empathy occurs when we suspend our single-minded focus of attention, and instead adopt a double-minded focus of attention,' adding that, 'Empathy is our ability to identify what someone else is thinking or feeling, and to respond to their thoughts and feelings with an appropriate emotion.'[105] That way one needs to distinguish between 'recognition and response'. Baron-Cohen identifies an 'empathy spectrum,' along which and at either end of the spectrum there are individuals with very high levels of empathy, or hyperempathy, and also those with little or zero empathy.

For Baron-Cohen then 'Zero degrees of empathy means you have no awareness of how you come across to others, how to interact with others, or how to anticipate their feelings or reactions.'[106] Baron-Cohen adds that at this extreme it is 'a lonely kind of existence, a life best misunderstood, at worst condemned as selfish. It means you have no brakes on your behaviour, leaving you free to pursue any object of your desires, or to express any thought in your mind, without considering the impact of your actions or words on another person.'[107]

Clearly, many of McDonagh's characters, both male and female, appear to have little or no impulse control and there seems to be 'no brakes' to be applied to their behaviours. As Baron-Cohen suggests, because one cannot successfully connect with others, on any level, whether it is a simple conversation, tasks that require teamwork, the expression of collective aspirations and values, or the acknowledgement of personal ambitions in terms of intimacy. The pathological Kid in *Six Shooter* and Harry Waters in *In Bruges* display many characteristics and behaviours that are consistent with Psychopathic Personality Disorder or Zero Empathy. In particular, Ray's grief and guilt in *In Bruges*, after he accidently kills a child in the process of murdering a priest, are especially significant in relation to empathy and in how he differs from the Kid and Harry or Mairead and Padraic in *Inishmore*. In addition, the film also blends a counterfeit gangland system of justice with a blended Christian/fairytale perspective on punishment, judgement and damnation.

Seven Psychopaths' main character Marty wants to move away from a form of screenwriting that is obsessed with psychopathic violence, but the movie ends up confirming the impossibility of avoiding such a fixation. The film is also about the processes of writing and drafting, and pushes ideas of inspiration, originality, intertexuality, plagiarism and pastiche in many directions, as irony comes to the fore, while also raising the notion of the writer not as a creative force but as an exploiter or voyeur, watching and waiting to manipulate the trauma and mayhem of others for creative purposes. The film seems to be a response to many of the issues raised in *The Pillowman* as to the nature of writing, in terms of inspiration, autobiography and formative experiences.

Additionally, in Part 3 there are general connections to be made between self-harm, suicidal behaviors and self-sacrifice across the plays generally and both Hans's final narrative in *Seven Psychopaths* and Katurian's final story from beyond the grave in *The Pillowman* centralise self-sacrifice in optimistic, almost heroic terms, that cannot be undermined by either the provisionality or irony of a postmodern sensibility. Thus, issues of sympathy, self-sacrifice and altruism emerge in a way very different from the earlier plays as the characters are in a morally complex and confused place of sorts. For Pinker, 'a key insight of evolutionary psychology is that human cooperation and the social emotions that support it, such as sympathy, trust, gratitude, guilt, and anger were selected because they allow people to flourish in positive-sum games'.[108] He proposes that humans are neither innately good nor evil, but are equipped with motives that can orient them away from violence and towards cooperation and altruism, through empathy, self-control, reason and moral sense formed by cultural norms and taboos that determine interactions.[109] Part 3 considers the impact of positive sum gains, not so much based on the prisoner's dilemma (in terms of defections/co-operation) that is central to Pinker's arguments, but the pacifist's altruistic dilemma. If the early plays almost sideline the challenges of altruism, the later ones foreground it in especially complex ways.

OVERVIEW

The subtitle of this book makes reference to the setting for *The Leenane Trilogy*, but it is an imagined, fictionalised and sensationalised place, with little or nothing to do with the real village. *Seven Psychopaths* opens with two characters under the iconic sign of L.A.'s Hollywood and the film interrogates the role of the film industry in shaping both writing practices and a popular cultural consciousness: it deconstructs its tricks of the trade, its formulae and templates, how it markets its products, how it fascinates and influences global audiences through its emphasis on sensation, romance and vicarious pleasures, and how it makes use of psychopathology and violence. (There are also the real spaces of Spokane and Bruges and the indeterminate fictional spaces of Tarlington and Kamenice.) Not only do the plays make reference to television programmes, films and actors, but on occasion, some work is at the fringes of a film world as in *Inishmaan* and *In Bruges*, both the city and the film in the making serve as a *mise-en-abyme*.

Television detective series mould an understanding of the world of the characters and romantic and temporary departures in train stations from an endless list of films shape Maureen's narration of a deluded love scene in *Beauty Queen*. So throughout this book a myth of the west of Ireland is deconstructed, and Hollywood's general mythologising of violence and false enabling justice is also interrogated.

The intentions of this book are to be especially innovative in terms of the various theoretical frames brought to bear on both the texts and performances, and where theoretical arguments need to be made I hope I do so in ways that are readable and comprehensive. Decisions had to be made in terms of cohesiveness to cluster the plays into three parts and to start discussions in one part that are continued on at a later stage, leaving the initial discussions incomplete of themselves. While I do make links across the three parts, I try to avoid making too many regular comparisons across the plays, and instead assume that once an earlier point is made, and when there are obvious continuities, it is sometimes unnecessary to remind the reader of them again. While I often draw on the increasing mass of critical commentary currently out there about McDonagh's output to date, I am not inclined to contest much of this work with any great rigour, for there is much with which I would disagree, so I am happier to make my own arguments.

I come to the published plays and to a series of performances – many of the premieres – as a spectator first, and a theatre scholar second. I tender selective snapshots and limited glimpses into what I see as the key textual and dramaturgical patterns, anomalies, tensions and potentials in the work. I make use of productions of the work that I have seen.[110] When I make reference to a particular production in many instances I use the endnotes to contrast it with other productions that I have seen. As Patrice Pavis notes *mise-en-scène* needs not to be tied to the intentionality of those who create it as, 'it is based very much on the end product of working processes, however incomplete and disorganised it may be'. Additionally, he argues *mise-en-scène* is not only about 'production', it is equally about 'reception' as it 'never comes ready-made and complete'.[111] I approach the film work as a dedicated fan of the screen rather than as any sort of proficient expert in the field, where I rely more on experience, instinct and intuition.

As for the relationship between text and performance, performance is not simply derived from a text, and the text is not a blue print which mobilises a performance.[112] Equally, the performance does not contain the text or simply stage the text, and while all productions and all individual performance are independent in many ways of the text, they are still informed, even controlled by dominant textual and tonal imperatives, so those cannot be displaced. As W.B. Worthen asks 'What are dramatic performances performances *of*?'[113] 'The text is absorbed into the multifarious verbal and non-verbal discourses of theatrical production, transformed into an entirely incommensurable thing, an event', is his response.[114]

And in that absorption, Worthen asks 'How can dramatic performance be conceived not as the performance of the text but as an act of iteration, an utterance, a surrogate standing in that positions, uses, signifies the text within the citational practices of performance.'[115] (Pavis's work offers an excellent theorisation of the relationship between both, and on some of it I would disagree.[116]) My own view is that texts and performances are two very different things, yet they share a relationship partially based on causality, but also on the ability of *mise-en-scène* to facilitate, accentuate, contradict, interrogate, undermine, ignore, supplement, foreground or repress aspects of its source text. At the end of the day it is a performance of a playscript written by a playwright who is seen as the initial source of the work, however it is staged, and secondly, the legal issues of rights and permissions give the writer a fair degree of control over productions of the work.

In terms of audiences, as Helen Freshwater notes, 'The common tendency to refer to an audience as "it" and, by extension, to think of this "it" as a single entity, or a collective, risks obscuring the multiple contingencies of subjective response, context and environment which condition an individual's interpretation of a particular performance event.'[117] Nationality, age, gender, ethnicity, class, personal mood, biases, attention span, disposition towards writer, actors, director, theatre company, theatre building, attitudes towards certain genres and novelty, one's relationship, if any, with the people with whom one experiences a performance, the time and day of the experience, what one has heard or read about the show before seeing it, one's seat in the auditorium, the price paid for the ticket and the food and alcohol one has consumed prior to the event – these all impact on reception.[118] When I cite either the responses of theatre reviewers or indicate the responses of audiences, I accept that not only is each performance unique, but it is also individualised in the mind and bodies of the spectator, so there can be no homogenous audience, and no ideal spectator.

While McDonagh has directed all of his three films to date, the various approaches of directors John Crowley, Wilson Milam and in particular Garry Hynes to the work, and their collaborators, will be essential to my analysis. Hynes's role in the development of the early scripts has been well noted, without anyone thus far tracking revisions and the details of such inputs through the various drafts of the script. Additionally, the contributions of two scenographers, Scott Pask in his collaborations with Crowley, and Francis O'Connor's work with Hynes and Milam, have been hugely influential in terms of my experiences and responses to the work. This book recognises the creative inputs of a range of other theatre artists, like lighting designers Ben Ormerod and Hugh Vanstone, sound designer Paul Arditti and composer Paddy Cunneen.

The extraordinary acting performances that are discussed throughout this publication are also noted and all have contributed to my responses to the work. These would include brilliant and often award-winning performances by Marie Mullen, Anna Manahan, Mick Lally, David Wilmot, Brián F. O'Byrne, Maelíosa Stafford, Dawn Bradfield, Tom Murphy, Peter McDonald, Elaine Cassidy, Domhnall Gleeson, Lalor Roddy, Frank McCusker, Kelly Condon, Aaron Monaghan, Tadgh Murphy, Dearbhla Molloy, David Pearse, David Tennant, Jim Broadbent, Rúaidhrí Conroy, Colin Farrell, Brendan Gleeson, Ralph Fiennes, Anthony Mackie, Sam Rockwell, Linda Bright Clay and Christopher Walken.

The fact that McDonagh's work has had such acting talent at its disposal speaks not only to how his work draws actors of great standing, but also indicates their willingness to embrace the very obvious challenges of the dramaturgy and of performing regularly across a production run. Since 1996, McDonagh has amassed a critical mass of work, which is not only performed regularly around the work, but is present on reading lists for second and third level students internationally. I hope that some of the challenges, dilemmas and pleasures I have had as a reader, spectator, critic, and as a teacher of this work carry through in the discussions that are to follow.

Endnotes

1 Patrick Lonergan confirms that 'his plays have been translated into more than 40 languages'. See *The Theatre and Films of Martin McDonagh* (London: Methuen, 2012), p.xvi.

2 John Michael wrote the script for *Ned Kelly* (2003), which is directed by Gregor Jordan and stars Heath Ledger and more recently he is the writer/director of the multi-award winning *The Guard* (2011), which has Brendan Gleeson, Don Cheadle, Mark Strong, David Wilmot and Liam Cunningham amongst its cast. Nick Curtis notes that '*The Pillowman*, with its depiction of an author with a mentally impaired brother, seemed to me to be full of sibling in-jokes and cheeky fraternal slurs.' See 'Brit's short rise to fame', *Evening Standard*, 7 March 2006, http://www.thisislondon.co.uk/film/article-21913927-brits-short-rise-to-fame.do (Access 23/2/2013)

3 F. O'Toole, 'A Mind in Connemara: The Savage World of Martin McDonagh', *New Yorker* 6 March, 2006, http://www.newyorker.com/archive/2006/03/06/060306fa_fact_otoole (Accessed 10/10/2009)

4 Diasporic communities not only have multifaceted identities, but they comprise temporary, cyclical or permanent residencies and traditionally have included skilled and unskilled workers, domestic servants, nurses, navvies and people employed in the services sectors. There were few white-collar professionals. As Liam Harte puts it, there is a fundamental need to purge 'any lingering traces of the myth of homogeneity that clings to the diffuse entity "the Irish in Britain".' See L. Harte, *The Literature of the Irish in Britain: Autobiography and Memoir, 1725–2001* (London: Palgrave Macmillan 2009), p.xix.

5 See O'Toole, 'A Mind in Connemara'.

6 Eventually he 'got a part-time job as an administrative assistant in the Department of Trade and Industry, but he drifted into his early twenties without acquiring either a girlfriend or a career'. Ibid.

7 D. Clarke, 'Psycho thriller', *The Irish Times*, 7 December 2012, http://www.irishtimes.com/newspaper/theticket/2012/1207/1224327589235.html (Accessed 7/12/2012)

8 R. Lyman, 'Most Promising (and Grating) Playwright', *New York Times*, 25 January 1998, http://www.nytimes.com/1998/01/25/magazine/most-promising-and-grating-playwright.html?pagewanted=all&src=pm (Accessed 20/11/11)

9 See O'Toole, 'A Mind in Connemara', p.44.

10 P. Pacheco, 'Laughing Matters', *The Los Angeles Times*, 22 May 2005, http://articles.latimes.com/2005/may/22/entertainment/ca-pillowman22 (Accessed 14/9/2011)

11 David Gritten reports McDonagh as saying '"The BBC puts on turgid, middle-class, humdrum, whiny stuff. I was trying to change their output in a major way, so it was natural for them to reject me."' See 'The Enigma of South London', *Los Angeles Times*, 25 October 1998, http://articles.latimes.com/1998/oct/25/entertainment/ca-35842 (Accessed 22/8/2011)

12 On these radio plays Michael Coveney reports in 1996: 'each and every one [...] was rejected by the BBC radio drama department, an unusual blunder, one assumes,

by the institutionalised safety net and seedbed of so many great dramatists (Pinter and Stoppard among them). "I had a play set in heaven," McDonagh recalls, "a mad science fiction story, one set in the back of a car and so on. Ten are really good. Listening to what the BBC did put out, in preference to my stuff, horrified me. Any approach from them now will be met with, well, tactful indifference."' See 'The Week in Reviews: Backstage: He Compares Himself With the Young Orson Welles. Oh Dear', *The Observer*, 1 December 1996, p.13. http://www.lexisnexis.com/uk/nexis/results/docview/docview.do?docLinkInd=true&risb=21_T12577053696&format=GNBFI&sort=BOOLEAN&startDocNo=1&resultsUrlKey=29_T12577092600&cisb=22_T12577053699&treeMax=true&treeWidth=0&csi=143296&docNo=6, (Accessed 22/8/2011)

13 See Pacheco, 'Laughing Matters.'

14 D. Dromgoole, *The Full Room: An A-Z of Contemporary Playwriting* (London: Methuen, 2000), pp.198–9.

15 McDonagh claims that he has only one piece of unperformed work *The Banshees of Inisheer*, but his agent, the Rod Hall [now Knight Hall] Agency, had previously listed a number of other plays on their website, namely, *The Retard is Out in the Cold* and *Dead Day at Coney*. Some previous articles on McDonagh also mention a play titled *The Maamturk Rifleman*. His agent also lists unproduced screenplays: *Barney Nenagh's Shotgun Circus*, *Suicide on Sixth Street*, *Three Billboards Outside of Ebbing*, which he recently suggested will be his next film. A screenplay called *Missouri* is no longer listed but had been in 2006.
See http://www.rodhallagency.com/index.php?art_id=000026 (Accessed 18/7/2011) David Gritten reports 'McDonagh has also written a screenplay commissioned by Hollywood producer Scott Rudin, called *First Day Out of Folsom*. "It has a lot of characters, many of whom end up dead," said Hall, who added he did not expect the script to be filmed.' See 'Grittten, The Engima of South London'.

16 See O'Toole, 'A Mind in Connemara', p.44.

17 See the biographical note in the programme for the National Theatre's production of *Inishmaan* in 1997.

18 M. McDonagh, *The Beauty Queen of Leenane, A Skull in Connemara, and The Lonesome West* in *Plays 1* (London: Methuen, 1999). (Page references to the plays in this collection will appear in parentheses within the main text and heareafter abbreviated to *Beauty Queen*.)

19 M. McDonagh, *The Cripple of Inishmaan* (London: Methuen Drama, 1997). (Page references will appear in parentheses within the main text and heareafter abbreviated to *Inishmaan*.)

20 M. McDonagh, *The Lieutenant of Inishmore* (London: Methuen, 2001). (Page references will appear in parentheses within the main text and heareafter abbreviated to *Inishmore*.)

21 M. McDonagh, *The Pillowman*. (London: Faber and Faber, 2003). (Page references will appear in parentheses within the main text.)

22 M. McDonagh, *A Behanding in Spokane* (New York, Dramatists Play Services Inc, 2011). (Page references will appear in parentheses within the main text and heareafter abbreviated to *Spokane*.)

23 *Six Shooter* (A missing in Action and Funny Farm Films Production in association with Fantastic Films, financed jointly by Film Four Lab (UK) and the Irish Film Board.)

24 *In Bruges*, (Blueprint Pictures, Film4, Focus Features and Scion Films). See further film details at http://www.imdb.com/title/tt0780536/companycredits. M. McDonagh, *In Bruges* (London: Faber and Faber, 2008). (Page references will appear in parentheses within the main text.)

25 *Seven Psychopaths*, (Film4, Blueprint Pictures, British Film Institute (BFI)).

26 Numerous academics include McDonagh's work in their discussions of the Irish tradition. *The Methuen Drama Anthology of Irish Plays* (2008) edited by Patrick Lonergan includes *The Cripple of Inishmaan* and *The Methuen Drama Guide to Contemporary Irish Playwrights* (2010), edited by Martin Middeke and Peter Paul Schnierer, includes an entry on McDonagh, justified on the basis that he is a London-Irish writer.

27 The hyphenated Anglo-Irish identity is one which has been used in very different ways traditionally, mainly to categorise those of the Irish Ascendancy class. Writers like Oscar Wilde and George Bernard Shaw crossed the Irish Sea decades earlier to establish careers in England. But there is a vast difference between finding oneself in Oxford as Wilde did and belonging to a highly educated class, in contrast to finding oneself in the less salubrious conditions of the predominantly working-class areas of London, such as Camden, Kilburn, Cricklewood, Elephant and Castle or Camberwell where many Irish emigrants ended up, initially at any rate.

28 A. Godfrey, 'Seven Psychopaths: "You can't kill dogs in Hollywood"', *The Guardian*, 1 December 2012, http://www.guardian.co.uk/film/2012/dec/01/seven-psychopaths-martin-mcdonagh?intcmp=239 (Accessed 19/12/2012)

29 Ania Loomba notes 'It has been suggested that it is more helpful to think of postcolonialism not just as coming literally after colonialism and signifying its demise, but more flexibly as the contestation of colonial domination and the legacies of colonialism. Such a position would allow us to include African-American or people of Asian or Caribbean origin in Britain as "postcolonial" subjects although they live within metropolitan cultures".' See *Colonialism/Postcolonialism* (London and New York: Routledge, 1998), p.12.

30 Gritten reports: 'And on arriving in Manhattan before his two plays were staged there, he told a journalist: "New York is sort of ripe for the picking. I mean, it's not like there are lots of really good plays over here right now".' See 'The Enigma of South London'.

31 An incident with the actor Sean Connery, best known for his roles in James Bond franchise movies at London's *Evening Standard* Theatre Awards ceremony, which was held at the Savoy Hotel in November 1996, earned McDonagh a certain notoriety in the tabloid press, when he and his brother refused to toast the Queen. See also R. Lyman, 'Most Promising (and Grating) Playwright', *New York Times*, January 25, 1998, http://www.nytimes.com/1998/01/25/magazine/most-promising-and-grating-playwright.html?pagewanted=all&src=pm (Accessed 20/11/11)

32 P. Lonergan, 'Commentary' to Student Edition of *The Lonesome West* (London: Methuen, 2010), p.lv.

33 J. McKinley, 'Suffer the Little Children', *New York Times*, 3 April 2005, http://www.nytimes.com/2005/04/03/theater/newsandfeatures/03mcki.html?_r=1&scp=2&sq=The%20pillowman&st=cse

34 Ibid.

35 Ibid.

36 See Clarke, 'Psycho thriller'.

37 D. Rosenthal, 'How to slay 'em in the Isles', *Independent*, April 11 2001, http://www.independent.co.uk/arts-entertainment/theatre-dance/features/how-to-slay-em-in-the-isles-681030.html (Accessed 10 October 2009)

38 Even in a very recent interview with Jason Zinoman in 2010, McDonagh shows that he has not lost the knack of controversy, taking major offence to unconfirmed comments attributed to Conor McPherson. But what might read as the first blows in a theatrical spat, did not materialise. I have heard that the only follow through were attempts by McDonagh to distance himself from the remarks. See 'Is He

Mellower? Ask the Guy Missing a Hand', 7 March 2010, *New York Times*, http://www.nytimes.com/2010/03/07/theater/07mcdonagh.html?partner=rss&emc=rss (Accessed 16/04/2012)

39 See Godfrey, 'Seven Psychopaths: "You can't kill dogs in Hollywood".'

40 J. Utichi, 'It's a mad, mad world', *The Sunday Times*, 9 December 2012, pp. 16–17.

41 N. Curtis, 'Brit's short rise to fame.'

42 Ibid.

43 A. Sierz *In-Yer-Face Theatre: British Drama Today* (London: Faber and Faber, 2001), pp.1–9.

44 P. Taylor, 'The Leenane Trilogy Royal Court, London', *The Independent*, Monday, 28 July 1997, http://www.independent.co.uk/life-style/theatre-the-leenane-trilogy-royal-court-london-1253000.html# (Accessed 20/11/11)

45 Ibid.

46 The title *A Skull in Connemara* comes from a line in Beckett's *Waiting for Godot* (1953) and that of *The Lonesome West* is from Synge's *The Playboy of the Western World* (1907). See A. Roche, 'Re-Working *The Workhouse Ward*: McDonagh, Beckett, and Gregory', *Irish University Review*, 34.1 Special Issue: Lady Gregory (Spring-Summer, 2004), pp.171–184. http://www.jstor.org/stable/25504965 (Accessed: 13/4/ 2011)

47 Further, for McDonagh, the specific landscape of the Aran Islands is equated with a 'lunar quality', with 'remoteness', 'wildness' and 'loneliness', according to Fintan O'Toole. See 'A Mind in Connemara'.

48 See Clarke, 'Psycho thriller'.

49 G. Whybrow, 'Introduction' to *The Methuen Book of Modern Drama* (London: Methuen, 2001), p.x.

50 C. Morash, *A History of Irish Theatre 1601–2000* (Cambridge: Cambridge University Press, 2002), p. 269.

51 D. Dromgoole, *The Full Room: An A-Z of Contemporary Playwriting* (London: Methuen, 2000), pp. 199–200.

52 Ibid., pp.199–200.

53 In contrast, Martin Middeke suggests that 'the everted world in McDonagh's plays challenges traditional authorities and expectations and, ultimately, strives to set reader and audience from ensuing forms of fear, veneration, piety or etiquette in a carnivalesque counter-world in which the boundaries between the real and the surreal are constantly blurred'. See 'Martin McDonagh', in M. Middeke & P. P. Schnierer (eds), *The Methuen Drama Guide to Contemporary Irish Playwrights* (London: Methuen, 2010), pp. 213–233, pp. 228–9.

54 P.J. Mathews suggests: 'Brian Friel's *Dancing at Lughnasa* in 1990 as a moment which marks the beginning of this period of incredible cultural accomplishment (beating by a number of months Ireland's World Cup miracle of 1990). This was followed closely by Oscar nominations and awards for Irish films such as *The Crying Game*; numerous Eurovision Song Contest wins; the *Riverdance* phenomenon; Seamus Heaney's Nobel Prize; Roddy Doyle's Booker Prize; the successes of a new generation of dramatists[...]; the rebirth of Irish pop with Boyzone, Westlife and The Corrs; the burgeoning of a crop of new Irish comic talent epitomised by the success of *Father Ted*; the wider appeal of traditional Irish music, as demonstrated by the soundtrack to the film *Titanic*; and the unprecedented success of Irish popular fiction in the work of Patricia Scanlan, Marian Keyes and Cathy Kelly, not to mention Frank McCourt.' See P.J. Mathews. 'In Praise of "Hibernocentricism": Republicanism, Globalisation and Irish Culture.' http://www.republicjournal.com/04/pdf/mathews004.pdf (Accessed 1/6/2010)

55 Billy Roche's *Wexford Trilogy*, comprising *A Handful of Stars* (1988), *Poor Beast In The Rain* (1989), *Belfry* (1991), all of which are set in the town of Wexford, where characters are interconnected as if they lived in a small village, and these works have a pastoral community structure at its core.

56 See T. Gifford, *Pastoral* (London: Routledge, 1999), pp.7–8.

57 M. O'Sullivan, 'Raising the Veil: Mystery, Myth and Melancholia in Irish Studies', in P. Coughlan and T. O'Toole (eds), *Irish Literature Feminist Perspectives* (Dublin: Carysfort Press, 2008), pp.245–278, p.247.

58 In terms of Science 'over time, colour, hair type, skull shape and size, facial angles, or brain size were variously taken up by scientific discourses as the most accurate index of racial differences.' See Loomba, *Colonialism/Postcolonialism,* p.63.

59 In the classic British series *Fawlty Towers*, Mr O'Reilly (David Kelly) the useless and wily builder is but one example of many representations of Irish characters in British popular culture. The television series *Father Ted* is a further example where the clichés are re-cycled but also cleverly deconstructed. Then there is the 'Irish episodes' of the likes of *Family Guy*'s 2007 episode called *Peter's Two Dads* and *The Simpsons* 2009 one called *The Name Of The Grandfather*, set on St Patrick's Day. These sorts of shows represent Ireland nostalgically and simplistically, and are over-reliant on re-cycling almost seamlessly classic clichés. Both of these television shows normally display an ironic disposition, but in their representations of Irishness, seem to lose temporarily that sensibility. Apart from delving into the origins of such stereotypes, there is a further imperative to look at how the Irish themselves both exploit and perpetuate those stereotypical associations.

60 Loomba suggests: 'If in [Frantz] Fanon's writing colonial authority works by inviting black subjects to mimic white culture, in Bhabha's work such an invitation itself undercuts colonial hegemony. Whereas Fanon's black mimics are dislocated subjects here, as also in a wide range of writings on postcolonialism, mimicry has the effect of undermining authority.' See *Colonialism/ Postcolonialism*, p.178.

61 See H. Gilbert and J. Tompkins, *Post-colonial Drama: Theory, Practice, Politics* (London: Routledge, 1996).

62 See D. Negra, (ed)., 'The Irish in Us: Irishness, Performativity and Popular Culture', in *The Irish in Us: Irishness, Performativity and Popular Culture* (Duke University Press, Durham and London, 2006), p. 1.

63 G. Meaney, 'Dead, White, Male: Irishness in *Buffy the Vampire Slayer* and *Angel*', in *The Irish in Us*', p.255.

64 U. Chaudhuri, *Staging Place: The Geography of Modern Drama* (Ann Arbor: The University of Michigan Press, 1995), p.8.

65 The hotel room, a temporary home away from home, is also a common enough feature, notably in *Inishmaan*, *In Bruges* and *Spokane*.

66 D. Hughes, 'Reflections on Irish Theatre and Identity', in E. Jordan, (ed.), *Theatre Stuff: Critical Essays on Contemporary Irish Theatre* (Dublin: Carysfort Press, 2000), pp.11–13.

67 Colin Graham contends, the notion of Ireland is always 'underwritten by an utopian trope which propels its completion always into the future.' See *Deconstructing Ireland: Ireland, Theory, Culture* (Edinburgh University Press, 2001), p.x.

68 M. Billington, 'New Themes in Synge-song Land: *The Beauty Queen of Leenane*', *The Guardian*, 8 March 1996.

69 See Patrick Lonergan's comments on spatial inaccuracies and inconsistencies in *Theatre and Globalization: Irish Drama in the Celtic Tiger Era* (Basingstoke: Palgrave, 2008), p.109, and Anthony Roche's reflections on temporal anomalies in *Contemporary Irish Drama* (Basingstoke: Palgrave, 2009), p.243.

70 B. Brantley, 'A Gasp for Breath Inside an Airless Life', *New York Times*, 27 February, 1998, *http://theater.nytimes.com/mem/theater/treview.html?html_title=&tols_title=BEAUTY%20QUEEN%20OF%20LEENANE,%20THE%20(PLAY)&pdate=19980227&byline=By%20BEN%20BRANTLEY&id=1077011432270* (Accessed 29/4/2013)

71 B. Richardson, 'Introduction: The Struggle for the Real-Interpretative Conflict, Dramatic Method, and the Paradox of Realism' in W.W. Demastes, (ed.), *Realism and the American Dramatic Tradition* (Tuscaloosa, University of Alabama Press, 1996), p.2.

72 As a direct contrast to Hynes's approach, Joe Hill-Gibbins directed the play to great acclaim in 2010 and in 2011. In this performance, these actors deliver their lines with a great measured, lucidity; the individual characters are more singularly focused psychologically, less inter-dependently aligned and less given to embellishment.

73 F. O'Toole, 'Introduction', *Plays: 1* (London, Methuen, 1999), p.xv.

74 Hanna Scolnicov's comments, on the early notionally realistic works of Harold Pinter, are worth keeping in mind: 'We understand the words because they resemble the things we say every day, just as the room in which they move resembles a familiar room [....] Although the superficial impression created is of theatrical realism, the disparate elements do not coalesce into a meaningful mimetic structure.' See *Woman's Theatrical Space* (Cambridge: Cambridge University Press, 1994), p.137.

75 W. W. Demastes and M. Vanden Heuvel, 'The Hurlyburly Lies of the Causalist Mind', in *Realism and the American Dramatic Tradition*, pp.255–274, p.273.

76 P. Healy, 'Please, No More Mr. Bad Guy Roles! (But Creepy Is Fine),' *New York Times*, February 21, 2010, http://www.nytimes.com/2010/02/21/theater/21walken.html?ref=theater (Accessed 15/8/2011)

77 Ibid.

78 S. Pinker, *The Better Angels of Our Nature: A History of Violence and Humanity* (London: Penguin Books, 2011) p.xxiii.

79 Ibid., p.742.

80 Ibid., p.xxi.

81 Ibid., p.xxi.

82 Ibid., p.580.

83 Ibid., p.xxiii.

84 Ibid., p.xxiv.

85 Ibid., p.xxiv.

86 S. Žižek, *Violence* (London: Profile Books, 2009), p.1.

87 Ibid., p.2.

88 Laura Eldred makes the connection between *Beauty Queen* and Alfred Hitchcock's *Psycho* (1960), the horror genre and contemporary gothic. See 'Martin McDonagh and Contemporary Gothic', in R. Rankin Russell, (ed.), *Martin McDonagh, A Casebook* (London: Routledge, 2007), pp.111–130.

89 Catherine Rees deals with violence and comedy and makes mention of Grand-Guignol in 'Representing Acceptability: Power, Violence and Satire in Martin McDonagh's *The Lieutenant of Inishmore*', in Lisa Fitzpatrick (ed.), *Performing Violence in Contemporary Ireland* (Dublin: Carysfort Press 2009), pp.85–103. Clare Wallace also raises the issue of Grand-Guignol in terms of torture and dismemberment, the absurd, the histrionic and farce, in *Suspect Cultures: Narrative, Identity and Citation in 1990s New Drama* (Prague: Litteraria Pragensia, 2006), pp.138–40. And Maria Doyle theorises the relationship between Grand-Guignol and *Inishmore* in 'Breaking bodies: The presence of violence on Martin McDonagh's stage', in R. Rankin Russell, (ed.), *Martin McDonagh, A Casebook* (London: Routledge, 2007), pp.92–110.

90 R. J. Hand and M. Wilson, *Grand-Guignol: The French Theatre of Horror* (Exeter: University of Exeter Press, 2002), p.71.
91 Ibid., p.xii.
92 Ibid., p.x.
93 McDonagh quoted in S. O'Hagan, '*The Wild West*', *Guardian*, 24 March 2001, p.32.
94 S. Richards, '"The Outpouring of a Morbid, Unhealthy Mind": The Critical Condition of Synge and McDonagh', *Irish University Review*, 33–1, (Spring-Summer 2003), pp.201–14, p. 211.
95 F. O'Toole 'Murderous Laughter – The Leenane Trilogy', *The Irish Times* 24 June 1997, p.12.
96 See Pinker, *The Better Angels of Our Nature*, p.692.
97 B. Bettelheim, *The Uses of Enchantment: The Meaning and Importance of Fairy Tales* (London: Penguin Books, 1976, reprinted 1991), p.31.
98 Ibid., p.12.
99 Ibid., p.15.
100 Ibid., pp.33–4.
101 Speaking against himself and perhaps a little tongue in cheek, McDonagh notes, 'It's all mathematical to me', he said. 'I don't really have a sense of other people's horror, because I'm just there trying to get it right: that joke to work or that horrific moment to work. I think there's something a little bit broken in my psyche that doesn't quite allow me to see it as other people do.' See J. McKinley, 'Suffer the Little Children'.
102 See Pinker, *The Better Angels of Our Nature*, p.691.
103 Ibid., p.695.
104 Ibid., pp.692–3.
105 S. Baron-Cohen, *Zero Degrees of Empathy*, pp.10–11.
106 Ibid., p.29.
107 Ibid., p.29.
108 See Pinker, *The Better Angels of Our Nature*, p.161.
109 Ibid., p.xxiv.
110 When I write about productions I have decided to use the present tense. Moreover, in a way, revisiting productions on video that I have seen live, or in seeing revivals or subsequent productions of work, there are complex interfaces going on, including changes in my own circumstances and perspectives which interface with my own evolving thoughts on the work that are inspired in part by the scholarship of others, which I use to explain, elaborate, challenge and construct my own arguments.
111 P. Pavis, *Analyzing Performance: Theatre, Dance, and Film*, David Williams (trans.) (Ann Arbor: University of Michigan Press, 2004), p.2 and p.17.
112 The importance of drafting and the rehearsal process are vital, but I have had no opportunity to pursue these.
113 W. B. Worthen, 'Drama, Performativity, and Performance', *PMLA*, 113.5, (Oct 1998), pp.1093-1107, p.1101. http://www.jstor.org/stable/10.2307/463244 (Accessed 8/4/2013).
114 Ibid.
115 Ibid., p.1102.
116 See my analysis of this in *Dissident Dramaturgies* (Dublin: Irish Academic Press, 2013), pp.19–24.
117 H. Freshwater, *Theatre and Audience* (Basingstoke: Palgrave, 2009), p.5.
118 See S. Di Benedetto's, *The Provocation of the Senses in Contemporary Theatre* (London: Routledge, 2012) for an examination of the interface between performance, reception and neurology.

PART 1

Fictional Places, Genre, Performance and Randomness

1 | Introduction: Welcome to the West

McDonagh's plays speak to each other in a variety of ways, as they share many commonalities in terms of dramatic form, stylistic dispositions and repetitive theatrical tropes. This part covers three plays from the early part of McDonagh's career, *Inishmaan*,[1] *Connemara*,[2] and *Beauty Queen*.[3] In relation to his characters generally, this part starts by looking at *Inishmaan* and investigates how this work deconstructs particularly negative stereotypes of Irishness, many of which seem to align themselves with traditionally aggressive colonial stereotypes, of which McDonagh is sometimes accused of perpetuating. McDonagh finds ways of foregrounding the processes by which certain texts can disseminate idealistic, antiquated, reductive, pejorative, transhistorical and fantastic forms of Irishness.

McDonagh highlights in particular the issues of whiteness in relation to Hollywood's representations of Irishness and its alignment with disability and subsistence living in both the scene where Billy Claven rehearses a sentimental script set in a dingy rooming house in Los Angeles, and in the referencing of Robert J. Flaherty's, the Irish-American's problematic, if iconic documentary-film *Man of Aran*,[4] which serves as an intermedial intertext and as a *mise-en-abyme*.[5] Through the intermeshing of this documentary-film, Mark Phelan argues that the script's humour 'derives from the hilarious collision between Hollywood fantasy and local reality' and that what is exposed is how 'nationalist myths of the "wild" west have been reclad and reified by the nostalgic idealisations of the Irish Diaspora'.[6]

McDonagh's five west of Ireland plays are predominantly set in, with the exception of the Osbourne shop, in cottage spaces, arranged in the 'old style' and they also exhibit stage objects conventionally associated with an older Ireland.[7] Such iconography is often viewed as a form of shorthand, in terms of establishing the sensibility of the plays and invoking attitudes, expectations and the dispositions of audiences to characters in such spaces. Productions of the work will of course re-construct, disregard, misconstrue or evade these dramaturgically 'Irish' contexts, but it is fair to say that in general, most performances maintain hypothetical or speculative Irish environments, idioms and sensibilities in their various *mise-en-scène*. (Patrice Pavis states that *mise-en-scène* 'is always, to one degree or another, a staging of the unconscious'. Whose unconscious it is however is the question that needs to be asked: the authorial or textual unconscious, the production's unconscious, the socio-political unconscious or the unconscious of the spectator?[8]) Such a 'vectorisation' of Irishness shapes the expressivity, pulse, rhythm, ambiance and performance idiom in a variety of ways that cannot be easily accounted for.[9] While reflections on Irishness will dominate the early parts of this section, it will become less and less of a focus as my argument progresses through this book.

In terms of space, Gay McAuley argues that 'playtexts can be read and their spatial content analysed, but "textual space" is made really meaningful only in performance. The playtext contains the potential for many spatialisations, and that of course entails many different meanings.'[10] (Anne Ubersfeld argues that 'the theatrical text is even flatter than any other: it does not describe its own spatiality'.[11]) McAuley's taxonomy distinguishes between the above mentioned 'textual space', 'stage space', 'presentational space', 'fictional space' and 'thematic space'. The latter over-arching category 'incorporates both text and performance'. 'Stage space' is considered in terms of 'width, depth, its degree of separation or integration with the auditorium, the number and position of its exits, the nature of the back wall or division between on and off stage', in other words, the basic architecture of the building and how it provides a 'physical grounding for the performance'. 'Presentational space' extends far beyond 'the scenery and decor', as the mere physical presence of actors on even a bare stage transforms it into a 'presentational space'. 'Presentational space' includes the

> actual physical occupation of the stage space by the actors as well as the set (if any), its furniture and props, the spatial demarcation established by the lighting, the number, nature and position of the exits, and the way the offstage areas are signalled physically [….] The physical presence of the actors, their comings and goings, movements and proxemic groupings, their body behaviour within the space are crucial to the presentational space.[12]

'Presentational space', can represent either 'a single fictional place or multiple places,' either 'alternating or succeeding one another or simultaneously present in different parts of the stage space'.[13] *Beauty Queen* shifts from

Leenane to London, *Connemara* from a domestic to a graveyard space and *Inishmaan* has multiple locations on the island, ranging from shop to parish hall, seashore to a squalid hotel room in Los Angeles, all of which need to be incorporated within a flexible, fluid scenography.

'Fictional place' refers to 'the place or places presented, represented or evoked onstage and off'.[14] Thus 'fictional place is "conceived space" whether it is on or off.' Onstage fictive place can 'be physically represented, or presented through the actor (the chair on the table is a mountain because the actor is climbing it), or it can be simply spoken.' 'Fictional place' is further separated into 'localised off' as in the case of accessible or inaccessible rooms or bedrooms, signalled by doors to suggest their presence, or more importantly 'unlocalised off,' meaning places like the west of Ireland, Connemara, Leenane or the Aran islands in McDonagh's work, and thus function as part of a play's 'dramatic geography.'[15]

The 'fictional place' is also one onto which audiences project their own understandings, expectations, desires, thus it is co-constituted, by performance and reception. In the most general terms, the west of Ireland is perceived as an area that is primarily rural, remote, relatively unspoilt, and significantly under-industrialised .[16] Additionally, there is often a loose association with tradition, the pagan and the mystical, and, simultaneously and without much contradiction, with Christian doctrines. Since the foundation of the Abbey Theatre in 1904 there have been consistent attempts to align west of Ireland plays in particular, with that which is authentic.[17] According to Richard Allen Cave, when the Abbey Theatre first toured in 1906 the company produced a series of 'Irish Plays' in London, which provided 'a kind of constellation of specific terms and epithets' that 'steadily defines the company's claim to originality as lying in its concern for a scrupulous authenticity', as audiences were assured that locals had been consulted in order to confirm the exactness of the details of the space, costumes, language and accent.[18]

Further, Nicholas Grene argues 'in its greenness, its littleness, its location as the offshore-island alternative to the major metropolitan societies of Britain or America,' Ireland is always available as a pastoral site.[19] Grene stresses the links the pastoral has with the 'archaic, traditional and originary', with a 'wholesome jollity' and with a 'harmony with nature,' and adds that it is a space often 'marked by quaintness, the charm, the lyrical otherness of Hiberno-English.'[20] Notions of home and belonging are also central to that authentic framing of 'fictional place'. A great example of this impulse can be seen in John Ford's romantic comedy *The Quiet Man* (1952), starring John Wayne, Maureen O'Hara, Victor McLaglen and Barry Fitzgerald. This film affirms Ireland's lush, romantic pastoral qualities, as Ireland also functions as a redemptive space. Gerardine Meaney regards Ford's film as the 'paradigm-setting Irish American fantasy of Ireland'.[21] Further Meaney notes that a form of 'recoverable' masculinity that is 'threatened by industrial society' could be achieved through 'ethnicity', as 'a return to pastoral values' and this has been 'a key element of US representations of Ireland'. She continues that John Wayne (as Sean Thornton) in Ford's film 'recovers his manhood by becoming Irish',[22] as he reclaims his connection to land and to his mother's family home. Further, she adds: 'At the heart of this is the paradox that Ireland is sold as that which cannot be sold, as a place where relationships with persons and place cannot simply be reduced to transactions between commodities and where gender, familial and communal relations have an authenticity or atavism (inflections vary) lost in contemporary society.'[23] Additionally, Meaney contends that the film 'marks the simultaneous erasure and fetishisation of Ireland's history and locality, the advent of Ireland as simulacrum of the object of another's desire'.[24]

Further to these discussions on fetishised 'Fictional place' it is necessary to include Michel Foucault's ideas on heterotopic spaces, concepts that also link in with the notion of damaging funerary practices that Nina Witoszek and Pat Sheeran have reflected upon.[25] The interlinking of these aspects allows the connecting of the transcendent and its opposite, immanence, the sanctified and the de-sanctified, the imaginary or fictive and the notionally real in my discussions on the production of *Connemara* by Druid in 1997. This play's premiere situated the drama beside and against these debilitating Irish funerary practices that are also very evident in Irish playwriting more generally, as Hynes's *mise-en-scène* achieves a necessary irreverent and sacrilegious vigour.

Across the west of Ireland plays, although the Hiberno-Irish dialect of the characters seems somewhat consistent with the patterns and inflections of regular west of Ireland speech, an analysis of the language reveals something more intricate and convoluted. Nicholas Grene cites McDonagh from a 1998 article: 'In Connemara and Galway, the natural dialogue style is to invert sentences and use strange inflections. Of course, my stuff is a heightening of that, but there is a core strangeness of speech, especially in Galway.'[26] Fintan O'Toole claims that 'Gaelic is just a pale ghost behind the vernacular English of the characters, its dead forms clinging on to an empty afterlife in the baroque syntax of their speech.'[27] Nicholas Grene attests to the same things but does not value them in the same way: 'where Synge put this Hiberno-English strangeness to defamiliarising poetic effect, in McDonagh it characteristically comes across as uncouth, ungainly and deflationary'.[28] In her analysis of the use of Irish-English and its 'grammatical and lexicographic particularities', Lisa Fitzpatrick uses Loreto Todd's book *Green English* to argue that 'many of the key linguistic markers identified by Todd are strikingly absent' in McDonagh's work.[29] Fitzpatrick goes on to state that 'those quirks of dialogue construction that seem Irish, such as the repetition and inverted word-order, occur also in *The Pillowman*, suggesting that they are typical of the rhythmic cadences of McDonagh's plays, rather than attempts to recreate Irish speech patterns.'[30] And O'Toole in his analysis of Garry Hynes's approach to *The Leenane Trilogy*, suggests that she '[…] takes the elements of literary Western speech and writes them out with the kind of fluorescent pens that Maryjohnny Rafferty […] uses for doing bingo.'[31] Putting it differently, Clare Wallace notes that McDonagh 'creates his own language and a style that is recognisably Irish, but also underscores its own artificiality'.[32] Clearly, the words and syntax used are neither authentic imitation nor a mutilation; the language is more a mongrel, heightened, strange and artificial form.

Also within the 'fictive place' of McDonagh's west of Ireland plays there are references to the murder of the politician Airey Neave, the miscarriages of justice of both the Guildford Four and the Birmingham Six, the events of Bloody Sunday and other historical incidents, such as the recent war in Bosnia. Furthermore, the early plays hint at the broader social realities of emigration, clerical abuse of children, bishops having babies with Americans and qualification by the Irish football team for major championships. Indeed, in many respects, *The Leenane Trilogy* seems to be utterly anachronistic to what was happening socially and economically in the progressive Ireland of the times of their setting, estimated as the early 1990s. Such issues raise the problematic notion of representation and, although the work identifies real places, people and incidents, it does not necessarily follow that there is an obligation to be accurately representative or to contextualise appropriately.

In terms of dramatic form, McDonagh's plays vary a great deal in some respects: *Lonesome* is predominantly farcical, as is *Inishmore,* while *Connemara* and *Inishmaan* are black comedies as much as they are farces and *Beauty Queen* seems to be a strange blend of naturalism, tragicomedy and melodrama. Regardless of this these plays tentatively disclose some of the specific conventions associated with the broad stroke expectations of naturalism or realism as I will discuss later.

The early reception of McDonagh's work is of particular interest in terms of genre expectation. The social commentator John Waters struggled with concepts of reality and realism, arguing that in the *Leenane Trilogy* what is experienced 'is a distorted reality, yes, but reality of a kind nonetheless.'[33] Later, he elaborates: 'McDonagh's plays are not "real" in the sense of being naturalistic representations of reality. Rather they are impressions of reality, from a certain angle or vantage-point.'[34] Somewhat differently, O'Toole contends that the writing 'takes the conventions of kitchen sink drama and exaggerates them into a kind of *dirty naturalism* [my emphasis]'.[35] Yet O'Toole evades the limits and implications of this 'dirty naturalism' by providing another rationalisation, identifying the intermeshing of two opposing sensibilities:

> [one] is a black-and-white still from an Abbey play of the 1950s: west of Ireland virgins and London building sites, tyrannical mothers and returned Yanks [....] But the other picture is a lurid Polaroid of a postmodern landscape, a disintegrating place somewhere between London and Boston, saturated in Irish rain and Australian soaps.[36]

O'Toole's array of insightful and occasionally contradictory comments capture both the slippery nature of the play's genres and the challenges to be faced in order to explain the layering, disjunctions, anomalies, superimpositions, double-takes, dialogical connections, slippages and shattered expectations of causality, proportionality, sequencing and dimensionality evident both in the textual details and in many of the performances of the work. However, O'Toole seems to blemish these substantial awarenesses with overstatement: 'Before these plays, no one had quite managed to describe the mental universe of people who live on the margins of a globalised culture.'[37]

In relation to *Beauty Queen*, Heath A. Diehl picks up on 'generic innovations',[38] 'generic rupture',[39] and on the 'interpretive dilemmas' that occur when critics 'ignore the radical generic break with realism which splits the two acts of McDonagh's play'.[40] (While I go along with the ruptures and innovations, I would not agree with the 'radical generic break' that splits both acts.) Comments by Ondřej Pilný also show an awareness of such genre complications, noting how 'this type of satire constitutes a specific mimetic dimension of McDonagh which is, needless to say, distinctly different from any realistic mirroring: McDonagh's plays ironically reflect constitutive themes of Irish culture and satirically explore the expectations of particular audiences.'[41]

On this issue of audiences, Anne Ubersfeld argues that generally 'Spectators have come to believe that the stage locus reproduces a real location. This idea – that the stage locus represents a "real", concrete space with its own limits, surface, depth and objects, a fragment of the world suddenly and integrally transported onto the stage – is relatively recent in the theatre and is encountered only in the West, or more precisely in bourgeois Western culture.'[42] She adds, 'the spatial structures reproduced in the theatre define not so much a concrete world, but rather the image people have of spatial relationships and the conflicts underlying those relationships in the society in which they live'.[43] In effect, Ubersfeld's argument is that: 'The stage locus is independent of any mimesis of a concrete space that [it] reproduces, whether transposed or not, symbolically or realistically, a particular aspect of our real universe; stage space is an area of dramatic action (or a locus for ceremony), it is a place where something happens that does not refer to some elsewhere.'[44] Ubersfeld is suggesting something radical, but the notion that the 'stage locus' is 'independent of any mimesis' seems to go against the inclinations of many spectators.

However, Ubersfeld's argument becomes more clearly nuanced through her usage of Umberto Eco's term '*iconicity*'. Ubersfeld reports that Eco concludes 'the iconic sign does not possess the properties of the represented object', and, secondly, that it reproduces 'some of the conditions of perception common to both the iconic sign and the represented object, according to normal perceptual codes'.[45] That way performances have multiple referents: the textual referent and 'the referential universe constructed in the dramatic setting', whether it is an imaginary Leenane or the Aran Islands.[46] Thus an iconic west is a more appropriate way of considering the reconstituted and transactionary relationships between the real and fictional worlds. McDonagh's west of Ireland plays share authentic appearing stage environments and the nominal ways that the characters inhabit performance spaces and interact with each other also suggest something close to the real, despite the fact that the plays consistently sacrifice a significant degree of 'psychological credibility.'[47]

On first inspection Hynes's best work nearly always seems to be on a realist continuum, whether it is her work on John B. Keane's folkloric, rural melodramas, or Tom Murphy's heightened naturalism in plays like *Conversations on a Homecoming* (1983) or *Bailegangaire* (1985), where realism is a springboard into something altogether different and more complex. McDonagh's work adds a layer of complication, as a style simultaneously consistent and inconsistent with the expectations of realism seems to be evident in the published texts, whereby tensions between familiarity and estrangement, 'visibility' and 'concealment' (terms I will come to later) along with representation, theatricality, misrepresentation and artifice are evident and provoke potential tensions within any *mise-en-scène*. In an interview with Cathy Leeney, Garry Hynes states: 'There's this issue about Martin and authenticity – the response that his [vision] is not Irish life now and it's not Connemara life. Of course it isn't. It's an artifice. It's not authentic. It's not meant to be. It's a complete creation and in that sense it's fascinating.'[48] Such comments have to be balanced by others she made to Michael Ross about her production of *The Lonesome West*, where Hynes maintains that the actors and directors 'have to absolutely believe that Valene will not allow his brother to eat a packet of his Tayto [crisps]. If you think of that as a joke, and take that attitude to it in rehearsal, then the play doesn't exist.'[49] That sense of 'absolute' belief in terms of actions must be inter-digitated with an expression of artifice and the theatricality within a *mise-en-scène* that does not necessarily validate the real.

2 | Performing Irishness with Illegitimacy in *The Cripple of Inishmaan*

CLOSE ENCOUNTERS OF A COLONIAL KIND

Garry Hynes's *mise-en-scène* for her productions of *Inishmaan* in 2008 and in 2011, in a combined Druid Theatre Company and Atlantic Theater New York production,[50] demonstrate how complex textualisations of Irishness are given shape by stage action and characterisations, in terms of accents, clothing, physicality, psychological and ideological dispositions and in the presence and usage of stage objects.[51] Hynes's two different *mise-en-scène* share a performance styles appropriate to McDonagh's particular challenging of the essential features of traditional and colonial stereotypes. Francis O'Connor's expressionistic scenography substantiates the dialectical relationship between the play's main dramatic arc and the various intertexts it co-opts.[52] In fact, Francis O'Connor's two designs for the family-run shop have little depth, they are elongated and flattish, almost forced forward, losing characteristic dimensions of depth and proportionality. As Ben Brantley notes of Hynes's 2008 production, 'it's hard to imagine an interpretation that makes this play's singular melding of sentimentality and savagery feel more organic than this one does'.[53] These two productions were not just made with Irish audiences predominantly in mind, as these productions toured a number of American cities.[54] (The 2011 production toured under the umbrella of Imagine Ireland – a Culture Ireland Initiative.[55])

While, much has been made of McDonagh's simplistic deployment of negative stereotypes and their ostensible single or double dimensions, I would argue that his apparently limited palette disguises a far greater complexity. Most of the critical discussions around character are based on their relationship with traditional colonial stereotypes. Throughout the history of the world, colonisation has occurred in a variety of forms and with considerable variations in terms of practices, impacts and consequences.

For close to 800 years Ireland was a colony of Great Britain. One crucial feature of Irish colonisation entailed the substantial settlements of British citizens on Irish lands and the banishment of some indigenous populations towards the western seaboard, for which the Aran Islands were a sort of last outpost. Given Ireland's close proximity to Britain, material goods and people moved more easily between both places. On the most basic of levels, colonial contact entails variations on, as Ania Loomba notes, 'trade, plunder, negotiation, warfare, genocide, enslavement and rebellions', to which she also adds 'cultural decimation and political exclusion'.[56]

Loomba points out for instance that the word colonisation as defined by the *Oxford English Dictionary* not only 'avoids any reference to people other than the colonisers, people who might already have been living in those places where colonies were established. Hence it evacuates the word "colonialism" of any implication of an encounter between peoples or of conquest and domination.'[57] (The myth of the relative scarcity or absence of indigenous peoples implies virgin territory and few evictions.) And when the existence of indigenous populations cannot be obscured, on the one hand, the summative narrative that colonisers tell to themselves is that imperialism is an appropriate and relatively benign activity. This activity is justified in part by myths of mutuality and reciprocity on the one hand, and, on the other, such foundational narratives establish the colonised as naturally inferior and the coloniser as innately superior.

Yet it has to be remembered that each experience of colonisation is different and that all colonisers are not equal, as one can be a citizen of a colonising country and/or agent of colonisation, participating in but not benefitting materially to any significant extent from it, as those who are socially privileged did and do. Just as clearly, one can be a victim of colonisation and still benefit somewhat from it, as some of Ireland's population did, and not just the elites, but other sections of the population who colluded openly or in secret with the foreign power.

Colonisation impacts on the material level very obviously; however, its effect on the colonised nation's psyche, on how its people think, respond to and circumvent the realities of colonisation are something altogether different again. Thus, colonial discourse studies evaluate, as Loomba notes, 'how stereotypes, images and "knowledge" of colonial subjects and cultures tie in with institutions of economic, administrative, judicial and bio-medical control'.[58] There is widespread evidence of such methodologies across 'a wide range of cultural texts and practices such as artworks, atlases, cinema, scientific systems, museums, educational institutions, advertisements, psychiatric and other medical practices, geology, patterns of clothing, ideas on beauty', claims Loomba.[59] Equally, travel logs, 'newspaper stories, government records and reports, memoirs, journals, historical tracts or political writings' must also be considered Loomba suggests for 'their rhetorical strategies, their narrative devices', the negative representations and few challenges they posed to privilege and inequality.[60]

Effectively, these texts disseminated the notional objectivity of the sciences, and the superior insights on custom, food and cultural practices to justify ranked relationships, prejudicial articulations and the colonial projects themselves. But as with all power dynamics and with all textual and visual representations, they can be tested not only for their prejudicial constructs, displacements and transferences, but just as importantly for traces of their own anxieties and repressions and for breaches of containment.[61] Importantly then, Declan Kiberd illustrates the notion of Ireland as 'patented as not-England',[62] and how Ireland traditionally functioned as England's 'unconscious'[63] – but one should not only view the unconscious as a repository of negativity only; there is also the repression of positivity, pleasure and creativity as well, for example. Kiberd demonstrates how Edmund Spenser in the late sixteenth century regarded the Irish as 'wild', 'hot-headed, rude and nomadic, the perfect foil to set off their own [English] virtues'.[64]

Equally, Mathew Arnold's attempts to put a positive spin on Irishness are flawed: Kiberd underlines the inherent prejudice in Arnold's comments that 'The Celtic genius had sentiment as its main basis […] with love of beauty, charm, and spirituality for its excellence, ineffectualness and self-will for its defect.'[65] Kiberd continues: 'Thus, if John Bull was industrious and reliable, Paddy was held to be indolent and contrary: if the former was mature and rational, the latter must be unstable and emotional.'[66]

Loomba is not alone in highlighting the consistency of these practices transnationally: 'Thus laziness, aggression, violence, greed, sexual promiscuity, bestiality, primitivism, innocence, and irrationality are attributed (often contradictorily and inconsistently) by the English, French, Dutch, Spanish and Portuguese colonists to Turks, African, Native Americans, Jews, Indians, the Irish and others. It is worth noting that some of these descriptions were used for working class populations or women within Europe.'[67]

In Loomba's comments it is worth giving emphasis to the broader forms of stereotyping and the inclusion of women and the working classes more generally within the same frameworks of prejudice and subjugation. In addition, 'Colonialism intensified patriarchal relations in colonised lands, often because native men, increasingly disenfranchised and excluded from the public sphere, became more tyrannical at home. They seized upon the home and the woman as emblems of their culture and nationality', Loomba contends.[68] Ireland in these negative binary constructs is fetishised, marginalised, infantalised, made to feel inferior and feminised by Britain as the dominant imperial power.

That said, there are a variety of issues in the imposition of a post-colonial framework on either Irish writing more generally, and to McDonagh's work more specifically. As Anne Fogarty notes: 'In particular, the politics of this mode of cultural investigation have come under attack as critics accuse it of endorsing rather than dismantling neocolonial relations between the first and third worlds and of spawning false universals and ahistorical abstractions that impede rather than further literary analysis.' And she adds, 'Moreover, it is frequently pointed out that postcolonialism runs the risk of licensing a convenient anticolonial animus that masks the many ways in which Irish and British culture are interconnected.' She goes on to say that the two 'leading assumptions that are frequently cited as a litmus test of the anti-essentialist ontology that supposedly characterises postcolonial fictions, namely that they search out liminal spaces and hybrid identities and eschew fixities and epistemological limits'.[69] McDonagh clearly sets out to stage 'liminal spaces' and 'hybrid identities', while challenging 'epistemological limits', with an awareness of inter-state interconnections. And McDonagh's characterisations are anything but 'ahistorical'.

Eoin Flannery notes Colin Graham's interrogation of David Lloyd's theoretical failure 'to sanction any telos other than perpetual discontinuity and fragmentation'. Thus 'Lloyd constructs a corollary fetish of the subaltern itself by "ethically endowing" the notion of subalternity.' [70] In McDonagh's work by contrast there is a refusal of such endowment of the subaltern characters, and more importantly, those on the periphery are neither romanticised nor uncontaminated marginal figures. There is no celebration of defiance or of indigenity and their blind spots to the external world are a direct challenge to how people can be both comfortable with limited knowledge, but incapable of discerning systemic changes as they are building momentum.[71]

The obsessions of *Inishmaan*'s characters with elsewhere, with information on global incidents and events, on the positive implications of international peoples settling in Ireland and fundamentally on how they are represented in Flaherty's documentary-film, all incite a fluidity to traditionally conceived stereotypes. Secondly, character dispositions and expectations established as part of the dramaturgical set-up are seldom the same as the ones with which the play concludes.

GREASY GROCERESSES

The opening two scenes of *Inishmaan* are set in a shop owned by the Osbourne sisters, Kate and Eileen, who share their home with [Cripple]

Billy, whom the sisters have adopted, after the deaths of his parents.[72] The family lives under the same meagre conditions as almost all of the community and such frugality is suggested in part poignantly and in part comically by the fact that the shop is under-stocked, as peas and flour are the dominant and essential provisions on display. Other products for sale are taken in lieu of payment for gossip by Johnnypateenmike, consumed by Eileen even before they hit the shelves or broken before sale, like the Henman's eggs. The shop is obviously an interpersonal, transactionary and commercial place, but it is also connected to the off-stage, private family space.

Dearbhla Molloy (Eileen) and Marie Mullen (Kate) in Hynes's 2008 production are vital to the establishment of the tone and rhythm of the performance.[73] They rely on a slow precise delivery, a vocal register that is shrill and almost crone like; gestural mirroring establishes an artificially constructed comedic world, but even more importantly, their exchange indicates that notions of mimesis must be almost totally abandoned. Their anxiety-ridden exchanges are marked by exaggeration and by the way that they elaborate on each others' comments.

Equally, the sisters de-emphasise the notion of a subtext, where socialisation has in a sense suppressed or repressed another voice or disposition, in effect when characters traditionally say one thing and think another. In this instance, it is more of a language beside a language, not beneath or within it. In these early exchanges, occasional shifts in emotion are delivered almost as internal comic asides. And on other occasions, there is subtle and sometimes blatant signalling of such fluctuations. Kate's and Eileen's later obsessions with sweets and talking to stones are consistent with McDonagh's and Hynes's overall non-naturalistic approach to characterisation.

Although there is accentuated comedy in Billy's centrality to their lives, their over-protectiveness of him seems to have some justification, given his near-death experience and his physical disability. The sisters callously and insensitively dismiss any hope of Billy ever finding a girlfriend: 'Kate: ... Billy does have a sweet face if you ignore the rest of him.'(p.3) The sisters want to keep him safe and to do so, it means that he remains not only local and within their grasp, but also not attached to anyone else. As they see it, Billy is dependent on them and their fatalism towards him contributes to their own sense of self-importance. Although their love for him is sentimental, nostalgic and sometimes misplaced, regardless of this it is their caring actions, rather than their words, which trump all their failings, inadequacies, transferences and displacements. Their home is Billy's home.

In this work, no one captures the instability of character more than Johnnypateenmike, the local gossip monger, who is almost a pantomime villain.[74] David Pearse in the 2008 production is almost 20 years younger than the age suggested for the character in the script. Pearse registers a greater level of sinisterness in his explosive terrorising of others. Gossip is not just something to trade, but is a form of control and exploitation. Ben Brantley's description of Pearse's performance is very apt: 'As pricelessly played by Mr. Pearse, Johnny is a spiteful creature, a stocky human fire hydrant as filled with resentment as with gossip.'[75] Despite Pearse's aggressive interference and manipulative qualities, by the play's end, he must be seen in a rather different light. By then, he is an enabling rather than disabling figure; he is more a hero than a parasite, who has been essential to Billy's survival.[76]

(Slippy) Helen McCormick is another example of this breaching of type: she is a great complex, comic creation; she is impatient, crude and aggressive; as well as being confident, assertive, challenging, destructive and rebellious. Helen is sometimes sadistic towards Bartley, her brother, she exploits others, offers to exchange kisses for travel. Helen has intimate encounters with stable boys who pretend to be film executives, yet Helen is contented with the pleasures that accrue rather than being disappointed by their deceptions. She kills a goose and a cat for money, paid for by two feuding gay men and has a passion for breaking eggs. Indeed, she may or may not have had an affair with the local egg man. Helen comments: 'Ah, do you know the egg-man's bed sheets are used to being eggy.' (p.57) Eggs can of course insinuate female fertility, but also hint at semen-stained sheets in the above instance.[77]

Helen is utterly insensitive to Billy's parents' deaths and even more so towards his disability. If Kate and Eileen sentimentalise pejoratively Billy's disability, Helen links it to a lack of phallus and lowly masculine status. Helen tells how Jim Finnegan's daughter keeps a chart to record the penis size of the locals that she has been with. While Billy is proud that he is not on such a chart, Helen accounts for it by the fact that he is not only 'mangled and fecked', but also that a woman would not be sure whether he 'had one' or 'not'. (p.18) She suggests that the only penises she has seen belong to priests: 'Helen: [....] They keep showing them to me.' (p. 19) She also talks of rupturing a curate at the age of six and claims that she threw four eggs at Father Barratt, who touched her 'arse in choir practice', and sees his behaviour as a measure of her attractiveness. (p. 12) Helen seems to take a casual approach to such inappropriate touching and appears not too wounded by the experience.

However, if the spectator is to regard her dismissal of the approach by the curate as predominantly if unnervingly comedic, Bartley's accounts of clerical encounters are far more uncomfortable: he tells her that it wasn't his 'arse' which was groped, that it is nothing to boast about, that it has nothing to do with being pretty and that the attention is more about 'being on your own and small' (p. 14). Laurence Kinlan as Bartley, in both of Hynes's productions, dispenses such challenging lines with great vulnerability, while at the same time he delivers his admission with a tone that neither encourages nor anticipates any response from other characters. So what might look like a context for the exposure of Bartley's abuse is also steered in another direction when Bartley suggests that Billy would never be a victim of such actions, as some line has to be drawn. That sense of Billy being somehow unworthy of paedophilic attention is starkly unsettling, but is also indicative of McDonagh's complex and risqué dramaturgy. Further, Bartley's revelations are almost directly followed by him asking Eileen if they have 'any Fripple-Frapples' for sale. (p.14) As such, the violence of abuse is not airbrushed out of consciousness, rather it is the capacity of the characters not to deny it, not normalise it, but to drift over it that is most important. The fact that Helen tells everyone ensures that there is not a conspiracy of silence. (Suppression and silence were part of the whole clerical abuse scandal to hit Ireland, England and America in more recent years.)

Lynn Gardner aptly describes Kerry Condon's performance as Helen in 2008 'as fierce as a polecat', for she is a young woman 'who has learned to ferociously protect herself'.[78] Condon is very experienced in performing in McDonagh's work, having already starred in the premiere of *Inishmore* in 2001 and is comfortable with the prerequisite levels of vulnerability and aggression.[79] Furthermore, Helen is one of the key figures in defining Billy's specific place in the community and how his disability is accredited, accommodated and appropriated. Helen, in different ways to the Osborne sisters, is a direct challenge to the stereotyping of Irish female characters. While much has been written about the idealisation of woman or representations of woman as sovereignty goddess in Irish cultural expression generally, it is as if McDonagh again seems to be intent on subverting such a trope. In a key scene Helen plays a game 'Ireland and England' with Bartley. She gives herself the role of England, and breaks eggs over his head. He is the enfeebled, static and vulnerable Ireland, which is a reversal of the usual alignment of the passive feminine with an oppressed Ireland and the aggressive masculine with the dominance of the coloniser. (Equally, this is a contentious representation of the colonial relationship between England and Ireland in this play first staged at Britain's National Theatre.)

BILLY GOAT'S GRUFF

Clearly, in both performances, it is Billy's body and his consciousness which are central to the construction of the *mise-en-scène*. Billy serves as the centrifugal force and the other characters are not so much there to create an ensemble, but are there almost to resonate with and against the play's main character in an expressionistic sort of way, in many ways like Hynes's production of Tom Murphy's *A Crucial Week in the Life of a Grocer's Assistant* at the Abbey Theatre in 1992.

In John Millington Synge's *The Playboy of the Western World* (1907) Christy Mahon's confidence increases thanks to the notoriety foisted upon him by the local community and it is the 'devil's own mirror' to which he turns in order to affirm that this impression is not a dream. Christy is motivated initially by the admiration of Pegeen Mike, who conspires with him to create a fantasy of betterment, however corrupt or misplaced it is, whereas from the start in *Inishmaan*, nobody seems to offer that sense of supportive enablement for Billy's journey towards self-discovery.

The general cultural insensitivity towards Billy's disability ranges from a disrespect towards his reading activities to Bartley laughing at his aspirations to be in the movies specifically because of his physical disability and from Babbybobby Bennett's (first played by Andrew Connolly and later by Liam Carney) fear of going out on a boat with a disabled person onboard, to the way that his sexuality and desires are so easily dismissed. The community collectively attempts to maintain Billy's marginalisation, but also to keep him as someone not comfortable in his own body, generating a sense of physical and psychic un-homeliness. Billy's disability is not specified in the text, but in performance all actors playing the part display apparent deformities.[80] It is important not to regard this disability as an easy form of enfreakment, more it is about making prominent the grotesque, as the play is also populated by a range of characters, all of whom are unaware or not concerned by their own idiosyncrasies, oddities, incongruities and strangeness. Equally, an emphasis on disability links in with the fixation of the community on what seems odd, strange and misshapen.

M. Beth Meszaros in a response to the connections between black comedy, disability and this play notes: 'The uncomfortable laughter that accompanies such humour is in part a response to a world in which *all* human beings are, at best, temporarily able-bodied.'[81] It is problematical, as Meszaros points out, to read impairment, disability and deformity as a general metaphor for human corruption, because such an analysis is 'insensible to the offensive construction of (whether physical or affective) as a signifier of moral weakness or turpitude' and does need to be confronted.[82] But as Meszaros notes: 'The modality of black comedy allows [Beth] Henley, as it allows McDonagh in *Inishmaan,* to attend to disablement in a fashion that is intellectually honest and aesthetically engaging.'[83]

In both of Hynes's productions Billy is played as if he is haunted or close to being overwhelmed by a sense of loss, as he constantly seems to circulate his own sadness, yet in each instance is not defined by his disability.[84] The doctor has little positive to say about Billy's parents, when asked, other than his father 'would rarely take a break from his fighting', (p.68) and that his mother was 'awful ugly', (p.69) had bad breath, but was 'pleasant enough'. (p.69) While Billy likes to believe that his mother had been punched by his drunken father while pregnant and that that led to his physical condition, the doctor corrects him – it was simply a genetic disease and warns him not to 'go romanticising it'. (p.69) Early on in the drama Helen challenges Billy with the accusation that his parents drowned '[....] trying to get away from' him, 'be distance or be death, it made no differ to them.' (p.15) Her explanation is a savage and insensitive assault, but she had more to say: 'Helen: They loved you? Would *you* love you if you weren't you? You barely love you and you *are* you.' (p. 16) It is not a passive fatalism that marks Billy's character most, rather his need to reflect on life, his mindfulness, the way that he responds to the challenges of his disability, his courage, ingenuity and assertiveness.

In Hynes's production, first Aaron Monaghan and later Tadgh Murphy as Billy create hugely influential and memorable performances. Monaghan's vocal delivery carries a particular vulnerability, low, forceful and touching, if slightly mumbled, which suggests a persistent scrabbling to make sense of his circumstances. There is hesitation, a consistent fractional stalling to his performance as his physical presence appears at times as less than resolute. Murphy brings a quieter, more measured approach to his interpretation: it is less pained perhaps, but at times more poignant and naively sensitive, and his performance is most effective in guiding the flow of emotions and responses, but it has less variation and fluctuation, as it is a little too dependent on a narrower if more consistent interpretative register. Of the two, Murphy's performance is the more gullible, and when he discovers the true facts of his parents' deaths, the disclosure is heartbreaking, whereas with Monaghan's performance it is as if such truth comes more as an affirmation of what he may have always suspected and the revelations offer a defining narrative to make coherent his own sense of his life, however illusionary it might have been up to now.

UNMADE IN AMERICA

By the end of Scene Two, almost all of Billy's aspirations and hopes seem to have been hindered or suppressed, but there remains his courage and self-determination regardless, a perseverance that is lost, it must be said, in some of the criticisms of the play. On the back of what appears like a serious lie about his health, Billy effectively forces Babbybobby to bring him on the boat across to the filming of *Man of Aran* – and even if is too late for the filming, Billy has taken to the seas, something he did not do before. Billy's actions suggest a desire to move on, a wish to embrace the outside world, even if that quest for otherness, difference and liberation takes the narrow, fictive and fanciful form of Hollywood and the movies. Later, throughout Scene Seven, the grim actualities for some who find themselves in Hollywood, hoping for a career in the film industry, are displayed. Billy is staying in a dingy hotel room rehearsing a clichéd-driven screenplay about an emigrant from Ireland dying from tuberculosis. Audiences may not be aware that this is simply a rehearsal, given that the scenario's details run close enough to Billy's circumstances as if to make them potentially believable, and equally, the sentiment that is foregrounded during this scene is not very far apart from the prospective sensibility of McDonagh's play at times itself. Some spectators may grasp immediately the subversive intent of the scene, others may be slower, and some others again may not get in on the joke until later when it is left to Billy to deconstruct the details himself. This leads to a particular type of complication, which some critics can put down as playfully and ironically indulgent and others as crudely manipulative.

Billy is rehearsing the part of a character, who is staying in a one-dollar a day rooming-house and who dying alone, uncared for, and is without medical treatment. While he has left behind a 'barren homeland,' he finds that America does not offer the prosperity and successes he so desired. The narrative emphasises the noble heart of the dying Irishman, whose body may be broken, but whose spirit is unbowed: 'Just an Irishman. With a decent heart on him, and a decent head on him, and a decent spirit, not broken by a century's hunger and a lifetime of oppression!' (p. 53) Notions of heaven and the memory of his mother are intertwined: 'Heaven could not be as beautiful as his mother', and crippled boys cannot get into heaven because they will uglify the place. (p. 53)

A crucial moment occurs here when Billy, in role, looks in a mirror and begins to sing 'The Croppy Boy'. And while the hero of the song dies, his resting place is in Ireland, but this scripted character is denied such a fate. He is companionless, and land-less, so to speak, whose identity as an Irishman is essential, but in its foregrounding, it overwhelmingly signifies lack. That sense of lack is partly about the inability to express his love for a woman, whom he has kept in the dark about his true feelings for her, and also, in part, about a silence brought into being by a history of oppression, dispossession and emigration. It is also about the inability to find or make a home in a place other than Ireland, but most importantly, it relates to his disability as essentially limiting or diminishing his sense of being. The songs of heroes might be on his lips, but these are of little comfort in his abandonment and displacement. Monaghan milks the moment, leaving it appear as if the scene is almost consistent with Billy's new-found distressing circumstances. (Murphy plays this scene with an apparent strength and physicality that suggest that his Billy remains in relatively good health, making the speech less probable.)

Billy does not get the part, as the film studio settles for an able-bodied (all) American boy from Fort Lauderdale. As Billy puts it pithily: 'the Yank said "Ah, better to get a normal fella who can act crippled than a crippled fella who can't fecking act at all". Except he said it ruder.' (p. 66) On his return home Billy opportunistically and cogently deconstructs the script, stating: '"An Irishman I am, begora! With a heart and a spirit on me not crushed for a hundred years of oppression. I'll be getting me shillelagh out next, wait'll you see. A rake of shite. And had me singing the fecking "Croppy Boy" then.' (p. 63)

And it is that sort of self-questioning of representation, that deconstruction of stereotypes that is also evident during the screening of *Man of Aran* in the local hall, as the islanders display no empathy towards the characters in the documentary-film. Instead they contest the sentiment and accuracy of the documentary-film, which sets out to make stoic, noble and heroic the lives of those on the margins. The film wishes to capture the authenticity, tenacity and survival instincts of the people, in the face of nature's onslaught and subsistence living. Some of the key moments in this work are repairing boats, gathering seaweed for fertiliser, scouring the crevices in the rocks on the island for soil, cliff face fishing in rock pools beneath and dangerously fishing for basking sharks for their liver oil that can be used in lamps. As one of many examples of native dissent, Karen O'Brien suggests that McDonagh has his characters purposefully 'reject the authenticity' of the shark hunting during their viewing of the film, as Aran's residents were not hunting basking sharks (also known as sunfish) 'in the 1930s when Flaherty filmed the documentary but nearly 100 years earlier'.[85]

Equally, in terms of gender, O'Brien correctly notes that 'The characters of *Inishmaan*, for example, do not relate to the assiduousness of the film's maternal figure, who tirelessly hauls heavy loads of water-soaked seaweed up the cliffs in order to cultivate a small patch of crops.'[86] The women in the play do not share that sense of obligation or enterprise. In terms of the feminine and the contestation of a patriarchal focus in the documentary-film's title, Helen wants a film to be made about herself, 'The Lass of

Aran', and not one simply 'some oul shite about thick fellas fishing' (p. 51) or 'wet fellas with awful jumpers on them'. (p. 60) (Mammy O'Dougal's husband was killed by a shark in 1871.)

Patrick Lonergan notes that 'Flaherty contrived and invented many of the film's most important moments. The cottage was built specially for the film, for example, – and the "family" were unrelated to each other.'[87] Secondly, instead of it being an authentic docu-film, it was a staged event that risked the lives of the actors, as Lonergan notes: 'Not only did Flaherty send the men out into the storm so that he could shoot the scene; he also made them return to the sea several times so that he could film them from different angles', which 'seems utterly unethical.' [88] What McDonagh does in this scene is to afford his characters the opportunity to deconstruct confidently O'Flaherty's work.

In the 2008 Hynes production Billy emerges, almost as if back from the dead, from behind the screen onto which the documentary is projected, dressed like a character from the movie. Interestingly, there is no screen projection in the 2011 production. Billy returns through a rear door to the hall. Instead of turning their backs on the audience to look at images projected onto a sheet on the hall's back wall, the actors look out into the theatre auditorium, as if they are watching the film. There are some aural indicators that suggest the showing of the film. And instead of Helen throwing an egg at the screen as she does in the 2008 production, she throws an imaginary egg into the audience, a detail which in some respects weakens the significance of the moment. Egg running down the suspended screen is potentially very funny. By having the actors in the 2008 production watch the piece with their backs to the audience, a different reality is constructed. The actors thus are not only responding, decoding and interpretative bodies, their liveness interrupts or disrupts the film's representative sensibility, as they interpret and reject aspects of it.

In contrast, the turning towards the 'audience off' in McAuley's terminology, 'can be a highly potent device in that it necessarily leaves the audience to identify the designated place with itself, but it is also strongly alienating of the fictional world'.[89] By having actors face out into audiences, and by reversing the gaze so to speak, Hynes implicates the spectator in the construction and transaction of Irishness, as a perceptive and culturally loaded activity, especially given the focus of the docu-film. As well as being emblematic of the returning, failed émigré, Billy's re-appearance represents that which is hidden, disregarded, and repressed of the documentary movie, but also confirms his subjectivity. Babbybobby's beating of Billy affirms this in a different way, when there is no excuse for Billy's exploiting of his grief and Billy suffers accordingly.

Paul Murphy's consideration of the early twentieth-century writings of John Millington Synge, William Butler Yeats and Lady Augusta Gregory offers a significant critique of the framing of marginalised, peasant or subaltern characters, both male and female, and the various dramaturgical functions they serve. Murphy's approach can enhance considerations of *Man of Aran* and is equally pertinent to any analysis of McDonagh's work more generally. Using Antonio Gramsci's work on subaltern figures, 'landless labourers and small cottiers,'[90] Murphy explains '*how* the subaltern is essentialised as a fantasy object which is symbolically central to dramatic and ideological representation,'[91] but marginalised socially, and that such centrality is designed 'to repress the continuing existence of class and gender hierarchies'.[92] Murphy argues that Gayatri Spivak's 'emphasis on the "mechanics" of the "constitution" of the subaltern informs the methodological approach' of his work, 'in the sense that, rather than essentialising the subaltern subject as "some *thing* that can be disclosed," the aim is to show that the subaltern is already essentialised within hegemonic discourse. The primary objective therefore is to explain *how* the subaltern is essentialised as a fantasy object which is symbolically central to dramatic and ideological representation.'[93]

Such centrality, Murphy argues, is designed 'to repress the continuing existence of class and gender hierarchies',[94] and to perpetuate 'social subordination.'[95] The peasant figure is essentially romanticised and deemed innocent in the work of Anglo-Irish writers, as dramatic action tends to 'affirm subordination,'[96] and conjure up an 'amnesia concerning inequality'.[97] Thus there is a fundamental gap between the representation and reality of their lives and a gap between how the dramaturgy acts on them and what is reinforced and legitimated through the symbolic centrality of the subaltern figure.

In relation to Yeats and Lady Gregory's *Cathleen ní Houlihan* Murphy argues how the peasant Michael morphs from '"a" peasant of historical specificity into "the" peasant of transcendent universality.'[98] In this instance, the notion of the '*Peasant* is constructed as the locus, or to put it in Lacanian terms as the *objet petit a*, of the cultural and political desires of the author.'[99] Equally, Flaherty's fisherman and his family in *Man of Aran* are in many respects fantasy objects and not too far from this perspective of naive 'transcendent universality'.

Yet it must also be said that Flaherty's island seems less like a pastoral landscape and more like a penitentiary. The struggles to subsist on very little also parallel the harrowing conditions of the Great Depression in America for instance. While there is a naive optimism as much as idealism perhaps in O'Flaherty's work, there is the further issue of whiteness to contend with. It is the apparent whiteness of Irishness that fundamentally complicates the application of the thinking of many theorists in relation to Ireland's circumstances, before and after colonisation.

In his examination of representations of whiteness Richard Dyer suggests that a number of categories of whiteness may be identified, in terms of 'pink, olive and grey' hues,[100] and these are further compounded by hair and facial features, body shape, gait and agility, and by that which is 'symbolically white'. Dyer is keen to point out the 'gradations of whiteness,' categorising those that are 'less securely white,' who include 'Latins, the Irish, and Jews,'[101] who are deemed as 'sometime white,'[102] or 'liminally white.'[103] Dyer's project is of a necessity to make whiteness 'strange,'[104] and McDonagh's work definitely does that with great regularity.

Through wide-ranging discussions of visual cultures, Dyer argues that the fundamental drives behind many of the representations of normative male whiteness are never without 'specific class, gender, or other socio-cultural inflections.'[105] Dyer connects advantage, privilege, superiority, dominance, goodness, power and legitimacy to a normative male whiteness, seeing its expression also in religious iconography, objective neutrality, spiritual purity, in the subjugation of women and in imperial practices. For Dyer, whiteness is a by-product of 'enterprise and imperialism' – enterprise in terms of adventure, application, problem-solving, and wilfulness, and colonisation in terms of myths of civilisation and progress, predicated on racial difference, interaction and domination.[106]

Following on from David Lloyd's work, Dyer argues that what is crucial is 'the attainment of a position of disinterest – abstraction, distance, separation, objectivity – which creates a public sphere that is the mark of civilisation, itself the aim of human history,' and this perspective underpins the 'conception of white people [...] as everything and nothing.' In its realisation of a sense of '*dis*-embodiedness,' for 'to be without properties also suggests not being at all,' which he explores as 'pure spirit.' But this also hints at 'non-existence' as 'colourless', as 'dissolving transcendence', as 'narrative impotence' or as death itself, as instability distorts its claims of universality.[107]

So to quote Dyer:

> Whites must be seen to be white, yet whiteness as race resides in invisible properties and whiteness as power is maintained by being unseen. To be seen as white is to have one's corporeality registered, yet true whiteness resides in the non-corporeal. The paradox and dynamic of this are expressed in the very choice of white to characterise us. White is both a colour and, at once, not a colour and the sign of that which is colourless because it cannot be

> seen: the soul, the mind and also the emptiness, non-existence and death, all of which form part of what makes white people socially white. Whiteness is the sign that makes white people visible as white, while simultaneously signifying the true character of white people, which is invisible.[108]

To substantiate his argument dialectically, Dyer settles with reluctance on the term 'non-white', rather than on 'people of colour'.[109] Fundamentally, for him, 'the equation of being white with being human secures a position of power.'[110] Further, Dyer cites Toni Morrison's work on the representations of African-Americans, how the projection of darkness and the unconsciousness, what is not within the realm of civility on the one hand, but on the other, what whites were aware of as also innate to them. Contradictory racial projections and displacements apply differently but with equal power to class and gender differentiations. Morrison notes: 'Whiteness, alone, is mute, meaningless, unfathomable, pointless, frozen, veiled, curtained, dreaded, senseless, implacable. Or so our writers seem to say.'[111]

Dyer profiles many examples of 'extreme whiteness', which when placed beside 'non-extreme, unspectacular, plain whiteness', illustrates 'a non-particular position of ordinariness' reserved from dominant white groups, united in their embodiment and recognition of a common consensual humanity, which can be addressed from a position of unremarkable disinterestedness, thus making its power dynamics intangible, invisible and affirming its privilege.[112]

But, Dyer argues 'the way in which this superiority is conceived and expressed, with its emphasis on purity, cleanliness, virginity, in short, absence, inflects whiteness once again towards non-particularity, only this time in the sense of non-existence'.[113] Further he suggests that 'the invisibility of whiteness as a racial position in white (which is to say dominant) discourse is of a piece with its ubiquity'.[114] On the other hand, non-whites are never afforded ordinariness, always marked as peculiar and exceptional, thus ensuring that whiteness is threatened by non-whiteness, by women, by homosexuality, by class disparities in terms of abundance, difference and finally by reproduction, which is central to the perpetuation of whiteness.

That said, within American popular culture Diane Negra has mapped the mobility of Irishness and its transactional qualities, and how its sensibility has altered over time. Currently it is more positively constructed, more wholesome subject than liminal object. Negra goes so far as to argue that 'Virtually every form of popular culture has in one way or another, at one time or another, presented Irishness as a moral antidote to contemporary ills ranging from globalization to postmodern alienation, from crises over the meaning and practice of family values to environmental destruction.'[115] Negra further notes the increasing use of 'Irishness as an ethnic code for reinstating social values perceived to be lost in millennial American culture'.[116]

Negra argues thus that, on the one hand, 'Irishness has become a form of discursive currency, motivating and authenticating a variety of heritage narratives and commercial transactions'.[117] and, on the other, how Irishness is not only 'reliably' and 'invariably, a form of whiteness', but that Irishness is a form of 'enriched whiteness'.[118] Negra suggests that 'Irishness may be both popular and comfortable precisely because it remains an identifiable (and presumably authentic) ethnicity that is nonetheless unthreatening and familiar.'[119] Negra highlights how Irishness oscillates between 'otherness' and 'whiteness', but just as substantially suggests that Irishness has 'become particularly performative'.[120] Amanda Third also reinforces Negra's idea that Irishness is a safe form of 'discursive currency', because it displays 'the necessary subaltern credentials that derive from a history of colonial otherness and circulating transnationality in essentialised and commodified forms'.[121] Traditionally, Third argues, 'as the Irish could not be distinguishable from the English in terms of skin colour, then red hair was demarcated as a distinguishing feature within the problematic category of whiteness, which enabled the singling out of the Irish and Celts as inferior [....] red hair was constructed as one characteristic of Irish otherness – in the colonial imaginary, it signalled their "off-whiteness" or their "not-quite-whiteness" [....] Redheads are produced, to use [Homi] Bhabha's phrase, as "almost the same, but *not quite*".'[122] Third continues as follows: 'The process of encoding Irishness as a restorative form of whiteness depends on the sublimation, and therefore the containment, of the more sinister and threatening dimensions of the history of Irish otherness.'[123] Third adds, however, that usually 'in current contexts it is that the subaltern, and often threateningly subversive, history of Irish otherness, rather than being disinterred, disappears'.[124] Third also stresses that Irishness 'offers a way of *performing whiteness* with legitimacy' (my italics).[125]

It is during *Inishmaan*'s final scene, where dialectical tensions between enriched and depleted, hegemonic and subservient, visible and liminal whiteness are made apparent, particularly, through the notion of romance, reproduction and death. Helen's change of heart and her kissing Billy results in Billy dumping the sack with which he had intended to kill himself, a gesture which is met by sustained applause from the audience on the evenings I saw it in 2008 and 2011.[126] And if success against the odds seems to be winning out, that a happy ending is within touching distance, then the tone abruptly switches again.[127] As Billy reaches to turn out the single hanging lantern, he coughs up blood. In both of Hynes's productions this is too hurried a moment, which may suggest an unwillingness to affirm the inevitable outcome of pulmonary tuberculosis.[128]

Regardless of this outcome, the play's closure is not emphasising romance, matrimony and potential offspring, but impending death. Here in this play, the inversion of the fertile potential of comedy maps onto the relative barrenness of the island, onto the future declines in the population of the island, and onto the impossibility of the budding romance to bring forth new life. In McDonagh's work more generally, and as Dyer has written about whiteness, there is no possibility of reproduction. (This is something to which I will return in the conclusion to this book.)

In this play in effect there are fictions within fictions, realities within realities, character within characters. By foregrounding theatricality, it is as if the characters are at all times conscious of performing for themselves, for their community and for an audience, as the range of emotions is pitched well beyond the registers of naturalism in Hynes's *mise-en-scène*. Johnnypateenmike, Helen and Billy are three of McDonagh's most optimistic characters. Each in different ways defies what their communities and theatre audiences have set out for them, in terms of gender, body ability and in terms of the most straight-jacketed stereotype of their theatrical type.

Rather than debilitating stereotypes, fixed essentialisms, or a 'transcendent universality' something fluid, flexible and unfixed materialises, as performativity opens up so many possibilities, including an undermining of the legitimacy of whiteness, disabling the superiority of whiteness, by equating it overwhelmingly with other, and with that which is not so different. It is my argument that what McDonagh potentially dramatises and what Hynes's work creates is that sense of having one's 'corporeality registered' in Dyer's words, while 'performing whiteness' and Irishness with illegitimacy. Writing about *Buffy The Vampire Slayer* and the character of Angel in particular, Meaney shows how death can be countenanced within the horror genre. In this genre, as Meaney suggests in her reading of Dyer's work, is the place where it is 'bearable for whites to explore the association of whiteness with death',[129] particularly for those that are 'liminally white' or pastorally white, as pastoral does a similar thing, with its elegiac function. In its blending of domestic and cemetery spaces, and in its enactment of a form of perverse second wake or deviant non-wake, *Connemara* sets out to interrogate the significance of the Irish funerary tradition and perhaps its destructive hold on the imagination.[130]

3 | In the Shadow of Living: Funerary and Heterotopic Spaces in *A Skull in Connemara*

Writing in 1967, Michel Foucault speaks of the fact that 'contemporary space is perhaps still not entirely de-sanctified (apparently unlike time, it would seem, which was detached from the sacred in the nineteenth century)' and that oppositions between 'family space and social space, between cultural space and useful space, between the space of leisure and that of work [...] remain inviolable,' as that inviolability is still 'nurtured by the hidden presence of the sacred'.[131]

Foucault distinguishes between 'real', 'utopian', and 'counter-sites',[132] which can be, in Foucault's terminology, 'spaces of illusion and of compensation'.[133] He goes on to identify 'Crisis heterotopias', which he aligns with primitive societies, and these are 'privileged or sacred or forbidden spaces, reserved for individuals who are [...] in a state of crisis'; however, these 'crisis heterotopias' are disappearing and are being replaced by what he calls 'heterotopias of deviation'.[134] Applying this terminology specifically in relation to graveyard spaces, Foucault notes that:

> Basically it was quite natural that, in a time of real belief in the resurrection of bodies and the immortality of the soul, overriding importance was not accorded to the body's remains [....] [But] from the moment when people are no longer sure that they have a soul or that the body will regain life, it is perhaps necessary to give much more attention to the dead body, which is ultimately the only trace of our existence in the world and in language [....] The cemeteries then came to constitute, no longer the sacred and immortal heart of the city, but 'the other city,' where each family possesses its dark resting place.[135]

Foucault is suggesting how the nature of graveyard spaces changes over time, in terms of significance, centrality and displacement, as the values of what these cemeteries house alters over time.

While pastoral spaces notionally can be some of the better examples of idyllic sanctified spaces, that sense of 'inviolable' divisions seems to no longer stand in relation to McDonagh, as he seems to be both evoking but also disputing that 'hidden sense of the sacred' in *Connemara*. How McDonagh frames this, as Foucault identifies, is through the 'juxtaposing in a single real place several spaces, several sites that are in themselves incompatible'.[136]

Of course, imbedded in almost all societies and cultures are strategies and rituals to deal with death and the remains of the dead, including last rites, prayers over the dead, wakes, cremations and burial ceremonies. Central to *Connemara* are the disinterring activities carried out annually by Mick Dowd, in order to clear an over-crowded graveyard on a rocky landscape and seven and a half years on from the death of his wife Oona, Mick Dowd faces the task of disinterring her skeletal remains. Both were involved in a motor accident which led to her death and he has served a jail sentence on a drink driving charge. Although having long completed his sentence, still hanging over Mick are rumours and innuendos that effectively maintain that his wife's death was not accidental, but that he purposefully drove a car into a wall in order to disguise the fact that he had fatally assaulted her prior to the accident.[137]

It is to be noted that disinterment is not a routine practice even in rural and rocky areas of Ireland.[138] Most cultures are generally resistant to the notion of exhumation and disinterment and usually one needs a court's permission to disturb a resting place. (However, in some countries due to spatial restrictions, corpses are exhumed and stored elsewhere in an ossuary, without compromises to the dignity of the dead.) Generally, the digging up of the dead carries with it all kinds of connotations and taboos and is often sensationalised by television and cinema in terms of autopsy scenes central to many cold case investigations.

In the Druid production, the opening exchanges between Mick (Mick Lally in one of his great performances) and Maryjohnny (Anna Manahan) display a mixture of shrillness, combativeness and defiance, with status shifting regularly between the characters.[139] Accusations may range from the incidental to the grievous, from cursing and cheating at Bingo to conning tourists, from providing misinformation about *The Quiet Man*'s film location to the non- attendance at confession and wife murder. Manahan's Maryjohnny is a wonderful presence, defiant and naive on the one hand, with a simplistic view of the world in response to things like cursing and urinating on consecrated ground, but, on the other, she is hugely exploitative and manipulative, and these do not benefit from moral consideration. For instance, the smile that Maryjohnny has for the audience at the end of the scene shows that while she is trying to settle Mick's anxieties about local gossip and intends somewhat to placate him with her words, her facial expression suggests that she knows more; even, perhaps that she is the source of those aspersions. She also remains ever willing to drink his poteen, as much out of selfishness as if it is some kind of perverted recompense.

Maryjohnny calls the act of disinterring a 'filthy occupation' and Mairtin Hanlon, her grandson, calls it 'The Graveyard Shenanigans', (p. 71) yet both remain obsessed and voyeuristic, regardless of their tendencies to see the task as morbid. Although Mick explains that the disinterring activities are overseen by both the church and the law, and makes clear that what he does is carried out with sensitivity, however, what happens to bones after disinterring remains a mystery, as Mick offers differing accounts as to what he does to dispose of the ancestors of Maryjohnny.

Mick settles on an account that appeases her; namely, exhuming, followed by bagging, the sinking of the bones to the bottom of the lake, accompanied by a 'string of prayers', and not submersion in the slurry pit that he had indicated previously. Ultimately, he is bound by oath to both the police and the clergy not to divulge what he does with the bones once they are removed from the graves. The disinterring chore is also an opportunity for Tom Hanlon, the local police officer and Mairtin's brother, to re-visit the circumstances surrounding Oona's death, as he is hoping to unearth some evidence to charge Mick belatedly with his wife's murder.

Whether it is characters inhabiting graveyards awaiting the dead to rise in Frank McGuinness's *Carthaginians* (1988), stories about grave digging experiences and paedophilia in Conor McPherson's *The Weir* (1997), the haunting presences of long dead children in Marina Carr's *Portia Coughlan* (1996) or Dermot Bolger's *The Passion of Jerome* (1999) or the dead coming back to life as in Hugh Leonard's *Da* (1978), Irish theatre often displays a greater obsession with death and dying, than with living. Of course, 'They give birth astride of a grave, the light gleams an instant, then it's night once more', is an often quoted line from Samuel Beckett's *Waiting for Godot* (1953).

Jonathan Swift's fascination, as Nina Witoszek and Pat Sheeran argue, with the 'morbid, the bleak and the repellent established Ireland as a pathogenic zone, as a "good place to die in,"'[140] something which Brian Friel exploits satirically in *The Mundy Scheme* (1969), where there is the idea of selling plots of land out west for the re-burial of the global dead. Central to this positioning is a 'vernacular funerary code' which has effectively and pejoratively 'reproduced and perpetuated the construction of Ireland as a place of death and fatality', according to Witoszek and Sheeran.[141]

This funerary tradition is shaped by 'folk representations, popular rituals, the rhetorics of the Irish media', and by a 'funerary mythology and experience' which underpins 'the Irish construction of place and landscape'.[142] This funerary tradition is also, they continue, 'reinforced by the memory of the Great Famine' and its 'accompanying horrors',[143] and 'it has also been further solidified by the response to the spiritual death in its various forms (despondency, resignation, passivity), threatening the Irish through the centuries of colonial oppression'.[144] Witoszek and Sheeran add that 'The loss of land and the displacement of the chief was very early on encoded in the metaphor of widowhood and conveyed through elaborate tropes of lamentation. It may well be that the anthropomorphisation of the country as a woman in bardic poetry lies at the basis of the funerary tradition.'[145]

COLD CASE COPPER

Scene Two opens at night with Mick halfway down into a grave, and the remains of two corpses are already extracted and bagged. In the initial Druid production, designed by Francis O'Connor, openings in the stage floor serve as two graves. Although the stage is bleakly lit to give the impression of night time, there remains on stage in the darkness, the dresser, stove, kitchen table and the sink with presses underneath whose presences are there not as simply shadows or as dimly lit objects, but simultaneously as strange, almost spectral presences of domesticity lingering over this public burial space.[146]

Mairtin is both a fool and a limited trickster figure, evident in the fact that when a local woman died, he put a werewolf comic alongside the body in the coffin and David Wilmot captures this superbly. The dark play imperative of Mairtin is seen in his ghoulish and puerile fascination with skulls, in his wish to contrast a newly uncovered skull with one already in the bag, later holding them to his chest as if they were two breasts. He also places the two skulls together as if they were kissing and also pokes a finger into an eye socket. The sexual dimension to such a gesture is further elaborated on when Mick talks about Mairtin inspecting the genital areas of both male and female deceased. Mairtin enquires as to what happens to the penis after death and Mick explains: 'Isn't it illegal in the Catholic faith to bury a body the willy still attached? Isn't it a sin in the eyes of the Lord?' (p. 86) and then goes further, stating that the penis is snipped off in the coffin and sold as dog food to Travellers. He adds that during the Irish Famine of the 1840s, the Travellers stopped feeding them to the dogs and started 'sampling the merchandise themselves'. (p. 87)

In the video recording of the play, little laughter greets Wilmot's Mairtin's playing with skulls and his holding of them as if they were breasts, but the audience did respond with laughter when Mick says it is hard to believe that Mairtin had a skull and a 'brain to go with it'. (p.85) When Mairtin pokes his finger into the eye socket of the skull, again there was little or no laughter in response, but during a non-scripted moment, when Mairtin pretends the skull to be a bowling ball and gestures to throw it towards the audience, there is a loud laugh.[147]

Discussions around castration and the extraction of genitals from corpses did bring a good deal of laughter. Mick's comment that 'the trouble with young people today, is they don't know the first thing about Irish history' is warmly responded to by the audience, in part comfortable with the exploitation of the cliché and the inter-generational comment, but all the more importantly, it is a response to the fact that what he is telling is a huge lie in the first place – Travellers eating phalluses removed from corpses before burial during the famine. (p.87)

This cemetery scene of course evokes the gravedigger's scene in William Shakespeare's *Hamlet*. Roland Mushat Frye notes that: 'Not only was there a broad tradition of showing a gentleman reflecting on a skull, there was even a visual tradition of setting that reflection specifically within a cemetery. In the fourteenth and fifteenth centuries, visual representations usually show the encounter of three living men and three dead. Sixteenth-century treatments come closer to Hamlet's exchange with the gravedigger.'[148]

Richard Fly, along similar lines, suggests that in *Hamlet*: 'The clownish gravedigger is a most formidable spokesman for the vanity and ephemerality of all human endeavour, and as Hamlet watches him working at his venerable trade he experiences in a new way the single irreducible fact of certain oblivion and general dissolution.'[149] While Hamlet's consciousness is further provoked by his experiences during the gravedigger's scene, [150] the same cannot be necessarily said of Mairtin and Mick. Neither undergoes any real sense of a *Memento Mori*, as their digging brings no encounter with a metaphysical ephermality, as there are no new awarenesses in the face of death. If as Witoszek and Sheeran suggest: 'The Irish omphalos is the graveyard, the centre of continuity and the meeting place between the worlds',[151] it can also be equally argued that the pastoralised Irish kitchen space is just as central. Now, it is McDonagh's meshing of both which becomes evident and so significant from this point forward.

Scene Three brings the play's action back from the graveyard to Dowd's living space. Mairtin and Mick move onto the next phase of the work. This scene opens with skulls on the kitchen table, with only Mairtin's head visible, at the same level as the table, so that his head is effectively amongst the skulls. Both actors smash up the remains with mallets, Wilmot's Mairtin with a certain transgressive or anarchic glee, Lally's Mick enraged by the knowledge that the remains of Oona have been stolen from her resting place. Mairtin claims that none of his friends would be body snatchers and he wonders if it were Travellers who did it: '[....] Maybe they were expecting another praitie blight and felt like something to be munching on ahead of time.' (p. 102) Again, there is evidence of prejudice and intolerance towards Travellers, but also something sacrilegious around mentioning the eating of dead flesh, which obviously hints at an extreme form of cannibalism. (In some cultures it is acceptable to eat dead flesh, but not remains that are seven years in the ground.) In the Druid performance, two drunken men smashing the skulls is now not framed as predominantly sinister or desecrating; it is only Mairtin's fear of being alone with the remains that offers any sense of a transgression of the sacred. Lally's Mick is very aggressive with the malleting and justifies his approach by suggesting that if the community endlessly gossips about him in the way that it has, what more should they expect when they wind up in his hands other than a 'batter'. (p. 103) As the scene progresses, there is something perversely de-ritualistic about this scene, something deviant is being revealed in their obsession and indifference towards the dead. And by the end of the scene there are pieces of shattered bone everywhere, and Lally's Mick also stamps on the bits of bone that have fallen on the ground. (Fragments at times have the potential to fly into the audience.[152])

This particular scene suggests a sort of deviant, de-sanctified second or even a non-wake that flies in the face of convention. Traditionally in Ireland, alongside Christian rites, pagan or indigenous practices of funeral wake games were enacted in such a way that the dead are grieved and celebrated, respected and disrespected, feared and embraced, during a period of time which eased the passing of the spirit from one dimension to another and accommodated a fear of the returning from the dead of those who have recently passed away. Wakes are in part to help 'alleviate the pain of bereavement' as Witoszek and Sheeran suggest.[153] And they add:

> While attempting to explain the eschatological basis of the wake, Seán Ó Súilleabháin has argued that its original purpose was not only to alleviate the pain of bereavement by means of a riotous feast but also to 'bribe' the spirit of the dead person, to keep him/her quiet and safely out of the way of the living.[154]

They suggest that the wake also served as 'a theatre of social rehabilitation in which useless praise was expended on those who are denied a good word during life. The wake had the power to transmute, to bring the dead person out of anonymity, disgrace even, and transform him or her into a local legend.'[155] Of the one 130 wake games and amusements documented by Ó Súilleabháin, of this 'ludic constellation' as Witoszek and Sheeran call them, 'the most prominent include storytelling, singing, dancing, card playing, athletic competitions, verbal sparring and fighting', and these go back to pre-Christian Ireland and the games of lamentation or 'cluiche caointech' celebrated to mark the death of a warrior.[156] (Mairtin's transgressive stories include a drunk in Salthill that drowned in his own urine (p. 106) and Mick tells of three of his uncles who 'drowned on sick'. (p. 106))

Quoting Lawrence Taylor, Witoszek and Sheeran observe that 'the Catholic Church's domestication and control of the libidinous and pagan element of the wake was a way to establish the Church's cultural hegemony in the nineteenth century',[157] but also 'wakes, viewed as folk spectacles that competed with church ceremonial for the control of death, may be interpreted as spasmodic acts of resistance to church hegemony'.[158] The wake's 'countercultural function as a "ritual of the people", in contradistinction to official ecclesiastical ceremonies, has proved irresistible to pupils of [Mikhail] Bakhtin and Foucault alike', Witoszek and Sheeran claim.[159] Traditionally, watching over the dead, and the 'blasphemous revelry with which the corpse was surrounded, launched a comic, even strangely alluring, *ars morierendi* [sic]', as Witoszek and Sheeran note.[160]

They also utilise Arnold Van Gennep's notion of liminal rites to suggest that the 'mourning process involves an identification between the bereft and the deceased in that both are situated "between the world of the living and the world of the dead"', and 'given this unresolved state, there are two choices. The mourners can either kill the dead a second time, so as to remove themselves from the realm of liminality, or preserve the dead and prolong their stay in the intermediate world.'[161] The texts Witoszek and Sheeran examine indicate a cultural reluctance to the killing of 'the dead a second time' and instead they remain in a state of inbetweenness.[162]

Although *Lonesome* opens just after Coleman's and Valene's father's funeral, what is remarkable is the indifference towards the dead and the absence of almost any of the signs of bereavement. The 'riotous feast' associated with the wake is swapped for a concern over vol-au-vents and the keeping of greedy locals away from the afters of the funeral. Van Gennep sees such meals after funerals as 'rites of incorporation'.[163] However, there is no need to 'bribe' the spirit to keep out of the way of the living and the traditional notion of the 'rehabilitation' of those just dead, does not seem to apply. Later the deaths of Tom Hanlon and Fr Welsh additionally challenge the brothers to encounters with grief, but there is neither real fear nor celebration of the dead, just feigned empathy, tokenism and indifference.

Here in *Connemara*, the removal of the bones from the graveyard to this domestic place complicates not only the liminal relationship between public and private, and between the living and dying, but even more importantly between the sacred and the un-consecrated, as Foucault suggests. It is not so much a refusal to kill the dead a second time, but instead the remains are strangely waked or non-waked for a second time and destroyed in such a way that they are not afforded a dignified re-location, but are scattered unceremoniously in a slurry pit, along with the waste from farmyard animals.[164] The grinding of the remains to dust also means that the skeletons are no longer individualised.

Van Gennep regards funerals as rites of separation, as survivors or the living emerge 'through rites of reintegration into society' (rites of the lifting of mourning). Often the dead do not pass to the afterlife, until they have been cremated or are decomposed and without flesh. Sometimes putrefaction can be accelerated by fire and followed by 'a second series for the burial of the skeleton'.[165] But the death and rebirth, death and resurrection, dismemberment and reconstitution that Van Gennep identifies in traditional rites of passage are disavowed here in the instance of this play. Both the rite of separation and passage into another dimension is interfered with by the digging up of the dead.

However, it is Mairtin's inability to control his own tongue that catches him out when he declares that the locket that Oona was buried with 'wouldn't fetch you a pound in the Galway pawn shop'. (p. 109) (It is a rose locket, with a picture of Mick inside.) Staggering drunk and unaware that he has revealed too much, Mairtin is readying himself to drive Mick's car. Mick leaves the scene carrying a mallet and the spectator wonders what fates await both men. Later that evening, with a bag in hand containing Oona's skull, which is in breach of all standard police procedures, Tom Hanlon comes round to coerce a confession from Mick to Oona's murder. Tom claims to have found the skull at the bottom of their family field, the same place where Mairtin supposedly came across the bones of a dead cow. Hanlon informs his police work by practices gleaned from television series like *Petrocelli, Quincy,* and *Starsky and Hutch* and prides himself on his detective's instincts and on his capacities to establish clear-cut differentiations between 'insults' and 'vague insinuations', (p. 95) but cannot tell the difference between circumstantial and hearsay evidence.[166]

This police officer is always on the look-out for problematic cases, having previously investigated the death of a fat man who was found naked in front of the television in his apartment, and his fridge only had a pot of jam and a head of lettuce. Such details call to mind the film *Se7en* (1995) written by Andrew Kevin Walker and directed by David Fincher.[167] In the Druid production, Brián F. O'Byrne is stiff in body and presents an affected voice, displaying the poise and status of what he expects a detective to be, driven by self-deception and over-confidence in his own abilities.

O'Byrne's slowness of body matches a lethargy of mind, and what he wants to pass off as measured deliberateness and deep consideration of facts and information, comes across as the exact opposite. Tom Hanlon as a character is less like television detective Columbo, mentioned by Mairtin in performance, but not in the script, and more like the corrupt but finally stupid detective Truscott in Joe Orton's *Loot* (1965).[168]

Indeed, Mick is ready to sign a confession to murder, but not to the murder of Oona, but to that of Mairtin, having left him for dead, for his part in taking Oona's remains from her grave. While Mick agrees to a confession, there is no pen readily available and in terms of grotesque humour, Maryjohnny produces one of her fluorescent bingo pens to solve the problem. Instead, Mick provides his own pen, his lucky lotto one, in order to complete the task. However, just like the father of Christy Mahon in Synge's *Playboy of the Western World* (1907) a concussed Mairtin re-enters the living area, all the while claiming his injuries were as a result of an accident and not assault. (Surreptitiously, Mick sets the confession alight.)

Mairtin is then struck by Tom on the head, once Mairtin admits to Tom's role in the digging up of the remains and in tampering with evidence, by carving a hole in the skull. Mairtin's inclination to squeal is because Tom had told him he would get ten pounds in the pawn shop for the rose locket, and all he got was a pound, which in many instances proves to be pathetic motivation, but nonetheless enough comic motivation for the piece.

During the final moments of the drama, Maryjohnny maintains to have seen something on the night of Oona's death, claiming that Oona will drag Mick's soul to hell after he dies. Again the suggestion is not backed up by fact. As she leaves, Mick caresses the cracked skull of his wife (as Maureen has done to her suitcase in *Beauty Queen*), kisses it gently and audiences are left without any confirmation as to how Oona died; watertight evidence is not put forward, only that which is uncorroborated, circumstantial and hearsay. His caressing of the skull raises all kinds of interesting suggestions around the erotic and death, even hinting at something unsavoury. In the Druid production, Mick Lally holds the skull for a long time, but it is less incisively sexual in its focus, and somewhat more to do with loss, absence and perhaps guilt, and is far more Grand-Guignol than necrophilic in its intentions.

Still, as Mushat Frye notes that the dramatisation of the *memento mori* in *Hamlet* 'did not trap a person in the spiritual cul-de-sac of a sterile preoccupation with death. On the contrary, one was directed toward life – toward the effective living of life which must, in every case, be lived under the shadow of death, and which, should be lived without anxiety, without dread, and without a preoccupation with transiency.'[169]

Susan Letzler Cole suggests that 'the grave is the birthplace of tragic drama and ghosts are the procreators', adding, 'tragedy is the performance of that ambivalence: the kind of ambivalence which ghosts emblemize' – and by that she means the ghost returning to haunt is 'the extending of life beyond the moment of death'.[170] If '*Hamlet* is the tragedy of a mourner in a world which provides no context for mourning',[171] as Letzler Cole suggests, then *Connemara* equally provides neither 'the extension beyond the moment of death' nor a 'context' for mourning. While the grave may be the 'birthplace of tragic drama', in *Connemara,* although the deceased may haunt, they are not ghosts and not 'procreators'. While *Hamlet* does foreground the maimed rite; for Mick Dowd, there is no closure by digging up the remains of Oona, as the digging up is no longer a maimed ritual, but a non-event on the metaphysical level, fundamentally, a non-wake.

McDonagh's realignment of the ritual of the wake, through morbid communal self-absorbing and self-defining narratives, transgressive disinterment and quasi-sacrilegious destruction of bones ensure the juxtaposition of 'incompatible spaces' that Foucault mentions and the mingling of discordant sensibilities. It could be argued that the Irish tradition of waking rituals constitutes forms of 'crisis heterotopias', which are a strange alignment of the sacred and the pagan, with a consistent belief in an afterlife, whereas in McDonagh's work generally, wakes are very much akin to 'heterotopias of deviation', where the belief in an afterlife is abandoned, where the remains of the dead have no sacred or symbolic value; they are either there to be smashed as part of a routine dis-interment, or else to be violated by a policeman as he tampers with potential evidence. The dead are exhumed and despoiled to contest their significance. While McDonagh seems to tempt his audiences initially with this pastoral myth of recovery and redemption, very soon audiences are wrong-footed. While pastoral spaces notionally can be some of the better examples of idyllic sanctified spaces, that sense of 'inviolable' divisions that Foucault mentions seems to no longer stand in relation to McDonagh, as he seems in his writing to be evoking but also disputing that 'hidden sense of the sacred' in *Connemara*.

In McDonagh's work, using Roger Sales's terminology of the pastoral as deployed by Terry Gifford, and as mentioned in my Introduction, 'refuge' becomes entombment, 'reflection' becomes thoughtlessness. There is no 'rescue' or 'reconstruction' for the characters, only repetition at best. 'Requiem' becomes a perverse exhumation of the dead, with grief predominantly absent. In the Druid premiere, such challenges are further complicated when deviancy is offset by the stupidity of the characters (as O'Byrne and Wilmot play them), the macabre undermined by the flippancy of the characterisations generally – the morbidity by the casual incongruity of the way that theatrical space functions and the grotesque is counterbalanced by the ridiculous fixations on the characters on quests for truths and facts in the face of fictions, lies, gossip and rural myths.

This approach brings to mind the already mentioned Orton's *Loot*, where there is a de-sanctified approach towards human remains, but also John Arden's *Sergeant Musgrave's Dance*: *An Unhistorical Parable* (1959). In Arden's play a group of soldiers brings back the bones of a colleague, Billy Hicks, to his homeplace and hang his remains in a public place in order to display the carnage of war and on a symbolic level the bones of imperialism and the community's effective complicity in colonisation. The pacifist inclinations of Musgrave and his troops and their rage at war and at soldiering prompt plans of a bewildering and gross retaliatory violence against the community.

In many respects, *Connemara* is McDonagh's 'Un-historical Parable', where he deploys an anarchic and unsanctified approach to Irish traditions of the dead, to obsessions with death and dying and to the debilitating hold of a funerary imaginary. Even more, I am suggesting that McDonagh's dramaturgy is a necessary challenge to the hold of the funerary tradition over diasporic communities and how they acknowledge home, exile and return, if it is seen in these terms, with exile as a form of living death. It is not the past, the draw of the grave or the call of eternity which matter, but existing not in the 'shadow of death', but in the shadow of living which is of substance.

4 | Theatricality and Unpredictable Determinism in *The Beauty Queen of Leenane*

THE FAIREST QUEEN OF ALL

The playtext of *Beauty Queen* contains quite detailed descriptions of what seems to be a relatively familiar, cottage space,[172] and while such specific details seem suggestive of something close to peasant or rural realism; however, in its blatant clichés and in its ironic, even kitsch cottage sensibility, something additional is being filtered through from the beginning. The performance style of Hynes's *mise-en-scène* evolved over time,[173] and jettisoned much of its earlier more naturalist approach.[174] My argument here will be on how her production engaged, negotiated and subverted many of the conventions, tenets and practices of traditional, peasant, realist dramas.

Central to both Naturalism and Realism are the notions of mimesis or verisimilitude. William W. Demastes suggests the following about critics of realism:

> (they) often reduce the term to signifying the use of real refrigerators, food, or other props on stage. Others identify it by observing common, unadorned language, and 'common' themes. Similarly guilty of over-simplification, proponents often argue that realism is predicated on 'objectivity', a faithful rendering of existence without biased impositions on the part of its creators.[175]

Demastes in his comments above captures many of the preconceptions. Christopher Innes points out that the term realism is broadly applied to an approach that is allegedly 'without editorializing or external commentary', as it deals with subjects in discernible social contexts, determined by authenticating details.[176] Innes prises the terms realism and naturalism apart, and his distinction is that naturalism refers 'to the theoretical basis shared by all the dramatists who formed the movement and their approach to representing the world', whereas realism then applies to 'the intended effect and the stage techniques associated with it'.[177] (This is a useful but limited differentiation, which I will further develop.) Demastes and Michael Vanden Heuvel cite William B. Worthen's comment that a 'realist theatre of disclosure is also a theatre of concealment', in its attempts to pass off 'acts of interpretation and dramaturgical shaping as neither subjective nor ideological'.[178] All theatre is subjective and ideologically motivated.

Under the influence of Charles Darwin's theory of evolution, early naturalist writers foreground the absence of choice for their characters, as they are pre-determined by their environments, by their psychological make-ups, and by their genetic inheritances. That way, as Demastes notes, 'predestination and fate have been reduced from religious or even romantic mystery to scientific inevitability', when incorporated into Emile Zola's theories of naturalism.[179] This sense of passivity or fatalism inherent in naturalist theatre practices gives rise to Raymond Williams's comment that 'the tragedy of naturalism is the tragedy of passive suffering and the suffering is passive because man can only endure and can never really change his world'.[180] (In contrast, realism to my mind, more in the mode of the work of Anton Chekhov and Henrik Ibsen, for example, is not as confined by passivity or inevitability in these same ways and although formally these plays tend to remain grounded in causality – with some exceptions – they leave space for difference, choice, challenges and change, however miniscule or ineffective character interventions may be.[181])

Additionally, Una Chaudhuri also notes the spatial arrangements of naturalism 'function according to a logic of *total visibility*',[182] reinforcing Worthen's notion of apparent 'disclosure'. She elaborates:

> The naturalist contract between spectator and performer is one of 'total visibility, total knowledge.' The promise of the well-stocked stage of naturalism is a promise of omniscience, indeed the transfer of omniscience from the dramatist to the spectator. Having been impregnated with 'reality,' in the form of all those little touches of 'innocent verisimilitude' that Bert [O] States memorably describes as 'the casual masquerading as the casual' (citing *Great Reckonings in Little Rooms: On the Phenomenology of Theatre* (Berkeley: University of California Press, 1985), p.67), the stage space of

> naturalism seems ready to deliver the whole truth, to dispel the enigmas of past and future from a firmly drawn present.[183]

These notions of 'visibility' and transparency are also disturbed once issues of concealment, suppression, repression, subjectivity and ideology are raised. Thus, dramatic naturalism and realism are regarded by many as pejorative, latently conservative and patriarchally compliant dramatic forms, capable of perpetuating specific race, class and gender biases.

UN-FORGIVEN CIRCUMSTANCES

For early realist or naturalist writers, acting styles, alongside scenic design, chimed with claims of verisimilitude and had little or no room for irony, satire, pastiche or theatricality. In effect, a 'minimalization of theatricality is very much a central gauge of realism, upon which rests a fundamental criterion of the realist mode', Demastes argues.[184] Today's audiences may accept certain levels of theatricality, but still regard the work as realist. Robert Gordon notes the idea that the actor 'should create the illusion that she *is* actually the character inheres in the project of the naturalistic theater to transform the pictorial realism typical of nineteenth-century theater into the perfect illusion of the slice of life'.[185]

Gordon notes, in essence, Stanislavski's evolving acting system, whether achieved through objectives and actions, consciously or unconsciously motivated, through lines, spontaneity, subtext, emotion memory and given circumstances, 'is based on the assumption that the aim of acting is the representation of the psychology of characters who function on stage as if they were real people'.[186] Emphasis is thus on self-effacement, there is no difference between actor and role, as mimicry is 'often combined with the use of introspective methods of characterization'.[187] However, theatricality complicates the visibility/concealment dichotomy and opens up an awareness of the input of designers, directors and actors, as well as announcing the active presence of the writer, who supposedly works under 'the illusion of absence' in the realist form.[188]

Pavis argues that in the theatre 'emotions are always manifested by means of a rhetoric of the body and by gestures in which emotional expression is systematized, even codified'.[189] Pavis decrees that the emotions of actors do not 'need to be real or lived: they must above all be visible, legible, and in compliance with the conventions relating to the representation of feelings', whether it is conventions 'of psychological verisimilitude', or 'of an acting tradition that has codified feelings and their representation'.[190] Pavis further elaborates: 'The greater the degree to which emotions are translated into attitudes or physical actions, the greater their freedom from the psychological subtleties of the unspeakable and of suggestion.'[191] Within the *mise-en-scène* Hynes's actors demonstrate the importance of 'kinesthetic sensations, awareness of the axis and body weight, of bodily structures and the location of their partners in space-time', which Pavis notes as being central to a style very much inconsistent with a realistic mode of acting.[192]

With her actors Hynes's approach seems to be less in the direction of the 'psychological subtleties of the unspeakable and of suggestion'– in Pavis's phrasing – and more towards a physicality that is predominantly grotesque or cartoon-like in attitude and disposition. Instead the characters become exaggerated types, whose actions are inflated, who are simultaneously playful and sinister, vulnerable and destructive, as well as being inhibited and licenced, contradictorily repressed and bold, in both their spontaneity and artificiality.

Additionally, as Pavis notes, the theatre director 'acts as a kind of tempographer for the performance: she controls its temporality and mediates between its propositions and our expectations',[193] and it is Hynes's sense of performance rhythm, alongside acting dispositions, which disavows the real as a default setting. So in *Beauty Queen*'s domestic space, where Mag and Maureen enact what appears as their daily routine, Hynes's production establishes a distinctive 'tempo-rhythm', through proxemics, kinesics, tonality and actor physicality.[194]

In fact, Marie Mullen admits to Peter Marks that 'her approach was too harsh in the production's early days. Maureen, sick to death of waiting on her mother, unloads on Mag from the moment she walks in from the rain in Scene 1, and Ms. Mullen made her too much of a harridan. "I was screaming my head off," she recalled. But she soon discovered the softer and funnier tones in a woman marked in life for defeat, the sort in whom an audience invests its fondest hopes.'[195] Anna Manahan's observation in the same interview is especially incisive: 'Every look, every nuance is like a stitch [...] If you drop one, you're in trouble, because it's all so interknitted.'[196] That sense of the Folans being interlinked suffuses the psychic and kinesic performance space shared by the actors throughout the production, where there is simultaneously so much and so little at stake.

Manahan as Mag and Mullen as Maureen confront each other in ways that only those locked into destructive patterns of co-dependency can. Initially, it appears as if Maureen is the more uptight, frustrated, hostile and provocative, and Mag the one who is more cunning, manipulative, malign and intentionally over-reliant on and over-controlling of her daughter. Mag seems to be attempting to maintain some form of authority over the family space, in a scenario that is a sort of 'latter-day Irish *Steptoe and Son*', as Nicholas Grene proposes.[197]

Although mother and daughter speak to each other in a form of shorthand, and they seem set in their ways, there is a very strong sense of something additional going on evident in how they speak to each other, as if it is the unsaid that binds them but also keeps them apart. This strange blend of interdependence, loyalty, dutifulness, excessive expectation, deceitfulness, harassment and guilt creates a good deal of frustration and negative reward for both parties. Manahan and Mullen play off each other with wonderful awarenesses and while there is a clear sense of a parasitic relationship, there are also, bizarrely, some more positive sentiments shared between them as well.

Their first significant battle over the nutritional supplement, Complan, captures their individual presentational, confrontational and manipulative methodologies. Mag's calling attention to her damaged hand is the initial deal breaker, with Maureen relenting and agreeing to prepare the Complan for her mother's consumption.[198] However, if Mag seems initially dominant, in part because of her seniority, the status shifts quickly when Maureen opts to confront her about the smell of urine coming from the kitchen sink. Indeed, Maureen raises the stakes higher by responding to Mag's story of a woman strangled by a stranger in Dublin. This is the type of man Maureen suggests that she would like to meet and to bring home with her. So what is momentarily suggestive and a little unsettling makes way for something far more complicated as Maureen takes strange delight in declaiming her gory fantasy of her mother's death: 'If he clobbered you with a big axe or something and took your oul head off and spat in your neck, I wouldn't mind at all, going first.' (p.6)

This exchange says as much about their aggressive, almost cartoon-like dynamic as it does about the tone of the writing itself, which is complicated further by the almost instant shift from aggression and intimidation evident in the gory details of a fantasised murder to the most banal sort of request when Mag asks for sugar to sweeten the porridge. There is possibly a growing awareness that their tensions seem a fraction too pre-determined, patterned and purposefully inconclusive. They may or may not be taking very seriously what is being said by each other. Such ambivalence is an essential part of the play's comedy.

Both actors accommodate subtle shifts in status, but also take a certain delight in their abilities to adjust from something quasi-psychologically antagonistic to a dynamic that is aggressively surreal, fobbing off the more serious emotional intensities through a heightening of the banal and the inconsequential. Indeed, the familiarity of their scheming, game-playing, status brokering, threats and intimidation mean that there is little need to be guarded about their individual intentions. They appear to be not only enacting a script, but that they could almost swap roles and perform each other's parts, such seems to be the twisted intimate bond of Mag and Maureen. However, when she pours her mother's tea down the sink and then dumps the half-eaten porridge in the bin, Maureen's reprisal to her mother's pressured demands may well startle the spectator, who may have been lulled into a false sense of comfort and expectation by the nature of the rapport up to this point, however belligerent it may have initially appeared.

Manahan has a fluent, flamboyant, declarative quality to how she performs, as if she has absorbed the rhythms of their exchanges and even appears to be somewhat more at ease with them, however traumatic some of the previous incidents may have been. It is not as if Manahan's Mag has made the trauma normal, but has internalised them in ways that can accommodate their shared world. Manahan's Mag appears to think that she knows how best to interact under these particular circumstances, and is partially deluded into believing that she can still be the dominant household figure. Mullen's Maureen disguises her instabilities behind her outward displays of shrill composure and order. Although frustrated by her mother, she sees herself as the dominant one, reassured by her physical strength, her mobility and by her previous victories. Mullen plays Maureen initially as if she believes that she has already triumphed in their battle or game. Therefore, it is as if she indulges her mother, inviting her to participate in their exchanges with a status well in excess of what Maureen believes it to be in actuality.[199]

A DEATH MATCH

Ray Dooley's introduction gives the play the opportunity to open out. Before Ray, Mag seems absentminded and a trifle difficult, but she is also more humane in her dealings with the nineteen- year-old, who is a strange mix of impatience, disrespect, petulance, aggression and naivety as Tom Murphy plays him in Hynes's first production. His juvenile frustrations and his ineffective anti-police sentiments are established by him in a very accomplished manner.

Mag's burning of Pato's invitation to the dance and Maureen's awareness of it leads to further extensive game playing, but the more sinister side of Maureen re-surfaces when she aggressively presses Mag into consuming hastily-prepared, lumpy Complan. The force feeding, under the threat of worse to come, displays Maureen's sadistic tendencies, but again these still seem to be under a good degree of conscious control.

Yet, as the cruelty of the exchange peaks between them with Maureen's threats and Mag's vocalising her objective to deny Maureen any form of life beyond her orbit, the focus switches again when Maureen offers to drive them both to Westport, with the intention of purchasing a black dress for the party. This maintains the pattern of intense confrontation followed by swift deflation and it probably now serves as the anticipated norm for the spectator: as such, it places again in serious doubt the exact nature of these venomous exchanges.

Having stayed over, Pato is exposed to Mag's spoiling tactics. Threatened by the potential implications of a budding relationship between Maureen and Pato – even at such an early stage of their romance – Mag informs Pato that Maureen has force fed her Complan and blames Maureen for burning her hand with hot oil. Mag also tells Pato of the time Maureen spent in Difford Hall, a mental institution in England, but this revelation does not unnerve him, rather he sees it as something which places Maureen in a positive, sensitive light.[200] Maureen guilefully acknowledges that she did have a mental break-down, leaving her free to repudiate Mag's account of the wound to her hand by claiming that her mother cannot tell the difference between fact and fiction. The great fear for Mag is to be abandoned, destitute and institutionalised in a nursing home.

Brián F. O'Byrne's Pato responds to their third-party directed performance with a strange mix of casualness, bemusement, fear, pity, compassion and respect. O'Byrne also poignantly captures a strong sense of his character's lonely, diasporic displacement in London. There is a level of genuineness to Pato, which is matched by passivity, gormlessness, fickleness, inconstancy and by a seeming unwillingness to assert or fight for what he desires. Before Pato, Mullen demonstrates a range of emotions that have not been displayed before, including sadness, insecurity, a blatant desire for intimacy and hope for the future. Equally, Mullen's Maureen embarrasses O'Byrne's Pato with her blatant and provocatively theatrical display of sexuality in front of her mother.[201]

Having done her best to ruin any budding relationship, Mag returns to her obsession with her porridge. Manahan captures this essential and recurring shift in focus quite brilliantly, as if to confirm that there are almost no continuities or consequences to the instinctive betrayal of the privacies of her daughter. Manahan indicates that both dispositions – an immediate focus on food and the need to damage her daughter – are seemingly operating on equivalent, undifferentiated registers. However, this inability or refusal to distinguish and the failure to understand proportionality and causality will have radical implications for Mag later.

On the evening of Pato's going-away party and not having had received the invitation to emigrate with him to America, Maureen, although moody, trivialises to the best of her ability the fact that she is not going to attend the event. However, in disclosing her knowledge about her daughter's enduring virginity, and by being mischievously incapable of withholding the slight, Maureen becomes determined to extract the extent and source of her mother's knowledge in ways that she knows best, readying her implements of torture – oil, chip pan and rubber gloves.

From this moment the play begins to move towards its inevitable, if not fully anticipated, conclusion. If audiences have doubted Mag's previous revelations about the scalding of her hand, here now is ample proof. If audiences had assumed that despite the interference of the elderly woman, youngish love would eventually win through, however, the instant Maureen pours hot oil on Mag's hand and then throws what remains over her, the play enters another altogether different dimension of consciousness.

While the stage directions in the text suggest a range of pained responses from Mag, it can be problematic for an actor to achieve these expressions successfully in performance. If this was a realistic work, then the actor would hope to demonstrate terror and heightened trauma. In the Druid production, there is little time for the oil to heat up to a realistically high enough temperature and the moment of torture passes quickly. The scene's horror equates with the moments of terror often found in Grand-Guignol and Manahan's Mag goes for the melodramatic and the sensational over the psychological.[202] Yet the performance emphasis is less on Mag and more on the composed, surreal calm and psychic daze that Maureen enters.

During Scene Eight in the Druid performance, Maureen is initially all positive and innocent, smiling while she recounts the romantic scenario of a last-gasp meeting and tender moments in a railway station, exchanged between the two lovers, who are only to be separating temporarily. Then bored of accounting for Pato's leave-taking, Maureen sinisterly raises the poker, only to lower it again, then easing the dead Mag forward with it so that her death is confirmed. (This is different to the script which has Maureen standing on her mother's back 'in thoughtful contemplation') (p.51).[203] The scene is further proof that Maureen has left one and arrived in another consciousness, a functioning madness. Regardless, Mullen's Maureen still maintains the capacity to cover over her own murderous tracks, with a crude explanation as to how Mag fell over a stile and then down a hill to her demise, as if from a children's rhyme. Still the justice and punishment models of fairytales await her.[204]

However, it is during her final encounter with Ray where the full extent of Maureen's delusions is exposed. Pato is not waiting for Maureen in Boston, as she herself wants to believe and the suitcase that she brings into the living space, will not be going anywhere soon. Indeed, on the night of Pato's leaving, he departed by taxi and not by train as Maureen had imagined and reported it to be. Pato is now engaged to Dolores Hooley or Healey and they are to be married the following year.

Luckily, Ray's anger on the discovery of the long-confiscated swing ball ensures that he closes down Maureen's impulse to strike him over the head with a poker in response to his use of the word 'loon'. (p.57) (Indeed, Maureen turns down Ray's offer to buy the poker, because of its sentimental, if sinister, value.) Increasingly, Maureen's disposition uncannily reminds Ray of that of her mother's and just as her mother had done previously, Maureen confuses Ray's name with that of Pato's.

Mullen's Maureen begins to take on more visibly some of the features of her mother. Her body movements slow down and she occupies the rocking chair, but also she is less and less able to interact with Ray, instead almost staring blankly into the distance, as she struggles, almost gives up on some levels of understanding and coherence.

In a traditional sense, Demastes and Vanden Heuvel argue that Zola's determinist naturalist model was also inspired by another of the dominant epistemes of his age – Newtonian causation – so the genre became 'associated with linear casuality, which proceeds from a classical scientific assumption that small and large causes begets effects of equal value to their causes'.[205] However, both critics argue that chaos theory and reflections on 'the butterfly effect' can be usefully exploited to explain both the unruly impulses and the randomness in some dramaturgical practices, loosely associated with realism.

Regardless, Demastes and Vanden Heuvel maintain that the chaos theory does not simply suggest that things are only chaotic, accidental and arbitrary, or that a belief in order is a delusion, but instead that prediction and casuality are not the dominant variables to any system or scheme. As they put it 'causal determinism, in short, is a lie created by humanity in its efforts to delude itself into believing it is in control of its surroundings'.[206]

Thus, in some of the quasi-realist works of Sam Shepard for example, Demastes and Vanden Heuvel argue for the abandonment of a casual coherence, in favour of something more disorderly and turbulent – an 'unpredictable determinism' – whereby randomness displaces the 'strict causal determinism of the many naturalist predecessors'.[207] To understand McDonagh's dramaturgy, it is essential to grasp how it embraces the 'unpredictable', the 'disorderly', the circular, the random, and the incidental. That way, indiscriminate motivations and emotional chaos lead to very unpredictable actions and equally capricious outcomes.

Ultimately, these effects are direct challenges to the assumptions of simple causality, visibility and coherence which seem central to the conventions of realism and to some of the expectations about the genre intentionality of a play like *Beauty Queen*. Demastes champions the confederacy and heterogeneity of realism, and I am with him when he argues that 'In many cases realism is not so much the tyrant as is the limited critical apparatus of reviewers and audiences who quickly identify superficial qualities in a play and instantly identify the work as being of a type that is intellectually unambitious, aesthetically primitive and culturally irrelevant.'[208]

While the spectator may have some serious explanations for Maureen's impulse to destroy her mother, apart from his name calling, it is difficult to find a clear-cut motive behind Maureen's impulse to kill Ray. Equally, and perhaps even more challenging is Coleman Connor's killing of his father in *Lonesome*; how can an insult about a hairstyle warrant patricide, a slight that is inexcusable and unforgivable according to Coleman? Motivation also becomes a problem in *Connemara*, where Mick's dissatisfaction with his wife is over small things, as he admits to nothing that might be a deep-seated motivation for a killing. Motivation is less and less apparent for the characters as we move through the early plays.

By the play's end, Mullen's Maureen vacates the rocking chair, and leaves it rocking, then picks up the empty and 'dusty' suitcase, as she readies herself to return it to her room. But she comes to a standstill and can get no further. (This is different in its detail to the published script where she exits into the hall.) As the lights fade, the rocking motion of the chair affirms Mag's absence, while Maureen is effectively incorporated within the consciousness of her mother and entombed, in the no-woman's-land of the domestic space.[209] In McDonagh's play there is only psychological incoherence in the form of her final madness, as subjectivity reaches a point of rupture, but not of 'desubstantiation'.[210]

In both the play-text and Hynes's production cause and effect make way for disproportionate theatricality, discontinuity and chaos, while the sequentiality, visibility, clarity, transparency and objectivity often aligned with the notionally real self-combusts. Using Jean Baudrillard's notion of the hyperreal, Brian Richardson argues, that 'The simulation displaces the real, the representation consumes and negates its referent.'[211] In many respects the focus on simulation and on the anarchic challenges to the conventions of realism seem to suggest that there is a form of combustion or self-consumption, a negation of 'its referent'. In *Beauty Queen*, McDonagh's characters can maintain simultaneously radically contradictory emotions and perceptions, which facilitates them in engaging inconsistently and incongruously with others.

The incorrigible performances of Manahan and Mullen are shaped by an amalgam of clowning, melodrama and Grand-Guignol, in a sensibility that combines the disturbing and the playful, horrific excesses and the mundane. That way, the exceedingly sinister becomes softened by their semi-casual, shrill approach to it all, as if the transactions between the main characters seem like a form of shared, anarchic self-indulgence in many ways, a cruel, crude, futile way of passing time, that is almost Beckettian in a sense. The harsh menace and threats between the main characters seem like a game that they have been playing for far too long, while they no longer know what is real and what is performed. It is both a crisis of identities as much as a crisis of unhomeliness.

5 | Conclusion

Chaudhuri notes that 'the crisis of the concept of home appears as the collision therein of two incommensurable desires: the desire for a stable container for identity and the desire to deterritorialize the self.'[212] For Chaudhuri, the status of home, 'as both shelter and prison, security and as entrapment [...] is crucial to its dramatic meaning.'[213] And she adds that modern drama generally employs 'as one of its foundational discourses, a vague, culturally determined symbology of home, replete with all those powerful and empowering associations to space as are organized by the notion of belonging.'[214] The pastoral rendering of space is a very significant component of this. Chaudhuri adds, 'The dramatic discourse of home is articulated through two main principles, which structure the plot as well as the plays' accounts of subjectivity and identity: a "*victimage of location*" and a '*heroism of departure*'.[215] And in the dramas of Chekhov, Chaudhuri suggests that 'the discourse of home is deconstructed to produce the image of a *static* exilic consciousness, experienced by the characters as a feeling of being homesick while at home'.[216] Equally, a notion of belonging unravels as:

> the logic linking belonging with exile is revealed to be not a logic of opposition but rather one of supplementarity: the emotional structure that is most familiar, most habitual and homelike to these characters is the feeling of somewhere else. They are not exiled *from* where they belong but exiled *to* where they belong.[217]

By the end of all three plays in this part home is not a sanctuary but a prison. Thus, Maureen, Mick and Billy are neither 'exiled *from* where' nor 'exiled *to* where' they belong, they are trapped in liminal places, between sanity and madness, life and death, freedom but also captivity.[218]

Gay McAuley has interesting comments on the Freudian term, 'negation', where one both admits and denies something simultaneously, where 'something is real and not real at the same time'.[219] She cites Anne Ubersfeld's notion of 'Denegation,' whereby audiences 'see a physical reality of what is happening on stage, accept it as reality, while knowing (or forgetting only for brief instances) that this reality has no consequences outside the confines of the stage space'.[220] McDonagh's play scripts affirm the mythic, symbolic, social, political and psychological constitution of the west of Ireland, however, there is also a form of 'denegation', evident in the use of stage or performance objects, icons and images and in the overlain ironic, kitsch or postmodern sensibility.

Hynes's major achievement in her productions of *Beauty Queen*, *Connemara* and *Inishmaan* is to make visible a sensibility that exploits notions of verisimilitude, while at the same time sanctioning less depth and less cohesion, by giving almost equal weighting to the petty and the complex, to that which has depth and that which is on the surface, while maintaining, in the instance of *Beauty Queen*, some of the aggrandised archetypal energies of mother and daughter dynamics in terms of bond, connection, duty, authority, dominance, surveillance and struggles for autonomy.

Connemara subverts many notionally sanctified associations held about isolated rural places or more particularly pastoral spaces. Any notion of spiritual dimension is almost eradicated, a corpse is just a corpse, a skull on a kitchen table is just a skull, with no real fears or anxieties surrounding the presence of remains. McDonagh confronts the funerary longing, the being with death rather than the being with life that is often sentimentalised within the pastoral. By his carnivalesque subversion of the funerary tradition and its embedded practices, there is a radical confrontation of nostalgic and romantic associations of Ireland with both innocence and death.

Peter Crawley suggests in his 2011 review of *Inishmaan* that 'Flaherty's film was beautiful, often entertaining and preposterously unreal. The same can be said for Druid and Atlantic Theater Company's co-produced revival.'[221] Crawley adds, 'But when its inhabitants seem either infantile or monstrous […] there's no shock of exposed taboos, no tang of revealed hypocrisy, just a cynical cackle.' And he continues, 'It is an ersatz world that denies investment; as cruel and twisted as a puppet show.'

The idea that Hynes's *mise-en-scène* is 'preposterously unreal' is absolutely accurate, across all three plays. While the stage worlds that Hynes creates have an 'ersatz' component, it has more to do with artifice and play and nothing to do with 'cynical cackle'. Instead of denying an audiences an 'investment' in the stage world, Hynes's directorial approach has far more to do with a different type of engagement, one beyond the real, beyond the simple exposure 'of taboos'. Some best qualities of puppetry cannot be glossed over, particularly its foregrounding of interpersonal and collective violence. (As Hand and Wilson note, as cited in the introduction,

Grand-Guignol is effectively a 'Big Puppet Show or a Puppet Show for Grown-Ups'.)[222]

What Hynes effectively does in these three productions is that she finds different ways of allowing intense emotions to either be self-contained, internally combust or to detonate behind a sort of invisible screen surrounding the characters. Audiences are aware of the emotion, sense it, perceive it, register it, but do not simply feel the impact of the emotions, as there is little follow through, to use a sporting analogy.

Like the sense of licence associated with much of stand-up comedy, Hynes creates a *mise-en-scène* where the performers can get away with almost anything, whatever they say or do, however grievous and cruel, not so much because there is a lack of straightforward judgment, but because there is a postponement of judgement to a point where the contrary can be countenanced, and where seriousness and intent are sacrificed on the altar of the surreal. Characters are perversely energised by failure, loss, and even by oppressiveness, and it is not at all debilitating.

Endnotes

1 The premiere of *The Cripple of Inishmaan* in 1997 is directed by Nicholas Hytner and designed by Bob Crowley. It starred Rúaidhrí Conroy and Aisling O'Sullivan, as Billy and Helen respectively. Conroy, who is slightly built, plays opposite O'Sullivan's very tall, physically strong Helen, who has to duck down her head when leaving through the door. On one occasion, she stands astride a sitting Billy, while she sexually intimidates him. Bob Crowley's portable design included a stone-washed cottage, with windows that were angular in shape; a Man of Aran poster hung on the back wall and it had an image of the Aran Islands as a backdrop. The mobile set could be altered easily to evoke a different location. I viewed a video recording of the National Theatre production in May 2011, which was recorded on 31 January 1997.

2 *A Skull in Connemara* was initially directed by Garry Hynes and designed by Francis O'Connor. It starred Mick Lally as Mick, Anna Manahan as Maryjohnny, David Wilmot as Mairtin and Brián F. O'Byrne as Tom Hanlon. I have seen a video recording courtesy of Druid, which was recorded in July of 1997 at the Town Hall Theatre, Galway.

3 *The Beauty Queen of Leenane* was directed by Garry Hynes, designed by Francis O'Connor and starred Anna Manahan as Mag Folan, Marie Mullen as her daughter Maureen, Tom Murphy as Ray Dooley and Brián F. O'Byrne as his brother Pato. After opening in Galway and after a short national tour in Ireland, the production relocated to the Royal Court's Theatre Upstairs in London on 5 March, before transferring to the Duke of York's in London's West End in November of the same year. Amongst the production's numerous awards were the Evening Standard Award for Most Promising Newcomer, Writers' Guild Award for Best Fringe Theatre Play and the George Devine Award for Most Promising Playwright. In 1998, the play opened in New York, first at the Atlantic Theater Company on 11 February, before transferring to the Walter Kerr Theater, where it ran from 23 April until 14 March 1999. This production was nominated for six Tony awards, winning four and it drew very particular attention to the work of Druid, Hynes, the actors and McDonagh. Garry Hynes became the first woman to win a Tony directing award (Julie Tabor also won that same evening for her direction of *The Lion King*). Marie Mullen won Best Actress Award and Anna Manahan in Best Featured Actress category, while Tom Murphy also got a Feature Actor Award. Bŕian F. O'Byrne also got a nomination for his performance as Pato and the drama was nominated in the best play category. See for details http://www.ibdb.com/show.php?id=1891. (Accessed 20/6/2012)

Additionally, H. A. Diehl reports that Marie Mullen, won an 'Obie Award – the Off-Broadway equivalent of a Tony – for sustained excellence of performance' and the play won several other prestigious American theatre awards, including: Theater World Award for Outstanding Ensemble Cast and Best New Play, Outer Critics Award for Best Broadway Play, Drama League Award for Best Production of a Play and the Lortel Award for Outstanding Play and Direction. See 'Classic Realism, Irish Nationalism, and a New Breed of Angry Young Man in Martin McDonagh's *The Beauty Queen of Leenane*,' *The Journal of the Midwest Modern*

Language Association, 34. 2, (Spring 2001), pp.98-117, p.113. http://www.jstor.org/stable/1315142 (Accessed 10/6/2012)

4 The currently unpublished and unperformed *Banshees of Inishsheer* also has an Aran Island setting as has *The Lieutenant of Inishmore* (2001). Sisters Eileen and Kate in *Inishmaan* and of Donny and his son, Padraic, in *Inishmore* share the surname Osbourne and Mairead and Davey have the surname, Claven, as Billy in this play.

5 The documentary-film functions somewhat like the fantastical film-within-a-film in *In Bruges* (2008) that is not quite a homage to Nicholas Roeg's *Don't Look Now* (1973).

6 M. Phelan, '"Authentic Reproductions" Staging the "Wild West" in Modern Irish Drama', *Theatre Journal*, 61. 2, (May 2009), pp. 235–248, pp.247–8. (Assessed 1/3/2011)

7 These cottage-based plays are not like the one in Cumbria in Bruce Robinson's film *Withnail and I* (1987) and they do not have the utopian fantasy of Thomas Kinkade's pastoral cottages. See (http://www.kinkadeusa.com/content/p/7/catid/1034/Cottages) (Accessed 29/1/2013)

8 P. Pavis, *Analyzing Performance: Theatre, Dance, and Film*, trans. David Williams (Ann Arbor; University of Michigan Press, 2004), p.88.

9 For Pavis, vectorisation is the 'methodological, mnemotechnical, and dramaturgical means of linking networks of signs. It consists of associating and connecting signs that form parts of networks, within which each sign only has meaning through the dynamic that relates to other signs.' Ibid., p.17.

10 G. McAuley, *Space in Performance: Making Meaning in the Theatre* (Michigan: University of Michigan, 1999), p.32.

11 A. Ubersfeld, *Reading Theatre*, trans, Frank Collins (Toronto: University of Toronto, 1999), p.95.

12 See McAuley, *Space in Performance*, p.29.

13 Ibid., pp.29–30.

14 Ibid., p.29.

15 Ibid., pp.30–31.

16 In advertising, Carmen Kuhling identifies how the pre-modern and the postmodern collide in advertisements for Irish products abroad: 'These brands and their advertisements appeal to a pre-modern Celtic culture or traditional solidarity while simultaneously exhibiting a postmodern, hybridized and aspirational cosmopolitanism. Ad campaigns for Ballygowan Water (which formerly used the slogan "the power of purity" and Celtic mythology) now represent Irishness through exuberant, young street dancers and a diverse urban culture.' See '"Liquid Modernity" and Irish Identity: Irishness in Guinness, Jameson, and Ballygowan Advertisements', *Advertising & Society Review,* 9.3, (2008), http://muse.jhu.edu/journals/advertising_and_society_review/summary/v009/9.3.kuhling.htm (Accessed 4/4/2010)

17 Note how Colin Graham rejects notions of authenticity and states that within popular culture 'Ireland' can be seen to have a '"liminal", affiliated and active existence at once within and without the systems which try to define the concept "Ireland."' See *Deconstructing Ireland: Ireland, Theory, Culture* (Edinburgh University Press, 2001), p.xi.

18 See R. Cave, 'The Abbey Tours in England' in N. Grene & C. Morash (eds), *Irish Theatre on Tour* (Dublin: Carysfort Press, 2005), pp.9–34, p.15.

19 N. Grene, *The Politics of Irish Drama: Plays in Context from Boucicault to Friel* (Cambridge: Cambridge University Press, 1999), p.212.

20 Ibid., pp.211–14.

21 G. Meaney, 'Dead, White, Male: Irishness in *Buffy the Vampire Slayer* and *Angel*', in D. Negra (ed.), *The Irish in Us: Irishness, Performativity and Popular Culture* (Duke University Press, Durham and London, 2006), pp.254–281, p.255.
22 Ibid., p.256.
23 Ibid., p.256.
24 Ibid., p.256.
25 See N. Witoszek and P. Sheeran, *Talking to the Dead: A Study of the Irish Funerary Traditions* (Amsterdam-Atlanta, GA: Rodopi, 1998).
26 N. Grene, 'Ireland in Two Minds: Martin McDonagh and Conor McPherson', *The Yearbook of English Studies*, 35:1, January 2005, pp.298–311, p.307, quoting from Joseph Feeney, 'Martin McDonagh: Dramatist of the West', *Studies*, 87 (1998), p.28.
27 F. O'Toole, 'Introduction,' Martin McDonagh's *Plays 1* (London: Methuen, 1999), p.xv.
28 See Grene, 'Ireland in Two Minds,' p.307.
29 L.Fitzpatrick, 'Language Games: *The Pillowman*, *A Skull in Connemara*, and Martin McDonagh's Hiberno-English,' in L. Chambers and E. Jordan (eds), *The Theatre of Martin McDonagh: A World of Savage Stories* (Dublin: Carysfort Press, 2006), pp.141–154, p.145.
30 Ibid., p.145.
31 F. O'Toole, 'Murderous Laughter' – 'The Leenane Trilogy,' *The Irish Times*, 24 June 1997.
32 C. Wallace, *Suspect Cultures: Narrative, Identity and Citation in 1990s New Drama* (Prague: Litteraria Pragensia, 2006), p.158.
33 J. Waters, 'The Irish Mummy: The Plays and Purpose of Martin McDonagh' in D. Bolger, (ed.), *Druids, Dudes and Beauty Queens: The Changing Face of Irish Theatre* (Dublin: New Island, 2001),pp.30–54, p.40.
34 Ibid., p.40.
35 See O'Toole, 'Murderous Laughter.'
36 F. O'Toole, '*The Beauty Queen of Leenane*', *The Irish Times*, 6 February 1996.
37 See O'Toole, 'Introduction', p.xv.
38 H. A. Diehl, 'Classic Realism, Irish Nationalism and a New Breed of Angry Young Man', pp. 98–9.
39 Ibid., p.101.
40 Ibid., p.101.
41 O. Pilný, 'Martin McDonagh: Parody? Satire? Complacency?', *Irish Studies Review*, 12:2, (2004), pp.225–232, p. 228.
42 See Ubersfeld, *Reading Theatre*, p.97.
43 Ibid., p.97.
44 Ibid., p.97.
45 Ibid., pp.100-1, citing Umberto Eco, *La Structure absente: Introduction á la reserache sémiotique*, trans. Ucciol Esposito (Paris: Mercure de France 1972) p.176.
46 Ibid., pp.101–2.
47 W.W. Demastes, ed. 'Preface: American Dramatic Realisms, Viable Frames of Thought' in *Realism and the American Dramatic Tradition*, (Tuscaloosa, University of Alabama Press, 1996), p.xi.
48 See Garry Hynes in an interview with Cathy Leeney in L. Chambers et al., *Theatre Talk: Voices of Irish Theatre Practitioners* (Dublin: Carysfort Press, 2001), pp.195–212, p. 204.
49 M. Ross, 'Hynes Means Business', *The Sunday Times*, 18 May 2003, cited by Patrick Lonergan, 'Commentary', to the Student Edition of *The Lonesome West* (London: Methuen, 2010), p.lii.

50 In 2009, the Druid and Atlantic Theater co-production of *The Cripple of Inishmaan* was awarded a total of nine prestigious theatre awards from the US, UK and Ireland. See http://www.druid.ie/productions/the-cripple-of-inishmaan#awards (Assessed 1/ 3/2011)

51 My discussions of the play are primarily based on the 2008 production, which I saw at the Olympia Theatre in October of that year during its run at the Dublin Theatre Festival. I will mention this production's revival, which I saw at the Gaiety Theatre in Dublin in March 2011, mainly by way of contrast. Sara Keating distinguishes: 'While this touring revival is excellent on many levels, it is ultimately more slick than subversive, more crowd pleasing than critical and the play loses something in the process.' Review, *Sunday Business Post,* 27 February 2011. An example of this may be the beating that Billy receives from Babbybobby: six blows are delivered before the lights dim and the sounds that are evoked by Billy are muted, reserved and not consistent with those in response to an actual beating. The moment is accompanied by harsh music. (In the 1997 Hytner production, when Babbybobby beats Billy, the scene change happens and there is no crying, only a couple of blows are heard.)

52 Francis O'Connor notes: 'What's really important is that design isn't about creating a backdrop for the space; it's not about creating a picture. It's about creating a whole world in which these characters exist. It means you must be aware of all aspects of it, the way people move in the space, they way it smells and feels. It's not a picture you're looking at, it's an entire world. Doing scenery doesn't interest me, doing plays really interests me.' See F. O'Connor 'In Conversation with Charlie McBride.' 26 August 2004, http://www.druidsynge.com/inconversation/in-conversation--oconnor (Accessed 12/6/2010)

53 B. Brantley, 'On a Barren Isle, Gift of the Gab and Subversive Charm', *New York Times*, 22 December, 2008, http://theater.nytimes.com/2008/12/22/theater/reviews/22bran.html (Assessed 1/ 3/2011)

54 Note the comments of David Pearse, who played Johnnypateenmike on Broadway in 2008–9, that 'we had to change our delivery for the American audience, but did not drop our accents or it would have been all wrong'. See 'Stargazing in the City of Towers', *The Sunday Times*, 21 October 2012, Section 5, p.3

55 See P. Lonergan, *The Theatre and Films of Martin McDonagh* (London: Methuen, 2012), p.163.

56 A. Loomba, *Colonialism/ Postcolonialism,* (London and New York: Routledge, 1998), pp.2–10.

57 Further, Loomba points out that the term 'colonisation' is difficult to pin down, in part 'due to the inter-disciplinary nature of postcolonial studies which may range from literary analysis to research in the archives of colonial government, from the critique of medical texts to economic theory, and usually combine these and other areas'. Ibid., p.xii.

58 Ibid., p.54.

59 Ibid., pp.47–8.

60 Ibid., p.81.

61 Effectively colonial violence is not simply physical, as 'it also includes an "epistemic" aspect, i.e. an attack on the culture, ideas and value systems of the colonised people'. Ibid., p.54, citing G. Spivak, 'The Political Economy of Women as Seen by a Literary Critic', in E. Weed (ed.), *Coming to Terms* (London: Routledge 1990), p.226.

62 D. Kiberd, *Inventing Ireland: The Literature of the Modern Nation* (London: Vintage, 1996), p.9.

63 Ibid., p.17. Conversely, in Conor McPherson's *The Seafarer* (2006) Mr Lockhart is the unconscious of the Irish character Sharkey. In performance Lockhart was

played with an English accent in both Abbey productions opening in May 2008 and December 2009, directed by Jimmy Fay and Conor McPherson respectively.

64 Ibid., pp.9–10.

65 Ibid., p.31.

66 Ibid., p.30.

67 A. Loomba, *Colonialism/ Postcolonialism,* p.107.

68 Ibid., p.168.

69 A. Fogarty, 'Other spaces: Postcolonialism and the politics of truth in Kate O'Brien's *That Lady', European Journal of English Studies*, 3:3, (1999), pp.342–353, pp.342–4.

70 E. Flannery, 'Outside in the Theory Machine: Ireland in the World of Post-Colonial Studies', *Studies: An Irish Quarterly Review*, 92.368, (Winter 2003), pp. 359-369, p363, citing C. Graham, 'Subalternity and Gender: Problems of post-colonial Irishness', *The Journal of Gender Studies: Special Issue: Gender and Post-Colonialism*, 5.3, pp.363–373, p.367.

71 In that vein, Victor Merriman suggests that in *The Leenane Trilogy* not only is there little done to conceal a negative disposition towards the marginalised, but also the work is complicit in perpetuating the worst stereotypes of imperialism, for the delectation of globalised bourgeois audiences, from whom the marginalised function as that which is repressed within bourgeois living. See '"Decolonization Postponed": Theatre of Tiger Trash', *Irish University Review*, 29.2, (1999), pp.305–17, p.312, and 'Heartsickness and Hopes Deferred', in S. Richards (ed.), *Twentieth Century Irish Drama*, (Cambridge: Cambridge University Press, 2004), pp.244–57, p.253.

72 Parental absence is a notable pattern, the father of the Folan household in *Beauty Queen* is never referred to, the mother figure in the Connor household in *Lonesome* is mentioned once throughout the whole play, and the dramaturgical implications of the fact that the Osbourne family in *Inishmaan* has no patriarchal figure are also many.

73 Molloy again plays Eileen and Ingrid Craigie performs Kate in 2011.

74 Johnnypateenmike fancies himself for a part: 'what with me fine oratory skills could outdo any beggar on the Dublin stage, only as ye know, I have me drunkard mammy to look after.' (p.8)

75 See Brantley, 'On a Barren Isle, Gift of the Gab and Subversive Charm'.

76 In the 2011 production, Dermot Crowley is successful in capturing the insidious eavesdropping nature of the character, and in the fact that Johnnypateenmike takes great pleasure in his communal role, bartering information for consumables. Vocally, Crowley is very precise, but has little emotional nuance.

77 K. O'Brien overstates it when suggesting that the egg breaking perhaps indicates the symbolical 'shattering [of] any means of reproduction and thus forecasting the decline of the Aran population'. See 'Ireland mustn't be such a bad place so': Mapping the "Real" Terrain of the Aran Islands', *Journal of Dramatic Theory and Criticism*, (Spring 2006), pp.169–183, p.176, https://journals.ku.edu/index.php/jdtc/article/viewFile/3554/3430 (Assessed 1/ 3/2011)

78 L. Gardner, 'Review,' *The Guardian*, 10 October 2008.

79 Clare Dunne in the 2011 production is somewhat the more seductive Helen, while her verbal aggression seems less in tandem with her overall characterisation. Of the two, Condon is the more marauding and seems to haunt her Billy far more, because of a sense of their shared and mutual desperation.

80 In 1997 Rúaidhrí Conroy performed with a Polio calliper on his leg and needed regular physio treatment for the way he held his gait according to notes on file in the National Theatre's archive. Aaron Monaghan accounts of his preparation for the part, and how he alternates sides for every second performance in his interview

with Theatre Development Fund with the un-credited staff journalist: 'Monaghan, clearly a detail-oriented actor, noted that with certain kinds of muscular dystrophy, "One of your calf muscles can almost explode. So automatically your foot is raised; you turn your leg in, and I'm standing over my foot. That developed into the walk that I have. And your spine can get quite curved. So I tightened the muscles on my arms."'See http://www.tdf.org/TDF_ShowsDetail.aspx?ShowId=5709 (Accessed 1/3/2011)

81 M.B. Meszaros, 'Enlightened by Our Afflictions: Portrayals of Disability in the Comic Theatre of Beth Henley and Martin McDonagh,' *Disability Studies Quarterly,* Summer/Fall 2003, 23. 3/4, http://dsq-sds.org/article/view/433/610(Accessed 3/2/2013)
82 Ibid.
83 Ibid.
84 The irony of course is that in most productions of this play that I know of, able-bodied actors get to play Billy's role. Note also the obvious fact that more able-bodied actors get the roles and win Oscars for physical and psychological representations of disability. For some, this disabling up is similar to the traditional blacking up.
85 K. O'Brien, See 'Ireland mustn't be such a bad place so,' p. 174.
86 Ibid., p.175.
87 P. Lonergan, *The Theatre and Films of Martin McDonagh* (London: Methuen, 2012), p.62.
88 Ibid., p.62.
89 See McAuley, *Space in Performance*, p.32.
90 P. Murphy, *Hegemony and Fantasy in Irish Drama, 1899–1949* (Basingstoke: Palgrave, 2008), p.22.
91 Ibid., p. 12.
92 Ibid., p. 10.
93 Ibid., p. 12.
94 Ibid., p. 10.
95 Ibid., p.20.
96 Ibid., p.22.
97 Ibid., p.26.
98 Ibid., p.26.
99 Ibid., p.23.
100 R. Dyer, *White* (London and New York: Routledge, 1997), p.44.
101 Ibid., p.12.
102 Ibid., p.19.
103 Ibid., p.210
104 Ibid., p.10.
105 Ibid., p.xv.
106 Ibid., p.13.
107 Ibid., pp.39–40.
108 Ibid., p.45
109 Ibid., p.11.
110 Ibid., p.9.
111 Ibid., p.80, citing Toni Morrison's *Playing in the Dark: Whiteness and the Literary Imagination* (Cambridge MA: Harvard University Press, 1992), p.59.
112 Ibid., pp.222–3.
113 Ibid., p.70.
114 Ibid., p.3.
115 D. Negra, (ed.), 'Introduction', *The Irish in Us: Irishness, Performativity and Popular Culture* (Duke University Press, Durham and London, 2006), p.3.

116 Ibid., p.4.
117 Ibid., p.1.
118 Ibid., p.1.
119 Ibid., p.2.
120 Ibid., p.2.
121 A. Third, '"Does the Rug Match the Carpet?" Race, Gender and the Readheaded Woman,' in *The Irish in Us,* pp.220–253, p.224.
122 Ibid., p.221.
123 Ibid., p.224.
124 Ibid., p.224.
125 Ibid., p.224.
126 Hynes also achieves a specific mirroring, as text suggests (p.42), when Billy goes missing early on, the actor playing Kate holds the sack as a sort of comfort blanket, and now as he contemplates suicide, Billy holds the sack in a similar sort of way, caressing if he is at last united with a belated destiny of sorts. The sack, which the published play direction suggests is displayed prominently on the shelf throughout the performance, is filled with tins of peas by Billy. In the Hynes productions, the sack is on the side of the counter and therefore its presence is less blatant.
127 Helen buys Bartley his longed-for telescope, an affirmation of his phallic status, and her kiss is perhaps an affirmation of Billy's as well.
128 In the 2011 Hynes production, Billy exits the stage through the back room through a hanging divide. The back space is light in a harrowing yellow and a silhouette of Billy grows larger in that isolated lit space. There is less use of red lighting which was used in the first production by Hynes.
129 G. Meaney, 'Dead, White, Male', p. 273, citing Dyer's *White*, p.210.
130 See the image by Hulton Getty on the published text of the play of a young boy leap-frogging a grave stone.
131 M. Foucault, 'Of other Spaces', trans. Jay Miskowiec, *Diacritics*, 16.1, (Spring 1986), pp.22–27, p.23.
132 Ibid., p.24.
133 Ibid., p.24.
134 Ibid., p.24.
135 Ibid., p.25.
136 Ibid., p.25.
137 Maureen Murphy suggests *'A Skull in Connemara* also has much in common with Maírtín O'Cadháin's *Cré na Cille (Churchyard Clay)*, a 1949 novel set among the dead in a Connemara cemetery – where the deceased natter about life and question each new arrival about the goings-on in the world above. Whereas McDonagh's dialogue is comic in its repetitions and banalities, O'Cadháin's characters speak in the richly nuanced local Irish dialect from a generation ago. Yet both works subvert traditional romantic attitudes towards the west of Ireland with portrayals of the mean-spiritedness and petty jealousies below the surface of rural Irish life – which even reach beyond the grave.' See 'Martin McDonagh: Prodigy of the Western World' http://www.roundabouttheatre.org/fc/spring01/martin.htm (Accessed 13/4/2011)
138 J. FitzPatrick Dean's comments are notable: 'There is no practice of routine disinterment, even in the rockiest terrain in Connemara, for example.' She regards the action of the writer as motivated by a need 'to distort any easy alignment with the real'. See 'Martin McDonagh's Stagecraft' in R. Rankin Russell (ed.), *Martin McDonagh, A Casebook* (London: Routledge, 2007), pp.25–40, p.38.
139 Decadent Theatre did an excellent production of the play in 2013, but it was too late to incorporate it into my argument.
140 See Witoszek and Sheeran, *Talking to the Dead*, p. 72.

141 Ibid., p.41.
142 Ibid., p.13.
143 Ibid., p. 38.
144 Ibid., p. 38.
145 Ibid., p.38.
146 David Gallo's design for the play's Broadway production is significantly different to that of Francis O'Connor, but what both do is to provide a space that can cater for the play's dramatic action and for performance idioms. David Gallo states:
'There's a murky sky-surround which will be lit a number of different ways to give it various kinds of character. The living room floats in the middle of this landscape, with no walls and no particular architecture. When it becomes the graveyard all the props go away and a series of tombstones pop up – again in perspective so there's a sense of depth. The doors on the sides vanish. Hopefully the graves floating on the ceiling above complete the idea that we're in this scary graveyard [....] In Seattle we did the production in the round and you could actually touch the gravestones from your seat. Here they're no closer than 17 or 18 feet and the perspective continues: as the house rakes back, the graves rake back as well. You can even read some of the names on the tombstones', including that of Mag Folan. See 'Gordon Edelstein and David Gallo in Discussion: Grave Matters', http://www.roundabouttheatre.org/fc/spring01/grave.htm (Accessed 13/4/2011) B. Brantley describes the design: 'That a classy warped cartoonishness is the aim here is signalled by the first glimpse of David Gallo's set. Granted, the scene on the stage itself is what we have by now come to identify as standard-issue Leenane: a simple, shabby room with desolate-looking furniture and the requisite central crucifix. But look up and you'll see, mounted upside down on the ceiling, rows of turfy grave plots with classic spookhouse tombstones. It's hard not to grin, like a child anticipating Halloween, at this inversion of the sacrosanct.' See, 'Leenane III, Bones Flying', *New York Times*, 23 February, 2001, http://theater.nytimes.com/mem/theater/treview.html?html_title=&tols_title=SKULL%20IN%20CONNEMARA,%20A%20(PLAY)&pdate=20010223&byline=By%20BEN%20BRANTLEY&id=1077011432186 (Accessed 4 April 2011)
147 Early on, the revelations about digging up ancestors and about the Hanlon family feasting on meat from a cow that lay dead for years in their field did not draw the laughter that I had anticipated in the recording of the production I have seen. (I say this in no way suggesting that such a single recording offers any sort of conclusive proof.) In some ways, I am suggesting that transgressive humour can be sometimes more obvious on the page than on stage, or at least easier to respond to when reading the work.
148 R. Mushat Frye, 'Ladies, Gentlemen and Skulls: Hamlet and the Iconographic Traditions', *Shakespeare Quarterly*, 30.1 (Winter 1979), pp.15–28, p.26. http://www.jstor.org/stable/2869658 (Accessed 13/4/2011)
149 R. Fly, 'Accommodating Death: The Ending of Hamlet,' *Studies in English Literature, 1500-1900*, 24.2, (Spring, 1984), pp. 257–274, p.266, http://www.jstor.org/stable/450527 (Accessed: 13/04/2011)
150 Mushat Frye argues that 'If we view the graveyard scene in Elsinore only or even primarily in terms of those typically twentieth-century attitudes which seek to ignore or euphemise death, we may regard Hamlet at this point as morbid in soul and sick in mind. But if we re-establish the sixteenth-century context and recall representative examples of the raw materials upon which Shakespeare's imagination worked, we see a Hamlet here thinking through the ultimate realities of death to arrive at what becomes, for him as it had for others, a new sanity and

even serenity.' See 'Ladies, Gentlemen and Skulls: Hamlet and the Iconographic Traditions', p.28.

151 See Witoszek and Sheeran, *Talking to the Dead*, p.78.

152 Brantley opens his review of Roundabout Theater Company's production of the play directed by Gordon Edelstein, at the Gramercy Theater, tongue in cheek: 'Excuse me, but is that a piece of tibia that's just landed in my lap?' He adds 'it's only natural that some of those soiled white fragments would fly beyond the proscenium arch. Audience members should be prepared to duck. On the other hand, who could possibly take his eyes off such a mordant, morbid and oddly ecstatic spectacle?' See 'Leenane III, Bones Flying'.

153 See Witoszek and Sheeran, *Talking to the Dead*, p.28.

154 Ibid., p. 27.

155 Ibid., p.28.

156 Ibid., pp.27–8.

157 Ibid., p.28.

158 Ibid., p.9.

159 Ibid., p.28.

160 Ibid., p.26.

161 Ibid., p.8, citing Arnold Van Gennep, *The Rites of Passage*, trans M.B. Vizedom and G. L. Coffee (Chicago: Chicago University Press, 1960), p.147.

162 Ibid., pp. 8-9.

163 A. Van Gennep, *The Rites of Passage*, p. 164.

164 In *The Lieutenant of Inishmore* there is the blatant dismemberment of the bodies on stage, with no sense of a wake, no sense of trauma, just shallow indifference both to the task meted out by Mairead and Padraic and towards the bodies that Donny and Davey are forced to desecrate. In relation to *Inishmore*, that from the nineteenth century forward, 'funerary symbols were increasingly used in political contexts'. (See Witoszek and Sheeran, *Talking to the Dead*, p.33.) In *Inishmore* the dead bodies are denied their funeral rights and instead the bodies are hacked to pieces, so that the deaths are provided with no symbolic resonance, as notions of martyrdom and self sacrifice are not afforded to McDonagh's terrorists.

165 See Van Gennep, *The Rites of Passage*, p. 149.

166 Mairtin accuses Tom of battering Ray Dooley. Tom says that Ray's broken toe was from him kicking the cell door and had nothing to do with police brutality.

167 And later, in the same vein, Mairtin accuses him of not being able to arrest a shop lifting child, whose face is covered in chocolate and that if he did arrest him 'you'd arrest him for killing the Kennedys'. (p. 121)

168 For instance, Declan Hughes sees McDonagh as 'a Connemara Orton.' See M. Kurdi, 'American and Other International Impulses on the Contemporary Irish Stage: A Talk with Playwright Declan Hughes,' *Hungarian Journal of English and American Studies*, 8.2, (2002), pp.76–7.

169 See Mushat Frye, 'Ladies, Gentlemen and Skulls: Hamlet and the Iconographic Traditions', p.28.

170 S. Letzler Cole, *The Absent One: Mourning Ritual, Tragedy, and the Performance of Ambivalence* (Pennsylvania, Pennsylvania University Press, 1985), pp.4–7 Sourced: http://books.google.com (Accessed 4 May 2011)

171 Ibid., p.6.

172 The stage objects indicated to appear in the performance space include, a 'long black range [...] with a box of turf beside it,' dinner table and two chairs, rocking chair, sink, a small TV, as well as 'a crucifix and a framed picture of John and Robert Kennedy.' Along the back wall there is 'a touristy-looking embroidered

tea-towel' which bears the inscription 'May you be half an hour in Heaven afore the Devil knows you're dead.' (p.1.)

173 I saw Hynes's production in 1996 at the Watergate Theatre in Kilkenny city and again saw it in the summer of 2000, with a revised cast in Dublin at the Gaiety Theatre. Manahan and Mullen were still involved, but Peter Gowen replaced O'Byrne and Rúaidhrí Conroy took over the role of Ray. As the main focus is on Manahan and Mullen's performances, my analysis is primarily based on the 1996 production and on an undated video recording of this first production, courtesy of Druid Theatre. It is details from this recording that I rely on to confirm my recollections and notes of the performance style, but this recording appears to be no longer in the Druid archive.

174 A direct contrast to Hynes's emphasis on a heightened artifice and a lack of concern about authenticity in her *mise-en-scène* is evident in Joe Hill-Gibbins's acclaimed production for the Young Vic in 2010, with Susan Lynch as Maureen, Rosaleen Linehan as Mag, with Frank Laverty as Pato and Johnny Ward as Ray. This production toured in 2011, coming to the Gaiety Theatre in Dublin in late May, with Derbhle Crotty replacing Lynch. In this performance, all four actors deliver their lines with a great measured lucidity; their exchanges are dependent on the actors bringing to their roles a decisive psychological clarity. Michael Coveney conveys his experience of the play at the Young Vic as follows: 'The audience enters the rural cottage in Connemara through dark corridors, a rain-sodden patch of scuffed grass and vast swathes of plastic sheeting. And Ultz has designed the dingy kitchen to perfection, with paint peeling off the red door, and a photograph of the Kennedy brothers conjuring the Irish diaspora that awaits Maureen Folan, the doomed beauty queen.' See 'Review', *What's on Stage*, 22 July 2010, http://www.whatsonstage.com/reviews/theatre/london/E8831279790437/The+Beauty+Queen+of+Leenane.html (Accessed 10/8/2010)

175 W.W. Demastes, 'Preface', in *Realism and the American Dramatic Tradition*, p.x

176 See C. Innes, (ed.), 'Introduction', in *A Sourcebook on Naturalist Theatre* (London: Routledge, 2000), pp.4–6.

177 Ibid., pp.4–6.

178 W.W. Demastes and M. Vanden Heuvel, 'The Hurlyburly Lies of the Causalist Mind: Chaos and Realism of Rabe and Shepard', in *Realism and the American Dramatic Tradition* (255–74), p.256, citing W.B. Worthen's *Modern Drama and the Rhetoric of Theatre* (Berkeley: University of California, 1992), p.17.

179 W.W. Demastes, *Beyond Naturalism: A New Realism in American Theatre* (New York: Greenwood Press, 1988), p.15.

180 R. Williams, *Modern Tragedy* (London: Chatto and Windus, 1966), p.69.

181 While naturalism stresses consequences and proportionality, inevitability and a rational order, realism accommodates improbability, the mythic or symbolic subtext in something like Henrik Ibsen's *The Wild Duck* (1884), *Hedda Gabler* (1890) or *The Master Builder* (1982). Mystery is seen in effect through the absence of certainty or inevitability and breaches in proportionality and cause and effect have profound implications in all of these three plays.

182 U. Chaudhuri, *Staging Place: The Geography of Modern Drama* (Ann Arbor: The University of Michigan Press, 1995), p.xii.

183 Ibid., p.29.

184 See Demastes, (ed.), 'Preface', p.x.

185 R. Gordon, *The Purpose of Playing: Modern Acting Theories in Perspective* (Ann Arbor, University of Michigan Press, 2006), p.38.

186 Ibid., pp.56–7.

187 Ibid., pp.355–6.

188 See Demastes, 'Preface,' p.xi.
189 See Pavis, *Analyzing Performance*, p.56.
190 Ibid., p.56.
191 Ibid., p.56.
192 Ibid., p.55.
193 Ibid., p.147.
194 In Irish theatre generally, mother/daughter or father/daughter relationships are seldom mythologised. Normally, it is male/male relationships.
195 P. Marks, '*Depicting The Hurt Of Love Curdling Into Hate'*, *New York Times*, April 21, 1998, http://theater.nytimes.com/mem/theater/treview.html?res=9C05E4D6113CF932A15757C0A96E958260 (Accessed 12/6/2010)
196 Ibid.
197 See N. Grene, 'Ireland in Two Minds', p.301.
198 This moment hints at broader, though mainly unreported, social violations of the elderly in family and care homes that range from people being left in beds for lengthy periods or in dirty soiled clothes to deprivation of food and medication, force feeding and other forms of violence. Amanda Phelan notes, 'Like child protection and domestic violence, elder abuse remains a difficult topic, shrouded in secrecy, particularly as most abuse occurs within the home environment and by family members. Thus, disclosure is mired in issues of family allegiance, embarrassment, anxiety regarding legal entanglement and if the perpetrator is the main care-giver, forced admission to a nursing home may be a fear. Defining elder abuse is challenging but there is a professional consensus that it may be perpetrated in many ways, such as physical abuse, sexual abuse, psychological abuse, financial/material abuse and neglect.' See 'Time to face up to reality of elder abuse', *The Irish Times*, 15 June, 2012, http://www.irishtimes.com/newspaper/opinion/2012/0615/1224317977647.html (Accessed 15/6/2012)
199 However, in the opening scenes of the Hill-Gibbins's production, the tensions between Crotty and Linehan are far more full-on from the start. Linehan and Crotty are aggressively committed to score points off each other and there seems to be a more desperate desire to compete and dominate. Linehan captures brilliantly the defiance, the malevolence, the fears and the bitterness of Mag, as she expertly grounds the trauma in ways that one might associate with someone who despises her daughter's energy and who is also a victim of persistent carer abuse late in life. Linehan includes a precise, calculated hesitation into her characterisation, as if she is consistently judging transactions and estimating responses. (Linehan's furtive burning of Ray's note is over-signalled and is a bit at odds with her more consistently pained, troubled and generally uncomfortable demeanour.) With Crotty's Maureen, one sees where the torment is coming from, as it seems primed to explode, and hers is by far the more aggressive and sadistic Maureen, displaying a strong sense of disjointedness, confusion and instinct for havoc. Sara Keating's review suggests that Derbhle Crotty plays Maureen 'with compelling psychological commitment. She is pushed to the limit of patience and sanity by her carping mother, and the sterility and poverty of Leenane.' See 'Review Beauty Queen of Leenane,' *Sunday Business Post*, 22 May 2011, http://www.sbpost.ie/the-guide/theatre-56347.html (Accessed 31/5/2011)
200 In *Seven Psychopaths*, Hans, having taken peyote, has a vision of Myra and she is 'not in a great place'. Mary asks: 'Like Enlgand?,' to which he responds 'It seemed a lot worse than that.'
201 In the Young Vic production, Crotty's Maureen wanders about in a bra and a short slip before her Pato and her mother, implying more of a predatorial, frustrated sexuality, whereas Mullen's Maureen is less confident about her body and uses her hands to shield herself on occasion.

202 In the Young Vic production, there is greater deliberateness: Crotty forces Mag over to the range and places her in the rocking chair close by. Resistance seems futile. As Maureen pours the oil, a sizzling sound is amplified to suggest the burning of flesh. Linehan's Mag expresses deep guttural sounds in response to the pain.
203 In the Young Vic production, Crotty's Maureen steps over her mother on the floor, signalling her transition into another dimension of entrapped irrationality.
204 Rebecca Wilson not only draws attention to the significance of Grand-Guignol, but also highlights the importance of melodrama and fairytales to this play. See 'Macabre Merriment in *The Beauty Queen of Leenane*', in E. Weitz (ed.), *The Power of Laughter: Comedy and Contemporary Irish Theatre*, (Dublin: Carysfort Press, 2004), pp.129–144.
205 W.W. Demastes and M. Vanden Heuvel, 'The Hurlyburly Lies of the Causalist Mind,' p.255.
206 Ibid., p.265.
207 Ibid., pp.263–5.
208 W.W. Demastes, 'Preface' in *Realism and the American Dramatic Tradition*, p.x.
209 Crotty remains in the rocking chair and there is also some sort of evident reward in her state of defiance and in her displacement of her mother.
210 Elinor Fuchs recognises 'desubstantiation' and the 'decentering of subjectivities' within a postmodern frame: 'The interior space known as the subject was no longer an essence, an in-dwelling human endowment, but flattened into a social construction or marker in language, the unoccupied occupant of the subject position.' See *Death of Character*: *Perspectives on Theater After Modernism* (Bloomington: Indiana University Press, 1996), p.3.
211 B. Richardson, 'Introduction: The Struggle for the Real-Interpretative Conflict, Dramatic Method and the Paradox of Realism' in *Realism and the American Dramatic Tradition*, p.14.
212 U. Chaudhuri, *Staging Place*, p. 8.
213 Ibid., p. 8.
214 Ibid., p. xii.
215 Ibid., p.xiii.
216 Ibid., p. 11.
217 Ibid., p. 11.
218 In her consideration of Teresa Deevy and Marina Carr, Cathy Leeney argues that under patriarchy, 'The boundaries around Irish women's realities define containment as a form of exile: exile from self-expression, from self-determination.' See 'Ireland's "Exiled" Women Playwrights: Teresa Deevy and Marina Carr', in S. Richards (ed.), *The Cambridge Companion to Twentieth-Century Irish Drama*, (Cambridge: Cambridge University Press, 2004), pp.150–63, p.150.
219 G. McAuley, *Space in Performance*, p.40.
220 Ibid., p.40, citing Anne Ubersfeld's *Termes Clés de l'analyse du théâtre* (Paris: Seuil, 1996), p.23.
221 P. Crawley, *The Cripple of Inishmaan*, *The Irish Times*, 25 February, 2011.
222 Likewise the cursing exchanges between Johnnypateenmike and Mammy O'Dougal are almost Billingsgate in their sensibilities.

PART 2

Slapstick Cultures, Dismembering Farce and Grand-Guignol Incorrectness

1 | Introduction: Uncompromising Contexts

In Part 1 I mapped how McDonagh's plays capture the prejudicial, systematic and epistemic violence of colonial and media stereotyping in terms of ethnicity, race, disability and gender, and I mapped the archetypal violence of *Beauty Queen*'s mother–daughter relationship, while raising issues around motivation, proportionality and 'unpredictable determinism.' Part 1 additionally reflected on the tragic-comic violence evident in an attempted infanticide and in the beating of a character with disability in *Inishmaan* and on the anarchic violence expressed against a funerary tradition in *Connemara*. In Part 3 I will deal with the moral sentiments of gangland violence in *In Bruges,* and in relation to *Seven Psychopaths*, I will also consider the implications of filmic representations of violence and psychopathology, and the potential challenges to many of the routine conventions in the traditional action or adventure genres. Ideologically inspired state violence will also be contemplated in relation to *The Pillowman*, as will the relationship between violence and retributive justice found in fairytales.

Now, here in Part 2, I will examine sibling violence and the minimal motivation for patricide in *Lonesome* and I will also discuss how Fr Welsh's self-harming may have mythic, sacramental, altruistic and ironic overtones. In relation to *Inishmore* I will consider the paradox of McDonagh's anarchic and pacifist motivated stage violence as a response to the pugnaciousness of the 'armed struggle' tradition of Irish Republicanism. Finally, in my discussions on *Spokane,* I will look at the violence associated with slavery, racism and a lack of social integration, as well as also considering primeval myths of racial distinction, alongside fantasies of self-serving heroism as a response to a fictionalised high school massacre.

In this part, pathological, allegorical, melodramatic, surreal and archetypal variables of violence coalesce under the rubrics of Farce, Grand-Guignol and the postmodern brutalism that is central to the *In-Yer-Face* style of theatre. The consequences of the various forms of violence are frightening when they appear, on the one hand, as omnipresent threats, ploys or actions, and, on the other, almost as reckless, casual, unmotivated and not premeditated. And if there is a trajectory in the dramaturgy of McDonagh, it is not so much the journey from violence to peace, but more the accommodation of both tendencies, additionally laced with the incongruities of satire.

Violence is often identified, according to Steven Pinker as 'an animalistic impulse, as we see in words like *beastly*, *bestial*, *brutish*, *inhuman* and *wild*, together with depictions of the devil with horns and a tail'.[1] As for a human fascination with violence, Pinker suggests, 'a likely explanation is that in evolutionary history, violence was so probable that people could not afford to understand how it works'.[2] Thus Pinker's thinking on the matter is, if you want peace, you must be prepared for war.

For Pinker, the human brain is 'a swollen and warped version of the brains of other mammals'.[3] Thus 'human nature accommodates motives that impel us to violence, like predation, dominance and vengeance, but also to motives that – under the right circumstances – impel us toward peace, like compassion, fairness, self-control and reason.'[4] He suggests that accounts of violence cannot simply be about the 'few bad apples and that everyone else is peaceful at heart', or that the majority are generally 'adverse to violence'.[5] The question is less about what makes us violent, but more about what makes us non-violent, according to Pinker. Yet, Pinker suggests that in the modern world there are great attempts to deny the darker side of human nature.

Prompted by Roy Baumeister's work in his book *Evil*, Pinker suggests that people who do evil things do not see themselves as that way inclined. However, 'the mindset that we adopt when we don moral spectacles is the mindset of the victim. Evil is the intentional and gratuitous infliction of harm for its own sake, perpetrated by a villain who is malevolent to the bone, inflicted on a victim who is innocent and good.'[6] The evildoer is an adversary – the enemy of good – and the evildoer is often foreign. Ultimately, this myth 'bedevils our attempt to understand real evil'.[7]

Distinctions between the narratives of the perpetrator and the victim of violence demonstrate 'how human psychology distorts our interpretation and memory of harmful events'.[8] (The confessional sequence between the two brothers in *Lonesome* demonstrates this, as does the anomalous thinking of the paramilitaries in *Inishmore*.) So Pinker asks 'Does our inner perpetrator whitewash our crimes in a campaign to exonerate ourselves? Or does our inner victim nurse our grievances in a campaign to claim the world's sympathy?'[9]

For Pinker, a great deal of human violence is cowardly, comprising 'sucker punches, unfair fights, pre-emptive strikes, predawn raids, mafia hits, drive-by shootings'.[10] In contrast, the savage and brutal frenzy of rampage, that is 'an unstoppable fury' that leads to senseless torture, mutilation, rape, massacre and genocide, is a good example, where 'rage gives way to ecstasy, and the rampagers may laugh and whoop in a carnival of barbarity'. This rage shows that 'the human repertoire includes scripts for violence that lie quiescent and may be cued by propitious circumstances, rather than building up over time like hunger or thirst'.[11] (In contrast, the pacifying process involves self-control, an ability to sympathise with others, and a 'sensitivity to norms and conventions', Pinker summaries.[12])

Pinker identifies a Rage System in the brain, noting, one of 'the oldest discoveries in the biology of violence is the link between pain or frustration and aggression'.[13] Added to the Rage System are the following: a Seeking System, a Fear System and a Dominance System. Yet it is clear, that in most 'hostile encounters' either between humans or animals, the antagonists 'usually back down before either of them can do serious damage to the other'.[14] So while the rage circuit controls aggression, people back down, not out of kindness, but often out of restraint and discretion.

Neuroanatomy suggests that in 'Homo sapiens primitive impulses of rage, fear and craving must contend with the cerebral restraints of prudence, moralisation, and self-control – though as in all attempts at taming the wild, it's not always clear who has the upper hand.'[15] So the processing looks like this, according to Pinker: 'Visceral feelings of anger, warmth, fear and disgust are combined with the person's goals, and modulating signals are computed and sent back down to the emotional structures from which they originated. Signals are also sent upward to regions of the cortex that carry out cool deliberation and executive control.'[16]

Scholarship cited by Pinker has shown that damage to the orbital cortex leaves people with a range of challenges, including impulsiveness, disinhibited and socially inappropriate behaviour, and they are 'susceptible to misinterpreting others' moods', are often 'unconcerned with the consequences of their actions' and are 'irresponsible in everyday life'. These individuals also lack 'insight into the seriousness of their condition' and are 'prone to weak initiative'.[17] From the work of Angela Scarpa and Adrian Raine, Pinker adds to this list for patients with frontal lobe damage, 'argumentativeness, lack of concern for consequences of behaviour, loss of social graces, impulsivity, distractability, shallowness, lability, violence'.[18] The hardware of the brain fosters and inhibits violence, but in the software 'the *reasons* [why] people engage in violence', are to be found.[19]

Pinker's taxonomy of violence is an expanded version of Baumeister's: first of all there is predatory violence, also called, 'practical', 'instrumental' or 'exploitative' violence, driven by greed, lust or ambition (Seeking

System), but without destructive motives like 'hate or anger' and has no 'inhibiting factor like sympathy or moral concern'. It can also be defensive and pre-emptive violence. Secondly, there is the violence of dominance, a striving for supremacy over another (Dominance System). Thirdly, there is the violence of revenge. Pinker notes, 'Yet for all its futility, the urge for vengeance is a major cause of violence. Blood revenge is explicitly endorsed in 95 percent of the world's cultures.'[20] While our psychotherapeutic culture portrays revenge as a disease and forgiveness as the cure, revenge is part of the Rage and Seeking circuits; after the brain is scanned it is the same regions that light up when a person 'craves nicotine, cocaine or chocolate. Revenge is sweet, indeed.'[21] And the Bible's Old Testament is in part driven by a notion of recriminative justice, an eye for an eye, and a tooth for a tooth.[22] (In *Inishmaan* it is a cat for a goose and such a tit-for-tat value system is raised in *Seven Psychopaths*.) In many films there are punishments doled out by Mafia or Triad-type criminal gangs as warnings, but also as retributions for the breaking of certain codes of behaviour or honour, which both *In Bruges* and *Seven Psychopaths* consider.

Fourthly, there is the violence of sadism, the pleasure found in hurting another, whereby 'the motive, puzzling and horrifying in equal measure, may be a by-product of several quirks of our psychology, particularly the Seeking System'.[23] Finally, there is the violence driven by ideology – 'the most consequential cause of violence', in Pinker's estimation.[24] *Spokane* is an example of ideological violence, and of the destructive unwillingness to accept racial difference. *Inishmore* also captures ideological violence, paramilitary rather than state violence, as well as aspects of a sadistic or pathological violence. *Spokane* is also driven by a thirst for revenge, as is *Lonesome*. And all three plays in this part, and the three discussed in the previous one, exhibit the characteristics of dominance and predatory violence. Fundamentally for Pinker, 'organisms are selected to deploy violence only in circumstances where the expected benefits outweigh the expected costs'.[25] Thus the expression of violence is not simply irrational, random, incoherent, but fundamentally strategic.

Slavoj Žižek distinguishes between subjective and objective violence as I have already mentioned in my introduction. He separates 'objective violence' into two further categories, 'symbolic' and 'systemic'. 'Symbolic violence', is that which is 'embodied in language and its forms, what Heidegger would call "our house of being"'. He notes that 'symbolic violence', 'is not only at work in the obvious – and extensively studied – cases of incitement and of the relations of social domination reproduced in our habitual speech forms: there is a more fundamental form of violence still that pertains to language as such, to its imposition of a certain universe of meaning.'[26] Systemic violence is 'often the catastrophic consequences of the smooth functioning of our economic and political systems'. Systemic violence is thus something like the notorious 'dark matter' of physics, the counterpart to the all too visible subjective violence.[27] And this systemic violence needs to be accounted for in order to make sense of the 'very public "irrational" explosion of subjective violence'.[28] What Žižek tracks is the 'systemic violence' of capitalism, which is much more 'uncanny than any direct pre-capitalist socio-ideological violence: thus violence is no longer attributable to concrete individuals and their "evil" intentions, but is purely "objective", systemic, anonymous.'[29] He distinguishes, using Lacanian terminology between reality and the Real: '"reality" is the social reality of the actual people involved in interaction and in productive processes, while the Real is the inexorable "abstract" spectral logic of capital that determines what goes on in social reality.'[30]

And while Pinker suggests that violence is fundamentally strategic, there are some things about which he cannot be so clear-cut. Following Sigmund Freud, Slavoj Žižek argues, 'The true evil, which is the death drive, involves self-sabotage. It makes us act *against* our own interests.'[31] (This self-sabotaging cannot be strategic in Pinker's model, yet it is often paramount to McDonagh's characters and their unwillingness to fulfil the imperatives of natural selection.)

For instance, during the Parisian suburban riots of autumn 2005, Žižek wonders why 'the protesters' violence was almost exclusively directed against their own. The cars burned and the schools torched were not those of richer neighborhoods. They were part of the hard-won acquisitions of the very strata from which the protesters originated.' [32] These actions are not rooted in specific protest, but 'what is most difficult to accept is precisely the riots' meaninglessness: more than a form of protest, they were what Lacan called *passage a l'acte* – an impulsive movement into action which can't be translated into speech or thought and carries with it an intolerable weight of frustration.'[33] Žižek elaborates: 'Lacan's *passage a l'acte* is akin to a lack of 'what cultural analyst Fredric Jameson has called "cognitive mapping," an inability to locate experience of their situation within a meaningful whole.'[34] Although capitalism is

> global and encompasses the whole world, it sustains a *stricto sensu* 'worldless' ideological constellation, depriving the large majority of people of any meaningful cognitive mapping. Capitalism is the first socio-economic order which *detotalises meaning*: it is not global at the level of meaning (there is no global 'capitalist worldview' no 'capitalist civilisation' proper – the fundamental

> lesson of globalisation is precisely that capitalism can accommodate itself to all civilisations, from Christian to Hindu or Buddhist, from west to east); its global dimension can only be formulated at the level of truth-without meaning, as the 'Real' of the global market mechanism.[35]

While Pinker is in favour of a 'Gentle Commerce', Žižek's theoretical frame is particularly useful, in that it identifies the dominant mechanisms of first world capitalism as a potentially spectral driver of violence, that while invisible, in terms of its indeterminability, it is ever present. Such a force drives disparities and inequalities, controls, discriminates, corals and dominates citizens and determines social, political and cultural expressions of identities through various forms of violence, physical, psychological, verbal, mythic and symbolic.[36]

In Jean-Marie Muller's written work for UNESCO, Žižek discusses how violence is presented here as 'a radical perversion of humanity' and language is a means of its refutation.[37] Žižek goes against this position, and asks, 'What if, however, humans exceed animals in their capacity for violence precisely because they *speak*?'[38] For Žižek, language gives a place to violence, as he argues, 'when we perceive something as an act of violence, we measure it by a presupposed standard of what the "normal" non-violent situation is – and the highest form of violence is the imposition of this standard with reference to which some events appear as "violent". This is why language itself, the very medium of non-violence, of mutual recognition, involves unconditional violence.'[39] He adds, 'What Lacan calls *objet petit a* is precisely this ethereal "undead object", the surplus object that causes desire in its excessive and derailing aspect. One cannot get rid of this excess: it is consubstantial with human desire as such.'[40]

Effectively, if all violence is to be rejected, there is never justification for it. But from Žižek's point of view there sometimes is a justification. On revolutionary violence, I would disagree with him fundamentally, as I would with his simplistic take on the collateral damage caused by violent revolt or Stalinist state terrorism. However, that the violence of colonisation is accounted for in part through language as Part 1 suggests as an 'epistemic violence,' but Žižek's over-burdening of language as an 'unconditional violence' is inaccurate. Equally, he makes no space for the more positive side of nature, that is, Pinker's 'Better Angels', or for the potential of non-violent resistance to be incorporated into language narratives and the imagination, which *Seven Psychopaths* superbly demonstrates. Regardless, he does identify the systemic violence of capitalism with a certain, if overstated, brilliance and it offers a good counter to Pinker's perspectives.

The different types of violence identified above must of course link in with theatre practices and the significance of dramatic form. Of course, McDonagh's theatrical palette shares many things in common with the already mentioned *In-Yer-Face* style of writing and performance which Aleks Sierz has appropriately illustrated, such as the tactics of offence, controversy, provocation, sensation, humiliation, shattering moral taboos and shock. This style he notes fundamentally challenges the binary distinctions 'we use to define who we are: human/animal; clean/dirty; healthy/unhealthy; normal/abnormal; good/evil; true/untrue; real/unreal; right/wrong; just/unjust; art/life'.[41]

The dramatic genres of Farce and Grand-Guignol are raised in some criticism of *Connemara* and *Beauty Queen*. The smashing of the skulls in a domestic setting in the former and the torture scene in the latter appear indicative of both genres. Martin Middeke describes *Connemara* as 'a turbulent Farce ', and as a 'hyberbolic Farce'.[42] Rebecca Wilson suggests in relation to *Beauty Queen* that:

> McDonagh has intermeshed a double-edged, interlocked retention and inversion of much ideology, iconography and topography of 'classic' melodrama; thematics of Gothic melodrama flavoured with elements of Grand-Guignol; a macabre 'gallows humour' and streaks of lasciviousness recalling those lode veins of the Irish comic tradition delineated by Vivian Mercier in *The Irish Comic Tradition*.[43]

Here in this part, I take the opportunity to theorise more substantially on both styles and their relationships with violence, as well as how they are evident in the three plays under consideration.[44] Jessica Milner Davis notes that 'Farce favours direct, visual and physical jokes over rich lyrical dialogue (although words are not unimportant in Farce and can be crucial to its quarrels, deceptions and misunderstandings) and it declares an open season for aggression, animal high spirits, self-indulgence and rudeness in general.'[45] Additionally, in terms of comic techniques, Milner Davis contends that 'Farce like other forms of comedy makes ready use of things such as burlesque (referential mockery of characters and situations known to the audience from outside the play itself) and slapstick (physical but stylized beatings and the humiliation of agelastic targets) and improbable co-incidences (often based on a reduction ad absurdum of some initially realistic event).'[46] For her, the characteristic which distinguishes Farce from other comic styles is that it does not set out 'to point out any particular lesson for its audience'.[47] (I will disagree with her on this point.)

Furthermore, Farce, according to Milner Davis, deals with 'the inescapable facts that all human dignity is at the mercy of the human body and its appetites and needs',[48] meaning it is driven by basic desires for food, sex, territory, power, dominance and control, something that connects with Pinker's thesis. Nominally, in terms of sex, Farce is often about attempts to seduce or to pursue illicit desires by those who are constrained by marriage or relationship commitments. In general, while there may be opportunities created for characters to be unfaithful, more often than not such desires remain unfulfilled, suggesting, in part, that the endings of Farce rely on a conservative dramaturgy of sorts.

Verbal aggressiveness or threats of physical destructiveness are commonplace in Farce, motivated by sibling rivalries, excessive competitiveness, petty jealousies, sheer self-absorption and self-indulgence. In classic Farce generally, the targets of aggression, if they are authority figures, tend to be represented as being:

> largely responsible for inviting their own fate (being misfits, killjoys, selfish, mean, hypocritical, exploitative and/or just plain stupid enough to fall for being fooled). They are frequently iconic figures, representative of general groups (such as parents, members of the opposite sex, country yokels lacking civilised manners, unsympathetic guardians, rival lovers of both sexes, self-invited visitors, over-educated, boring pedants and professionals, masters and bosses, or just plain annoying wimps).[49]

In the generic category of Farce, the figures that are the focus of aggression tend to be family members, colleagues, and neighbours, interpersonally close rivals rather than public figures per se. (These would include young clergyman in *Lonesome,* the policeman in *Connemara* and paramilitary figures who mould mythology in *Inishmore*.)

It is what Farce offers in terms of violence that most interests me in this part. However, in classic Farce Milner Davis argues, although 'violence is omnipresent', it is 'often more sound and fury than actual harm, more symbolic gesture than potent action'.[50] In *Lonesome*, the Valene and Coleman Connor are driven mainly by resentment, hatred, hostility, rage and revenge. Their violence always appears to be on the cusp of something more extreme.[51] (Yet, in their world view, violent conflict is an expression of care, which is bizarrely at odds with Pinker's model.) Through different expressions of violence McDonagh splinters away from that classical tradition, informed more by the licence and chaos that figures like Joe Orton provide, in *Loot* (1965) for example. Eric Bentley has tellingly emphasised the abstractness of the violence in Farce whereby 'Prongs or a rake in the backside are received as pin pricks. Bullets seem to pass right through people, sledge-hammer blows seem to produce only momentary irritations. The speeding up of movement contributes to the abstract effect.'[52]

Milner Davis also distinguishes between humiliation or deception farces, slapstick farces, burlesque farces, snowball farces, reversal farces and equilibrium or quarrel farces.[53] *Inishmore* is both a humiliation and snowball farce, driven by one small incident, after which the difficulties get bigger and bigger. The humiliations are reserved as much for the characters like Padraic and his republican colleagues as for the pieties of politically-motivated paramilitarism.[54] The mayhem on the stage in *Inishmore* is not a negotiated settlement but is an act of anarchic de-commissioning of sorts, by destroying almost all of those who have caused havoc, as it fits neatly with Bentley's notion that Farce is additionally 'a question of the speeding up of human behaviour so that it becomes less human'.[55] Moreover, Bentley goes so far as to claim that Farce is 'the theatre of the surrealist body'.[56] The dismembering of the dead paramilitaries in *Inishmore* or the smashing of the exhumed remains in *Connemara* are also exemplary of this sort of abstraction.

Milner Davis aptly contends that characters in Farce are '[d]oomed to repetitiveness in both behaviour and mental processes [...] display exactly that aspect of "*du méchanique plaqué sure du vivant*" ("something mechanical plastered onto the living") which for [Henri] Bergson defined an event as being comic.'[57] However, in any discussions of Farce it is vital to keep J.L. Styan's comments always in mind: 'Farce does not elude analysis in terms of its mechanical plot and characterization, which are generally implausible anyway and arguably of least importance to its effect. The style of Farce, or more precisely its degree of stylizing, is inseparable from its workings, and it is this key element which is hardest to recognize in reading and all but impossible to describe. The usual critical tools do not help, and our ignorance of its true mechanism – the way it energizes an audience – may be the reason why we undervalue it.'[58]

In their writing, Richard J. Hand and Michael Wilson consider the tradition of the Théâtre du Grand-Guignol, which was established in 1897 by Oscar Méténier and ran on Paris's Rue Chaptal, in the notorious and atmospheric Pigalle area. Grand-Guignol is a form of theatre that traditionally alternates comedies and darker dramas, bringing together melodrama and naturalism,[59] yet it also 'owes a great deal to expressionism and its influence in particular can be seen in the early horror films',[60] Max Maurey 'rebranded the Grand-Guignol as a "Theatre of Horror",' whereby 'much time, effort and expense was invested in creating effects that were as realistic as possible: while a victim may die a melodramatic death, the means by which they met that death were as naturalistic as possible', Hand and Wilson suggest.[61] However, Grand-Guignol's 'unique mixture of the horrific and the erotic, of the graphic and the morally dubious, of *sang, sperme et sueur* (blood, sperm, and sweat),' while the stuff of legend, is in reality 'less colourful than its reputation'.[62] The more comedic pieces appertain 'to mortifying experiences of sexual humiliation and embarrassment', but they are different to the gruesomeness and the essential moments of horror found in the darker pieces to which Hand and Wilson give ample consideration in their work.[63]

Although the dominance of the Grand-Guignol style faded from the late 1940s forward, the theatrical style can be linked to McDonagh's work generally in a number of ways. Firstly, in terms of a grotesque sensibility evident in the obsession with hands and mutilations,[64] secondly, in terms of how the cinematic horror genre informs his own playwriting (whether it is James Whale's *Frankenstein* (1931) or Nicholas Roeg's *Don't Look Now* (1973), which in turn, as previously mentioned, has been influenced by Grand-Guignol and thirdly, in McDonagh's broader utilisations of the violent excesses of anarchic postmodern and popular cultural susceptibilities, where distinctions between fantasy and reality, truth and illusion, pleasure and pain, and fear and exhilaration do not easily hold.

Hand and Wilson show how Grand-Guignol can be read back, by looking at current theories of the cinematic horror genre. In terms of horror in particular, Hand and Wilson utilise Philip Brophy's concept of 'Horrality', and apply it to Grand-Guignol. For Brophy the term is 'a compound of horror, textuality, morality and hilarity', which entails 'the construction, employment and manipulation of horror – in all its various guises – as a textual mode [....] "Horrality" is too blunt to bother with psychology, traditionally the voice of articulation behind horror, because what is of prime importance is the textual effect, the game that one plays *with* the text, a game that is impervious to any knowledge of its workings.' (Note it is the effect rather than the psychological motivation for it which matters.)

Despite audiences' knowledge of the codes and despite the fact that they know what is going to happen, Brophy notes: 'the cheapest trick in the book will still tense your muscles, quicken your heart and jangle your nerves', adding 'its effect disappears with the gulping breath, the gasping shriek, swallowed up by the fascistic continuum of the fiction'. Brophy continues:

> the reader [...] has no time for critical ordinances of social realism, cultural enlightenment or emotional humanism. The gratification of the contemporary Horror film is based upon tension, fear, anxiety, sadism and masochism – a disposition that is overall both tasteless and morbid. The pleasure of the text is, in fact, getting the shit scared out of you – and loving it; an exchange mediated by adrenaline. In the abandoning of the 'ordinances of social realism' and 'emotional humanism,' 'adrenaline' becomes the mediating force.[65]

While it is not my argument that a play like *Spokane* simply borrows or parasitically mimics that governing style, or that Grand-Guignol provides the only dramaturgical stylistic template, my analysis instead will focus on how this play might be best understood by grasping its substantial relationship with the norms and forms of Grand-Guignol, and how the work accommodates its influences. Carmichael's gory obsessions with his missing hand and his fetishistic collection of limbs speak not simply to the excesses and sensations of Grand-Guignol, but also are central to a criticism of racist practices. As I will argue, throughout this part, essential social appraisals are made through the frameworks of Farce and Grand-Guignol, forms not traditionally associated with such broad-ranging socio-political critiques.

2 | Unnatural Selection: *The Lonesome West*

In recent scholarly debate on masculinities and Irishness, general discussions have focused on the ideological mechanisms of patriarchal dissemination, control and preservation and on the need to contest the systemic reliance on and manipulation of 'hegemonic, heteronormative masculinities' (R.W. Connell's much-cited term).[66] In relation to theatre practices, Brian Singleton's work also considers how masculinity 'not only lorded itself over women, but also subjected subordinated groups to its authority and control. Hegemonic masculinity then operated through a performance of patriarchy.' Singleton further emphasises, again following on from Connell, the substances of subordinate, oppositional, 'non-hegemonic masculinities', evident in illustrations of diverse sexualities and in class, religion, race, ethnic and gender differentiations.[67]

In their considerable non-embodiment of 'hegemonic masculinities', McDonagh's characters generally appear to be a long away from forms of representational masculinities that are firm agents of patriarchy or significant benefactors of its dividends – including the 'material', status and the 'honour, prestige, and the right to command'– that Connell identifies.[68] *Lonesome* is a good way to begin interrogating such ideas.

The first production of *Lonesome* directed by Garry Hynes, has Maelíosa Stafford as Coleman, Brían F. O'Byrne as Valene, Dawn Bradfield as Girleen (Mary Kelleher) and David Ganly as Fr Welsh. My comments on this play are based on seeing the play in the summer of 2001 at the Gaiety Theatre in Dublin, with almost the same cast, only with Tom Murphy replacing Ganly.[69] Francis O'Connor creates a kitchen/living area of a cottage/farmhouse in Leenane, with a strong claustrophobic feel to it. The stage design looks exceptionally dingy, almost derelict, encrusted in grime due to the ongoing negligence of the two bachelor and middle-aged brothers, Coleman and Valene, who seldom cook, and seem to have a diet, comprising crisps, alcohol and whatever they can scavenge after attending funerals.

Furnished with a table, chairs, and a single tattered armchair, the space also features Valene's fibreglass statues (figurines) of saints and popes which are prominently displayed on shelves. Over the cooker, there is a double-barrelled shotgun and above that again a crucifix. The photographs of the Pope and Robert and President John F. Kennedy present in *Beauty Queen* are substituted in this instance by a framed photo of a black dog, Lassie, which sits on a chest of drawers. The letter 'V' is embossed on most items in the space, indicating Valene's ownership of both the family home and of the objects resident therein. (Valene's branding is a further violation of the space itself. Later the arrival of a new, large orange cooker does not escape Valene's compulsion to initial everything, almost without exception.)

Stafford's Coleman is slovenly in appearance, is wearing a too-tight mauve or purplish shirt under an old three-quarter length leather jacket and looks underdressed for his father's funeral. (Coleman's shirt part co-ordinates with the purple trousers of Valene, whose sleeveless cream, Aran-patterned pullover has a purple band.) He appears driven by a provocative menace, as he swaggers with a bravado that springs from a strangely cynical, if pathological self-confidence. He is excruciatingly assured that he will not face the forces of justice over his very recent killing of his father. Physically and emotionally, Stafford seldom pays much heed to any form of personal boundary. His Coleman is predominantly without sensitivity, while curiously and frequently vexed by the petty grievances he holds against his neighbours, and his general disdain seems to have no particular individual target. The opening exchanges between Fr Welsh and Coleman are also marked by Coleman's casual disregard for the clergyman's status, who has just presided over his father's funeral. Reluctantly feeling obliged to pour a drink of poteen for the priest, Coleman aggressively rips off some sellotape that Valene has wrapped around a biscuit tin to seal it from his brother. On Valene's return, it only takes a moment for the rowing and the swearing to kick off between the two siblings.

O'Byrne's Valene appears to be the physically weaker of the two brothers, and is allegedly traumatised by Coleman's persistent negative behaviour towards him. His Valene has an obsessive habit of rubbing his hands over his knees three times, and many of his exchanges are marked by inappropriate interventions that discontinue the flow of a conversation. O'Byrne's Valene also displays the demeanour of someone who has a newly-acquired status, is strengthened by this misplaced confidence and his verbal aggressiveness and petulant challenges to Tom Murphy's out of his depth and exasperated Fr Welsh are brilliantly realised. As a spectator, one quickly grasps where this need to brand the space and objects in it comes from. Valene resists the priest's sermonising and believes that the priest's focus should be not on him and his sibling, but more on the likes of Maureen Folan and Mick Dowd, both locally and widely known as murderers.

When pulled apart by the drunken priest, it appears as if they are performing for him, affirming his anxieties, but also strangely expecting him to take individual sides. However, for the brothers, Fr Welsh needs to grow up, cast aside his maudlin, vulnerable, sentimentality, because currently, he takes things 'too much to heart'. (p. 140) Out-manipulated and team-tagged by the brothers, Fr Welsh is then targeted for his apparent lack of compassion, prompting him to increase his self doubts. These anxieties are framed perversely by Valene as Fr Welsh's regular and notorious crises of faith. Murphy brings a vulnerability to the role of priest, meshing defencelessness, confusion, exasperation and distress with a physicality that indicates low levels of self-esteem and self-awareness, while at the same time Murphy's priest-figure takes some ressurance from his imprecise and erroneous understanding of the tenets of the Catholic faith.

Although Murphy's Fr Welsh may seem to be the polar opposite of the two brothers, he is never too much at odds with the play's dominant tonality, indeed, he perversely compliments it. In Hynes's production every miniscule transaction, every micro gesture the characters perform emphasise the fact that they believe fundamentally, whether accurately or not, that there is so much at stake in every instance. As Ben Brantley notes in his review of Hynes's New York production, these 'two middle-aged brothers whacked away at each other like a liquored-up Punch and Judy.'[70] (Tellingly, in the Hynes production, they share a pair of reading glasses.)

In Hynes's productions all encounters are transactional – based on interdependence, indebtedness, threats, manipulation and psychological ascendancy. Their notional present is distorted by the impact of previous slights, the petty snubs and vendettas that are essential to distrustful and revenge fuelled interactions. They are pained by each other's successes however minimal and are of similar mind only when they both have the same targets in their community.[71]

'QUERULOUS DYADS'

Nina Witoszek and Pat Sheeran argue that so many writers in Irish literature generally, especially in theatre, have relied on 'Querulous dyads', characters who 'live in a state of negative symbiosis: while they trade insults they are yet dependent on one another'.[72] They also note how such a structure is 'diametrically opposite' of the buddy system so pervasive in 'American culture'.[73] Such Irish dyads, Witoszek and Sheeran continue, 'are part of a community of hatred which observes a "taboo on tenderness,"' a phrase coined by Ian D. Suttie.[74] Consequently, Witoszek and Sheeran suggest:

> Vernacular hatred and its various verbal and behavioural manifestations (calumny, detraction, etc.) is a diffuse, low-voltage, insidious process of dealing with death [....] At its most virulent – and Ireland is a pathogenic zone in this regard – it destroys personal identity and maims for life. It is in this sense that the manifold manifestations of the vernacular hatred may be treated as tropes of funerary culture, ways of willing and wishing death. Like the funerary tradition itself, vernacular hatred has a double aspect. It too provides a bond, but one that is scarcely worth having. It empowers literature, but blights life. It creates identity but one that is found, at bottom, on death.[75]

What they identity clearly applies to Coleman and Valene.[76] Furthermore, they contend that not only is it 'hatred which energises the famous Irish wit: verbal assassinations, sneers, jeers, lampoons and venomous satires',[77] but it also originates in religious belief, through its renunciation of the 'world, the flesh and the devil: a requirement which inevitably refined the arts of self-hatred. Then it demanded the impossible: love one's neighbour as oneself. Most, it seems, resolved that contradiction by hating their neighbour as they hated themselves.'[78]

While I do agree with the way they connect religion, self-hatred and the funerary tradition and indeed these are interlinked strands that this play confirms, I do not accept their overarching and unduly negative summary of Irish wit as it leaves little room for playfulness, subversiveness, irony or de-contextualisation, and it does not address the role of either a reader or theatre audiences in resisting or contesting such destructive dispositions when they are on display. McDonagh takes this funerary tradition to task as mentioned in Part 1. Catherine Rees argues that 'the brothers live together in a pseudo-marriage with seemingly no female interaction', and she also sees them like the 'masculine pairing of Beckettian characters such as Vladimir and Estragon and Hamm and Clov, relationships of interdependence and frustrated ambitions'.[79]

AN INGLORIOUS SACRIFICE

The two suicides in the play do raise particular issues around self-worth, self-hatred, religion and a curious belief in self-sacrifice. Fr Welsh gets very upset by the fact that neither Valene nor Coleman could even 'bat an eye' at the revelation that Tom Hanlon had just taken his own life. (p. 150) There is a great moment when O'Byrne's Valene pretends to copy the priest's gestures and to mirror his physicalisation of grief. Murphy's Fr Welsh drops his head on the table, spreads his arms across it, Valene mimics him, only to be distracted by a bag of Tayto crisps on the ground, which he sneakily drags towards himself and raises with his feet to his hands. But despite his low-level efforts to feign empathy, O'Byrne's Valene cannot hold the pose for very long, as his recently arrived new cooker keeps catching his eye.

Later, Coleman's casual admission to the murder of his father over an insult about his hairstyle, which was compared to that of a drunken child's, Valene's confession to the covering up of the deed, and the spectacle of the two brothers wrestling on the floor for control of the bullets for the gun leave Fr Welsh in a state of absolute consternation. Fr Welsh's impulsive response to such transgressions is to plunge his hands into the liquefied fibreglass figurines that Coleman had destructively placed earlier in a hot oven in order to antagonise Valene. Welsh's deed, a be-scalding of sorts, is intended to put a stop to what they are doing to each other. The gesture is, however, deeply comical in performance. Pain is rightly abstracted in the way that Bentley talks about in terms of Farce, as Tom Murphy's Fr Welsh revels in the comic and downplays the traumatic implications of what he has just done to himself, when he becomes exasperated by the fact that they persist in getting his name wrong.

However, the generally confused emotional landscape of all three males in *Lonesome* is complicated by the presence of the 17 year-old female Girleen, who on first appearance in the Druid production wears a school uniform. Somewhat like the youthful Helen McCormick in *Inishmaan*, but unlike the bored, frustrated, almost psychopathic or sadistic Mairead in *Inishmore*, Girleen is consistently the challenge to male self-obsession and toxic thinking. She is in part their object of desire, but is also especially assertive, verbally aggressive and very funny.[80] Girleen initially is also far more playful than any of the others and this is evident in her discussions about having sex for money, a proposition which leads in a circuitous way to a situation where she wonders whether or not Fr Welsh could afford to pay her for sexual services.

Equally, Girleen is the more mobile, grounded and self-aware of the four characters. But that does not make her either the reality principle or the figure that simply compensates for the male void of empathy, that she gives access to or recognition of emotions and sensations that the male characters cannot find within or acknowledge as important for themselves. (At one point Coleman's lie that Girleen paid him in drink for sex is exposed, but this detail says less about Girleen as a simplistically objectified figure, and more about the inappropriate fantasies and delusions maintained by the brothers more generally.)

Girleen's despair after Fr Welsh's death is the only grief of apparent substance in the play. Valene reports that she is close to a mental breakdown after the death, something that may be less about her state of mind and more about the male characters' unwillingness to embrace grief. From this perspective, trauma has more to do with mental frailty, rather than a response to loss. Girleen has a foothold in that strange male world, insisting on a participative and confrontational presence in it, on the one hand, but, on the other, she also maintains an easily distinguishable distance from it. In fact, Girleen is the most complex character in this play, and is realised in the affectionate, tactile, spontaneity of Bradfield's deeply engaging performance. Girleen's heightened levels of empathy and self-awareness, which when pitted against the limited and inappropriate instincts of the male characters, creates a dialectically complex sensibility for the play's audience. Girleen gives voice to non-hegemonic femininity and to subordination per se.

Additionally, the contradictory attitudes of the brothers to women generally, whether they are neighbours, visiting nuns, or images of women from around the world is striking; there is fear, awe, desire, desperation and major anxieties about intimacy, commitment and engulfment. (The only mention of the brothers' mother is in relation to a figurine given to her by an American, so in that sense woman is effectively an unmentionable, unfathomable absence.)

Equally, their own virginal states lead to accusations that are deeply homophobic: Coleman calls Valene 'ya little virgin gayboy', and Valene calls Coleman the same thing later. (p.147) Coleman punctures the logic of Valene's ownership claims, suggesting that there is no way he could move around the space by levitating, like 'them darkies', This comment invites further inappropriate reflections on 'darkies', 'Pakies', and 'whistling at the snakes'. (p.142) Most of the misogyny, homophobia and racism seem grounded in fear and not in the experience of contact between those of different genders, sexual orientations or races. Yet, if Fr Welsh's self-harming is one form of bizarrely altruistic, if misguided, sacrifice on behalf of (an) other, then his later suicide extends its significance further, as its gestural and symbolic relevance are de-substantiated and de-ritualised within the farcical frame. In many ways the hold of this funerary tradition is both affirmed but also substantially destabilised by these two key moments of apparent self-sacrifice.[81]

In the Druid production, as the two brothers return from Fr Welsh's funeral they are dressed in suits. There is a great awkwardness between them when they move to shake hands. Interestingly, they swap their usual places around the kitchen table. To start, they share the food brought home from the funeral. Indeed, when Valene pours two drinks, he gives Coleman the by far fuller measure of poteen. The admissions to destructive deeds in the past and the seeking of forgiveness appear to be on their agenda, prompted by Fr Welsh's wishes recorded in his letter to them.

As Valene, O'Byrne's mode of admission about the past seems almost genuine and the traumas associated with these incidents appear relatively grounded, but his motives are not beyond suspicion. Stafford's approach as Coleman to the apologising routine is somewhat in earnest, but also involves a good degree of cynicism and calculation, as he soon sees further opportunities to transgress and to be disagreeable. As the confessions to past deeds progress, they are prompted less and less by sincerity and remorse, and are increasingly guided by one-up-manship. And the deluded belief that Catholicism's sacrament of confession effectively means you can do anything you want, once forgiveness is sought, soon emerges as Coleman's constricted world-view. So in the Connor household, their version of the sacrament of confession, the seeking forgiveness for one's sins, and the penance and absolution that follow becomes instead, and by degrees, a de-sacramentalized power play. This sensibility is confirmed by Coleman's comment: '[....] Okay, it's my go. I'm winning.' (p. 185)

It is Valene's divulgence of his part in the injuring of Alison O'Hoolihan in school that led to the end of Coleman's friendship with her and her engagement with the doctor who treated her, which initially seems like something that cannot be trumped. The revelation incites Coleman to sling sausage rolls at him. Mairtin Hanlon was long the chief suspect in the harming of Lassie, but Coleman now admits to having been the perpetrator. Initially, Valene is inclined to believe the admission to be untrue, and affirms with some conviction that lying is not within the rules.

Stafford's Coleman slowly and theatrically takes the ears from a bloodied brown paper bag and then places the ears of the dog on O'Byrne's head, who leaves them there temporarily before easing them onto the table, at which point, Stafford offers a marker so that O'Byrne might have the opportunity to initial them. O'Byrne slowly descends into a hysterical rage, ensuring that the stand-off which follows, with Valene armed with a knife and Coleman with a gun, looks as if it is heading only in one direction, towards a violent climax, following the template of *Beauty Queen*, where death follows a destructive revelation.

Pinker notes that 'Even though nothing tangible is at stake in contests for dominance, they are among the deadliest forms of human quarrel',[82] as small altercations can result in homicide, or nations going to war 'over nebulous claims'.[83] Having a spectator to many a row is often all that is needed to make matters worse, as Pinker notes of the research in the area. Fr Welsh then is that audience member as hinted at earlier. Between rival males, testosterone is often the problem, as are high or deludedly high rather than low-levels of esteem, which is normally assumed to be the case in terms of poor self-image. Further the confession exchange is not only about dominance, but equally is about revenge.

For Pinker, 'Vengeance is not a disease: it is necessary for cooperation, preventing the nice guy from being exploited.'[84] And he adds, 'forgiveness and contrition, are necessary for social organisations to reap the benefits of cooperation'.[85] What transpires between Coleman and Valene captures the complexity of revenge as a major driver of violence. Revenge is only cranked down when the relationship 'with the perpetrator is too valuable to the server', or, when the perpetrator 'has become harmless', that is when one can persuade another that it was unintentional, or that the harm was not foreseen and that a person will not do so again, with guarantees and re-assurances and with a willingness to make retribution.[86] Apologies can easily 'mollify a rankled victim', so can demonstrations of shame, guilt, embarrassment.[87] To avoid these apologies from being cringeworthy or excessive grovelling is a tough task and the religious pathway of forgiveness, offers some sense of critical and reflective distance. Fr Welsh's solution is a solid enough form of restorative justice.

But after a destruction of the final showdown, Coleman invites Valene for a drink, just after having again apologised, with a bit more sincerity, for what he did to the dog, his second go at destroying Valene's figurines, their general fighting and the killing of their father. This almost heartfelt invitation offers a sort of bizarre closure. By this play's end, there is neither an affirmation of the repetition compulsion that drives the characters nor does the work offer a form of closure that inspires optimism. The inconclusiveness is captured in Valene's attempt to structure something symbolic out of fragments: the crucifix, Fr Welsh's part-burned letter and Girleen's chain, purchased as an expression of affection for Fr Welsh, but also broken and discarded by her. Fr Welsh's last wishes initiate something different but the brothers could never kick-start a fundamental shift in consciousness. Forgiveness and retribution are not really possible and peace between them is as futile as the suggestion of superglue as a solution to the destruction that Coleman has caused during the play's final scene.

There is a moment close to the end when they almost embrace each other in performance, yet it is more Coleman's tendency to placate Valene after he has done something to harm him which seems like the pattern being exposed. They share numerous near-death moments. Indeed, central to their shared value system seems to be the belief in the merits of conflict, which is evident in Coleman's remark that: '[....] And what's wrong with fighting anyways? I do like a good fight. It does show you care [....]' (p. 194)

Rees notes that 'McDonagh's representation of males seems to deliberately subvert the narratives of normative representation associated with male behaviour, especially narratives constructed around violence, rurality and nationalism. In confronting these issues, McDonagh "marks" masculinity as a political subject within the plays, but does not allow the audience to reach stable conventional conclusions about "typical" or normative masculine behaviour.'[88] Thus through loneliness, jealousy, deviance, isolation, disempowered, enfeeblement, excessive interdependency, the absence of intimacy and subsistence living, the subordinate or subservient masculinities of all three male characters in *Lonesome* are especially foregrounded, in ways that challenge hegemonic heteronormativity.

But just as crucially is the fact that while the focus is on masculinity, McDonagh also illustrates a subservient humanity that is not simply gender, religion, race and class specific. Subordination, rather than equality is the experience for the majority of the world's population, even amongst the relative privilege of first world cultures. Audiences perhaps acknowledge their own subservience, their own subordinate status in first world democratic societies that preach opportunity, choice, agency and the promise of equality, but equivalent status and the appropriate 'dividends', patriarchal or otherwise, will never accrue for the majority of people, whether male or female, apart from those who are relatively wealthy.

In the Druid production considered here, through getting even, attempting to dominate, chasing, pushing, name calling, fighting, and hiding and destroying things that belong to each other, the two actors, who play Coleman and Valene, express brilliantly the tensions between them and luminously expose the utterly interdependent worlds of their characters. As Hynes directs her production, the performances are cartoon-like, impish, defiant and what is amputated is a real sense of depth; truncated, then, is this third dimension associated with something that is notionally akin to the real, a dramatic world that bears the weight of excess and exaggeration, without seeming unnecessarily false, but that does not make it representative of something real. It establishes an environment where morality is provocatively limited to a phrase like 'Against God' (which I will return to in Part 3) and personal awarenesses are apparently absent. Indeed, the farcical energy of the performance highlights a destructive funerary sensibility, but a considered playfulness destabilises many of the negative implications of such a tradition as tabulated by Witoszek and Sheeran.

Indeed Milner Davis proposes that 'Farce is comedy with *self-awareness* left out',[89] and, in many ways, that is the case for the characters in *Lonesome*. But I also think that there is room for Farce to bring on board complex awarenesses, through its 'primitive vitality' that Joan FitzPatrick Dean identifies in her analysis of Orton's work.[90] The positioning of the work could be seen to place a greater onus on the spectator, particularly in terms of a depleted or almost 'zero-empathy' demonstrated by the characters in *Lonesome* and the responses it might initiate,[91] and this is something I will also address in Part 3.[92]

In McDonagh's work non-conformity to the traditional expectations of the farcical genre must be embraced. Equally, in the toxicity, ill-discipline and in the oddness of the characters there are major challenges to hegemonic ideological inscriptions and a confrontation of the framing of Ireland in a positively naïve, pastoral fashion. Therefore the combination of an inverted pastoral, a contestation of a funerary consciousness that is not simply just an Irish phenomenon, non-hegemonic masculinities and femininities, and a re-tabulating of Dyer's term 'liminal whiteness', ensure the significance of subordination of McDonagh's disenfranchised, immutable, stigmatised characters, while always othering, but equally other to themselves, offer the further potential of a transgressive whiteness and not the perversity of a funerary whiteness, obsessed by death and its consolations.

3 | Suspect Devices: *The Lieutenant of Inishmore*

When Martin McDonagh was growing up in London, a large number of individuals from Northern Ireland and the Republic of Ireland that belonged to the Irish communities across Britain identified with the plight of a Catholic minority in Northern Ireland during 'The Troubles' period (from the riots of 1968 to 1998's Good Friday Agreement); this empathy had often at its root views on their place of origin's colonial history. Diasporic communities can sometimes persistently and more easily reinforce viewpoints of historical injustices and, then passionately, if somewhat inaccurately, contemporise them, seeing them as being repeated in the present. Very narrow, simplistic assessments and perspectives were sometimes made on what was seen as the extended military and imperial rule of Northern Ireland and thus the perpetuation of a cycle of historical occupation and injustice. Often certain social and political prejudices experienced by Irish citizens in Britain reinforced such viewpoints. Many others had more complex understandings of the impact and legacy of a divided island.

A tiny minority within these diasporic communities were financially and militaristically supportive of Republican paramilitary actions, including the brutal murders of innocent victims, while the majority, despite a nationalist outlook, stated unequivocally 'not in my name' to acts of paramilitary violence in Ireland, Britain and elsewhere. Many were probably even more repulsed by the persistence of state, police and militarist violence against a Catholic or Nationalist minority in Northern Ireland.

The Provisional Irish Republican Army's (PIRA) military campaign in Britain coincided with McDonagh's formative years. In 1974, the PIRA planted a number of bombs in the United Kingdom. For example, on 4 February a bomb exploded on a coach occupied by army members and their families, killing 12 people on the M62 motorway. On 17 June a bomb detonated at London's Houses of Parliament and on 5 October 1974 explosive devices set off in two public houses in Guildford left five dead and over 50 injured.[93] Twenty-one died in two bombs planted in pubs in Birmingham on 21 November, and by 29 November the British government passed the Prevention of Terrorism Act.[94] Both the Guildford and Birmingham bombings led to miscarriages of justice for the Guildford Four, the Maguire Seven and the Birmingham Six. The British judicial systems forged ahead with criminal proceedings based on unreliable and distorted evidence gathered by the police and relied on statements made during illegal interrogations.

For many of the first and second generation Irish living in Britain at that time, not only did they regularly experience hostility, suspicion and racism, but equally, there was a sense for many that the British political and legal structures were systematically prejudiced against the Irish and the draconian powers granted to the police under the new legislation amounted in their application to breaches of their human rights. There also existed of course real fears of paramilitary attack amongst the broader British populace. Any paranoia about Republican paramilitary activities was added to by the mass media reporting on the acts of violence in Northern Ireland, the Republic of Ireland and Britain. Frequently, much of the reportage painted the situation as a sectarian conflict and not as one of the legacies of colonisation, and not one that grew from the partitioning of the island of Ireland in 1922 into the 26-county Free State and six out of the nine counties of the province of Ulster, forming Northern Ireland, which remained under British rule.[95] Henry McDonald notes that 'McDonagh was not sucked into the "Brits Out" bar ballad culture that used to exist in north London and south Boston.'[96]

According to McDonagh's own accounts, and as I mentioned already earlier, the Warrington bombing on 20 March 1993, which led to the deaths of Jonathan Ball (aged three) and Tim Parry (aged12) – a year prior to the kick-starting of the formal Northern Irish Peace Process in 1994 – was what provoked him into the writing of *Inishmore*. In relation to this bombing, McDonagh states, 'hang on, this is being done in my name [and] I just feel like exploding in rage'.[97] While the PIRA admitted to the planting of the Warrington bomb, in their minds however, as Richard English reports, the fundamental responsibility 'lies squarely at the door of those in the British authorities who deliberately failed to act on precise and adequate warnings'.[98]

In a somewhat similar situation, Martin McGuinness's statement in *An Phoblacht/Republican News* in 1988 after an PIRA bomb killed nationalist civilians in a trap set for British soldiers is telling: 'The tragedy of this war is that IRA Volunteers, British forces and, sadly, also civilians will continue to suffer and die as long as Britain refuses to accept its fundamental responsibility for what is happening in our country.'[99] If civilians are collateral damage, then that has to be a regrettable but inevitable part of warfare, springing from unjust circumstances, as McGuinness viewed it.

While *Inishmore* is set on Inishmore, one of the three Aran Islands off County Galway, and while it does address aspects of paramilitary violence and collateral damage, the play clearly does not wish to deal realistically, dispassionately, accurately or objectively with the causes and circumstances of 'The Troubles'. This play instead attempts to subvert the justifications for and the logic behind Republican paramilitary violence carried out by the likes of the PIRA and Irish National Liberation Army (INLA), the latter group which is the focus of this play.[100]

McDonagh claims: 'I was trying to write a play that would get me killed. I had no real fear that I would be, because paramilitaries never bothered with playwrights anyway, but if they were going to start I wanted to write something that would put me top of the list.'[101] In a more circumspect and earlier interview, he recounts, 'having grown up Catholic and, to a certain degree, republican, I thought I should tackle the problems on my own side, so to speak. I chose the INLA, because they seemed so extreme and, to be honest, because I thought I'd be less at risk. I'm not being heroic or anything – it was just something I felt I had to write about from a position of what you might call pacifist rage. I mean, it's a violent play that is wholeheartedly anti-violence.'[102] That sense of 'pacifist rage', and that sense of the drama being also 'wholeheartedly anti-violence' are interesting insights.

McDonagh also states in an interview that *Inishmore* is 'much more in the Joe Orton tradition than in any tradition of Irish drama. This is the furthest I'm going to push this whole violence, black-comedy thing, because I don't think it can get much blacker or more violent.'[103] According to C.W.E. Bigsby, it was Orton who redefined Farce, as it 'became both an expression of anarchy and its only antidote',[104] and McDonagh appears to follow this Ortonesque trajectory: an anarchic alignment of sex, violence and politics rather than the conservative tendencies of Classic Farce as Milner Davis proposes them to be.

Inishmore's outlandish plot has Mad Padraic Osbourne's cat, Wee Thomas, supposedly killed by three of his ex-paramilitary colleagues in a ploy to lure him back home so that they can assassinate him,[105] only for him to be rescued by a 16 year-old local girl, Mairead – a marksperson par excellence – who also has a sentimental yearning to fight for Ireland's freedom, a romantic interest in Padraic, and she is even more infatuated with her own cat, the ginger Sir Roger (Casement).

The play opened at the Royal Shakespeare Company's Other Place, Stratford-upon-Avon on 11 April 2001, then had a short London run at The Pit, at the Barbican, before returning to London's West End on 26 June 2002 at the Garrick Theatre, with a somewhat different cast, but with Wilson Milam directing on each occasion.[106] The Garrick production, which won the Olivier Award in 2003 for best comedy, stars Peter McDonald and Elaine Cassidy, both having replaced David Wilmot and Kerry Condon as Padraic and Mairead. In the revived production at the Garrick, Trevor Cooper remains cast as Donny and Domhnall Gleeson takes over from Owen Sharpe as Davey. Supporting cast includes James (Paul Lloyd), Christy (Peter Gowen), Joey (Glen Chapman), and Brendan (Luke Griffin).[107]

The Garrick production is exceptionally dark, funny and seriously farcical in sensibility and is the one that I will emphasise in my discussions in order to illustrate how genre is signalled and how audiences might be steered in their engagement with the work.[108] During this production's opening moments, Gleeson's Davey Claven desperately holds out some forlorn hope that despite the fact that a cat's brains are dripping out, he still wants to seek out a veterinary surgeon for a second opinion. He has also gormlessly admits to the breaching of best medical practice by moving the victim (cat) from the scene of the accident.[109] Further, the production's grotesque sensibility is reinforced when Gleeson stupidly, gruesomely and forlornly scrapes a placemat in order to swipe the dislodged innards back into the remains of the cat. Gleeson's Davey is a long red-haired young man who cycles about the island on his mother's pink bicycle, which is too small for him and he brilliantly captures the naivety, innocence, earnestness and foolhardiness of his character.

Trevor Cooper's Donny is the slovenly patriarchal figure, who is driven by a complex mix of fear, conniving and indifference, who takes a back seat and watches Gleeson's Davey dig a bigger and bigger hole for himself. Cooper evokes brilliantly the maniacal waywardness of his son, Padraic and exploits his son's violent reputation for his own purposes by drawing out Davey's growing sense of foreboding. From Donny's perspective, Davey is either a suspect or accessory to the crime of cat murder and Donny is going to do his best to implicate him, in order to protect himself. In picking up the cat from the roadside, Davey's well-intentioned, Good Samaritan-like deed may now put him in extreme danger, as he is in a dramatic world where 'moral sense' and the norms of poetic justice simply do not appear to apply. Both actors are clown-like figures, in some respects, that are going to be unintentionally drawn into a world of paramilitary conflict and chaos.

Later, with Padraic's impending arrival home, Davey expects to be one step ahead as arrogance and naivety interplay. By pre-programming his brain to wake up, Ninja-style, Davey intends to rise early in order to put in the final preparations. But the cross made to mark the burial place of Wee Thomas remains on the floor and Davey's hands are still black from the polishing task. And the black shoe polish will of course fail to disguise the orange mane of his sister's cat, which Davey hopes to explain away by the fact that Wee Thomas has an exotic disease that has both turned him orange and leaves him smelling of shoe polish. Gleeson's performance gets absolutely right his character's disastrous creativity and limited improvisatory intelligence and the gaps between reality and wishful thinking are evident for all to see. As loyalty is of little merit in farces such as this, the initial allegiance between Donny and Davey is quickly cast aside as they comically turn on each other in face of Padraic's interrogation of them, as they face the Clown's rather than the Prisoner's Dilemma, which I will explain later.

An audiences' first encounter with Padraic is to witness him torturing the trussed-up James Hanley in a Belfast warehouse – just after Padraic has extracted two toenails from one of James's feet. Padraic is working his way towards one of his nipples, which he threatens to force feed to him.[110] The torture is interrupted by a phone call, during which Padraic casually gives to his father a summary account of his day-to-day activities, such as tormenting a drug dealer or putting bombs in a couple of chip shops that 'didn't go off'. (p. 13)[111] McDonald's Padraic earnestly behaves just as a professional might do if a consultation is interrupted by a phone call. The casual discussion between father and son about how well the PIRA makes their bombs, in contrast to the INLA is exceptionally provocative, leaving a certain level of distaste, by exposing a perversely destructive logic. Altering his priorities, Padraic sets James free, casually, if gormlessly, offering post-torture advice about tetanus injections and the need to avoid the wound turning septic; he even gives James the bus fare to get to the hospital. James, who has feigned an interest in cats and conceals his real loathing of Padraic, gives Padraic advice as to how to treat his cat for ringworm and makes up the name 'Dominic' for his own imaginary cat – a name that references either Dominic McGlinchey or Dominic Behan perhaps.

In this scene, McDonald captures his character's sadistic inclinations, but also his goofy playfulness, in a manner that obscures easy forms of spectator resistances to or objections towards the character's behaviours.[112] For McDonald's Padraic, destructive single-mindedness, callousness and nostalgia go hand in hand, while such seamlessness is difficult, McDonald succeeds. As a consequence, on believing his cat to be dead, McDonald's expression of losing purpose in life registers the requisite sentimental and challenging ambivalence that generates strangeness: '[....] No longer will his smiling eyes be there in the back of me head, egging me on[....] as I'd lob a bomb at a pub, or be shooting a builder'. (p. 44) Incongruity and exasperation towards the twisted and destructive logic of Padraic are central to this production's ambiance as the gap between his boundless empathy for his cat and his brutal indifference towards the suffering he causes to others is of most interest. (Part 3 will pick up on this pathology in a more sustained fashion.)

Elaine Cassidy's cropped-haired Mairead, wears combat trousers and carries an air-rifle. Cassidy allows her character a strong, self-deluding and devious presence, as she is initially overly self-assured, manipulative and sexually confident.[113] When she fearlessly fills the role of heroic rescuer, by initially blinding three paramilitary assassins, Brendan, Joey and Christy, she becomes increasingly attractive to Padraic. Unseen by their rivals, Mairead and Padraic waltz into the house and execute them one by one, driven by an erotic glee as much as by sadism. The killings bind them temporarily as a couple. (Later, he kisses her, while holding the dug up remains of a cat against her back, bloodying her dress.)

THE LITTLE GREEN BOOK

So, to pick up again on one of the arguments initiated in Part 1, that a fundamental grand narrative of imperialism is that it is an appropriate and relatively benign activity, reliant on myths of mutuality and reciprocity. From the prevailing Irish perspective, and in contrast, the grand narrative of colonisation over a significant 800-year period accounts for conquest, dominance and control, abject material conditions and cycles of political protests and often badly armed rebellions, which were almost always followed by desolation after the quelling of insurrection through the use of brutal, 'strategic,' military force. The self-sacrifice of indigenous individuals was seen not only as heroic, but also as having both mythic and religious significances. Most critics suggest that the colonial subject does not have easy or ready access to strategies of resistance, whether linguistic, political or military, as more often than not 'resistance is simply pathologised' by the imperial power, as Ania Loomba has noted.[114]

While the partitioning of Ireland in 1922 was carried out in order to appease a Unionist–Loyalist majority in the northern region of the island, it has been in effect one of the most substantial and complex legacies of the island's colonisation. Clearly, the majority of the citizens of these six counties wanted to remain part of the Union, but it left a significant Nationalist and predominantly Catholic minority feeling excluded from what they would have naturally regarded as their national allegiance. Neither the political division of the island nor the minority's acute perception and experience of themselves as second-class citizens were adequately addressed by successive British governments from the 1920s onwards, who were most keen to appease the Unionist majority and to maintain the status quo. Social issues in terms of housing, education, employment, segregation and gerrymandering led to civil protests in the 1960s, but demands for change were resisted. There was a strong Republican influence on the Northern Ireland Civil Rights Association.

On 14 August 1969 the British army took to the streets in order to quell civil unrest.[115] State militarism was seen at its worst during the events of Bloody Sunday on 28 January 1972, when a civil rights protest march in Derry was met by British military violence, leaving initially 13, and later 14 people dead and many others wounded.[116] After this event paramilitary activities began to escalate further, with Loyalist paramilitaries defending what they saw as their rights and Republican organisations responding to British military and Loyalist paramilitary intimidation and acts of violence and murder.

In late 1969 the PIRA was set up, partly as a response to the perceived weaknesses of the old IRA, which was an increasingly immobile and spent force. Initially, the PIRA did not attack soldiers, as it was violence as self-defence, but by March 1971, the strategy had moved towards 'all-out resistance,' according to Malachi O'Doherty.[117] Richard English suggests 'that while there was a need for Catholic self-protection in the late 1960s (and beyond)', however, 'the Provisional's defensive record has, in practice, been a poor one'.[118] Internment, the fraudulent findings of Widgery, which was set up to investigate Bloody Sunday, the Diplock Court system of 1973 and increasing Loyalist paramilitary activities only added to the problems in Northern Ireland.

For some in Nationalist or Republican areas, guerrilla warfare, freedom fighting or armed resistance was seen as a righteous and inevitable response, with the aim to break the will of the British crown forces. For many Republicans, clearly it was believed to be a violence of last resort and therefore a morally and politically legitimate response to the notion of serial injustices, threats and illegal occupation. Republicans emphasised their over-arching allegiances to figures of history, such as the revolutionaries of 1916 in order to suggest the continuity of their struggle; they also aligned themselves with victims of conflict internationally. For someone like Frantz Fanon, 'Decolonization is always a violent phenomenon';[119] thus English argues: '[I]t is not difficult to hear the echoes in IRA thinking of a Fanonist argument that the violence of the colonized can only be understood within the context of the colonizer's own prior violent actions.'[120] Thus the actions of the PIRA evolved from the defence of the Nationalist or Catholic communities to acts of retaliation and then later to guerrilla warfare, including attempts to take the war off the island of

Ireland and to the rest of the United Kingdom and sometimes Europe, as briefly mentioned earlier.

Later in the early 1980s, republicans adopted a twin strategy of the armalite and the ballot box, the PIRA with its paramilitary campaign and its political wing, Sinn Féin with its participation in politics. The crossovers from and interchanges between politics and fiction are inordinately complex, but it is essential to say that a writer should not be under any obligation to represent accurately, but that the creative freedom of the writer still can be tested for its ideological leanings and imperatives.

SECOND TIME AS KARL MARX

So if one evaluates the language of most colonial conflict situations, the rhetoric employed regularly distils down to the same essences; imperial authority expresses the need for order and civility and revolutionaries emphasise the facts and incidents of oppression and injustice and argue the need to fight violence with violence, with claims that a retaliatory violence is the only message that a major power will understand, before it eventually becomes obligated to enter any sort of negotiations. Each will skilfully find the gaps in the rhetoric and propaganda of the other side.

History, of course, often is a site that offers propagandistic evidence, validates insurgency and affirms the continuities of a tradition. The alleged Irish Republican lineage ranges from Wolf Tone and Padraig Pearse to James Connolly and Bobby Sands, and links internationally to the thinking and actions of the likes of Karl Marx, Ché Guevara and Nelson Mandela. Speaking specifically about Gerry Adams and Martin McGuinness, Kevin Rafter notes: 'The self-claimed purity tradition is central to their narrative for Sinn Féin and the [P]IRA. These Republicans trace a direct line of succession from the 1916 Easter Rising right through to their own political and military organizations. The sequence of historical events is arranged to provide a narrative for Republican theology.'[121]

The propagandist justification for Republican paramilitarism has been spun with a mixture of conviction, fluency, evasiveness, soft sentiment, hard bargaining, threats and special pleading. These articulations often went hand in hand with the refusal to denounce certain atrocities. The strategists of the PIRA, were, according to Ed Maloney, 'longsighted, bright, talented, dedicated, determined, pragmatic, cunning and all too often duplicitous. They were also utterly ruthless in their mission, which above all else was to survive and prosper.'[122] That mix of strength, determination and belief, alongside pragmatism and duplicitousness are publically side-stepped by those who express blind faith, publically at least, in the purity of republican principles.

Furthermore, according to these modes of resistance and the craft of warfare, legitimate targets were determined to be soldiers serving in the UK and Europe, police officers, informers and colluders, including builders, maintenance people and the suppliers of services to the British Army. In the play, Padraic self-determines what constitutes legitimate targets and this puts him at odds with his colleagues. Now he is a valid target of theirs. Padraic's own list of valid targets was carelessly lost on a bus. In addition, Mairead's blinding of cattle is a self-legitimated action, a position she later revises. By so doing, McDonagh is confronting the problematic processes of ideological legitimisation.

And it is through discussions around a campfire that McDonagh further attempts to invalidate the logic of these paramilitary practices, by deconstructing the rhetoric of armed struggle and its justifications of violence through historical precedents. Joey, McDonagh's somewhat sensitive paramilitary, is disconcerted by the fact that there had to be a feline fatality; but for Christy, the ends justify the means. There is a certain governing logic, but in his false attribution of the line to Karl Marx, the cracks in his thinking are exposed. All that Brendan can say in response is that Marx was not the source of the quotation, but he cannot confirm who coined the phrase. Rather than there being a seamless ideology shared by this band of brothers, their collective narrative is represented as lacking any cohesion.

Joey, however, cannot be distracted from his main contention – that he did not join the INLA in order to kill cats and states: 'That sounds like something the fecking British'd do. Round up some poor Irish cats and give them a blast in the back as the poor devils were trying to get away, like on Bloody Sunday.' (p. 28) Brendan asks Christy to clarify as to whether or not such cat-killings took place on Bloody Sunday. Joey's train of thought as it waywardly moves to a simplistic politics of attribution suggests a level of ignorance, indoctrination and mental short-circuiting that is as unnerving as it is frightening.

By way of priming Joey, Christy wonders if his colleagues are aware of the number of cats Oliver Cromwell assigned to the black hole of history, and if so, they themselves could be comforted by the fact that they could never be in Cromwell's league. Historically, Cromwell's soldiers murdered thousands in his campaign in Ireland (1649–53). The cultural and political memory recognises the name and apportions censure accordingly, but the governing detail is forgotten, unknown or ignored. These three freedom-fighting characters do not possess the historical particulars to legitimate their actions. Instead, they improvise with the facts and construct narratives based on inaccuracies and self-indulgent details. Even greater quandaries are raised by Joey's later intervention. The INLA has gone down in his estimation for killing Airey Neave,[123] who was the INLA's most high-profile assassination: 'Joey: [....] You can't blow up a fella just because he has a funny name. It wasn't his fault.' (p. 29) (While other murders are hinted at this is the only occasion when a real casualty of 'The Troubles' is directly named in the play.)

Equally exchanges between Padraic and Mairead offer further elaborations of the governing paramilitary ideology previously propounded by Christy, Joey and Brendan. On his return to the island, Padraic is first greeted by Mairead, who is singing Dominic Behan's 'The Patriot Game' – a song about a 16 year-old boy who, in the face of imperialism's injustices, joins the cause. The song is her calling card so to speak, as she communicates her desire to align herself with the figure in the song. Padraic's response to the song is interesting: 'If they'd done a little more bombing and a little less writing I'd've had more respect for them' (p. 32) – 'they' meaning Dominic and Brendan Behan. Although Mairead asks him out, Padraic refuses to socialise until Ulster is free: 'Not while there was work to be done riding Erin of them jackboot hirelings of England's foul monarchy.' (p. 33) The language alone exposes modes of ideological indoctrination and the rhetoric used to give paramilitarism its particular focus. Padraic will not recruit her, because women are barred, except for pretty ones. (His rejection raises the issue about the significant number of women who were on active service during the Troubles period, much of which has gone unrecognised.)

Interestingly, Mairead provokes Padraic by suggesting that his rejection of women's advances may be because of his sexual orientation. He firmly assures her that there are 'no boy-preferers involved in Irish *terrorism*'. (My emphasis) (p. 33) The alignment of patriotism with 'hegemonic heteronormativity' to the exclusion of subordinate 'boy preferers', exposes homophobic anxieties and broaches the subject of homoeroticism which is often aligned with groups of men in conflict or war situations, while also signalling the importance of a hyped-up, warrior-styled masculinity. This point is extended by the fact that Mairead's cat is named after Sir Roger Casement who was charged with treason for gun-running and was hanged in 1916. Many suggest that *The Casement Black Diaries*, in which Casement's homosexuality is divulged, were counterfeited by British counter-intelligence.

THE TERROR DIVIDEND

If McDonagh deconstructs the rhetorical rationale of paramilitarism, he also contentiously links republican paramilitarism to criminality and vigilantism, with the inclusion of punishment beatings and the relationship between paramilitary characters and drug dealing.[124] Many people were tortured by Republican paramilitaries, including enemies, informers, infiltrators, those colluding with the British army and those accused of anti-social behaviour. The crimes of those frequently tortured for anti-social behaviour were joyriding, disturbing the peace, along with petty and major drug dealing. (Teenagers supposedly terrorising neighbourhoods were not without role models.) In many punishment beatings, apart from baseball bats and pickaxe handles, guns and knives are often used. There were also 'tar and feathering', kneecapping or the notorious 'Six pack' or 'mixed grill', comprising two bullets into the two ankles, knees and elbows or wrists. Such naming gives little indication of the levels of incapacitation that ensues from such torture. Of course, many communities welcomed these interventions as they felt that they could not turn to the police to protect their neighbourhoods. Žižek's comments on fear and systemic violence are worth recalling.

It is easy to regard punishment beatings as simply the filling of a sort of policing vacuum, but they left their victims with neither the presumption of innocence nor the right to a defence, and many people were left dead, seriously mutilated and permanently disabled. Richard English notes also that 'intercommunal vendettas and power struggles played their part in these gruesome IRA policing methods'.[125] Both the Provisionals and the INLA were very active on that front. These punishment beatings did not end with the Good Friday Agreement. During the post-1995 period, according to Rafter, 'There were over 1,200 so-called punishment attacks [...] which were attributed to the IRA.'[126] English notes that in 1996 Martin Doherty, a Belfast teenager was 'nailed by Republicans to a wooden fence with metal spikes through his knees and elbows',[127] and in February 1998, Brendan Campbell another alleged drug dealer, was also killed.[128]

In effect, the torture Padraic carries out on James is very much on the lenient side. This petty drug dealer is guilty of indiscriminate drug dealing. If they were not so drugged up, Republican-inclined juveniles would be on the streets throwing stones at the police, according to Padraic. For Padraic's group, James is a legitimate target of their community policing policy, but Skank Toby is the tolerable face of drug dealing, as he donates a cut of his sales to the cause. This money finances ferry crossings and 'chip-shop manoeuvres', (p. 45) and in Christy's estimation, Toby does a great 'community service'. (p. 29) Disregarding Christy's thinking, Padraic had cut off Toby's nose and fed it to a cocker spaniel; the dog then choked on the nose. As a consequence Padraic is to be eliminated in part because he cannot distinguish between Toby's and James's activities.

The overall connection between paramilitarism and drug-dealing has long been a contentious and broadly disputed one. Patrick Magee claims that 'personal aggrandisement and enrichment, often through drug trafficking, is frequently the slander of next resort'.[129] However, in most people's estimation, paramilitary groups were well known for setting up anti-drug campaigns and for removing some drug dealers from local communities, only to facilitate their own distribution networks or to licence others to trade, under their control. Rafter adds that '[t]here have been claims that Republicans have constructed and operated an arm's length drugs policy whereby they effectively "license" their territories to drug dealers in return for a share of the proceeds of their illegal activity'.[130] However, Rafter notes that 'paramilitary groups in Northern Ireland have also been active in the drugs trade', although the Independent Monitoring Commission 'did not list drug income as a source of [P]IRA revenue'.[131]

By most accounts paramilitaries had and still have strong links with other criminal behaviours through vigilante activities, extortion, exiling, smuggling, kidnappings, fuel laundering, betting scams, currency exchange, illegal property purchase and rental, tax and welfare fraud, dealing in replica goods, protection rackets through the setting up of security companies, money laundering through public houses, taxi and courier services, along with bank robberies, including two in particular: The Northern Bank Robbery in Belfast in December 2004 and the failed robbery that led to the murder of the police officer, Gerry McCabe in Adare, County Limerick in 1996. There is a perception that such illegal activities also generated a cluster of untouchable terrorist elites in many instances. Although the burden of proof seems to fall short, there is disbelief in thinking that it is not the case. However, 'according to a 2003 Garda report, no direct link can be established between the [P]IRA and criminality, but that individuals associated with the organisation are active in these areas. Allegations are difficult to substantiate, but it does not mean that they are not there', Rafter notes.[132] Throughout the play McDonagh intentionally aligns the republican cause with criminality, with punishment beatings and collusion with the drug trade, which they supposedly avidly oppose. However, it is questions about the representations of the relationship between paramilitarism, resistance motivations and pathology are the most important issues in this the play. And this is what I wish to focus on now.

Mary Luckhurst argues that the play 'broadly depicts an orgy of random violence, and individuals fuelled by a mixture of Puritanism, sentimentality, and mindless fanaticism, whose political aims have long been subsumed by a desire to terrorise for its own sake', and by so doing, 'political substance' is all 'but air-brushed away'.[133] Later in the article Luckhurst's concerns move from the work to the criticism, arguing that despite all of the perceived failings of the writing, 'None of this would matter but for the fact that many English critics, while arguing that [*Inishmore*] can be laughed off as a clever joke, also claim that it is a play of political gravitas. Their reasoning for this conviction is invariably vague and more than imbued with a guilty compulsion to speak in its defence.'[134] Not everyone shares that view and in McDonagh's defence, Catherine Rees confronts Luckhurst. Rees sees McDonagh as using 'cruelty not to titillate middle-class audiences and create an enfant terrible reputation, but to expose the cruelty and pointlessness of the terrorism he is criticising'.[135]

Tom Maguire's response to the play is built in part around Patrick Magee's 'survey of the representation of Republicans in prose fiction', in order to confirm that '[t]he representation of the composite Republican was to reach its nadir' in *Inishmore*.[136] Magee's position is that 'the composite Irish Republican to materialise was a Mother-Ireland fixated psycho-killer, aka a Provo-Godfather, readily discernible with recourse to an identikit indebted to Tenniel's "Irish Frankenstein" and other images from *Punch* redolent of Victorian racism.'[137] For Maguire and Magee, those sorts of misrepresentations need to be confronted. (Patrick Magee was sentenced to five life sentences for planting the bomb in 1984 in the Grand Hotel in Brighton which was housing the British Conservative party's annual conference.)

To substantiate his argument, Maguire utilises Seamus Deane's contentions from 1985 that 'the language of politics in Ireland and England is still dominated by the putative division between barbarism and civilisation',[138] Deane has suggested that for centuries there were huge attempts to integrate the Irish into British ways, in business, politics, religion, in custom and practices, and within the law. However, those who remained outside the law were deemed barbaric, uncivilised and undisciplined. They were effectively criminalised, suffering 'the condition of homo criminalis',[139] a position from which 'the quaint Paddy or the simian terrorist arise quite naturally from the conviction that there are criminal types, politically as well as socially identifiable to the state and to all decent citizens'.[140]

Deane claims that the military wings of the Republican movements are framed as terrorists and are seen as uncivilised barbaric criminals, while state terror is effectively legitimised, that imperialism causes those on the side of civilisation and order to 'kill with impunity, because they represent, they embody the Law', whereas those that are deemed uncivilised do not have such 'impunity' and are regarded as illegitimate.[141] For him, the actual criminal activities of political or paramilitary organisations are seen only as a slandering propaganda strategy of the imperial state and not really for the violence or trauma that they cause as a secondary effect.

The arguments that Deane generate are at times subtle and I have absolutely no truck with the general sophistication of state terror to be so manipulative, of which Ireland's history has seen vivid evidence. However, if imperial state elides both the actuality and consequences of violence and the collateral damage violence brings,[142] a similar pattern surely is implicit but denied in his argument about Republican violence, which also evades the actualities of violence and the fallout for people's lives caught up in the realities of armed struggle; it deems imperialist violence as 'barbaric' and Republican violence as morally justified and to an extent civilised in a different fashion. Each side, not just the imperial one, evades its own distinctive barbarism.

As English reminds us: when the state, 'in Weberian manner, identified itself as holding a monopoly over legitimate force' but when it uses its 'force in arbitrary and extra-legal ways, killing members of its population in dubious circumstances and then refusing adequately to investigate those circumstances, how can distinctions between legal force and illegal paramilitarism remain crisp after such episodes?'[143] English has in mind the shoot to kill policy and the collusion of police and military forces with Loyalist paramilitaries, who 'considered the Republican and Nationalist threat to their state, a sufficient justification for carrying out appalling actions'.[144] All sides stress their own sufficient justifications and target ideologically the illegitimacy and corruption of their enemies' positions.

More specifically, the linking of paramilitary actions with animal-like behaviour, for example, is a recurring trope deployed towards an enemy with real frequency. Patrick Lonergan argues, informed by Lionel Pilkington's scholarship, that 'by presenting the enemy as animal-like, one denies their cause a political legitimacy. An animal does not have a political view: it instead behaves unpredictably and irrationally – and it can be put down if it becomes uncontrollable.'[145] While the naming of paramilitary figures as animal or animal-like, while it is one tactic of a pathologising imperial power and the representation of behaviours as barbaric, it is also important to recognise the significance of collegial nicknaming, self-branding and self-promotion within paramilitary groups and how these can generate reputations and auras of fear. This dialectic is a complex one.

Real paramilitary figures on both sides bore particular nicknames. The 'dog' was also the '[P]IRA's nickname for Republican Brian Keenan', as Ed Maloney points out.[146] There was the 'Border Fox' Dessie O'Hare, 'Mad Dog' Dominic McGlinchey, and 'Mad Dog' Johnny Adair.[147] Here in this play there is of course (Mad) Padraic, who is seen as sentimental, brutal, barbaric, with little empathy and pathological. Equally, Padraic demonstrates many of the characteristics of psychopathology that Pinker and others note, and to which I will return more fully in Part 3, namely, having no capacity for sympathy or remorse, high levels of unearned narcissism.

Before Mairead kills Padraic, he is making promises of marriage to her, but of course, not until Ireland is 'free'.[148] They still plan to be together, to go to Northern Ireland and to fight for the cause. It is additionally provocative when we hear of her mother's only hope that her daughter's planned move up north will not leave innocent children dead. Pragmatic Mairead cannot, however, make that promise.[149] Upon discovering the remains of her Sir Roger, Mairead shoots Padraic with two pistols, with blood spraying all over her dress and the rear stage walls.[150] McDonagh allows Mairead's rage to supersede her desire for him, as passion is displaced by an assassin's calculation. By killing him, she is completing the destruction of this specific splinter group. Her cold calculation seems utterly sadistic.

Crucially, in Cassidy's performance there seems to be no regret, just indifference in the aftermath of these events.[151] Sadism is 'an acquired taste', according to Pinker.[152] More generally, sadism is evident in torture, in entertainment where humans or animals are harmed, where people watch executions. In war zones, soldiers can do grievous harm when they are on the rampage, as the American soldiers do during the Mỹ Lai massacre as it is central to the mindset of the Buddhist figure in *Seven Psychopaths*. Pinker identifies four aspects of nature that lead us to the possibility of taking pleasure from another's pain. Firstly, the macabre, 'a fascination with the vulnerability of living things,' rubbernecking, pulling limbs from animals; secondly there is dominance, in how the mighty have fallen, if they have been 'among your torturers', or in the downfall of rivals, of those we envy or those of a higher class that fall on hard times, or if someone is accused of guilt, even when innocent. We want to see them squirm, suffer, see what it is like from another person's vantage point. The third one is pay-back, or 'the sanitised third-party version we call justice', and finally, sexual sadism.[153]

In terms of heinous depravity, for Pinker 'if genocide is the worst by quantity, sadism might be the worst by quality', as to deliberately inflict pain 'for no purpose but to enjoy a person's suffering is not just morally monstrous but intellectually baffling, because in exchange for the agony of the victim the torturer receives no apparent personal or evolutionary benefit'.[154] Pinker notes, 'the development of sadism requires two things: motives to enjoy the suffering of others and a removal of the restraints that ordinarily inhibit people from acting on them'.[155]

Harold Schechter, according to Pinker, distinguishes between male and female serial killers; male killers' sadistic violation of bodies has a strong sexual component, but female psychopaths 'are no less depraved than their male counterparts. As a rule, however, brutal penetration is not what turns them on. Their excitement comes – not from violating the bodies of strangers with phallic objects – but from a grotesque, sadistic travesty of intimacy and love: from spooning poisoned medicine into the mouth of a trusting patient, for example, or smothering a sleeping child in its bed. In short, from tenderly turning a friend, family member, or dependent into a corpse – from nurturing them to death.'[156] While McDonagh's psychopaths are ruthless killers, they seldom show a sadistic violation of the bodies in a sexual sense, apart from Padraic shoving a cross into Christy's mouth. Initially, Padraic and Mairead oversee the dismemberment, but in this play these acts are not carried out by the perpetrators, but simply delegated to Donny and Davey. There is no reward in the actions. After all the deaths, Mairead expresses little pleasure in what has occurred, indeed boredom is a strange response, but in her plans to further investigate what has happened there is little doubt but that she may only be temporarily satiated by all the blood and carnage.

McDonagh does not give us the typical sadist serial killer after all. While it is easy to argue that McDonagh intentionally pathologises his paramilitaries, that they all share in different ways puritanical streaks, sentimental allegiances and a mania for violence, it does not imply that McDonagh illegitimates or makes redundant his own intentionalities by so doing. His framing of paramilitary violence is not as a violence of last resort, instead, it is under-motivated, driven more by the sentiments of a cause, the inclinations of which are disguised by them rowing in behind a political agenda that partially facilitates their own destructive drives.

McDonagh also takes one final and perhaps most contentious approach to this paramilitary tradition, by contesting, as he had done in *Connemara* in a slightly different way, the significance of the funerary practices in the perpetuation of republican ideology. When Donny and Davey are given the task of dismembering the remains of Christy, Joey and Brendan in order to erase their identities, the manner in which they approach this is another absolute confirmation that in performance this play has nothing to do with verisimilitude. The responses or emotions, if we are to call them that, from the two actors Cooper and Gleeson playing Donny and Davey respectively, are not consistent with sensitivities one might associate with such a dastardly, abject task.[157] There is a layer of blood on the stage, and it can be found to be often dripping over the lip of the stage into the auditorium.[158] The actors move slowly around the stage and it sticks to their footwear.

However, any sense of bodily or taboo violation is offset by the fact that the bodies and limbs on stage are clearly props, and in Milam's Garrick production, there is absolutely nothing done to hide that fact. The kitchen table is upturned as it serves less as a sort of provisional, grotesque coffin and more as an improvised container for residual remains. Still one may think tangentially of death camps or ethnic cleansing.

Witoszek and Sheeran have argued that 'vernacular narratives of death',[159] have a substantial hold on Irish writing and politico-cultural and funerary practices. Both argue that the Easter Rising of 1916 is 'the founding funerary event of the Irish Republic'.[160] Traditionally, they suggest, 'Under colonial circumstances, the argument runs, funerary rites establish themselves as rites of the powerless. Mourning becomes a sign of opposition to power, a reclamation of identity.'[161] In Northern Ireland, Loyalist and Republican groups have made the most of funerals of civilian casualties and those who have died on active service. Kris Brown and Elisabetta Viggiani note how rigorous Republicans were 'in memorialising their dead throughout the conflict, with commemorative parades and militarised, politicised funerals: similarly, the material culture of remembrance – wall murals, plaques and monuments – dot the urban and rural landscapes of Republican areas'.[162] Or as Malachi O'Doherty puts it, 'Catholicism and Republicanism offer a form of immortality in the memory of those who honour the martyrs.'[163] McDonagh is clearly subverting this funerary aspect, as the dead paramilitaries in his drama are denied the usual pomp and ceremony of traditional funeral rites.[164] Cooper's Donny has little or no reaction to the death of his son, only a resistance to the chopping up of the body. Grief, loss and trauma are taken out of the equation in order to display forms of de-humanisation evident in sadistic violence. Also evident is the connection between the mechanical, surreal corporeality of Farce that Bentley and Milner Davis mention.

STALEMATES

However, the return from the dead, so to speak, of Wee Thomas, a regular McDonagh trope, leaves Donny and Davey facing a final test. Gleeson's Davy fretfully wonders with great implausibility: 'So all this terror has been for absolutely nothing?' But, unable to execute the cat, Donny and Davey instead feed him Frosties, as a faux farcical closure ensues and the issue of mistaken identity is resolved. There is also the potentially more complex awareness as to how the connection between cause and effect again breaks down, how violence begets violence and how the innocent get anarchically drawn into a world of subjective, systemic and barbaric violence.

The PIRA ceasefire was declared on 31 August 1994 and Combined Loyalist Military Command (CLMC) ceased operational hostilities on 13 October 1994, but these declarations were not the end to the violence.[165]

The Good Friday Agreement in 1998 was the landmark moment in the peace process. The decommissioning of weapons which followed after protracted negotiations were less gestures of assurance and were due more to political pressure from the White House, according to many commentators.[166] However much one takes up a pacifist and constitutionally political position, one of the real challenges is to acknowledge that a peace process in Northern Ireland only came about by bringing to the negotiating table many of those who were central to Loyalist and Republican paramilitarism. Globally and historically, there is nothing unique in that.

Of course, McDonagh does not deal with the political realities and collective traumas that actually drove people towards violence, to lack compassion for the suffering of others, to refuse to accept that many of the killings were cold-blooded murders. No hiding behind the idea of a just conflict could ever disguise certain unpalatable truths. For example, despite the high degree of media professionalism and spin doctoring, one of the things that Republicans could not get right was their handling of issues surrounding the disappeared – those taken out, interrogated, killed and buried in unmarked graves, depriving their families of a proper burial.

This play sets out to expose ambivalence and the conspiracy of tacit approval that some had, including members of the Irish diaspora and key public commentators in the media and academia towards paramilitary actions. While there is little doubt that McDonagh is attempting to nullify the political motivation of Republican freedom fighters in an armed struggle, a distinction has to be made between this tactic and a recognition of the fact that he is not simply invalidating responses to injustices and the suffering of the minority community, frequently, if not persistently terrorised by the state, through police, army, and Loyalist paramilitary groups.

Furthermore, while many people had strong and indisputable motivations for their paramilitary behaviours and genuinely framed those actions as a reaction to and retaliation against, rather than as the initiation of the violence, many others had very dubious motivations. The perpetuation of violent activities long after the peace process established itself, the licencing of ex-paramilitaries to partake in criminal actions, the maintenance of paramilitary elites and the financial dividends that accrue to these individuals to this very day all raise an array of different questions about power, control, domination and exploitation of the social classes that paramilitary groups set out to defend and protect. As already stated, McDonagh takes the side of constitutional politics. Who truly can know the conditions of suffering and trauma without having lived them? There is also the privilege of distance.

Regardless, McDonagh notes that: 'I think a lot of the stuff that has happened in the past 25 years has been a sick joke. I'm not trying to solve anything, the same way as I am not trying to damage anything; just looking at it in a different way. I mean, how else can you react to all that has happened through writing, or art or whatever you want to call it, if not through absurdity?'[167]

To me, there is something radically significant in his anarchic dramaturgical approach, whose purpose is not to efface the role of imperialism or to excuse it, more it is to contest the fundamental justifications of paramilitary violence and 'freedom fighting'. And while that argument is one-sided, incomplete and purposefully inaccurate in that it does not afford any depth, dignity or sincerity to his characters' motivations, it still does not demolish his argument nor does it make suspect his utter resistance to Republican violence and its ideological narratives, which McDonagh sees as clever and fatalistic propaganda. I believe that it is within the playwright's remit to focus on one side only, making it less a betrayal of Republicanism and a distortion of history, and more an anarchic expression that is a core freedom for writers and for citizens of democracies to write as he or she sees fit, without censorship.[168]

4 | A Grand-Guignol Phenomenon: *A Behanding in Spokane*

A REVENGER'S COMEDY?

A Behanding in Spokane premiered on 4 March 2010 at the Gerald Schoenfeld Theatre, New York, starring Christopher Walken as Carmichael, Zoe Kazan as Marilyn, Anthony Mackie as Toby, and Sam Rockwell as Mervyn. The play is set in a dingy hotel room in the notional Tarlington, America, and it is part thriller, part caper comedy and part horror Farce, with the play's promotion material stating: 'Martin McDonagh transplants his Grand-Guignol-style comedy from Ireland to Washington State.'[169]

John Crowley has a Grand-Guignol sensibility very much in mind for his *mise-en-scène*, inspired in part by his prior experiences of working on *The Pillowman* in London (2003) and New York (2005) which I will discuss in Part 3. Scot Pask's scenography establishes a sort of off-kilter stage environment for the performance, which Ben Brantley eloquently describes as one 'that might have been decorated by Edward Hopper in partnership with Stephen King'.[170] As the play begins a tattered stage curtain is drawn back to reveal a poorly maintained, dilapidated hotel room, with unfashionable wallpaper on the walls. Exposed plumbing connected to a radiator runs along the side-wall, stage right and a damaged high ceiling is visible overhead. This curtain and a row of antique, part-broken footlights are additional attempts to determine an old-fashioned, Grand-Guignol sensibility.[171]

It is a world that is otherworldly, decaying, non-descript, a non-localised environment of sorts, made all the more bizarre when two small-time cannabis dealers, Marilyn and Toby – echoes of Skunk Toby in *Inishmore* – find themselves way out of their depth when they try to scam Carmichael out of 500 dollars. They are attempting to pass off the hand of an old Australian aborigine, which they have stolen from the local museum of natural history, as Carmichael's long-sought-after amputated limb.

In the play's premiere, Christopher Walken's Carmichael is the dishevelled, weary, journeyed-out stranger, who is hardened by encounters in America's underworld.[172] He is dressed in a long black coat, with trousers just a little too short, his hair, straggled and uncared for, reaches to the lower part of his neck and is shoved behind his ears. Brantley captures the play's opening atmosphere-setting moments especially well: 'For there before you sits Mr. Walken, looking baleful and unwashed as only Mr. Walken can [....] Man and milieu understand each other here, and they exhale a shared, crusted loneliness and a thick funk of impure thoughts and deeds. "Nothing good can possibly happen," you think, eyeing the gloom with giddiness, "and isn't that wonderful?"'[173]

From the off, Walken's Carmichael seems uncomfortably trapped in a twisted quest and vengeance narrative, however perverse this happens to be. There is vulnerability but also a charming mania to Walken's performance, as he extracts the sinister and the playful with each movement, each gesture, each nuanced gradation of his voice.[174] Walken was not alone in generating this effect. Patrick Healy notes Walken's comments: '"Every character in this play, I like them. They're outcasts. Struggling, but decent," "They're not crazy, they're just..." he said with a pause, "strange".'[175] While one would run with the notion of 'outcasts', one does struggle with the idea that Marilyn and Toby are 'decent', and it is Mervyn, the receptionist that is the potentially more interesting of these three.

Mervyn struggles less with an innate sense of decency and more with his deviant inclinations and impossible fantasies. Rockwell plays Mervyn as goofy, creepy and especially sinister in his voyeurism; his potential malevolence is always close to the surface. He remains persistently snide, intrusive and stupidly self-possessed. Mervyn is a sort of forerunner for Rockwell's Billy Bickle in *Seven Psychopaths*.[176] (Because Toby had 'stiffed' Mervyn in a 'speed deal' two years previously (p.22) – he has some measure of retributive revenge on his mind throughout the play.)

Like Carmichael, Mervyn has constructed some sort of a mission for himself, however suspect and crazed it happens to be. He fantasises about scenarios of corruption and mass murder, rescue and redemption, up to now without ever having come close to such graphic situations, and without ever having an opportunity to be heroic.[177] Having heard a gunshot, Mervyn admits that he is excitedly drawn to the room because of his fantasies of significance, believing that: 'If I worked here long enough and kept my eyes open, something was gonna happen[....] a bunch of guys wearing *cloaks* checked in, their only luggage was *harpoons* .... Or some guy from Nigeria checks in, he wants to sell you a rollercoaster .... Or if a giant panda checked in.' (p.8) At another point he reveals his high school massacre fantasy; after 12 victims are murdered, he saves the rest of his school colleagues. As with most fantasies of rescue and redemption there are also potentially less altruistic motives to be discerned.[178]

THE PHANTOM MENACE OF HISTORY

Carmichael's racism is apparent from the off, evident in expressions like 'a coon's age' (p.8),[179] but more substantially in the disregarding attitude he displays in his shooting at and imprisonment of Toby, the African-American character, who is initially locked into a cupboard. Carmichael has described Toby as 'suspicious'. (p.8) Additionally, Toby is first presented in homophobic terms by Carmichael because he has fainted when a shot is fired in his direction. Late in the play when Mervyn wants to drive the police away he will tell them of a white girl being chased by a black male and that is another explicit indication of perceptions and biases within society and policing, as Mervyn knows the police will more than likely react to that story. There are other broader hints of racist practices, but also challenges that complicate simple binary perspectives that might suggest all white people are racist – Carmichael and his mother are, but to differing degrees, Mervyn is casually racist and Marilyn is perhaps the most offensive in her narrow political correctness.

Equally it would be wrong to assume given a historically subordinated role that African-Americans are either free of racist practices or that they will not exploit politically correctness for their own ends. There is a hint of the latter in Toby's reply to the accusation of Mervyn that he had double crossed him: 'It wasn't me, Mervyn. It just wasn't me. You ain't one of these cats who think all black people look the same, are ya?' (p.30) In some ways these comments and actions are evidence of the 'subjective' racism of the characters, but more than that, McDonagh also exposes 'systemic' racism.

Racial differences and the history of slavery and violation are foregrounded in exceptionally complicated ways by the dramaturgical significance given to the black hand that Marilyn and Toby try to pass off as Carmichael's missing limb. In her attempts to lie to Carmichael, Marilyn has the ridiculous explanation as to why the hand is black: according to her it is due to the length of time it has been removed from Carmichael's body. (There are echoes here of Davey's attempts to polish the orange cat with black polish.) Toby, realising the ineptness of her explanation, passes it off as a mix-up, stating that Marilyn has retrieved the second hand stored in their accommodation — 'Tyrone Dixon's hand'. (p.13) However, Toby's guess that a 'distinguishing feature' of the missing hand is the word 'Hate' on the knuckles entices Carmichael to go out and locate it, leaving Marilyn and Toby imprisoned in a room, primed to explode.

Of course, the sight of the African-American Toby chained to a wall cannot but remind an audience of the many terrors of slavery and, equally, the image of him covered in petrol sparks off associations with the torturous and murderous actions of the Ku Klux Klan and with the horrors and discriminations that drove civil rights protests in America's relatively recent past. Pinker notes that between the sixteenth and nineteenth centuries the following occurred:

> at least 1.5 million Africans died in transatlantic slave ships … [and] millions more perished in forced marches through the jungles and deserts to slave markets [….] At least 17 million Africans and perhaps as many as 65 million, died in the slave trade. The slave trade not only killed people in transit, but by providing a continuous stream of bodies, it encouraged slaveholders to work their slaves to death and replace them with new ones. But even the slaves who were kept in relatively good health lived in the shadow of flogging, rape, mutilation, forced separation from family members and summary execution.[180]

Thus, slave owners brutally carried out murders, whippings, disfigurements, defacements and amputations as forms of ruthless discipline and punishment. Tongues were cut off for supposed dissent, hands were chopped off for real and alleged theft and legs maimed for attempts to escape. Rape, castration and genital mutilation were frequently used as forms of control, domination, humiliation and punishment. Furthermore, under systems of both slavery and colonisation, individuals were denied subjectivity and agency, were accredited as being not fully human, and thus could be mutilated, branded, purchased and sold.

Consequently, the aboriginal hand is symbolic of not only the appalling treatment of aboriginal peoples in Australia, but also of broader injustices, oppressions, violations and objectifications and Carmichael's attitude towards it reinforces white supremacist, even imperialist, thinking. (Linked to this is Mervyn's fixation on the gibbon in the zoo, given the racist alignment of those colonised with monkeys, including Africans and indeed the Irish.) There is something beyond coincidence in the fact that Carmichael's 27-year search for his hand, as detailed in the script, coincides with Toby's age.

The black hand is also associated with actions of protest and empowerment through the symbol of the raised fist and the Black Panther movement's campaigns against discrimination and injustice. After Toby cries at one point in the play, Marilyn retorts: '[….] where's all your Black

Panther shit *now*, cry-baby? Where's all your "Fight the powers that be" now, huh?' (p.15) Marilyn also pulls Carmichael up on the use of the word '"Nigger"' and confidently suggests an alternative term – '"The hand of a person of colour."' (p.12) Marilyn is also very unhappy that Toby didn't assertively confront Carmichael's racism. Toby's response to her is telling:

> [....] Yeah, I got a thing about calling a cracker white supremacist motherfucker who's got a gun in my face and my girlfriend's face, who's waving a nigger's hand around like it's a motherfucking Kentucky Fried motherfucking *chicken-wing*, *yes*, I've got a thing about picking the dude up upon his offensive mis-usage of RACIAL MOTHERFUCKING EPITHETS!. (p.17)

On the two occasions I saw the play, audiences responded with a mixture of incongruity and laughter to her naive assertiveness and immaterial political correctness in the context in which they find themselves. While Kazan's performance as Marilyn does have an unduly persistent and domineeringly shrill quality to it, she suitably captures the limitations of her character; there is little or no character progression for her, and nor should there be an expectation of it in this genre. Despite her bravery, Marilyn's inability to see beyond the instant moment stands out and this disposition is regularly played for laughs. (Marilyn is no Girleen or Helen.) Mackie's somewhat cowardly Toby is equally naive, far too confident in his assumptions that, unlike his girlfriend, he does see the bigger picture.

However, despite the ways that McDonagh seemingly and knowingly exposes the racist slights of Carmichael, and despite the ways that both Mackie and Walken respond to and frame Carmichael's racism and accompanying homophobia, Hilton Als opens his review of the production as follows: 'I don't know a single self-respecting black actor who wouldn't feel shame and fury while sitting through Martin McDonagh's new play [....] Nor do I know one who would have the luxury of turning the show down, once the inevitable tours and revivals get under way.'[181] Als continues: 'like any smart immigrant, McDonagh knows that by going after Toby's otherness he becomes less of an outsider himself'.[182] These comments appear to be serious indictments of the work on racist grounds.

Als also interrogates the language of the play, noting that '*A Behanding* isn't the least bit palatable; it's vile, particularly in its repeated use of the word "nigger".'[183] He continues: 'Toby's characterization is as offensive as the language used to describe him. While Carmichael's "nigger" talk could be put down to an attempt of McDonagh's to expose the nastiness of a segment of the population's use of racist comments – many writers have used ugly language to paint an honest portrait of racism in this country.'[184] However, Als notes 'the caricature he presents in Toby, the young black male as shucking, jiving thief, can't be excused on those grounds, or by the slick professionalism that coats the play's intellectual decay'.[185]

For me, the 'N' word is not simply used in a palatable way; it is utilised to expose racism not to perpetuate it. The short answer to questions surrounding Toby's criminality is that there is no explicit or simple relationship between criminality and race in McDonagh's work – there may well be in terms of class and that is another argument[186] – indeed Carmichael is by far the greater criminal and if one were to run with Als's argument, then any ascription of race to any negatively drawn character would be almost impossible, for by its nature it would almost always be simply prejudicial.[187]

Als has other angles of attack: 'The sad fact is that, in order to cross over, most black actors of Mackie's generation must *act* black before they're allowed to act human.'[188] This raises immediately the question, as to which character is actually acting 'human' in this piece? Als stacks the cards in a very particular way, assuming that Mackie 'hasn't the luxury of turning down the role'. One expects that Mackie probably did have a choice whether to play the role or not. I assume that like Als, this fact cannot be proved either way, but most actors have a choice as to accept any role they are offered, and simply as one of the stars of Kathryn Bigelow's Oscar-winning, *The Hurt Locker* (2008), one might expect that numerous opportunities were coming Mackie's way at that time.

One further example of the dramaturgical complexities as to how racism is handled by McDonagh can be seen in the exchange between Carmichael and his mother. Carmichael's injured mother, who has fallen from a tree, having climbed up to release a balloon, has probably broken her ankles and is now coughing up a lot of blood, or so she claims.[189] She refuses to call the emergency services because of the content of a trunk in his bedroom, about 20 pornographic magazines, with titles like *Finally Legal*. She gains access to these through the use of her 'stinking *hands*', (my emphasis) as Carmichael describes them (p.37). There are also images of black women and Carmichael is forced to come clean:

> [....] Alright, yes I *do* find some black women attractive [....] *That* doesn't mean I'm not a racist [....] Look, I'm standing here right now, okay, there is a black man chained to my radiator, and he's covered in gasoline, now that's hardly Affirmative Action, now is it? (p.38)

In this comment alone, the spectator gets the humour, paranoia, gender and race objectifications and access to the contradictions of Carmichael's self-deceiving behaviour, as well as an awareness of his need to answer the challenges laid down by his mother. When Toby is obliged to confirm to Carmichael's mother that he is no friend of her sons, she calls him 'nigger' and hopes that he dies. Carmichael retorts angrily to that exchange: 'Oh she did, did she? Hey Ma, *I'm* the one decides if the niggers die around here, okay? I don't need *your* goddam racist advice!' (p.39) For me, it is difficult to conceive as to how such exchanges cannot be seen but as significant interrogations of racist practices through the use of comedy, absurdity and inversion.[190]

Furthermore, in Carmichael's racial and homophobic offensiveness, Walken's mode of delivery structures what is being spoken as if he is a voyeur, commentator, dissenter and aloof critic of his own character's tendencies, thereby framing the offensive remarks with an awareness that underscores their inappropriateness. Effectively, in my experiences of the performances, the self-awareness and self-framing or blatant bracketing off by the actor of such comments highlight his resistance to and undermining of the language and mindset of his character.[191]

In their contemporary performances of Grand-Guignol dramas, Hand and Wilson have found that the more 'traditional Stanislavskian approaches to the actor and rehearsal are useful, but only up to a point', as the Grand-Guignol form 'breaks away from conventional naturalism as often as it embraces it'.[192] (This aspect tallies with some of my previous comments on Hynes's directorial approaches to performance in her productions of *Beauty Queen* and *Inishmaan*.) For Hand and Wilson, in this dark world of performance, 'it is acknowledged by the actor that the violence on stage is not an abstract violence that exists in some fantastic realm far away from our everyday lives, but is an action [...], which we all are at any given moment, but a step away from (whether as potential victims *or* potential killers).'[193]

In this premiere of *Spokane*, Walken is central to the jettisoning of naturalism and in the foregrounding of different forms of violence. With someone as adept as Walken, it is easy to see how the other performers could be submissive towards and overwhelmed by his performance energy. To their credit each performer finds a non-naturalistic niche from which to operate, as the consciousness of this play, like that of *Inishmore* with Padraic, is predominantly in the grip of and defined by the force of Carmichael. When he leaves to track the hand in Toby's and Marilyn's place, Walken's absence from the stage creates a certain vacuum, but the play remains substantially reliant on his trace energy and on the threat of his imminent return.

Additionally, in Grand-Guignol, as Hand and Wilson note, audiences appear to be 'accessories to the act, and most crucially, willing witnesses',[194] – celebrity casting enhances this aspect – and even more tellingly perhaps, it is through use of direct address and the breaking of the fourth wall that the spectator is further implicated in the performance.[195] (The phone calls made by Carmichael to his mother and Mervyn's early monologue in front of the closed stage curtain confirm that breach.) However, it is an audience's responses to a production's moments of sensation and violence in Grand-Guignol that are especially interesting to Hand and Wilson, who note that actors have a very strong role in controlling the audience–performer dynamic, and while 'There are elements of collaboration, voyeurism and democratization, [...] we are never in any doubt as to who is in control.'[196]

THE LITTLE CASE OF HORRORS

Spokane's Grand-Guignol emphatic relationship becomes very evident in the play's crucial 'moment of horror', which not only shocks, but potentially obliges audiences to consider further the obsessions of Carmichael, and to wonder what motivations, if any, there may be for his behaviour.[197] When the throwing of the sneakers fails to quench the candle that is wrapped in a rag inside a gasoline can – in a scenario orchestrated by Carmichael – the content of Carmichael's suitcase becomes a potential source for possible objects that Toby and Marilyn might throw. The stage directions are specific.

The stinking (again that word associated with Angela's hand by Carmichael) case 'bursts open and out spill about 100 human hands and their *stinking* gloop; some decayed and wizened, some recent and blue, some bloody, some mostly bones, some with a wrist or part of an arm still attached, some just a couple of fingers hanging together with a strip of skin, and some the sad small hands of little children'. [My emphasis] (p.19) Once aware of the case's contents, Marilyn and Toby recoil in horror, and on both occasions I saw the performance, audience members were especially unnerved by the surprise. Later Toby and Mervyn aggressively sling some of the hands at each other, reminding one of cinematic slapstick or cream pie flinging scenes. Again when Mervyn hits Marilyn accidently with a hand, there is a further sense of intentional taboo violation. In addition, some of the hands almost inevitably end up in the auditorium. (This is somewhat like the consequence to the malleting of the bones in *Connemara.*)

The case's contents oblige Marilyn and Toby to speculate as to how Carmichael has come by his collection of hands and they presuppose that some were purchased, and others were violently chopped off. However, neither Marilyn nor Toby is inclined to believe the Hillbilly behanding narrative,[198] and Mervyn claims to have scanned six 'chopped-off hands websites' and, on that evidence, he has the audacity to tell Carmichael that his story lacks plausibility. One of the clear implications of the fact that Carmichael has made the hillbilly story up is that it strongly raises the possibility that he may have done the amputating himself or had it carried out by someone else. It is at that point, I have to rely on psychology and neuroscience in order to progress my argument and I will need to distinguish between phantom limbs, Body Dysmorphic Disorder (BDD) and Apotemnophilia or a condition better known as Body Integrity Identity Disorder (BIID), which was once identified as Amputee Identity Disorder. These conditions offer potential insights into understanding the obsessions of Carmichael, but they have broader socio-cultural applications as well. [199]

V.S. Ramachandran has written a great deal about phantom limbs and about the sensations and feedback that remains even after a limb is cut off.[200] Ramachandran notes that 'The entire skin surface of the left side of the body is mapped onto a strip of cortex called the postcentral gyrus running down the right side of the brain', but when the arm is amputated, there is 'no longer an arm, but there is still a *map* of the arm in the brain'.[201] Despite the missing limb, the brain map 'soldiers on' and, this complication, Ramachandran argues, means that 'the felt presence of the limb persists long after the flesh-and-blood limb has been severed'.[202] So in some respects, Carmichael is haunted by the 'felt presence' of his missing limb, and in some ways is unduly fixated on winning it back. Body Dysmorphic Disorder is a condition where 'the individual believes, incorrectly, that a part of their body is diseased or exceedingly ugly', as Tim Bayne and Neil Levy propose.[203] Christopher James Ryan suggests that it is a relatively common condition and 'it has been estimated that BDD sufferers may account for 7–15% of people seeking cosmetic surgery'.[204]

However, far more relevant is the rarer condition called Apotemnophilia, which occurs where able-bodied individuals believe that they will be more human and more complete or whole, if they have a limb or some other body part removed. It is not that this body part is gangrenous, malignant or deformed, but that the presence of the limb is creating psychological havoc; the individual believes in effect that being an amputee will create a state of fulfilment of sorts. Elliot D. Sorene, Carlos Heras-Palou, and Frank D. Burke suggest that those who have the Apotemnophilic condition, if unable to secure an amputation, 'can become increasingly anxious, depressed and, even, suicidal',[205] but it does not mean that they are delusional.[206]

Ramachandran and Paul McGeoch also note the condition is 'neither psychotic nor delusional,' as they 'know that these feelings are not normal'.[207] Indeed, 'in other respects they are mentally and neurologically normal'.[208] There are major ethical issues around the subject of procedural amputation and because the practice tends to be medically outlawed there are websites which give instructions as to how people might carry out such procedures on themselves and there are harrowing documentations of these practices and of the medical complications that can often follow botched jobs.[209] Mainly, people opt for hand and breast amputations, and frequently for amputations above the left knee.[210] There are also less frequent practices of castration and of eroticised genital mutilation. Explanations from Apotemnophilia range from regarding it as an attention-seeking condition to the suggestion that 'it arises from a Freudian wish-fulfilment fantasy, the stump resembling a large penis'.[211] Ramachandran explains it differently.

Crucial to Ramachandran's understanding of consciousness are a number of key components, namely unity, continuity, privacy, social embedding, free will, self-awareness and embodiment.[212] For Ramachandran the brain has 'an innate body image' and when that does not align with 'the sensory input from the body – whether visual or somatic' – 'the ensuing disharmony can disrupt the self's sense of unity as well'. Ramachandran extends further, 'nerves for touch, muscle, tendon and joint sensation project to your primary (S1) and secondary (S2) somato-sensory cortices in and just behind the postcentral gyrus. Each of these areas of the cortex contains a systematic, topographically organized map of bodily sensations. From there, somatosensory information gets sent to one's superior parietal lobule (SPL), where it gets combined with balance information from one's inner ear and visual feedback about the limbs' positions. Together these inputs construct body image: a unified, real-time representation of your physical self.'[213]

In his specific studies of Apotemnophilia, Ramachandran discovers that many patients have a sense of being 'overcomplete', or that the body part is regarded as 'intrusive'.[214] Therefore, 'mismatch aversion' provides the most relevant explanation, according to Ramachandran, because with Apotemnophilia, while there is 'normal sensory input from the limb to the body maps in S1 and S2, there is no "place" for the limb signals to output in the SPL body image maintained by the SPL'.[215] As there is no place in the body image for the undesired limb, and since the brain 'abhors internal anomalies', the limb is regarded as an 'overpresence', an excess that needs to be removed. With Apotemnophilia then, the elimination of the object of hindrance brings relief, and in many instances a sense of completion, once that which is regarded as an excess in terms of body image has been removed. This is not the case with Carmichael.

OBJET PETIT ART

The symbolic significance of the hand becomes even more problematic during the play's final moments, as the climatic gory expectations of a Grand-Guignol dénouement is not realised, in that there is no final moment of extreme sensation. Instead, helping to tidy the room, as police sirens are heard approaching from a distance outside, Mervyn discovers a hand, amongst the many scattered limbs, with the word 'Hate' written on it in pen. (The script suggests that the tattoos on Carmichael's fingers are initially covered by stickers, and when he returns from the apartment, the stickers are gone. A stage direction also indicates that the word 'Love' is clearly visible on Carmichael's right hand as the lights go down. This was not the case from where I was sitting in the theatre.)[216] Carmichael dismisses the idea that it might be his missing hand, that he has had ironically, the desired object in his possession all along and thinks that Toby may have done it to mess with his head. The non-tattooed, thus temporary nature of the markings, as noted by Carmichael, may suggest a lack of permanence, commitment, or even more challengingly, of all, pretence.[217]

Regardless, the Love–Hate dichotomy hints not only at the divided mind, but also perhaps at the choices of attitude or perspective that one makes in relation to the world in which one lives; Pinker's demons or better angels conundrum. Carmichael's specific desire to find his missing limb is seen by him primarily in terms of his love for his own limb, in terms of his hatred for his violators and in terms of his natural rights. But he is aware that only on retrieving it, despite its worthlessness, will he be able to return to his homeplace and achieve some form of closure. The phantom limb theory suggests a lack and irretrievability of a prior reality before some crisis, whether it is the loss of a limb or the symbolic loss of innocence that an over-determining American Dream cannot alleviate. The memory of a time before the behanding, deemed by Carmichael as idyllic and innocent is the phantom fantasy, that of the absent presence, something lost, irretrievable, but inexplicably ever present. However, the fact that his violators are 'hillbilly detritus' reverses what would be regarded as the anticipated targets of such supremacist mutilating activities.[218] (p.11)

Toby is notionally the gateway to or a gatekeeper of the certain excesses, but it is a sham after all. He pretends that it is in the deep-freezer in his garage where he keeps the '*excess* hands'. (p.13) However, in melting-pot, multicultural America, white supremacists see non-whites as inferior but also as excesses and as a challenge to their privileges. It is perhaps the 'over-presence' of the other, symbolic of Carmichael's sense of disharmonious over-completeness, that suggests that this multi-cultural reality does not equate with his internal maps, ones based on homogeneity and nothing can be done to keep its exponential growth at bay. (Note Žižek's earlier comments on objet petit a).

For Žižek, fear is the ultimate mobilising principle: 'fear of immigrants, fear of crime, fear of godless sexual depravity, fear of the excessive state itself, with its burden of high taxation, fear of ecological catastrophe, fear of harassment. Political correctness is the exemplary liberal form of the politics of fear. Such a (post-) politics always relies on the manipulation of a paranoid *ochlos* or multitude: it is the frightening rally of frightened people.'[219] So, on the one hand, he contends, liberal cultures promote tolerance, but on the other, such cultures want the other to remain at a distance, and by respecting the privacy of the other, which effectively is 'a right to remain at a safe distance from others'.[220]

Žižek argues that the 'Liberal capitalist fantasy is that the truth lies in the stories we tell ourselves about ourselves, but the reality is that the truth resides outside, in what we do.'[221] Carmichael's hillbilly story is a fiction. It is the truth 'outside' his narrative which is fundamental. Thus fear is a major issue for Carmichael, in terms of what has been lost and what he cannot get back, and in terms of his anxiety about the future, there is no quelling of it, as the 'overpresence' reappears to haunt him. The rejection of the racially othered and aboriginal hand, suggests that nothing can compensate for the void left by the absent left hand. Yet the compulsive accumulation of foreign or 'marked' objects stored in the case is evidence of an accumulative carnage of a history of violence, Carmichael's fetishisation of his own trauma and that of others, but also a certain absurdist redundancy of stored memory.

Hand and Wilson note that overall the Grand-Guignol style 'presents a provocative mixture of the horrific and the erotic, the satirical and the realist, the reactionary and the radical, the frightening and the funny, the thrilling and the theoretically determined. No one aspect is clear-cut [....] What one spectator watches as artful construction, another sees as an escapist "ride". One person's repugnant nightmare is another's outrageous comedy, while the same thing is yet another person's erotic fantasy.'[222] While the erotic is low-key in this McDonagh play, the satiric and the radical are very much in evidence in the way that the drama plays with horror and sensationalises socio-cultural and historical traumas by provocatively negating racist thinking and practices.

Walken's Carmichael is almost the mad scientist or grave robber figure from the Grand-Guignol or horror genres, plundering the underworld, 'haggling with street scum and shaking down corpse-dealers across the filth-lots and flea-alleys of this sad decaying nation'. (p.11) As Carmichael Walken is sinister and playful, so self-reflexive and self-aware, and he clearly knows how to exploit the moments of threat and terror in order to create the strongest of thrills and sensations for the spectator.[223] Effectively in Crowley's Grand-Guignolesque *mise-en-scène* there is a prioritising of sensation over psychology, adrenaline over intellect and the symbolic over the real. Ultimately, the symbolism of the hands is less about direct meaning and more about possibilities and potential, but the issue of race is central to its prospective significance. Thus McDonagh's play addresses in a very complicated fashion the refusal to accept, in Ben Pitcher's phrase, the 'facticity of difference', by which Pitcher means 'the sense in which the existence of cultural difference – whether understood in terms of race, ethnicity, or religion – has become fully acknowledged as a constituent part of the societies within which we live today'.[224] Carmichael's journey is driven by a 'phantom' revenge narrative, so that Carmichael's desire for a notional restorative justice becomes in McDonagh's idiom a Grail type-quest, in a Monty Pythonesque,[225] Grand-Guignol style.

5 | Conclusion

With in-yer-face theatre, according to Sierz, 'Violence becomes impossible to ignore when it confronts you by showing pain, humiliation and degradation [….] Violent acts are shocking because they break the rules of debate; they go beyond words and can get out of control. Violence feels primitive, irrational and destructive. Violence onstage also disturbs when we feel the emotion behind the acting, or catch ourselves enjoying the violence vicariously.'[226] With McDonagh's work the violence is also 'impossible to ignore,' there is often 'degradation' and 'humiliation' but the 'the pain', is not so easily shown, as Sierz sees it, and audience responses and potential 'vicarious' pleasures are sufficiently complicated as I have outlined in relation to all three plays discussed here. Furthermore, it is the blending of genre that complicates the issues raised by Sierz.

Milner Davis has argued that while Farce 's comic spirit 'delights in taboo-violation', it ultimately 'avoids implied moral comment or social criticism,' but my discussions in relation to these McDonagh plays argue for the opposite point of view.[227] Assisted by the work of Pinker and Žižek, I have discussed how inter-character or self-directed violence can be predatorial and merely attention-seeking, about dominance and puerile patterns of engaging, vengeful and self-indulgent, sadistic and trivially wanton, deeply ideological and triflingly juvenile in its rationale, and strategic and random, purposefully sensational and transgressively taboo breaking. There is also a rage against authority figures, parental figures, or paramilitary moulders of memory, clerical figures or policemen, which is in alignment with the broader aims of Farce.

I have also demonstrated systemic forms of violence that are both exogenous and endogenous. I have also discussed violence in terms of how mythic and cultural memory and historical injustices must not simply licence violence in the present or how the ideological rational of paramilitary republicanism in its responses to state domination, while remaining loyal to a concept of a violence of last resort and historical precedents, often, dutifully and effectively co-opted the psychopathological and the sadistic to carry out its actions, licencing paramilitary elites and rewarded them with a terror dividend. Additionally, racial violence is as much about a depleted and dysfunctional whiteness, as well as being about how the language of political correctness haunts most cultural expression and the problematic inability to deal with racial and gender integration under patriarchy and first world capitalism. It is not the 'gentle commerce' of Pinker's capitalism, but a rough and ruthless commerce that violently perpetuates marginality and subordination, by foregrounding acquiescence and obedience.

In addition, I have been proposing that McDonagh has a great deal to say about capitalism's ideological circulation through language, narrative fragments, songs and ballads, television programmes, magazines and other forms of popular culture. (The representations of violence that are endemic to these forms will be considered in the following section in relation to *Seven Psychopaths*.) McDonagh's perversion of liberal capitalist values of equality, progress, prosperity, and the future, evolves as a savage critique of his own unease with inequality. McDonagh's characters are radical in their disobedience and in their submissiveness only to the incidentals of liberal capitalism. Gender, class, race and ethnicity for example are systems of regulation and control, for which violence plays an essential role. For many, the challenge is against prescriptive and obligatory heteronormativity, as well as specific gender, class and race roles. McDonagh's work offers the challenge of compulsory and un-evadable marginality. Despite the general misanthropic sensibility of Grand-Guingol, in *Spokane* the performances suggest that something unusually positive is permitted to seep through the *mise-en-scène*; for despite all the gore connected to the case of horrors and despite all the serious threats of violence, no character is seriously harmed. Instead of punishing Toby and Marilyn, like the others before them who have double crossed him, Carmichael sets them free and even he may well feel imperceptibly reassured, perhaps even faintly comforted by the helping hand of a stranger, in the form of Mervyn, his doppelganger of sorts. (So there must be a certain caution in talking about a character like Carmichael as if he is delusional or simply psychopathic. The fact that he does demonstrate a capacity for empathy means that he would not be categorised as psychopathological under Baron-Cohen's terminology which I utilise in Part 3.)

Equally, the temporary truce between Coleman and Valene, together with the survival of Wee Thomas, offer some grounds for guarded optimism. Milner Davis notes that Farce 'tends to debar empathy for its victims'.[228] Again, my argument is contrary to this point of view. Instead of debarring empathy, Farce and Grand-Guignol complicate the divisions between victim and perpetrator, with the exception interestingly of McDonagh's paramilitaries.

In Part 3, violence will remain a central issue, as I tackle the predatory violence of the Kid character in *Six Shooter*, the violent imperative of retribution found in gangland moralities in *In Bruges*, totalitarian state legitimated violence in *The Pillowman*, and in *Seven Psychopaths* the obsessions of much of Hollywood screenwriting with psychopathology. I will examine the violence perpetuated against children in fairytales and across other cultural narratives, which are central to a tabulation of the significance of empathy. As I will argue that McDonagh's most controversial accomplishment is to find a means of formulating complex ways of evoking empathy for some of the strategic and non-strategic victims and perpetuators of violence. Ultimately it is a question not so much of natural selection,[229] but unnatural selection, sometimes the survival of the un-fittest, where there are so few offspring, where characters prefer to leave stories as their perverted legacy. Violence moves beyond deterrence, when it is murder in the name of protection of the innocent as in Michal in *The Pillowman*, or grotesquely, in the case of *Seven Psychopaths* when it comes to the welfare of a dog, Charlie Costello's 'beloved Shih Tzu' and the retributive justice of serial killers taking out serial killers. McDonagh does little or nothing to sanitise violence other than to frame it through genre, but only makes it visible on the margins of cultures and societies. That is his way of acknowledging its systemic omnipresence.

Endnotes

1 S. Pinker, *The Better Angels of Our Nature: A History of Violence and Humanity* (London: Penguin Books, 2011), p.599.
2 Ibid., p.584.
3 Ibid., p.584.
4 Ibid., p.581.
5 Ibid., pp.581–2.
6 Ibid., p.597.
7 Ibid., p.598.
8 Ibid., p.589.
9 Ibid., p.589.
10 Ibid., pp.586–7
11 Ibid., p.588.
12 Ibid., p.610.
13 Ibid., p.601.
14 Ibid., p.581.
15 Ibid., p.605.
16 Ibid., p.608.
17 Ibid., p.609, citing the work of J.R. Séguin, P. Sylvers, & S. Lilienfeld, 'The Neuropsychology of Violence', in D.J. Flannery, A. T. Vazsonyi, & I.D. Waldwan (eds), *The Cambridge Handbook of Violent Behaviour and Aggression* (New York: Cambridge University Press, 2007), p.193.
18 Ibid., p.609, citing A. Scarpa and A. Raine, 'Biosocial bases of violence', in D.J. Flannery, A.T. Vazsonyi, & I.D. Waldwan (eds), *The Cambridge Handbook of Violent Behaviour and Aggression*, p.153.
19 Ibid., p.612.
20 Ibid., p.639.
21 Ibid., p.640.
22 Countries governed under Sharia Law persist in public punishments, such as amputations for what would sometimes be regarded as minor misdemeanours in the western world. Reportage and video footage of such barbarous actions are frequently broadcast.
23 See Pinker, *The Better Angels of Our Nature*, pp.612–13.
24 Ibid., pp.612–13.
25 S. Žižek, *Violence* (London: Profile Books, 2009), p.39.
26 Ibid., p.1.
27 Ibid., p.2.
28 Ibid., p.2.
29 Ibid., p11.
30 Ibid., p.11.
31 Ibid., p.74.
32 Ibid., p.64–5.
33 Ibid., p.65.

34 Ibid., p.65.
35 Ibid., p.67–8.
36 Within his argument Žižek sets up a number of straw men and women labelled 'liberal communists', philanthropic global capitalists, whose private individual's endowments are a response to the failures of global capitalism, whereby the activities of their foundations are solutions to problems that they themselves conspire to create and extend the lifecycle of capitalism.
37 Ibid., p.52. See Jean-Marie Muller, 'Non-Violence in Education', http://portal.unesco.org/pv_obj_cache/pv_obj_id_594EB68AB5FE6A16278CD4386C32188A8CD40300/filename/fa99ea234f4accb0ad43040e1d60809cmuller_en.pdf (Accessed 31/1/2013)
38 Ibid., p.52.
39 Ibid., p.55.
40 Ibid., p.55.
41 A. Sierz, *In-Yer-Face Theatre: British Drama Today* (London: Faber and Faber, 2001), pp. 1–6.
42 M. Middeke, 'Martin McDonagh', in Martin Middeke and Peter Paul Schnierer (eds), *The Methuen Drama Guide to Contemporary Irish Playwrights* (London: Methuen, 2010), p.217.
43 R. Wilson, 'Macabre Merriment in *The Beauty Queen of Leenane*', in Eric Weitz (ed.), *The Power of Laughter: Comedy and Contemporary Irish Theatre* (Carysfort Press, Dublin, 2004), pp.129–144, p.131.
44 For Joan FitzPatrick Dean 'the term farce, even in its most sophisticated manifestations, still carries the pejorative connotations of facile amusement and limited vision.' See 'Joe Orton and the Redefinition of Farce', *Theatre Journal*, 34.4, (1982), pp.481–492, p.485.
45 J. Milner Davis, *Farce* (New Brunswick & London: Transaction Publishers, 2003), pp.2–3.
46 Ibid., p. 3.
47 Ibid., p. 3.
48 Ibid., p.3.
49 Ibid., p.4.
50 Ibid., p.3.
51 Enda Walsh's hugely successful *The Walworth Farce*(2006) is notable for its crazed, chaotic, farcical violence and Mikel Murfi directed its premiere.
52 E. Bentley, *The Life of the Drama* (London: Methuen, 1965), p.222.
53 See Milner Davis, *Farce*, p.7.
54 Ben Brantley acknowledges that *Inishmore* 'is brazenly and unapologetically a farce. But it is also a severely moral play, translating into dizzy absurdism the self-perpetuating spirals of political violence that now occur throughout the world. I kept thinking of Macbeth's forlorn recognition that "blood will have blood." In *Inishmore*, that maxim has become such a fact of life that people no longer evoke natural human responses in one another – well, irritation, maybe.' See 'Terrorism Meets Absurdism in a Rural Village in Ireland', *New York Times*, 28 February 2006, http://theater.nytimes.com/2006/02/28/theater/reviews/28inis.html?pagewanted=all (Accessed 18/11/11)
55 See Milner Davis, *Farce*, p.247.
56 Ibid., p.252.
57 Ibid., p. 4.
58 J.L. Styan, *Drama, Stage and Audience* (Cambridge: Cambridge University Press, 1975), pp.77–8.
59 In particular, the form of naturalism that evolved in nearby theatres of Paris, in André Antoine's *Théâtre Libre* (1887).

60 R.J. Hand and M. Wilson, *Grand-Guignol: The French Theatre of Horror* (Exeter: University of Exeter Press, 2002), pp.ix–xii.

61 Ibid., p.9.

62 Ibid., p.3.

63 Ibid., p. 34.

64 Hand and Wilson's book includes ten Grand-Guignol plays. *The Ultimate Torture (La Dernière Torture* (1904), by Andrè De Lorde and Eugène Morel, is set during the Boxer Rebellion of 1900 in the French consulate in Beijing and includes a scene where Bornin dies after having two of his hands cut off. *The Kiss of Blood* (*Le Baiser de Sang*, (1929)), by Jean Aragny and Francis Neilson, has a character called Joubert, who is desperate to have his finger amputated, the one that pulled the trigger on the gun that he believes murdered his wife. Joubert amputates it himself at the end of the first act. Later one of Joubert's staff tells Leduc and Doctor Volguine that Joubert has had a second finger removed, this time by operation. Finally, goaded by his wife, Hélène, who pretends that she is a ghost, Joubert chops off his hand with an axe, and dies almost instantly as the play ends. As Hand and Wilson see it, '*The Kiss of Blood* is a horror play but is never far from the world of farce, above all in the irony of Joubert's failed murder attempt and his attempts at self-destruction,' Ibid., p.247.

65 Ibid., p.70, citing P. Brophy, 'Horrality-The Textuality of Contemporary Horror Films' in Ken Gelder (ed.), *A Horror Reader* (London: Routledge, 2000), pp.276–84, pp.277–9.

66 Both Caroline Magennis and Raymond Mullen specifically emphasise the need 'to question the production and maintenance of hegemonic masculinity in Irish literature and culture' for instance. See 'Introduction', *Irish Masculinities: Reflections on Literature and Culture* (Dublin: Irish Academic Press, 2011), pp.1–10.

67 B. Singleton, *Masculinities and Contemporary Irish Theatre* (Basingstoke: Palgrave, 2011), p.8

68 R.W. Connell, 'The Social Organisation of Masculinity', Stephen M. Whitehead and Frank Barrett, (eds), in *The Masculinities Reader* (Cambridge: Polity Press, 2001), pp.30–50, pp.40–43.

69 I also viewed a recording made at the Town Hall Theatre, Galway on 6 October 2001 with the same cast.

70 See B. Brantley, 'Leenane III, Bones Flying', *New York Times*, February 23, 2001, http://theater.nytimes.com/mem/theater/treview.html?html_title=&tols_title=SKULL%20IN%20CONNEMARA,%20A%20(PLAY)&pdate=20010223&byline=By%20BEN%20BRANTLEY&id=1077011432186 (Accessed 4 April 2011)

71 The Lyric Theatre and An Grianán Theatre co-production played at the Lyric Theatre, Belfast, from 16 September to 15 October 2005, and at the Civic Theatre, Tallaght from 17 to 22 October 2005. I attended the Tallaght run.

In contrast to Hynes's production, Mikel Murfi's is faster in tempo, has a more sterile take on the character's emotional dependencies and is even more farcical in sensibility. Lalor Roddy played Coleman, Frank McCusker Valene, Charlene McKenna Girleen and Ian Kilroy featured as Fr Welsh. Murfi's *mise-en-scène* is full of the grotesque energy of clowning, inspired by his training at the L'École Internationale de Théâtre Jacques Lecoq, and by his work with Barabbas the Company. Even more so than in the Druid production, Murfi's characters thrive on the conflict. The sardonic, petulant anality of McCusker's Valene plays impressively against the more calculating intimidating figure of Roddy's Coleman. The glee that they take in each other's discomfort is apparent from the off. The characters of Roddy and McCusker are too self-absorbed and too self-obsessed to see little or anything beyond their own battles, displaying the sorts of tunnel vision of characters in Farce as signalled earlier by both Bentley and Milner Davis. Secondly, this pair of actors is committed far more to a physical rather than to the psychological embodiment of their conflicts, evident in them being even more reactive, provocative, unconcealed, and childlike in their actions and responses. For them, there seems to be no need to push things beneath the surface or to disguise their feelings. The sensibility of slapstick, aggression and false bravado are offset by the formidable darkness that both performers bring to their roles. Lisa Fitzpatrick notes of Dargent's design that 'Rather than reproducing a traditional, naturalistic cottage set, Dargent opts for a slice of a cottage, set at an angle, with bare stage exposed between the set and the wings. Inside the cottage, Valene's collection of plastic saints decorates the walls, which are painted pinkish-red and stained with damp, dark streaks and patches [....] The costumes comment upon the characters: Coleman is dressed casually, suggesting an aging would-be playboy, while Valene's tightly-buttoned shirts and too-short sleeves and trousers give a visual expression to his meanness.' See 'Review', *Irish Theatre Magazine*, 25.5, (Winter 2005), pp.81–2.

See production images at http://www.lyrictheatre.co.uk/media/185484788a9841 7490581dc3d5a93548The%20Lonesome%20West%20Pic%201.JPG (Accessed 4/6/10210)

72 In the Irish writing tradition, there is a persistent pattern of quarrelling friends, fighting brothers with split or divided selves evident in a range of Irish plays, for example in the work of John Millington Synge, Sean O'Casey, Brian Friel, Tom Kilroy, Marina Carr and Mark O'Rowe, in plays such as *The Well of the Saints* (1905), *The Silver Tassie* (1928), *Philadelphia, Here I Come!* (1964), *Double Cross* (1986), *Portia Coughlan* (1996) and *Howie The Rookie* (1999).

73 N. Witoszek and P. Sheeran, *Talking to the Dead: A Study of the Irish Funerary Traditions* (Amsterdam-Atlanta, GA: Rodopi, 1998), pp.157–8.

74 Ibid., p.158.

75 Ibid., p.146.

76 McDonagh's own relationship with his brother, John, was intense, and was characterised, McDonagh says, by 'love, love, love, and a tiny spark of hate'. One of his earliest memories is of his parents berating him for getting into a fight with John, who had to be rushed to the hospital with an injured foot. The incident, McDonagh says with a laugh, 'set off a strain that's been going ever since'. See F. O'Toole, 'A Mind in Connemara: The Savage World of Martin McDonagh', *New Yorker*, 6 March 2006, http://www.newyorker.com/archive/2006/03/06/060306fa_fact_otoole (Accessed 10/10/2009)

77 See Witoszek and Sheeran, *Talking to the Dead*, p.142.

78 Ibid., p.149.

79 C. Rees, 'Narratives of power' [Unpublished PhD thesis on Martin McDonagh's work, Aberystwyth University, 2007], pp.241–2.

80 Girleen comments aggressively to Valene: 'You're the king of stink-scum fecking filth-bastards you, ya bitch-feck, Valene.' (p. 138)

81 For Witoszek and Sheeran whether it is the figure of Cúchulainn or Cathleen Ní Houlihan, most if not 'all of the traditional images and narratives of identity resort to the motifs of suffering and endurance. These are necro-static', as for Witoszek and Sheeran, most Irish writers 'have been experts in brokenness and impotence, in diagnosing the symptoms of death-in-life'. See *Talking to the Dead*, p.4.

82 See Pinker, *The Better Angels of Our Nature*, p.621.

83 Ibid., p.621.

84 Ibid., p.644.

85 Ibid., p.645.

86 Ibid., pp.653–4.

87 Ibid., p.654.

88 See Rees, 'Narratives of power', p.273.

89 See Milner Davis, *Farce*, p. 143.

90 See J. FitzPatrick Dean, 'Joe Orton and the Redefinition of Farce', p.482.

91 Paul Murphy's analysis of the previously mentioned Murfi production at the Lyric Theatre reflects on the relationship between Farce and audience de-sensitisation and the fact that the 'emotional scarification' of the characters remains unaddressed by the writer. See 'The Stage Irish Are Dead, Long Live the Stage Irish', in L. Chambers and E. Jordan (eds), *The Theatre of Martin McDonagh: A World of Savage Stories* (Dublin: Carysfort Press, 2006), pp.60–78, p.73.

92 See S. Baron-Cohen's *Zero Degrees of Empathy: A New Theory of Human Cruelty* (London: Allen Lane an imprint of Penguin Books, 2011).

93 The Cain website notes: 'On 22 October 1975 Patrick Armstrong, Gerard Conlon, Paul Hill and Carole Richardson (who became known as the "Guildford Four") were found guilty at the Old Bailey of causing explosions in London in October 1974. The four were sentenced to life imprisonment. Following an appeal the four were released on 19 October 1989. The court of appeal decided that the "confessions" had been fabricated by the police. In a linked case, members of the Maguire family, the "Maguire Seven", were convicted on 3 March 1976 of possession of explosives (even though no explosives were found) and some served 10 years in prison before the convictions were overturned.' See http://cain.ulst.ac.uk/index.html (Accessed 13/11/11)

94 The Birmingham Six (Paddy Joe Hill, Hugh Callaghan, Richard McIlkenny, Gerry Hunter, Billy Power and Johnny Walker) were found guilty of the bombing, stayed in prison until their third appeal of their prosecution was accepted and their convictions deemed unsafe, based on irregularities in the prosecution case, dubious forensic tests, altered statements, forced confessions and suppression of evidence. They were set free on 14 March 1991. In *Beauty Queen* the Birmingham Six's miscarriage of justice is mentioned as evidence of corrupt policing practices in Ireland. In *Inishmore*, Mairead suggests going to see Jim Sheridan's *In the Name of the Father* (1993), a film about the Guildford Four. Padraic's version of things is that the Guildford Four should have accepted their convictions and not wasted time protesting their innocence. That way they would have served the cause best. The non-empathetic logic is so perverse, but utterly appropriate to McDonagh's dramaturgical aspirations.

95 The Irish team, led by Michael Collins, during the Treaty negotiations believed correctly that no more was on the table from the British government and that the treaty would be a temporary solution to the political and military impasse. It also led to a civil war between Pro and Anti-Treaty sides.

96 H. McDonald, 'The Guardian profile: Martin McDonagh', *The Guardian*, 25 April 2008, http://www.guardian.co.uk/film/2008/apr/25/theatre.northernireland (Accessed 13/11/11)

97 C. Spencer, 'Devastating Masterpiece of Black Comedy', *Daily Telegraph*, 28 June 2002, http://www.telegraph.co.uk/culture/film/3579406/Devastating-masterpiece-of-black-comedy.html# (Accessed 13/10/2009)

98 R. English, *Armed Struggle: The History of the IRA* (Basingstoke: Macmillan, 2003), p.280.

99 Cited by English, p.259.

100 The Irish National Liberation Army (INLA), a group with the same 32-county Ireland aspiration as the Provisionals, but driven by a fanatical Marxist ethos. The INLA, also called the People's Liberation Army (PLA), People's Republican Army (PRA), and Catholic Reaction Force (CRF) was set up in 1975 and was the military wing of the Irish Republican Socialist Party (IRSP). Estimates suggest that the INLA

was responsible for about 125 deaths in total during the Troubles, with 45 being members of the security forces. Internal feuding and killings accounted for about 20 of their own members. INLA also had a particularly violent reputation and was notorious for infighting. See CAIN website Service.

101 F. O'Toole, 'A Mind in Connemara: The Savage World of Martin McDonagh', *New Yorker,* 6 March 2006, p.45.

102 S. O'Hagan, 'The Wild West', *The Guardian,* 24 March 2001, p.32. http://www.guardian.co.uk/books/2001/apr/28/northernireland.stage> (Accessed 30/7/2012)

103 D. Rosenthal, 'How to slay 'em in the Isles', *Independent*, April 11, 2001, http://www.independent.co.uk/arts-entertainment/theatre-dance/features/how-to-slay-em-in-the-isles-681030.html (Accessed 10 October 2009)

104 C.W.E. Bigsby, *Joe Orton* (London: Methuen, 1982), p.17.

105 David McKittrick points out that Dominic McGlinchey introduced the concept of 'direct military rule', which 'In practice this seemed to give him licence to carry out summary executions without reference to the rest of the organisation.' See 'Obituary; Dominic McGlinchey.' *The Independent*, 12 February, 1994.

106 Seehttp://www.albemarlelondon.com/Archive/ArchiveShow.php?Show_Name=The%20Lieutenant%20of%20Inishmore (Accessed 19/3/2013)

107 I saw this Garrick production. In May 2011 I also viewed a video recording of the production which transferred from the RSC's The Other Place to The Pit, at the Barbican which was recorded on (16/1/2002), and a copy of which is held by the Victoria and Albert Museum. The play's New York run began at the Atlantic Theater Company on 27 February 2006, then transferring to Broadway's Lyceum Theatre on 3 May, with Alison Pill replacing Kerry Condon. The production closed on 3 September, gaining five Tony award nominations. A recording of this production is held at the New York Public Library, and I viewed it in April 2010. While the casts changed and these Milam productions took place in very different theatre spaces, at different locations, with dissimilar cultural contexts, it is still reasonable to say that all three productions harness a grotesque farcical sensibility, variously realised across different productions. Milam also directed the production of the play at the Olympia Theatre in Dublin, during the Dublin Theatre Festival in October 2003 and it had Barry Ward as Padraic and Aoife Madden as Mairead. This one appeared under-rehearsed and was without the irony and sinister playfulness that I had witnessed at the Garrick; consequently, the signature humour of the work was lost on many occasions.

108 Different to my own, Ashley Taggart's detailed account of his experience of seeing the play in performance at the Garrick Theatre is especially interesting. See 'An Economy of Pity: McDonagh's Monstrous Regiment' in L. Chambers and E. Jordan (eds), *The Theatre of Martin McDonagh: A World of Savage Stories* (Dublin: Carysfort Press, 2006), pp. 162–173.

109 Of the two British Davey's, Owen Sharpe's is the more composed and less shrill in comparison to Gleeson's. On occasions Sharpe is a little too earnest as Davey, whereas Gleeson has greater comic timing and has established a better distance from his character. Sharpe's Davey has long black hair versus Gleeson's long red mane.

110 It is important to note that when shots are fired during the warehouse scene there is no attempt to duplicate the sounds of real pistol fire; they sound more like an amplified cap-gun sound, thereby unhinging relationships with the real, but also contributing towards non-realistic framing of the violence that is to come.

111 Davey, points out that Mairead laughs at the news when she hears of bombs going off in England. (p.18) Public civilian spaces were used for bombs by both the Loyalist and

Republican sides. On the 23 October 1993, the bomb on the Shankill Road, whose target was Mad Dog Johnny Adair, killed nine Protestant shoppers and the bomber Thomas Begley, with a further 60 injured in the explosion in Frizzell's fishmonger's shop, but it is not a chip shop that is mentioned in the text. And as an example of tit-for-tat murders Richard English notes: 'On 5 February 1992, Loyalists of the UFF extracted revenge for the Teebane killings when they shot dead five Catholics in a crowded betting shop on Belfast's Ormeau Road.' See *Armed Struggle*, p.277.

112 David Wilmot's is an angrier, more determined and sinisterly aggressive performance.

113 Condon as Mairead has a more defined sense of flippancy and dismissal, but also displays a greater vulnerability.

114 A. Loomba, *Colonialism/Postcolonialism* (London and New York: Routledge, 1998), p.140.

115 *CAIN Web Service.*

116 It would not be until The Saville Inquiry (1998–2010) where the truths of those events were substantiated, and the failings of the army and soldiers acknowledged publically. (At the time of the play's transfer to the Garrick on London's West End, the Saville inquiry was also in session.) Malachi O'Doherty notes that after the incident many joined the PIRA not to protect but avenge, as they felt that 'the British had put their own legitimacy on the line through the transparency of the Widgery report's subsequent cover-up'. See *The Trouble with Guns: Republican Strategy and the Provisional IRA* (Belfast: Blackstaff Press, 1998), p.87.

117 Ibid., p.66.

118 See English, *Armed Struggle,* p.351.

119 Quoted in English, p. 234.

120 Ibid., p.235.

121 See Rafter, *Sinn Féin 1905–2005*: *In the Shadow of Gunmen* (Dublin: Gill and MacMillan, 2005), p.4.

122 See Maloney, *The Secret History*, p. xvi.

123 R. English notes 'Neave was killed with a car-bomb in London, as he drove out of the MP's car park in Westminster.' He had 'a secret service career and was Conservative spokesman on Northern Ireland; he was also a strong right-wing opponent of Irish Republican paramilitarism', see *Armed Struggle*, p.219.

124 As Henry McDonald suggests 'Watching the torture scenes [...] you are transported back to all those houses of horror across Ireland where informers and rivals were stripped, blindfolded, beaten, forced into confessions and eventually shot.' See '*The Guardian* profile: Martin McDonagh'.

125 See English, *Armed Struggle*, p.275.

126 See Rafter, *Sinn Féin 1905–2005,* p.27.

127 See English, *Armed Struggle*, p. 322.

128 Ibid., p.322.

129 See Magee, *Gangsters or Guerillas?,* p.2.

130 See Rafter, *Sinn Féin 1905–2005,* p.205.

131 Ibid., p.205.

132 Ibid., pp.196–7.

133 M. Luckhurst, 'Martin McDonagh's *Lieutenant of Inishmore*: Selling (-Out) to the English', *Contemporary Theatre Review* 14.4 (2004), pp. 34–41, p. 37.

134 Ibid., p.37.

135 C. Rees, 'The Politics of Morality: *The Lieutenant of Inishmore*', *New Theatre Quarterly* 21.1, (February 2005), pp.28–33, pp.28–9.

136 T. Maguire, *Making Theatre in Northern Ireland: Through and Beyond the Troubles* (Exeter: University of Exeter Press, 2006), pp.33–4.

137 P. Magee, *Gangsters or Guerillas? Representations of Irish Republicans in 'Troubles Fiction'* (Belfast: Beyond the Pale, 2001), p.2.
138 S. Deane, *Civilians and Barbarians: Field Day Pamphlet* No.3. Rpt. in *Ireland's Field Day* (Derry: Field Day Theatre, 1985) pp.33–44, p.39.
139 Ibid., p. 39.
140 Ibid., p. 39.
141 Ibid., p. 40.
142 In a guerrilla war, innocent people would occasionally be the collateral damage, but in the instance of Northern Ireland, the number of innocent people killed, who were not involved in paramilitary or military violence, was substantial. The fact is that during the Troubles more innocent civilians were killed than military or paramilitary; '[t]he so-called "war" left 3,600 people dead — the majority civilians', Kevin Rafter suggests. See *Sinn Féin 1905–2005*, p.3.
143 See English, *Armed Struggle*, p.238.
144 Ibid., p.99.
145 P. Lonergan, 'Commentary and Notes to *The Lieutenant of Inishmore*' (London: Methuen, 2009), pp.xvi-lviii, p.xlii. See also L. Pilkington, *Theatre and the State in Twentieth-Century Ireland, Cultivating the People* (London and New York: Routledge, 2001), p.146.
146 E. Maloney, *The Secret History of the IRA* (London: Lane, 2002), p.136.
147 H. McDonald notes that before Adair, McGlinchey 'during the mid to late 1980s, the first of the Troubles, "Mad Dogs" ran a terror campaign across Ireland whose victims ranged from postmistresses to police officers, fellow republicans to suspected informers.' See 'The Guardian profile: Martin McDonagh'.
148 Padraic's fantasy is for an Ireland free: 'Free for kids to run and play. Free for fellas and lasses to dance and sing. Free for cats to roam about without being clanked in the brains with a handgun' is of course an ironic take on Eamon De Valera's famous St. Patrick's Day 1943 speech, 'The Ireland That We Dreamed Of'. (p. 60)
149 McDonagh's favourite film is Terrence Malick's *Badlands* (1973) and of course Oliver Stone's movie *Natural Born Killers* (1994) also both sensationalises and eroticises the actions of killings carried out by two lovers.
150 When interviewed by Mike Wilcock, David Wilmot notes of the New York production:
'This is theatre that is potent – and potent beyond ideas. It physically shows you things that shock. It's a huge technical challenge, but when it's done well it turns the tables on television and cinema that supposedly can do things theatre cannot. We had a massive effect when Mairead shot me [Padraic] in the head with both guns, I had to press a button in the chair which was fitted with pumps and valves. Blood spurted out of the chair and literally covered the girl in blood so that all one could see was two white eyes.' See '"Put to Silence": Murder, Madness, and "Moral Neutrality" in Shakespeare's *Titus Andronicus* and Martin McDonagh's *The Lieutenant of Inishmore*', *Irish University Review*, 38.2, (Autumn-Winter 2008), pp.325–369, pp.342–3.
151 The ideological confusion that McDonagh provides for his paramilitary activists is repeated in similar ways in Chris Morris's 'jihadist comedy' *Four Lions* (2010), which also demonstrates the complexities of blending incongruity, naivety, violence, revenge and Farce and uses the twisted logic of a group of bumbling male terrorists plotting a suicide bombing mission during the London Marathon. The characters have the aspirations and some rhetoric of fundamentalists, but are amateur in their approach and flawed in their thinking and justifications. Graham Smith reports that producer Mark Herbert, from Warp Films, said: 'Chris's research has been

meticulous. It is fatwa-proof.' See 'Comedian Chris Morris faces new controversy over film about suicide bombers wearing fancy dress to target London Marathon', *Daily Mail*, 25 January 2010, http://www.dailymail.co.uk/news/article-1245887/Four-Lions-Controversial-Chris-Morris-jihadist-comedy-bumbling-suicide-bombers-premieres.html (Accessed 16/11/11)

152 See Pinker, *The Better Angels of Our Nature*, p.668.

153 Ibid., p.664.

154 Ibid., p.660.

155 Ibid., p.663.

156 Ibid., p.666, citing H. Schechter, *The Serial Killer Files: The Who, What, Where, How and Why of the World's Most Terrifying Murders* (New York: Ballantine, 2003),p.31.

157 For details on the complex preparations for the blood and gory on stage see D. Segal, 'Buckets of Blood Means It's Curtains: Stage Crew Concocts Gallons of Fake Gore For Theatrical Spatter Fest', *Washington Post,* 13 April 2006, http://www.washingtonpost.com/wp-dyn/content/article/2006/04/12/AR2006041202233.html (Accessed 7/3/2013)

158 Ben Brantley notes of the 2006 New York production 'The red stuff is splashed, spattered and smeared over walls, floors, furniture, clothes, skin and cat's fur. The fur is the main thing.' See 'Terrorism Meets Absurdism in a Rural Village in Ireland'.

159 See Witoszek and Sheeran, *Talking to the Dead*, p.6.

160 Ibid., p.10.

161 Ibid., p.9.

162 K. Brown and E. Viggiani, 'Performing Provisionalism: Republican Commemorative Practice as Political Performance' in L. Fitzpatrick (ed.), *Performing Violence in Contemporary Ireland* (Dublin: Carysfort Press 2009), pp.225–248, p.225.

163 See O'Doherty, *The Trouble with Guns*, p.22.

164 McDonagh's anarchic violence is also a type of revenge in a way, somewhat similar to Quentin Tarantino's *Inglourious Basterds* (2009) which uses graphic violence, grotesque elements and Farce to create a finale where the whole Nazi command is burnt alive in a French cinema, whilst they watch a piece of Nazi propaganda. Tarantino's movie is not historically accurate, but instead celebrates a visceral inclination towards anarchic forms of retributive destructiveness and fantastic revenge.

165 As the Peace Process established itself, the British government wanted to be seen in a positive light, as a contributor to a solution rather than the source of the problem in the first place. However, it was a bit late for the British to be a 'neutral arbiter', but equally 'British responsibility in a simple imperial-villain sense is harder to sustain', according to English. See *Armed Struggle*, p.357.

166 While the 'casual link between 11 September and the subsequent path taken by the IRA towards the actual decommissioning of arms should not be overplayed', yet there was increasing pressure for paramilitaries not to be aligned globally with Al Qaeda. After the 9/11 attacks and after the Colombian Three episode, where three Irish men were accused of training FARC guerrillas, the US State Department called for the IRA 'to totally dissociate from any terrorist activity', according to English. Americans were very quick to use the phrase 'terrorists' and not paramilitaries or freedom fighters. See English, *Armed Struggle*, p. 333, citing a report in *Belfast Telegraph,* 28 September 2001.

167 See O'Hagan, 'The Wild West'.

168 More recently, dominant republicanism has been rigorous in challenging any version of the troubles, even by former activists, that did not accord with its own and many have been put under intense pressure to stay on message, and if not, there have been firm campaigns to dismiss dissident narratives.

169 See http://www.applause-tickets.com/behanding-in-spokane.asp (Accessed 1/9/2011)
170 B. Brantley, 'Packing Heat, and a Grudge'. *New York Times*, 5 March 2010, http://theater.nytimes.com/2010/03/05/theater/reviews/05behanding.html (Accessed 15/8/2011)
171 Of course Sarah Kane's *Blasted* (1995) is set in a hotel room, where an explosion allows for another conscious to enter the space so to speak.
172 The significance of Walken as the main celebrity relies on a certain level of audience familiarity with his body of work, which is marked by a wide range of dark, intimidating and menacing performances that are balanced by often hilarious eccentricities and great comic timing and presence. Walken's major performances range from *Annie Hall* (1977) *to Deer Hunter* (1978) from *King of New York* (1990) to *True Romance* (1993) and *Pulp Fiction* (1994), from *Batman Returns* (1992) and *Sleepy Hollow* (1998) to *Catch me if you Can* (2002) and *Balls of Fury* (2007). His Captain Koon's gold watch monologue in *Pulp Fiction* stands out for many. His classic, poignant and brutally intense performance as the solider, suffering post-traumatic stress disorder, who turns to playing Russian Roulette earned him a best supporting actor Oscar in 1978 in *Deer Hunter*.
173 See Brantley, 'Packing Heat, and a Grudge'.
174 For Hilton Als, Walken's 'Carmichael isn't a character; he's Christopher Walken – the same Walken who has hosted "Saturday Night Live" and appeared in countless movies – with his intriguing (and then not) halting speech patterns and his sinister aesthetic.' Almost any Walken performance will be in intertextual dialogue with his many more notorious film roles, as would be the case with most famous actors, but Als's criticism did not hold true for me, because in many ways such awareness adds to rather than diminishes the performance. See 'Underhanded: *Martin McDonagh's slap in the face', The New Yorker*, 5 March 2010, http://www.newyorker.com/arts/critics/theatre/2010/03/15/100315crth_theatre_als?currentPage=2 (Accessed 10/3/2011)
175 P. Healy, 'Please, No More Mr. Bad Guy Roles! (But Creepy Is Fine).' *New York Times*, February 21, 2010. *http://www.nytimes.com/2010/02/21/theater/21walken.html?ref=theater* (Accessed 15/8/2011)
176 Martin McDonagh notes: 'Whenever I write an American character, I've always got Sam's voice in my head,' says McDonagh. 'He's so consistently surprising. You can never quite put your finger on him, whether he's the hero type or the bad guy. There's a danger and an edge, but he's got great comic timing too, which is perfect for this play.' See T. Shone, 'The loopy oeuvre of Sam Rockwell, America's sweetest badass', 28 February 2010, *New York Magazine* http://nymag.com/arts/theater/features/64269 (Accessed 18/8/1011)
177 In his individual narrative Mervyn tells of drunken visits to the zoo to visit a caged gibbon, when he would put his finger through the bars and the gibbon would pull his finger. Reflections on the life and dreams of a caged animal are followed by the revelations that he drunkenly imagined rescuing the animals, but that it never happened, and when he stopped going to the zoo, he started taking a lot of speed, got caught, and his bail conditions insisted on him working in the hotel.
178 Other variations on the same theme include: 'Maybe a prostitute would get stabbed and I'd have to go rescue her? Or some lesbians would get stabbed', and he would be awarded a 'protecting lesbians medal', for his efforts. (p.21)
179 This phrase also used by Uncle Bertie in *The Night of the Hunter (1955)*. And in *Inishmore*, Davey uses the term 'Black as a coon' to describe how the cat will look like after polishing. (p. 23).
180 See Pinker, *The Better Angels of Our Nature*, p.185.
181 See Als, 'Underhanded'.

182 Ibid.
183 Ibid.
184 Ibid.
185 Ibid.
186 Mike Cole's outline of Critical Race Theory (CRT) from a Marxist point of view is worth considering. He notes the influences of people like Frantz Fanon, whose distinctions between the 'governing race' and the 'zoological' natives offer particular insights on this work and links in with Mervyn's visits to the zoo. Cole also mentions the importance of civil rights and equal rights activists, particularly, the 'Black Power and Chicano movements of the sixties and early seventies' as well as 'radical feminism' in the articulation of such a theory. See *Critical Race Theory and Education: A Marxist Response* (Basingstoke: Palgrave, 2009), p.12.
187 The other answer to his accusation may be found in the Baltimore-based, five-season television series *The Wire* (2002–8) which does stress a strong criminal element in some predominantly African-American areas of socio-economic, class, gender and race disadvantage. However, the series highlights far more the blight of poverty and significant social injustices in politics, education, media, policing and broader society generally, than it ever simplistically aligns blackness or race with criminality.
188 See Als, 'Underhanded'.
189 Hand and Wilson note the significance of the monstrous maternal in many horror movies, noting Barbara Creed's application of Julia Kristeva's theory of abjection in relation to the construction of the maternal figure. See *Grand-Guignol*, p.110.
190 Of course, Carmichael's relationship with his mother, to whom he expresses the following, could point the argument in another direction: 'you never lifted a finger to help me in 27 years .... you never encouraged me once, you never did shit, you just left me to look for it all on my own, you never even did anything to stop 'em taking it in the first place so why don't you butt out, Buttinski? ....' (p.39).
191 Colin Farrell achieved a similar thing by different means in *In Bruges* (2008) with less irony and framing, but by openly inviting judgment of his character in terms of his racist slights.
192 See Hand and Wilson, *Grand-Guignol*, p.35.
193 Ibid., p.36.
194 Ibid., p.36.
195 Ibid., p.37.
196 Ibid., p.78.
197 Additionally, the proliferation of the multiple hands in the case does remind one of the trophies gathered by serial killing psychopaths and, on the other, of the work of Eugène Ionesco and the excesses of absurdist theatre practices.
198 Toby notes: 'I kinda had the feeling I saw that in a TV movie one time. That had Lee Majors in it. But maybe I'm getting it mixed up with the *Bionic*, I don't know' (p.31).
199 Acrotomophilia is where people are sexually attracted to those with amputated limbs, but have no wish to do harm to their own limbs. However, the trunk back home, so to speak, with the hidden pornography suggests that what Carmichael finds sexually arousing are black and younger women (as if, in part, to betray his mother's racism), but there is no mention of women with missing limbs.
200 Ramachandran notes patients with limbs missing from birth, still experience vivid phantom limbs, 'implying the existence of scaffolding that is hardwired by genes'. See *The Tell-Tale Brain: Unlocking the Mystery of Human Nature* (London: William Heinemann, 2011), p.256.
201 Ibid., p.26.
202 Ibid., p.27.

203 T. Bayne and N. Levy, 'Amputees By Choice: Body Integrity Identity Disorder and the Ethics of Amputation', *Journal of Applied Philosophy,* 22.1, (2005), pp.75–88, pp.75–6.

204 C. J. Ryan, 'Out on a Limb: The Ethical Management of Body Integrity Identity Disorder', *Neuroethics*, 2, (2009), pp. 21–33, p.24.

205 E.D. Sorene, C. Heras-Palou and F. D. Burke, 'Self-Amputation of a Healthy Hand: A Case of Body Integrity Identity Disorder', *Journal of Hand Surgery*, 31.6, (December 2006), p.593. http://jhs-euro.com/content/31/6/593.abstract (Accessed 10/3/2011)

206 Tellingly, Ryan suggests that the 'beliefs central to BIID are not delusions, however it is possible to say they have few of the features of the beliefs that are usually categorised that way', adding that 'Though psychotic illnesses usually manifest with more than just one delusion, monosymptomatic delusional disorders classically present as a single delusion in an otherwise normal individual.' Ryan believes those with BIID should not be seen as suffering from 'a monosymptomatic delusional disorder'. See 'Out on a Limb', pp.23–4.

207 V.S. Ramachandran and P. McGeoch, 'Can vestibular caloric stimulation be used to treat apotemnophilia?', *Medical Hypotheses*, 69.2, (2007), pp.250–252, p.251.

208 Ryan argues that there are many medical instances where healthy body parts are removed, when there is a high cancer risk, then prostate glands, breasts and ovaries can be removed. Organ donation is an obvious case and those suffering gender identity disorders are often 'offered sex reassignment surgery; so that their bodily appearance might better match the sex that they believe represents their true self.' See 'Out on a Limb', p.28.

209 Sorene, Heras-Palou and Burke note that 'Elective amputations of healthy limbs have been carried out in the UK in 1997 and 1999. However, after widespread publicity, such surgery has effectively been banned in the National Health Service.' See 'Self-Amputation of a Healthy Hand', p.593.

210 Some individuals resort to shot-gun blasts, knives or chain saws in order to destroy a limb or body part and in other instances, according to Ramachandran and McGeoch, attempts involve freezing the limb with dry ice in the hope that they 'will damage it to such an extent that an amputation is then mandatory'. See 'Can vestibular caloric stimulation be used to treat apotemnophilia?', p.251.

211 See Ramachandran, *The Tell-Tale Brain*, p.255.

212 Ibid., pp. 250–253.

213 Ibid., pp.254–6.

214 However, Ramachandran notes that in 'two-thirds of cases the left limb is removed', so this allows him to question the 'disproportionate involvement of the left arm', but he ignores the percentage of the population that are right handed – as Mervyn does – and instead likens it to somatoparaphrenia, a condition where after a right-hemisphere stroke, the patient not only 'denies the paralysis of the left arm but also insists that the arm doesn't belong to him'. Ibid., p.256.

215 Ibid., p.257.

216 *Night of the Hunter*, directed by Charles Laughton and written by James Agee, has its serial-killing character, Reverend Harry Powell played by Robert Mitchum has the words Love and Hate tattooed on the knuckles of his left and right hand and uses the hands to teach morality.

See http://tvtropes.org/pmwiki/pmwiki.php/Main/KnuckleTattoos (Accessed 20/11/11) Also Tim Dirks notes: '[Spike *Lee's Do the Right Thing* (1989) referenced the love-hate, left and right hand theme, when Radio Raheem (Bill Nunn) explained the love-hate dichotomy. In *The Rocky Horror Picture Show* (1975), LOVE and HATE were tattooed on Eddie's (Meat Loaf) knuckles, and in *The Blues Brothers* (1980), the two brothers (John Belushi and Dan Aykroyd) have their names tattooed on their knuckles. In *The Simpsons* episode "Cape Feare", the menacing Sideshow Bob (voice of Kelsey Grammer) had similar tattoos on each set of knuckles as well – but since the characters in the cartoon show had only three fingers and a thumb, the tattoos were humorously "LUV" and "HAT" - (with a bar over the A).]' See Tim Dirks ' The Night of the Hunter', http://www.filmsite.org/nightof.html (Accessed 20/11/11)

217 For side by side with this BIID condition, Bayne and Levy note there are also those who are labelled 'pretenders'; people who consciously fake a disability. Walken's fluid interpretation of the character leaves that possibility open that Carmichael may well be a pretender, as he consistently foregrounds a characterisation that is fundamentally performative. See Bayne and Levy, 'Amputees By Choice', p.78.

218 Cole argues that 'As long as CRT centralises "race" rather than class, and as long as it voices no serious challenge to United States and world capitalism, it will be tolerated.' See *Critical Race Theory and Education*, p.151.

219 See Žižek, *Violence*, p.35.

220 Ibid., p.35.

221 Ibid., p.40.

222 See Hand and Wilson, *Grand-Guignol*, p.78.

223 McDonagh is quoted as saying of Walken that he 'brings everything to it. There isn't anyone in the world who has humour and scariness at the exact same time. He always found the humour in the lines, and he always found the scariness, but he has a way different take on lines than any actor I've ever known, I think. But it works, you know [....] It's like a dream to hear the way he plays around with the stuff that I've come up with. It's a joy.' H. Haun, '*A Behanding in Spokane* — Watch Where You're Walken', 5 March 2010, http://www.playbill.com/features/article/137585-PLAYBILL-ON-OPENING-NIGHT-A-Behanding-in-Spokane-Watch-Where-Youre-Walken/pg2

224 B. Pitcher, *The Politics of Multiculturalism: Race and Racism in Contemporary Britain* (Basingstoke: Palgrave, 2009), p.2.

225 See the 1975 film *Monty Python and the Holy Grail.*

226 See Sierz, *In-Yer-Face Theatre*, pp. 8–9.

227 See Milner Davis, *Farce*, p.141.

228 Ibid., p.141.

229 For Robert Trivers, 'Natural selection refers to the fact that in every species, some individuals leave more surviving offspring than do others, so that the genetic traits of the reproductively successful tend to become more frequent over time.' See *Deceit and Self-Deception: Fooling Yourself the Better to Fool Others* (London: Allen Lane, 2011), p.1.

PART 3

A Moral Conundrum: Psychopathology, Empathy by Way of Fragmentary Stories

1 | Introduction: 'Against God'

In the plays and films, Christian and other religions, including Buddhism and Hinduism, are often called upon in attempts to mark distinctions between right and wrong, virtue and vice, choice and compulsion. In McDonagh's early work there is both a repetitive use of and struggle with the phrase 'Against God' that is prevalent across the body of work.[1] For example in *Inishmaan*, Helen remarks on a deed under consideration to unnerve an elderly woman, while it would not be a 'very Christian' thing to do, it would be 'awfully funny'. (p.48) In *Connemara*, Maryjohnny pettily deceives visitors by saying that it is in her 'Liam's place was where *The Quiet Man* was filmed', whereas Ma'am Cross is the precise location. (p. 67) Mick also reminds her of her regular habit of illegally playing ten books at bingo, a number which rises to 15 for the Christmas jackpot, well in excess of the general limit of four. While Mick is indulging in a certain level of playful banter with her over such venial and inconsequential incidentals, the tables are turned when she reminds him that it is not only seven-and-a-half years since his last confession, but also that it was his deceased wife, Oona, who last took him there; a comment which also effectively points towards his role in her death.

Maryjohnny is also enraged by 'a pack of whores' who have urinated in the churchyard. She believes that they have committed a great blasphemy and desecration by so doing. The target of her rage is five-year-old children, and the incident that took place 27 years previously: '... I'll tell you when I'll let bygones be bygones. When I see them burned in Hell I'll let bygones be bygones and not before!' (p. 65) In relation to one's neighbours, one's parents or one's siblings, there is no fundamental sense of togetherness or of community and there are very few expressions of love. Still there are perhaps twisted forms of affection expressed by Mag and Maureen, Padraic and Mairead and Coleman and Valene for each other. Regardless, as Fr Welsh remarks in *Lonesome*, 'It seems like God has no jurisdiction in this town.' (p.134)

Broad stroke discussions about morality are almost always problematic. It would be reasonable to suggest that cross-cultural moral cores, as Steven Pinker notes, include 'fairness, justice, the protection of individuals and the prevention of harm', but these are 'just one of the several spheres of concern that may attach themselves to the cognitive and emotional paraphernalia of moralisation'.[2] He continues arguing that ancient religions like Islam, Hinduism and Judaism 'moralise a slew of other concerns, such as loyalty, respect, obedience, asceticism, and the regulation of bodily functions like eating, sex and menstruation'.[3] Today, Pinker argues, there is a shifting of 'the allocation of moral intuitions away from community, authority and purity and towards fairness, autonomy, and rationality'.[4] Morality can be a brake on behaviour, but it can also lead to calls for ghastly punishments for small and large non-conformities. Morality can turn the other all too easily into the enemy, agent of Satan or agent of opposing ideology and thus legitimate all sorts of atrocities.

Pinker distinguishes between morality as a philosophical conceptualisation from a topic in psychology, that is 'moral sense.' So, why, he asks, is it that in different times and different cultures, standards of behaviour once acceptable, change? How can moral sense be compartmentalised? 'Why can morality be extended to thoughts as well as deeds?'[5] While philosophical morality can focus on moral objectivity and universal convictions, for Pinker, 'Moral psychology is about the mental processes that people *experience* as moral.'[6] So for him, 'There are important psychological distinctions between avoiding an action because it is deemed immoral,' such as killing, and 'avoiding it because it is merely disagreeable' ("I hate cauliflower"), unfashionable ("Bell-bottoms are out"), or imprudent ("Don't scratch mosquito bites").'[7] You don't mind if others eat cauliflower, but you do care if others kill.

Thus, for Pinker, 'Moralised beliefs are a*ctionable*': these are things that you do, and you don't need an ulterior motive or reward for doing or not doing something. When we breach a moral code, we seek to explain it away, as weakness, corruption or a lack of self control.[8] Additionally, from this perspective 'moralized infractions are *punishable*'.[9] Thus murderers must pay as a society makes that happen or individuals take it into their own hands and that gives us the clash in value systems in *In Bruges* between Ken and Harry for instance. Furthermore, Pinker notes many moral convictions 'operate as norms and taboos rather than as principles the believer can articulate and defend'.[10] Individuals can know something is wrong, without being able to articulate it.

Based on work by Richard Shweder and Jonathan Haidt, Alan Fiske devises a taxonomy, which Pinker adjusts slightly. Fiske's relational model emphasises first 'Communal Sharing', based on in-group loyalty, bonding and rituals of togetherness. It is a bonding based on care and protection. The second relational model is 'Authority Ranking', based on dominance, status, precedents, etc. The dominant figures take what they need and demand loyalty and in return they offer protection and assurances. The third model is 'Equality Matching', which 'embraces tit-for-tat reciprocity and other schemes to divide resources' as equitably and as fairly as possible. Fiske's final relational model is 'Market Pricing', and this is about money, and financial value, and is not as nearly universal.[11] Thus Pinker substitutes in the term 'Rational-Legal' as his final model. [12] For Pinker, 'no society defines everyday virtue and wronging by the Golden Rule or the Categorical Imperative. Instead, morality consists in respecting or violating one of the relational models (or ethics or foundations)', by causing communal disharmony, by undermining authority, by being violent without provocation, without matching another's contribution, without paying the cost of goods or services.

This taxonomy thus provides a 'grammar for social norms'.[13] 'Each moralized norm is a compartment containing a relational model,' reliant on one or more 'social roles', 'a context', and a 'resource'. So to be a 'socially competent member of a culture is to have assimilated a large set of these norms'.[14] Organ selling, trading your children for financial gain, and such like, are instances when no cost-benefit analysis can be applied. Then, as with Fiske's model, as Pinker notes, those that do not come under these relational models are deemed to be in 'null or asocial relationships', and are thus dehumanised, treated like 'inanimate objects' and open to 'predatory violence of conquest, rape, assassination, infanticide, strategic-bombing, colonial expulsions, and other crimes of convenience'.[15]

McDonagh's dramaturgy inconveniences these relational models, as his characters seem to breach these relational norms, by engaging in social roles in ways that are casual or thoughtless, unintentional, incompetent and subversive. There is a persistent perversion of contexts, situations and appropriate norms, and the characters' approach to resources in ways that are inappropriate, such as an unwillingness to share, or taboo breaking, in regard to personal hygiene (skulls on tables), saying or threatening the unthinkable, deriding historical or communal memories, such as waking traditions, or violating the most basic of expectations and norms, as in the aftermath of a funeral or the beating of a disabled character with a lead pipe.

Few things test moral sense or cultural values as much as the exploitation of children or the violation of innocence, which is central to fairytales generally and both to *In Bruges* and *The Pillowman* in particular.[16] In the former, an innocent child is killed during an assassination of a priest, affording the maniacal gangster Harry to express the belief that such a killing has only one result, extermination of the killer, even if he is the one who requested the contract killing in the first place. Central to both pieces of very different work is the issue of fairytale and how these tales inform 'moral sense', in terms of justice, judgment, sacrifice and the taking of sides. As always, while some of the theories used here are written about the disorders of individuals and groups, they do help to build a bigger picture about McDonagh's characters. All four works in this section mark the tensions between being casually and inconsiderately destructive towards others and displaying compassion, as well as between the breaching of relational models and altruistic behaviours and between empathy and pathological impulse.

ZERO POSITIVE V ZERO NEGATIVE

Most spectators easily identify the refusal, unwillingness or inability to empathise as one of the defining features of many of McDonagh's characters. For example, in *Lonesome*, Valene is described as nodding 'in phoney empathy'. (p.150) Simon Baron-Cohen argues that throughout the history of the world acts of cruelty, evil and objectification of others cannot be easily rationalised, so he prefers to substitute 'the term "evil" with the term "empathy erosion"', a state which effectively arises 'because of corrosive emotions, such as bitter resentment, or desire for revenge, or blind hatred, or desire to protect,' which are in theory 'transient emotions', thus making empathy erosion potentially reversible.[17] So 'depleted empathy'[18] or temporary blips in the empathy system can be addressed successfully by individuals themselves or with external assistance. But 'when our empathy is switched off, we are solely in the "I" mode. In such a state we relate only to things, or to people *as if they were just things*.'[19] For him, the dismissing of another's subjectivity, their dehumanisation and objectification occurs when empathy is switched off, but by the end of this discussion, it might be gleaned that this is not the only reason.

Baron-Cohen argues that the 'empathy circuit' in the brain involves ten regions,[20] and that any under-activity can be determined by functional magnetic resonance imaging (fMRI).[21] Cases of individuals whose personalities change due to brain injuries have proven that if certain parts of the brain are less active, then behaviour seems to change accordingly: some individuals lose a capacity for empathy or jettison social inhibitions after brain traumas.

However, some people's focus is so self-absorbed that 'a chip in their neural computer is missing', so there is potential danger in an 'enduring lack of empathy, as a stable trait'.[22] When in this particular frame of mind, such individuals have no sense of how they might hurt another, no sense of guilt or remorse for what they do; they do not seek to build trust, do not negotiate, and do not understand a social need to collaborate, as they simply demand their way, because the needs of others are neither apparent nor important. (These are many of the ways of violating Pinker's relational models.)

Baron-Cohen makes careful distinctions between 'states' and 'traits': the former being 'fluctuations in a psychological or neural system, induced by a particular context, [and these] are reversible', and include being drunk, tired, impatient and stressed, in other words, doing the wrong thing and regretting it: with the latter, these traits 'are permanent, crystallised configurations of a psychological or neural system, enduring across different contexts and are irreversible'.[23] Of course, the issue of permanence is difficult to affirm, but what he does suggest is something fairly fixed and predictable when it comes to individual 'traits'.

Some individuals who have experienced extreme neglect can be left with substantially depleted empathy levels; others of comparable experiences may not be damaged in the same way and maintain an enduring capacity for empathy. Not all individuals with low levels of empathy have suffered sustained neglect. However, Baron-Cohen cites the research of Dante Cicchetti and his colleagues, who discovered that eighty per cent of children who suffered abuse and neglect went on to develop 'disorganised attachment'.[24] (This term is of particular interest when it comes to a range of McDonagh's characters, from Billy in *Inishmaan* to Michal in *The Pillowman* and from Kid in *Six Shooter* to Billy Bickle in *Seven Psychopaths*.)[25]

Furthermore, for individuals, and again rather than dramatic characters, a range of environmental factors interact with specific 'genes for empathy', but these genes, Baron-Cohen acknowledges 'cannot code for a high level construct like empathy. Genes simply blindly code for the production of proteins, blissfully unaware of their ultimate long range effects.'[26] Additionally, Baron-Cohen's study shows how serotonin impacts on aggression, on the so-called 'warrior gene'.[27] (This is a gene which Pinker refutes.) There is also a gene which clears the serotonin from the synapse, there are genes associated with emotional recognition, genes associated with the sex hormone, testosterone, and with oxytocin (variously known as the love, trust or attachment hormone).[28] All of these genes and environmental factors impact variously on what Baron-Cohen describes as the 'Empathy Quotient (EQ).'[29]

For those individuals that have very low or no empathy, Baron-Cohen divides them into the categories of zero negative and zero positive: the zero negative cluster includes Narcissist (Type N), Psychopath (Type P) and Borderline (Type B), all of which are in his words 'psychological disorders.'[30] (He also distinguishes between psychopathic and Anti-Social Personality Disorders.) Zero-positives, associated with those on the autistic spectrum, are very different to Zero-negatives, and I will deal with that category later in relation to Michal in *The Pillowman*. The Zero-negative category is vital to an understanding of McDonagh's work.

On the Zero-negative side, those individuals categorised as 'Borderline' display a 'constant fear of abandonment, emotional pain and loneliness, hatred (of others and of themselves), impulsivity and self-destructive, highly inconsistent behaviour.'[31] Baron-Cohen argues that during the 'separation-individuation phase,' a child normally establishes their sense of self, which is crucial for later in life mental health, as this process normally balances the healthy needs for autonomy and for closeness, on the one hand, and the unhealthy fear of 'engulfment' and abandonment, on the other.[32] However, some people get stuck in this splitting stage, failing to achieve integration and enter a 'dissociative state'.[33] In *Beauty Queen* Mag intensely fears abandonment by her daughter, and her maternal ruthlessness can be seen as a consequence of such fear in many respects. Further, Maureen is her mother's equal in her inability to separate adequately, as separation notionally only comes to her by the killing of her mother, but it effectively results in her, as earlier argued, being entombed in her home place, engulfed by memories, locked into a 'dissociative state' and destined to become or replicate her mother.

In Baron-Cohen's theorising, Type N zero negative behaviours are evident in individuals who have notions of extreme entitlement and excessive expectations of being well treated, 'irrespective of how they treat others'.[34] These individuals regard themselves as very special, that they are better than everyone else, display an absence of humility, remain totally self-preoccupied and engage in 'monologues, not dialogues.'[35] While narcissism does lie on a 'spectrum of traits,' it is only pathological in extreme cases.[36] Pinker also notes that narcissists 'think well of themselves not in proportion to their accomplishments but out of congenital sense of entitlement.'[37] Pinker adds, resentment, 'whips up the emotions of thwarted dominance – humiliation, envy, rage – to which narcissists are prone.'[38]

In *Lonesome*, Valene's branding of the home with the initial 'V' is but one example of a form of 'loner narcissism', which is reinforced by his meanness. But, after the death of Fr Welsh, Valene's apparent willingness to change things complicates a reading of the character as simplistically narcissistic. In *The Pillowman*, Katurian's self-absorption, particularly in terms of the value he places on his writing and the significance of his legacy are indicative of high levels of narcissism. Indeed McDonagh has in interviews spoken not only about the narcissism of writers like himself, but also about the protection it offers in facing down rejection.[39] (And of course, as will be discussed later, in *The Pillowman* the narcissistic young girl in 'The Little Jesus Story' has a Messiah or Saviour complex.)

However, it is towards the very negative end of the empathy scale, and those that are pathological Zero negative (Type P), which is of greatest interest in relation to the characters in the plays, and in particular all three of the films. First of all, Baron-Cohen distinguishes between Anti-Social Personality Disorder and Psychopathic Personality Disorder. Individuals with Anti-Social Personality Disorder are primarily rooted in an intense personal preoccupation and will do whatever it takes to achieve their desires.[40] This tendency leaves them prone to 'violent reactions to setbacks or those that get in their way', but most substantially, there is a form of 'cold, calculated cruelty' evident in much of their behaviour.[41]

Baron-Cohen identifies the following characteristics: non-conformity to the law, deceitfulness, persistent lying, impulsivity and failure to plan ahead, irritability and aggression, reckless disregard for the safety of oneself or others, consistent irresponsibility by not honouring commitments and obligations, self-righteousness, the taking of pleasure in the suffering of others, and most of all, a set of behaviours marked by a lack of remorse.[42] In Baron-Cohen's estimation about '3 per cent of males (but only 1 per cent of females) have this condition, and in prisons, over half the male population and one quarter of the female population would be diagnosed with this disorder.'[43]

However, at a further extreme someone with Anti-Social Personality Disorder can also be psychopathic or have Psychopathic Personality Disorder, also called Zero Negative (Type P): Baron-Cohen asserts that this cohort comprises fewer individuals again, less than 1 per cent of the male population and about 15 per cent of the prison population.[44] To support his argument, Baron-Cohen uses Hervey Cleckley's research on psychopathology: Cleckley identifies the following dispositions: superficial charm, lack of anxiety or guilt, undependability and dishonesty, egocentricity, an inability to form lasting intimate relationships, a failure to learn from punishment, poverty of emotions, a lack of insight into the impact of their behaviour and a failure to plan ahead.[45] While the above list of behaviours does not directly lead to violence and criminality per se, a potential psychopathology can be evident in people that are ruthless in corporate worlds, on sporting pitches and in formal or informal groupings, being manifested in high levels of deception, manipulation and both verbal and physical aggression.

Additionally, these pathological individuals cannot easily determine someone else's stress levels, do not fear punishment, and lack resilience, mindfulness and insight, but they are also missing what Baron-Cohen describes as 'the internal pot of gold', an inner resourcefulness in the face of challenges afforded by a security of being.[46] Coleman in *Lonesome* ticks many of these psychopathological boxes, in terms of impulsivity, recklessness, inconsistency and a lack of remorse. As earlier argued, Mairead and Padraic, along with some of his paramilitary colleagues in *Inishmore* seem also to fall within this category. In *The Pillowman* policemen murder detainees with impunity, namely a writer who slaughters the cruel parents that torture and victimise his brother, and the rescued brain-damaged brother who turns out to be a serial killer of children. And the primary interactions of Ray, Ken and Harry in *In Bruges* offer an extraordinary insight into processes of thought and behaviour in this criminal underworld. Each of these characters presents a limited understanding of the gangland world in which they operate and each character's viewpoint is triangulated to challenge the perspectives of the others on 'moral sense', forgiveness and retribution. *Seven Psychopaths* proposes an evolved form of engagement with psychopathology, as there are particular challenges in McDonagh's contesting of the scripting of sensationalist and voyeuristic film violence.

In the first instance, I will look closely at how *Six Shooter* formulates a governing tension between empathy and psychopathology. Pinker argues that empathy is only significant if it results in the establishment of better rights for people; while initially empathy is good, it has to lead to adjustments to policy, regulations, fairness and equality. So empathy must happen in conjunction with reason, self control and 'abstract moral argumentation'.[47] Baron-Cohen would be in agreement with that.

2 | Unwanted – Dead or Alive: *Six Shooter*

HIS DARK MATERIALS

Filmed in Wicklow and Waterford and written and directed by McDonagh, *Six Shooter*, a 28-minute short action movie, won the 2006 Academy Award for Best Live Action short Film and a number of other Irish and British film awards.[48] In some ways, McDonagh said that he wrote and directed this short film so that he could learn about filmmaking. And despite the fact that he was learning off the hoof, it is a terrifically successful film, more in terms of its story, humour and characterisation and less in terms of its production values. Cinematically, the final product is anything but seamless, with some basic errors that are common to many novice directors, but such downsides do not significantly take away from this very clever, comedic, signature, apprentice piece.

The film's opening focus is on Brendan Gleeson's character, Mr Donnelly. The first significant facial shot is of him responding to the announcement that his wife has passed away at three o'clock that morning. He just lowers himself into a chair, before accepting an invitation from the doctor to sit with her remains. It is an eventful evening for this hospital, which has already dealt with two cot deaths and a mother who was shot and decapitated – a beheading of sorts. The piece's comedic frame is further established when Donnelly unthinkingly wonders if the woman has survived such an atrocity. This mood is reinforced when Donnelly addresses his dead wife, not knowing what to say to her and when he produces the photo of 'David', their rabbit, the tragic-comic mood is re-affirmed. Physically and emotionally, Gleeson registers a grieving, hapless, confused and incongruous character, who now has to find his way back home via public transport.

Although there are free seats on the train Donnelly chooses to sit down opposite another passenger, a young teenager named only as Kid (Ruaidhrí Conroy), who is wearing a beige leather jacket and luminous green shirt and carries with him a child's toy monkey, attired in a red waistcoat with a tambourine in its hands. This monkey or trickster figure seems to serve as a kind of guiding spirit for Kid. Conroy captures brilliantly the character's impatience with all social interactions, the inability to self-censor, and the instant capacity to twist conversations towards the strange. His reflections on the height of jockeys is indicative of that mindset, because it turns all too easily towards an aggressive challenge to something his mother has told him previously: that people can grow up 'to be whatever they want to be'. Such a homespun philosophy, also circulated by many motivational speakers and life coaches, cannot apply to taller people who would effectively be too heavy to be professional jockeys. He declares that he has not a 'friend in the world'. The aggression of the Kid character, his willingness to challenge social niceties, his indifference towards others and above all his insensitivity, combine to make him a outstanding pathological figure.

Many of the traits that Baron-Cohen has mentioned using Hervey Cleckley's research on psychopathology are initially evident, and more come into focus throughout the duration of this short film – particularly when he relates to a distraught couple sitting nearby. The Dooleys, played by Aisling O'Sullivan and David Wilmot, show a certain strain to their relationship, most notably when she rejects an attempt by her partner to touch her hand. While not keen for him to relay their grief to others, in her gesture there is an even stronger demonstration of an inability to keep their grief private. Instantly, the Kid notices such tensions, and wants to engage with them. Cursing is the first thing he uses to draw the couple within his ambit.

When the Kid hears from Donnelly that the couple's baby son has died the previous evening, the Kid's macabre curiosity and twisted take on the world get the better of him as he states: 'Maybe they banged it on something.' And things turn even stranger when he not only casually repeats the accusation, but he also suggests that if he had a child and if it was getting on his nerves, he would bang it on something. He is even surprised that parents do not kill their kids more often, as most kids are 'fucking rotten.' Calling the couple 'Fred and Rosemary' (the serial-killing West duo) is an offence that captures his unstoppable determination to agitate or discommode others emotionally. Non-conformity and above all an inability to either feign or demonstrate empathy are further notable markers of his behaviour and are consistently realised by Conroy.

EMERGENCY CORD

Having convinced the mother to give him a look at the photo of their dead child, Kid suggests that the baby looks like Jimmy Somerville, from the all-gay pop group Bronksi Beat. And having inspected the picture, the Kid remarks: 'no wonder you banged it on something'. Mrs Dooley is compelled to defend herself, stating that it was a cot death. His retort – 'that is what all yee mams say' – reveals a great deal. He smirks, knowing full well that he has fundamentally unnerved her, whilst he makes a face similar to that of the toy monkey. By this stage, it is evident that he is clearly a transgressive trickster figure, who goes beyond a limited playfulness and ambivalence towards something far darker, sinister and extreme.

Flustered, the mother falls when getting out of her seat past the Kid, and the picture of the child tears. The Kid wonders out loud, 'Was that a bit much now. I think you might have gone a bit overboard, fella.' This slight sliver of self-awareness comes as one of the few moments where he brings some degree of critical consciousness to his own un-empathetic actions. But such a thought passes all too quickly and if the spectator sees it as an indicator of a turn for the better in relation to this character, he or she will be proved wrong.

Kid's response to the mother's suicide is to close the carriage door, pick up the picture of the child and not to raise any alarm. The extent of Kid's delusions and psychopathology are clearly revealed by his inadequate response to this incident; there is his nonchalant and cavalier explanation to her husband that she 'flung herself off the train five minute back, dashed her brains to muck against a wall'. This revelation leads to initial disbelief, given the fact that he responds generally with such social insensitivity and given that such a potential situation could not possibly give rise to such a casual, callous and indifferent response. Again we are back to issues of proportionality, the collapse in cause and effect and to the utter breach of expectations surrounding basic social interactions. To Dooley's disbelief Kid retorts without compassion: 'Just look out along the train, she's dripping down the half of it.' Kid's summary of events in his witness statement to the policeman is that 'She was acting like an oddball from as soon as she sat down, all crying like a mad thing.' His empathy depletion is further affirmed.

In contrast, Donnelly demonstrates empathy for the couple's plight. During an earlier conversation with Donnelly, the grieving father wonders if Kid might be 'retarded', but that label is dismissed by Donnelly. However, both tentatively if naively agree that there is 'No harm in him.' How wrong they are. Later, Kid is prompted to ask why is Donnelly so distressed as he 'didn't even know the woman?' The Kid persists: 'Admit it fella, she was getting on your nerves too with her bawling.' Because of Donnelly's previous attempts to humour him, the Kid shows something like a flicker of empathy in Donnelly's direction as his distress starts to get the better of him. To Donnelly's admission that his wife has just died, the Kid retorts: 'Did she get murdered too?' And as Donnelly cries, he is encouraged to release his tears, prompted by the comment: 'Cry auld fella. She's up with God now, she's up with God now.' And although Donnelly expresses his lack of faith, Kid insists that he must have belief in God, as he is 'an auld fella'. And in terms of the Kid's own recent loss, he exclaims: 'My mam got murdered last night but you don't see me off wailing like a spa.'

At this point in the film the body count is high: there is Donnelly's dead wife, the Kid's murdered mother, the cot deaths and the suicide of Mrs Dooley, and when the police stop the train in order to arrest Kid, he is destined to join the register of the dead. There is nothing heroic in the Kid's anarchic last stand, leaving him less a rebel with a cause and more a murderous criminal without one. And in Kid's final admission that he 'Didn't hit one of them' there is the fundamental re-affirmation of the complex comedic sensibility of the piece. In this film, the killing of a parent, loss of a partner and a suicidal response to trauma raise issues of motivation, fortitude, choice, how pain can overwhelm and the matter of the 'internal pot of gold' that can determine the capacity to persist and endure. Less like Maureen in *Beauty Queen* and Coleman in *Lonesome,* both of whom could make some form of polite conversation, Kid is very much like Padraic in *Inishmore*, utterly fixated on himself.

Donnelly gets home and he readies himself to die. He faces the picture of the Sacred Heart upside down on the sideboard, a gesture which positions his psyche in relation to Catholicism and religious superstition. Ironically, having beheaded the rabbit with a single shot from the gun he had taken from Kid's body, now when Donnelly turns the gun on himself it misfires and explodes. *Six Shooter* frames the bereaved Donnelly's failure to kill himself as chaotic and tragic-comic and the mercy killing of the rabbit as absurd. So, in this film, there is, on the one hand, both the grotesque violence and the anarchic approach of the heartless, pitiless and insensitive Kid, and, on the other, the more charitable, benevolent, gracious and humane actions evident in the deeds of both the anguished couple and Donnelly. In the interactions of these two opposing perspectives a complex network of reactions, sensibilities and responses are formed, whereby the tensions between empathy and psychopathology are rooted in a very intricate fashion that complicates any 'moral sense'. And this dialectic is followed through in all of the three other works in this section.

3 | A Winter Solstice: *In Bruges*

While it would be too reductive to suggest that *Six Shooter*'s Donnelly functions in any substantial way as a template for Ken (again Brendan Gleeson) and the Kid for Ray (Colin Farrell) in *In Bruges,* still there remains some striking similarities between the short film and McDonagh's first full-length feature film, which he again wrote and directed.[49] A three-week rehearsal period prior to the film's shooting helped generate the great central performances. *In Bruges* won the Best Screenplay Award at the 2009 BAFTA Awards and received an Academy Award nomination in the Best Screenplay category, also in 2009. Colin Farrell won a Golden Globe Best Actor Award in a Motion Picture – Musical or Comedy for his performance and Gleeson was also nominated in the same category.[50]

Two London-based Irish gangland figures, Ray and Ken, are sent to Bruges by their crime boss Harry Waters (Ralph Fiennes) after Ray, during his first professional hit, while calculatedly and cold bloodedly killing a Catholic priest, Fr McHenry (Ciarán Hinds), also acccidentally murders a child who is waiting outside the confession box in the church in London. (The little boy's confessional list includes being moody, being bad at maths and being sad and has obvious echoes of the unhappy children in *The Pillowman*.)

The casting of these two Irish actors, Farrell and Gleeson, for parts not originally conceived of as Irish is particularly interesting.[51] They not only speak with Dublin accents, but repeatedly acknowledge their Irish and Dublin heritages.[52] (After the initial kill, Ken is supposed to call Harry on the public phone in the pub identified as 'Jimmy Driscoll's', another Irish name which again reinforces the importance of Irishness to the work. (p.40) And the bar in which they drink in Bruges is an Irish pub. When Ray is arrested on the train, the policeman asks, 'You Irish?' (p.63)) Also as Joan [FitzPatrick] Dean reminds us; at a crucial moment late in the play as Ken sacrifices himself, 'the soundtrack departs from Carter Burwell's accomplished score and gives us "On Raglan Road", performed by The Dubliners, with Luke Kelly singing with a very pronounced Dublin accent.[53] "On Raglan Road" was written by Patrick Kavanagh in 1946. The poem was originally published as "Dark Haired Miriam Ran Away" and was written about his love for Hilda Moriarty. It was Kavanagh's idea to set the poem to the air of the traditional song "The Dawning of the Day"' (Fáinne Gael an Lae).[54] Such a shift in the score to this love song, not only underlines the poignancy of the moment, but frames the death within a culturally and diasporically-aware Irish tradition. Some spectators will think of this song as relatively incidental, others might guess that the song has an association with the character or accept that the mood and tone of the song speaks to Ken's actions, while others will be not only familiar with the song, but will make strong associations between Ken and a passion for the city which partially defines him.

The film was shot on location in the Belgium city of Bruges,[55] which is a very well preserved, mainly medieval city, often called the 'Venice of the North'.[56] Although it is set in a contemporary reality, the screenplay suggests that 'We could be in any period of the last 500 years. We happen to be in the present day', (p.3) and by so doing, McDonagh evokes the timelessness of fairytales and such issues of non-time and non-place will also be important to reflections later in *The Pillowman*.[57] The backdrop of fog-laden parks, canals, bridges, cobble-stoned streets, museums, public squares, bell towers and gothic churches combine with a winter and Christmas-like setting to create a specific gothic, 'other worldly' atmosphere.[58] (Bruges is also the setting for an inter-cultural romance of sorts.)

Cosmo Landesman notes in his review: 'Instead of the urban jungle of anonymous modern cities, here we have two killers trapped in the chocolate-box beauty of a medieval town.'[59] Catherine O'Brien observes that:

> the city's architecture itself is deceptive: the little Bonifacius bridge, seen in one of the opening shots, appears to be medieval but dates back only to 1910; in their night-time tour of Bruges, Ray and Ken purportedly look at the exterior of the Gruuthuse museum but, in the reverse shot, the audience are actually shown the town hall on the Burg, with its statues of the counts and countesses of Flanders – 19th-century replacements for the medieval statues that were pulled down by French revolutionaries in 1792. Some of the apparently Gothic facades on the market place, which figure in the film's bloody climax, date from the 1950s.[60]

Apart from the tragicomic sensibility of the film, throughout, lighting and cinematography also play crucial roles in establishing the complex idiom and ambience of the piece. Geoff King notes how:

> McDonagh and cinematographer Eigil Bryld frequently employ lighting that generates a soft golden glowing effect, combined in chiaroscuro style with patches of deep shadow, further establishing the overall 'quality' impression of the visuals. This applies to many of the interior shots in the film. In some cases, overt motivation is provided for such forms of light. One night scene in Ken and Ray's hotel room, for example, is lit by strongly directional light coming from the bathroom, while a restaurant sequence has the appearance of benefiting from the relatively low-key lighting of the venue.[61]

While lying low awaiting instructions from Harry, Ray and Ken are not in agreement as to the beauty and significance of the place: Ken is pleased to have the cultural opportunity to experience the city, Ray however despises the place, in ways that reflects less badly on the city per se and represent more his deep distress.

Farrell's initial voice-over sets out not only the scenario of murder, the gloominess and frailty of his character, but establishes Ray's unease doing touristy things, together with his impatient and childlike disrespect for the beauty of the place.[62] So unlike such killers as the pathological paramilitary Padraic in *Inishmore* who has no sense of remorse, or Coleman in *Lonesome*, whose indifference to the killing of his father is staggering, Ray feels overwhelming remorse for his killing of the child, but not for that of the priest. Spectators witness Ray's sense of distress, before discovering the crime of which he is guilty, so it is more likely that the initial empathy incited in audiences will not instantly dissipate, but can potentially be sustained in a very complex fashion. Effectively and challengingly, how often do cinema audiences approve of child-killers?

Humour also further complicates matters. When the film production assistant and drug dealer called Chloë (Clémence Poésy) asks Ray on the night of their date what he does for a living, he replies that it is all about shooting priests and children. His response is designed as if not to be believed on the one hand, but on the other hand it is also a less than playful comment on the fact that he is a killer. She finds his response amusing and a bit perverse. She admits that she deals heroin and cocaine to film crews, but she is playing a different, more provocative and seductive game to his. Disclosure is both painful and perverse for him. Furthermore, Ray's joke that the Belgians 'only invented the chocolates to get to kids', is a bit tasteless. When she retorts with the fact that one of the girls killed in a series of murders was indeed a friend of hers, Ray is acutely unnerved. Chloë is only having him on, but her comments test broader sensitivities.

(Of course the deeper irony is that here is a child murderer casually joking about the sexual abusers and killers of children and his comments are dependent on a fundamentally false degree of differentiation.)

This fairytale, touristy, other-worldly space of Bruges slowly evolves into a more complex type of space, given over to include genuine reflections on guilt and damnation. There are also funerary and heterotopic dimensions to this city itself – as discussed earlier in relation to the rural quarters of Leenane in *Connemara*. Ray's guilt is exacerbated by the first painting he experiences in the Groeninge Museum – which is Jan Provoost's 'De gierigaard en de Dood' (The Miser and Death). This canvas imagines a final judgment set in a confessional box (or as the screenplay describes it 'a skeletal death comes to collect his due').[63] (p. 24) The museum also houses the gruesome diptych 'Judgment of Cambyses' and the even more gruesome 'The Flaying of the Corrupt Judge Sisamnes' by Gerard David.[64] It is a diptych that is both unflinching in its cruelty, as well as almost forensically voyeuristic in its detail which serves, more particularly, as stern warnings to corrupt public figures.[65] Margitta Rouse notes of this sequence that in the film 'The Judgement of Cambyses' 'is presented in hard cuts from photographic still to still; the limited camera movement after the series of stills simulates Ray's way of quietly taking in every single detail – the flaying of an arm, a face in agony, a cut chest and a skinned leg. Rolling his eyes he moves past scenes from the Legend of St George by an unknown [Flemish] master, depicting St George being tortured in various ways.'[66]

Soon afterwards, Ken's and Ray's attentions are turned to Hieronymus Bosch's famous 'The Last Judgement'. The punitive consciousnesses of Provoost's, David's and Bosch's visions of a judgment and justice mesh with Ray's own sense of guilt and damnation for the crimes he has committed, as the religious and moral significances of the penitential or tourist trip expand for these two lapsed Catholic Dublin characters.

A scene set in the Basilica of the Holy Blood confirms that Ray has little time for miracles. The church houses a phial of blood brought back 'by a Flemish knight from the Crusades in the Holy Land', and supposedly it is the blood of Christ. Legend suggests that the dried blood occasionally and miraculously liquefies.[67] Instead of a miracle of redemption or absolution, damnation seems to be Ray's destiny. Ken becomes increasingly willing to articulate his own moral contradictions and ambivalences; on the one hand, he holds doors open for old ladies and, on the other, he executes people, most of whom have deserved to die, in his estimation at least. However, he is still haunted by, but has gained a measure of control over, his killing of Danny Aliband's brother, who came at Ken with a bottle, in an attempt to protect his brother. As an enforcer for Harry, Ken is duty bound out of loyalty, indebtedness and honour to carry out such actions. The codes of honour of gangland are complex and contradictory.[68]

One of the fundamental paradoxes of McDonagh's gangland is that Harry seemingly sanctions contract killings without too many moral concerns, but when a child is killed accidentally, he goes ballistic. Breaches of expected modes of moral relating are obvious. It also raises the question as to what the Irish priest might have done to warrant his assassination? The lack of clarity in the film makes it all the more unnerving perhaps and all the more ambivalent morally as a consequence. On the other hand, audiences are tempted to believe that the priest is a target, as Ray thinks or wants to believe, because he is a paedophile. (Both *Lonesome* and *Inishmaan* raise issues of sexually abusive priests. As previously mentioned, Helen almost makes casual her experiences of unwelcome attention, but Bartley has a different pained response.) The priest acknowledges him as 'Raymond', so they know each other. (p.22) However, in a deleted scene, the priest is on an action committee that is opposed to a property development project in which Harry has a vested interest.

In another of the deleted scenes one discovers that Harry has been a victim of child clerical sexual abuse in Bruges in the Bell Tower. (Matt Smith played Young Harry in the scenes cut from the film.) This clerical figure sports a red signet ring, similar to the one worn by the assassinated priest. (A screenplay direction indicates 'The crucifix on McHenry's signet ring glints now and then', thus endowing it with some significance. (p.22)) This is qualified by the fact that the age gap between the priest in the flashback and the boy does not hold through in the age differences between Fiennes and Hinds, who are of a similar generation.

So in many ways, Harry's raging at the killing of the child by Ray may have this abusive experience as its source. There is something very strange in him sending Ray before he dies to the site of his own violation, an experience that is so wounding that it is distorted into a falsely positive one, by means of disassociation and objectification. Thus Harry's unhinged championing of the innocent must be seen in a different light. While the film itself does not ultimately provide this back story, there is enough perhaps in Fiennes's engagingly enraged performance to suggest that some sort of fundamentally damaging experience took place in Bruges.[69]

'BEYOND THE FRAGILE GEOMETRY OF SPACE'

Catherine O'Brien confirms that 'It is Catholic architecture that pervades *In Bruges* from the opening moments [...] and the film begins with a disorientating low-angle view of the Church of Our Lady, which dates back to the year 1220. Although the church is never named in the screenplay, it is described by Jimmy as "the pointy building" – the spire indicating the way to Heaven – but in the first sequence the audience are unaware that Ray's ultimate brush with death will take place in the precincts of this place of worship.'[70] And McDonagh responds in the following way to a question about the exploration of religious themes in the work, asking. 'How would I feel if I had done something so heinous? So yes, as I was able to explore – certainly explore, not come to any solutions about, but explore what I believe in[,] having been brought up Catholic and having rejected that, but still having those kind of tendrils of faith or what you were taught as a child still in your head.'[71] Ken remarks something similar: 'I was brought up believing certain things, I was brought up Catholic, which I've more or less rejected most of... But the things you're taught as a child, they never really leave you, do they?' (p.25). Whatever thoughts Ray has had about what he has done, whatever consolation there is to be had in Ken's guidance and reflections, and whatever distractions he can gain from a date with Chloë, Ray's overwhelming despair traps him within a suicidal state of mind and he has every intention of killing himself.

Notably, it is Ken's 'almost involuntarily' scream at Ray which puts a stop to the attempted suicide. (p. 53) The scream exemplifies Ken's divided loyalties, but also his growing sense of protectiveness over Ray. In this instance, Ken's instinctive or innate values trump duty and obligation.[72] Under Harry's instruction, Ken is there in the park to kill Ray, earlier having picked up a gun from Yuri (Eric Godon), a local associate of Harry. There is an obvious deep anomaly dramatised here – that is to be rescued by one's potential murderer.[73]

Having put Ray on a train so that he can disappear somewhere in Europe, and knowing what Harry's response will be, Ken's invitation to Harry is a simple and grotesquely comic one: 'I'll be here waiting. 'Cos I'm getting to quite like Bruges now. It's like a fucking fairy tale or something.' (p.60) And later, Ken effectively surrenders to Harry in the Bell Tower, and suggests his willingness to accept Harry's punishment and the justice of gangland for his act of disobedience. Unnerved by Ken telling him about his indebtedness and how he loves him, Harry asks him not to 'come over all' Gandhi-like. (p. 73)

If it looks as if there is a brief moment when Harry can be placated and dissuaded from his predominant intent, he gains control of the evolving situation: 'Harry: Like I'm not gonna do nothing to ya just 'cos you're standing about like Robert fucking Powell!' (p. 74) (Powell played Jesus in Franco Zeffirelli's *Jesus of Nazareth* (1977); so with this statement religion is further re-mediated through this television series.) Ken's first visit to the

Bell Tower is noticeable for the fact that Ken 'cocks his finger, shoots Ray with an imaginary gun, just for fun,' (p.8) a reference to Travis Bickle's similar sort of gesture in Martin Scorsese's *Taxi Driver* (1976). What is initially playful is effectively a foreshadowing of what is to come.[74]

When Harry first shoots Ken in the leg and then escorts him down the Bell Tower's stairs it seems to suggest that he has extracted appropriate and full revenge. But when Eirik (Jérémie Rénier) confirms to Harry that Ray is still *in situ*, Ken is shot in the neck, after failed attempts to stop Harry going after Ray. The fresh start that Ken had hoped for Ray is not possible in the world of movies generally, not in the world of Bosch, not in fairytales, and especially not in Harry's world. Seldom will a killer, especially of children, get away with his or her actions in Hollywood movies; they may later sacrifice themselves for someone else or they may confess and gain some morsel of forgiveness, but rarely will they be freed from punishment as a consequence of their actions. If there is blood on someone's hands, it tends to mean death. Edward Zwick's *Blood Diamond* (2006) is a good example.

To warn Ray, the wounded Ken throws himself from the top of the Bell Tower, having made a huge effort to climb back to the top, and having carefully dropped coins to clear the public out of the way. Even at the moment of poignant self-sacrifice, there is the obstinacy of McDonagh's comic impulse, for the gun that Ken has stored in his pocket to help Ray with his self-defence falls apart on landing, and of course this is similar to what happens to Kid's stolen gun in Donnelly's hands towards the very end of *Six Shooter*.

As Pinker suggests, while human sacrifice is evident in the mythology of almost all civilisations and that 'the most benighted form of institutionalized violence is human sacrifice: the torture and killing of an innocent person to slake a deity's thirst for blood',[75] but self sacrifice is of a different order. For Pinker, Christianity is based on a belief that 'God accepted the torture-sacrifice of an innocent man in exchange for not visiting a worse fate on the rest of humanity.'[76] Dennis Kreb's study of the 'empathy–altruism hypothesis', which Pinker renames as the sympathy–altruism hypothesis, is effectively identifying a motive that benefits 'another as an end in itself rather than as a means to some end'.[77] It is not about mutual benefits, nor is it a 'biological altruism', which is a behaviour that comes as a cost to oneself but to the benefit of another. This theory would refute the standard theory called 'psychological hedonism', in other words, that pleasure is the motivator for action, or 'psychological egoism', that people only carry out actions that are beneficial to themselves.[78]

Research has shown, according to Pinker, that 'sympathy can promote genuine altruism, and that it can be extended to new classes of people when a beholder takes the perspective of a member of that class, even a fictitious one.'[79] The actions of both Ken and later as we shall see of Hans in *Seven Psychopaths* are very similar.

Having been chased and wounded by Harry, a disorientated Ray finds himself on the snowy film set. As Ray staggers amongst the many film extras, the screenplay details are precise – the extras are 'in strange, nightmarish masked costumes, many frighteningly similar to the demons and those terrorised by them in Bosch's "Last Judgment".'[80] The script suggests that some performers have an identical bullet wound to that of Ray's, and they are 'dizzily, horrified'. (p.85) Although wounded, Ray still tries to warn others of the impending danger, but they do not understand what he says.

The extras are not sure as to whether the gun-wielding Harry is part of the film or not. For this final and late night of shooting of the film, 'The psycho-dwarf,' Jimmy [Jordan Prentice], 'turns out to be just a lovable little schoolboy and it was all some kind of Boschian nightmare.'(p.75) (The film in the making in the city is neither a homage to nor a pastiche of Nicholas Roeg's *Don't Look Now* (1973), according to Chloë, but this film does serve a significant intertextual purpose. Jimmy calls it a 'jumped up Eurotrash piece of rip-off fucking bullshit'. (p.45))[81]

As Harry extracts his justice on Ray, the dum dum bullets penetrate and then exit Ray's body, thereby blowing Jimmy's head off, similar to the way that the bullets fired at the priest kills the boy indirectly.[82] Despite Ray trying to explain to a horror-stricken Harry that Jimmy is an adult and not a child, as if such a differentiation should ultimately matter, Harry blows his head off, with the line 'You've got to stick to your principles'. (p.86)

As Ray lies on the ground, critically, if not fatally wounded, he is not alone however; there is Chloë and Marie (Thekla Reuten), the pregnant hotelier, close by to monitor him. (Earlier, the pregnant Marie had been robust, determined and defiant in the face of two mobsters, as both Harry and Ray had shared a common if predictable bond over concerns about her safety, which is not often the case for bystanders in many Hollywood movies.) Ray's mind wanders to Christmas presents that will not be opened and he thinks about going to visit the mother of the child he killed, to agree to whatever punishment she deems appropriate for him.

Ray's expressed aspiration, 'I really really hoped I wouldn't die', is at full remove from the suicidal thoughts he had a day previously, thus in the face of death, life is the preferred option. There is the sense that Ray has benefitted from Ken's gift and wishes to hang on to life. And if the tone is veering toward the emotive and the sentimental, it is undermined by Ray's final comments: 'Prison, death, it didn't matter. 'Cos at least in prison, and at least in death, y'know, I wouldn't be in fucking Bruges.' (p.87) That sort of swift swaying from emotion to emotion is the hallmark of the piece, and it says a great deal about how McDonagh wants to engage with an audience through his particular use of a tragic-comic sentiment.[83]

Such tragic-comedy both infects and inflects the interrogation of 'moral sense' and the construction of empathy. The establishment and maintenance of these dual elements are difficult to realise but vital to this film. In *Six Shooter*, the suicide of Mrs Dooley and Donnelly's attempted suicide are both driven by grief, whereas the suicide attempt of Ray is guided by his guilt and despair. There is a depth of feeling in both films that is hard to evade.

Yet, for Anthony Lane, 'Bosch and his contemporaries believed in the existence of the damned, and those painted, freakish sufferers were vessels of genuine dread, whereas *In Bruges* calls its characters to their final reckoning with no higher motive than to blow them merrily away.'[84] Lane adds: 'When a beautiful, pregnant woman tells him and Ken to lay down their guns, Harry replies, "Don't be stupid. This is a shootout." It's a gag, but also a giveaway: these people have no souls to lose, because they know they're in a movie.'[85] While Lane is right to suggest that there may well be no sense of moral final reckoning for McDonagh's characters, it does not mean that they are guilt-free and without that fundamental judgment.

And although Lane is correct to signal the self-awareness of performances, the intertextual and quasi or faux-postmodern sensibility, however, rather than weakening the piece, I think it adds to it significantly, as it is suggestive of a world where the grand narratives of religion can be negligible in their influence, and, if so, without those defining structures what is one left with? So why not interrogate these lingering and ineffective grand narratives of order and justice that a final judgment seems to affirm; why not layer in palimpsest-like contradiction, in order not so much to create specific meanings, but to suggest resonances, echoes, interconnections and elaborations – and no more than that. It is a universe without the comfort of either absolutes or of closure, whether it is redemption or damnation. The film's strength is in its denial of certainty. That said, there is still the lingering consolation of empathy, Ken for Ray, Chloë for Ray and Ray for her, in terms of intimacy, temporary connection, or even bonding.

To blend the comedy and the tragedy, the ironic awarenesses and the empathy, the acting needed to be particularly impressive. Interestingly, there are widely differing critical responses in relation to the performances. Philip French suggests that collectively, actors Fiennes, Gleeson and Farrell, the latter with 'his eyebrows constantly wrinkling like a pair of leeches limbering up for a fight', have 'rarely been better'.[86] Peter Bradshaw suggests that 'Farrell has brought his A-game to this cracking little comedy-noir

[....] He is absolutely superb: moody and funny, lethally sexy, sometimes heartbreakingly sad and vulnerable like a little boy. He radiates the star-quality that once made him the world's *It Boy*, and will do again.'[87]

Manohla Dargis however, sees Farrell's performance 'as crudely conceived as it is finally sentimental (the same goes for the film), but it's also winning because Mr. Farrell makes us see the goofy side of seduction'.[88] Anthony Lane is of the view that Farrell struck him 'as unfocussed and adrift, as he has so frequently in recent times, resorting too readily to twitches and tears. But Gleeson, who looks half like a whiskey priest and half like a pastry chef's mistake, holds our gaze without effort, not least when his own gaze is held by altarpieces, books and paintings in Belgian galleries.'[89]

The views of both Dargis and Lane do not at all tally with my response to Farrell's performance. I do not think that his characterisation is 'crudely conceived', rather it is broadly conceived: at times, it is painfully real, but again, at other times, it is a relatively un-grounded performance, pitched to be the opposite of Gleeson's more assured and circumspect character. Farrell more than Gleeson has to be capable of wild shifts in mood and emotional register. At times, it is as if they are more than alert to their own performances as performances, but Farrell in particular displays an open invitation to audiences to criticise his character. This is especially important for audiences, who must in many respects disassociate from Ray's deeds, as Ray himself does, yet the comedy and the irony invite something additional again into the transaction, a curious sort of twisted empathy.

The film is less about the 'goofy side of seduction', but perhaps more about an assessment of spectators, who warm all too easily perhaps to the 'goofy side' of violence in ways that are disassociated from the horrors of gangland injustices. In perhaps wanting the priest to be guilty of something and therefore make the killing a bit more palatable, McDonagh raises substantial issues about societal and filmic genre expectations. In McDonagh's work, unlike in some of Tarantino's films, death does have some significant consequences. I agree with James Rocchi's comments that 'McDonagh never loses sight of the fact that Ray and Ken are ugly men engaged in ugly business; more intriguingly, Ray and Ken never lose sight of it, either.'[90]

4 | Home Schooled and the Nation State: *The Pillowman*

The Pillowman is set in a prison cell of an unnamed totalitarian state,[91] where a writer, Katurian Katurian Katurian (KKK) – or Katurian for short – faces interrogation by two police officers, Tupolski and Ariel about a series of child murders. This play deals with zero empathy in different ways, as it is the state (Type S perhaps) which fundamentally has no little capacity for sympathy or empathy, despite its agents having personal narratives that seem to suggest so. Patrick Pacheco explains that during a lonely period in his late teens, McDonagh wrote 200 short stories, which he intended to fashion into a film titled *57 Tales of Sex and Violence*. However, only one was actually about sex – 'Anarcho-Feminists' Sex Machines in Outer Space' – the rest were about violence as McDonagh recalls . Of these, 'eight stories eventually made their way into *The Pillowman*'. These stories, Pacheco notes were tales written 'in a hothouse of anger and alienation. Unemployed, the fledgling writer spent most of his day at the typewriter when he wasn't watching Australian soap operas ("for the girls in the bikinis").'[92] The director of the play's premiere, John Crowley, suggests 'in its first incarnation *The Pillowman* resembled "stories strung together" '[....] In its revised form, those same stories "keep looping back on themselves", as a detail dropped here later pops up there, to create "a wilderness of stories."'[93] Indeed, Victoria Segal states that the play is a reworking of a '1995 submission to the Soho Theatre's Verity Bargate Award.'[94] An early version of the work got its first public reading at the Finborough Theatre, London in 1995,[95] and received a rehearsed reading in Galway in April 1997 as part of the Cúirt International Festival of Literature.[96]

The Pillowman premiered at the National Theatre's Cottesloe auditorium in London on 13 November 2003.[97] The National Theatre production won the 2004 Olivier Award for Best New Play. The New York production, which opened at Broadway's Booth Theater on 10 April,

2005,[98] won the 2004–5 New York Drama Critics' Circle Award for Best New Foreign Play, two Tony Awards, for lighting and scenography, received a Tony nomination for Best Play and the 2005 Drama Desk Award for Outstanding Sound Design. Since 2003 *The Pillowman* has had a number of other notable productions around the world, in Argentina, Germany,[99] Japan,[100] Canada, France, South Korea, Sweden[101] and again England and across America,[102] to name but a few.[103] Images from most of these productions alone would suggest that very different sorts of *mise-en-scène* are inspired by the text.

While the casts for both the London and New York productions are completely different, the creative team is relatively consistent. Both productions are directed by Crowley, Scott Pask is responsible for the set and costume design, Paul Arditti for sound and Paddy Cunneen the music. (Hugh Vanstone lights the London production and Brian MacDevitt the New York one.) Obviously, the American production builds on the creative team's experiences of working on the first one and the second becomes a good deal more sophisticated design-wise, helped obviously by a bigger budget; while both share considerable continuities in terms of their dominant sensibilities and theatrical style.[104]

My reflections on and analysis of the work are substantially prompted by Crowley's *mise-en-scène* for the London production, and at times I will consider how this differs to the New York one mainly by way of endnote, but occasionally within the main text when a substantial point needs to be made about the New York version.[105] Crucial to Crowley's London *mise-en-scène* is the approach to how the narratives are told and how those that are enacted are accommodated stylistically. The challenge is not so much to situate the quasi-real interrogation space alongside the worlds of these sometimes enacted gruesome fairytales, but how to interdigitate them in order to synergise an embellished, dialogical consciousnesses.[106] The surrealistic costuming and the confined and multiple performance spaces, as designed by Pask, eradicate notions of verisimilitude and blend superbly with the lighting and sound designs which are there to heighten sensation and to generate potentially unease or exhilaration for the spectator – it is a world where sensation, shock and adrenaline are the mediating forces.

For these narrative re-enactments, Pask's garish worlds combine with Crowley's deployment of a sort of monstrous and transgressive acting style that is not consistent with the more naturalistic approaches to performance evident in the interrogation scenes. Put simply, these re-enactments blend a Grand-Guignol style, as already defined in Part 2, with a harrowing carnivalesque sensibility. Mikhal Bakhtin's conceptualisation of Carnival is of course about the celebration of the real, while making space for difference, desire, reversals, transgression and temporary disorder.[107] Sue Vice articulates the parameters of Bakhtin's thinking on *mésalliances*, something which leads to strange combinations of the 'lofty with the low, the great with the insignificant, the wise with the stupid'.[108] Thus the mock trials, mock interrogations, mock crowning and mock deaths are clearly derivative carnivalesque components. Also central to carnival are functioning, reproductive and decaying bodies and of course the abject. As Vice argues, 'the abject confronts us [...] with those fragile states where man strays on the territories of animal',[109] to this it could be added the territory of the non-human.

In *The Pillowman* it is the pained and violated bodies of children, which are indicators of abject states and the straying into 'the territories' of animalistic behaviours. Thus, the meshing of the carnivalesque and Grand-Guignol is an appropriate way of framing the violence and the terror, but is also substantial in facilitating the fundamental fairytale consciousness of the stories themselves, as the dark horrors of fairytales meet the equally dark terrors of interrogation in this totalitarian space. On the one hand, by such intermingling the play demonstrates both the expressions of discernible if illegitimate power and authority, and on the other, it allows this space to facilitate the questioning of the purposes of individual creativity in response to ideologically shaped politico-cultural narratives and performances of power more generally.

Steven Pinker sees ideology as a fundamental form of violence, and he has in mind totalitarianism. For Pinker 'The really big body count in history pile up with a large number of people carry out a motive that transcends any one of them: an ideology [....] Ideological violence is a means to an end. But with any ideology, the end is idealistic: a conception of the greater good',[110] which leads to the elimination of opponents, all in the name of the greater good, through an insistence on 'means-ends reasoning, which encourages us to carry out unpleasant means as a way to bring about desirable ends'.[111] It is not so much the psychological, as the 'epidemiological: how toxic ideology can spread from a small number of narcissistic zealots to an entire population willing to carry out its designs.'[112] For example, 'Group think', polarisation, the moralisation of 'conformity and obedience,' the taking cues from others, allowing one's better judgment to be over-ridden by mutual consensus and collective delusions, pluralistic ignorance or the spiral of silence, when people think everyone else believes the opposite, all of these are part of the complex socio-political dynamic.[113]

So, when it comes to the naming of the characters in *The Pillowman* Ondřej Pilný states that:

> The linguistic mélange of names only underscores the fictitious nature of the setting: the writer's name appears to be Armenian in overdose [....] The brother is called Michal – Czech, Slovak or Polish; the victims are Andrea Jovanovic – Serb, Croat or Slovene and Aaron Goldberg – a credible Germanic-Jewish name for the Central European region. The detectives' names, Tupolski and Ariel blend Polish with Shakespeare.[114]

In terms of location, the town in which the play is set, Kamenice, is, according to Pilný, 'Czech, but features a Jewish quarter with the non-Czech name of Lamenec (besides, Jewish quarters vanished from Czech towns after the Holocaust)'.[115] (There is also a town in Albania bearing that name.) The almost similar name of 'Kamenica', is not only Czech, but is also common in Poland, Slovakia and in Serbia, a 'Kamenica' was recently the site of ethnic political struggle leading to ethnic cleansing, as both Hana and W.B. Worthen note.[116] While Pilný argues that the play is set 'probably sometime in the mid-twentieth century',[117] most other critics are less inclined to give the play such temporal specificities.

Žižek's reflections on the particular violence of totalitarianism are of specific interest in relation to *The Pillowman*; he notes that one of the strategies of totalitarian regimes is to have legal regulation (criminal laws) so severe that, if taken literally, *everyone* is guilty of something. But then their full enforcement is withdrawn. In this way, the regime can appear merciful: 'You see, if we wanted, we could have all of you arrested and condemned, but do not be afraid, we are lenient [....]' At the same time, the regime wields the permanent threat of disciplining its subjects.[118] Thus for Žižek, 'Here we have an overlap of potential total culpability (whatever you are doing *may* be a crime) and of mercy (the fact that you are allowed to lead your life in peace is not a proof or consequence of your innocence, but a proof of the mercy and benevolence of an "understanding of the realities of life", of those in power).'[119]

Thus the state is both all-seeing, and monopolises a capacity for empathy. The state also circulates narratives that justify violence, encourage prejudice, disguise inequalities and rationalise the denial of rights. Prejudice, bias and above all sentiment are central to any regime's incitement of complicity or the alignment of its citizens with its dominant values. A justification of totalitarian rule is the governing or master narrative, and all of the stories in this play dialogue with that ideological disposition.

Having lived under Russian totalitarian rule until the collapse of the Hungarian party-state in 1989, Péter P. Müller notes that he clearly 'experienced a rather different world in this East Europe and dictatorship than the one depicted' in *The Pillowman*.[120] Müller continues however, 'although the play does not get its verification from a comparison to historical, political features and events of particular countries, it does not mean that the world in and of *The Pillowman* cannot be considered to be a valid and authentic one'.[121] So despite situating the play in a notionally totalitarian space, the socio-political realities of totalitarianism are not substantially evident, indeed nor should they be expected to be as such, yet in its more abstract depictions of the mechanisms of the manipulation and control of its citizens, McDonagh's world cannot be dismissed simply for its socio-political inaccuracies as Müller proposes. McDonagh offers a theatrically licenced totalitarianism; it is more a world where totalitarianism can symbolise anything from imperialism to state oppression, and even perhaps dogmatic academic or critical interrogations of dramaturgical and performance practices.[122]

ARRESTED DEVELOPMENTS AND AN ETERNITY OF STORIES

In contrast to totalitarian states, democracies generally, and the mutual philosophies that govern them, are based on basic freedoms and rights, particularly in relation to arrest, detention and interrogation. In many countries there are very strict procedures – otherwise, evidence gathered or confessions made cannot be deemed admissible. In most judicial processes there is the expectation of and entitlement to a fair trial, to impartial, objective justice, and to the presumption of innocence in very many jurisdictions. However, during Katurian's interrogation by the seemingly measured Tupolski and psychotically aggressive Ariel, these basic rights do not seem to apply, as threats, intimidation and torture occur during the process.

Although pressured early into giving the impression that he is socially compliant, not a dissident and not a subversive, Katurian still endeavours to maintain the facade of an edgy, defiant writer. (While the dissident role of the writer in the totalitarian state has often been romanticised, McDonagh delights in undermining that approach.) The police wish to tease out the link between Katurian's stories and the nature of the killings of Andrea Jovacovic, whose body has been recovered on a heath with blades down her mouth and Aaron Goldberg (echoes of one of Harold Pinter's characters in *The Birthday Party* (1958)) whose body was found dumped behind the Jewish quarter. The discovery of Aaron's amputated toes in the home of Katurian and his brother, the brain-damaged Michal, has them both now in detention. Another child Maria, a mute girl, is also missing, and presumed dead. [123]

In the first production, Jim Broadbent as Tupolski and Nigel Lindsay as Ariel perform in ways typical of some of the interrogation scenes in

Harold Pinter's work, particularly in *The Birthday Party*, a play in which Stanley Webber is interrogated by Goldberg and McCann. Broadbent and Lindsay blend successfully the sinister, the asinine and a threatening playfulness; regardless there is a sense of their performances having a strong connection to a realistic context that is evident in the actors' approaches to how they motivate or justify the actions of their characters. Broadbent's performance is relaxed, low key, sub-textually astute and rich by way of implication, ominous in his intentional verbal throwaways, but also strikingly ambivalent in his calculation.

Broadbent's inflections suggest that his character is attuned to the nuances and manipulations of ideology, but also to the fact that he morphs and adapts to the circumstances as he sees fit. He is more a player than an ideological believer. Equally, the details surrounding the death of Tupolski's child and his lengthy story of rescue and safety are his attempts to humanise himself primarily for himself, but the spectator may be aware of him or her being tricked into a false complacency by his capacity for compassion, by a faux-empathy.[124] Nigel Lindsay's East End-accented Ariel appears as if he is on a lead from the start and seems to be perpetually enraged or close to the edge. Lindsay successfully affirms Ariel's obsession with the protection of children and he fantasises about retirement and children coming up to give him sweets in order to reward his good deeds.[125] The aggressive dominance of Broadbent and Lindsay is eased by a sense of casual routine or of the everyday mundanity of ceaseless interrogation.

In the London production from the earliest stages, and in the face of such intimidation, David Tennant's extraordinary performance as Katurian demonstrates a consistent strained exaggerated fervour, not so much as wide-eyed innocence in the face of a pressured interrogation, more a wide-eyed demented and defensive reflex. His acting style is radically different to that of the other two main actors. Tennant successfully reveals the deviance and the casualness of someone who is pressured to adjust relentlessly one's tone and disposition, as he attempts to make sense of his interrogation and to placate however possible his interrogators. Although intensely expressive, Tennant often sits on his hands in order to establish a level of control over his gestures, as he seems afraid of leaking information through non-verbal means. He is attentive to the fact that his writing career may be at an end and a degree of narcissism emerges around the merits of his stories.[126]

FOOD FOR THOUGHTS

Stories, in their various forms are ways of sharing or gaining insight into how 'other people' think, live and do. So as Richard Kearney suggests: 'The art of storytelling [...] is what gives us a shareable world,'[127] and that 'every human existence is a life in search of a narrative.'[128] Bruno Bettelheim believes that fairy tales are far better than myths, legends, folk fables, parables or biblical stories in unlocking the questions and answers offered by other forms of narrative.[129] In his application of a psychoanalytical approach to fairytales, Bettelheim then uncovers aspects of the preconscious, conscious and unconscious minds in such stories. For both adult and or child, he argues, the unconscious 'is a powerful determinant of behaviour'; so when things are temporarily denied, suppressed or repressed, 'eventually the person's conscious mind will be partially overwhelmed by derivatives of these unconscious elements,' otherwise, one 'is forced to keep such rigid, compulsive control over them', to such an extent that one's 'personality may become severely crippled' by the pressure.[130] (While Pinker is all for self-control, this raises the implications of it for some.) 'If we hope to live not just from moment to moment, but in true consciousness of our existence then our greatest need and most difficult achievement is to find meaning in our lives,' Bettelheim adds.[131]

In order to 'find deeper meaning, one must become able to transcend the narrow confines of a self-centred existence and believe that one will make a significant contribution to life – if not right now, then at some future time'.[132] This may inform the belief of a writer like Katurian in his work. For Bettelheim, children have irrational mindsets, and for a story or fairytale to capture truly a child's attention in the first instance, it must entertain, it must encourage a form of curiosity. Yet if fairytales are to work on a deeper level, and to assist in maturation, it must do so by stimulating the imagination, in order to 'help him [sic] to develop his intellect and to clarify his emotions; be attuned to his anxieties and aspirations; give full recognition to his difficulties, while at the same time suggesting solutions to problems which perturb him.'[133]

The admission of the unconscious, the personal and collective, and not just the socio-political, through fairytale can potentially 'ensure that the negative dispositions are transformed into other more positive purposes' Bettelheim claims.[134] In dealing with anxieties, and in highlighting complexities, stories can offer solutions to unresolved issues. As the imagination and stories can accommodate the repressed as well as the allegorical and metaphorical, the potential of the unconscious to wreak havoc is reduced, in terms of the impact on the self or on how the self transacts negatively with others.[135]

Bettelheim continues that if modes of socialisation attempt to either overwhelmingly deny or downplay a child's aggressive, selfish, chaotic or destructive disposition, then the child is denied permission to access his or her 'own contradictory states' or to see the ambivalence of his or her behaviour from another's vantage point; whereas in fairytales generally, 'evil is as omnipresent as virtue', and therefore these stories accommodate both simultaneously.[136] However, Bettelheim makes a vital distinction:

> The figures in fairytales are not ambivalent-not good and bad at the same time, as we all are in reality. But since polarisation dominates the child's mind, it also dominates fairytales. A person is either good or bad, nothing in between [....] The juxtaposition of opposite characters is not for the purpose of stressing right behaviour, as would be true of cautionary tales. Presenting the polarities of character permits the child to comprehend easily the differences between the two, which he could not do as readily were the figures drawn more true to life, with all the complexities that characterise real people.[137]

Polarisation also shapes Pinker's concept of 'moral sense' and clarifies the relational models. Bettelheim adds then that: 'a child's choices are based, not so much on right versus wrong, as on who arouses his sympathy and who his antipathy.'[138] So, Bettelheim suggests: 'The question for the child is not "Do I want to be good?" but "Who do I want to be like?",[139] and he adds 'In fairytales, as in life, punishment or fear of it, is only a limited deterrent to crime. The conviction that crime does not pay is a much more effective deterrent, and that is why in fairytales the bad person always loses out. It is not the fact that virtue wins out as the end which promoted morality, but that the hero is most attractive to the child, who identifies with the hero in all his struggles.'[140] Bettelheim claims morality is not the essential issue in these fairytales, rather, the 'assurance that one can succeed'.[141] But the central existential problem for him is 'Whether one meets life with a belief in the possibility of mastering its difficulties or with the expectation of defeat.'[142] Baron-Cohen's 'inner pot of gold' determines so much.

The first story narrated by Katurian, 'The Little Apple Men', is in part revenge-fairytale and in part a surrealistic Grand-Guignol version of Greek tragedy, but it can also seem potentially to have a political agenda of sorts, but it initially appears to be on the 'child's side'. It seems to offer the diametric oppositions of fairytales, but it has a twist. Revenge in 'The Little Apple Girl' story could simply be read as an anarchic or subversive gesture by the child directed either towards the phallic rule of the father or the totalitarian state. It is a state, in the first instance, which does not protect her from paternal violation.[143] The follow on punishment of the little girl by the little apple men's friends may be regarded as a perpetuation of a cycle of retribution rather than justice. (Indeed the systemic failures of some social services and voluntary organisations to protect all the young, vulnerable and innocent in first world cultures more generally, and Britain specifically, hang over the play more generally.)

'The Tale of the Town on the River', Katurian's only story to be published, also features the figure of a violated child and is a re-working of 'The Pied Piper of Hamelin'.[144] However, the Pied Piper figure is not simply all 'evil'. In Katurian's version a toe-less child survives when all the other children are led away to their doom by the Pied Piper, suggesting that an initial act of brutality by a stranger, with whom the child had kindly shared his meagre rations, brings with it a perverse sort of unanticipated salvation. It could indicate that the child must be philosophical and pragmatic, and neither name nor be shaped by traumatic incidents. Occurrences cannot be seen as simply good or bad, but instead to be viewed from a more distanced perspective, however brutal those encounters might initially appear to be. But by focusing on the child's survival, it could also be argued that the story's twist is not subversive at all, because it substantiates forms of power and violation transacted in totalitarian states, whereby it is less the immediate outcome and more the long-term good that must be the collective focus.

Read this way, this may well be why it is publishable, but it is also the story most easily aligned with Tupolski's story 'The Story of the Little Deaf Boy on the Big Long Railroad Tracks In China', where the child's survival is dependent on the discriminate knowingness of a benign authority figure, who is in this instance beholden to the upholding of the power of the state and to be dispassionate and objective in judgment and calculation and, by implication, in its rule of law. The superior knowledge of the man in the watch tower (Michel Foucault's Panopticon perhaps) is in a way a justification of actions that are non-democratic.[145]

The particular fantasy of the writer unfettered by circumstance appears to be an increasingly deluded one as the evidence of Katurian's family's past begins to accumulate. There appears to be very obvious similarities and cross contaminations between the circumstances of his dysfunctional family and the work of the writer, which is best seen in the crucial story, 'The Writer and the Writer's Brother', where the line between fact and fiction is crossed over too many times for comfort, which also happens with Hans's and Myra's story in *Seven Psychopaths*. While notionally a fiction, Katurian's story is very similar to the ways that he and Michal were separately and diametrically parented and socially oriented. But like a fairytale, the oppressor is destroyed and the protagonist is rescued. Rather than a happy ending, the story is extended by the fact that the fairytales of the rescuer are transformed into something else. (By extension, families are not simply independent of the state, as more often than not, they either mimic the structures of that state or play a role in affirming and legitimising the state, consciously or unconsciously. Family structures and values are perpetuated through rituals, ceremonies, institutional practices and parenting strategies, including, of course, bedtime stories.)

As this story 'The Writer and the Writer's Brother', is the first story to be enacted, how it is staged is very important. Tennant narrates the short story from the cell, while 'the mother, in diamonds, and father, in a goatee and glasses, enact' it. (p. 31) In both of Crowley's productions the scenes from the story take place initially on elevated platforms, with the bedroom spaces opening up from behind screens, backstage left and right. The actor playing Michal has the role of the teenage Katurian in the flashback/narrative sequences and a young male actor plays the younger Michal. In both London and New York performances, the rooms overhead are exceptionally small and cramped spaces, with the actors' heads almost touching the ceilings. In both productions while the actors in the enacted sequences perform the gestures in silent alignment with the gory soundscape, Tennant and Crudup provide the character voices. And in both productions there is a similar use of eerie noises, drillings sounds, and the muffled sounds of a gagged and bound child. A body of the child arches in the bed at one point as it experiences electrocution.[146] Clearly these brief descriptions of the staging suggest that this is anything but a conventionally realistic universe.

The other story that is performed in this style is 'The Little Jesus' narrative, which draws on Christian iconography, and there is perhaps a certain blasphemy to it, despite its ironic playfulness. It is a story about a little girl, who believes that she is the 'second coming of the Lord Jesus Christ.' (p.68) The narrative is a sort of Snow White meets the Jesus Christ of the New Testament, who as a child attended the synagogue, debated with the learned elders and wanted to be independent of his parents, before setting good example, performing miracles and dying on a cross. Effectively, the girl believes herself to be Jesus – a sort of messiah complex of sorts, as noted earlier, and it ties in with the crucifixion and martyrdom fantasies that coexist as both optimism and perversion across the works more generally, whether it is the blood sacrifice of paramilitaries or the perverse self-sacrifice of Fr Welsh.

While both productions share a similar sensibility for 'The Little Jesus' story, they are realised in slightly different ways. For both, this story is enacted on the main playing space, with the confining walls of the holding cell removed, as the second part of the performance begins. The nice parents and the cruel foster-parents in 'The Little Jesus' story are played by the actors who initially played the Katurian parents and the character shifts are indicated only by slight adjustments to costume. The little girl wears a large false beard and carries a doll initially. (The text suggests that the blind man should be performed by the actor playing Katurian, while in performance it was the actor playing Michal who took the role in both.) In the London production, a diorama rotates behind the actors, illustrating the key scenarios. The New York performance involves a more elaborate staging and the story is performed initially against a stained-glass background.

As the young girl heads off on her spiritual journey, there is a miming of an encounter with drug addicts injecting themselves in an exaggerated style. The car and the meat lorry collision that kills her parents, who are beheaded – another example of this mutilation trope in the work more generally – is accompanied by the garish sounds of carnage. In the New York production two gravestones appear on the stained-glass backdrop, before the focus shifts to a forest with eerily coloured trees and then shifts to include sounds of broken glass. When the girl is tortured by the parents there are beating gestures, but no sounds are heard; her head moves from side to side to indicate a response to the blows, but without any register of pain, so the blows are grotesquely contrived.[147]

The appearance of the blind man is accompanied by liturgical sounding music. With the girl's return to the house, back-dropped by a distorted tableau with green armchairs, purple lamps and crooked paintings, she is fitted with the crown of thorns. She is whipped, accompanied by raucous sound effects, but there is again no register of pain, all the blows are deliberately fake, and she drags with exaggerated feebleness and with great difficulty the wooden cross around the room. The foster parents crucify her and then bury her alive in a glass coffin, with the ironic invitation to return from the grave within three days if she truly is who she believes herself to be. There is no knight in shining armour, no noble prince, no rescue, no redemption, and most of all no resurrection for her from the grave. (Yet, the little girl victim in 'The Little Jesus' story is of course resurrected as the girl whose fate is in the hands of Michal, who enacts not this story but that of 'The Little Green Pig' tale instead.) Bettelheim's model is psychoanalytical and developmental, but I have been suggesting that Katurian's narratives blurs distinctions between protagonist and antagonist, good and evil, and his stories offer no closure, no happy ever after. I have also been suggesting throughout a way of reading the stories allegorically as well.

Before his interrogators, Katurian rejects the idea that the figure of the child signifies the general populace, that there is any semblance of subversive justice when the adult figures get their 'comeuppance', and that whatever the outcome there is for the children, good or bad, the stories are less about preaching a moral message and more about the creativity of the writer to twist anticipated, expected, easy or unearned endings.[148] Throughout Katurian's grilling, his interrogators seem only interested in what his stories might mean, and whether or not the stories are a codification of anti-state sentiment. In terms of allegory Worthen and Worthen note that 'Tupolski reads allegorically but not dialectically: to Tupolski, the particulars of Katurian's stories are not mediated by narrative form and seem hardly to achieve the status of artistic *signs* at all; the stories are merely irritating murder manuals. Katurian, on the other hand, refuses allegory altogether and so refuses its generalising potentiality.'[149]

Katurian denies, almost forbids, the notion of deconstructing his narratives for patterns, tropes, obsessions or aspects of the repressed. He believes that his stories possess no subtextual, socio-political comment or subversive agenda, thus there is no need to seek out metaphoric, allegorical or symbolic significances. Katurian appears willing to withdraw anything in the work that might be deemed politically insensitive, offensive, seditious, dissident or merely out of line. It is as if Tennant's character is saturated with the same crazed energies of the stories, as if he is in a way possessed by them or they by him.

Michal's harrowing responses to Katurian's stories illustrate not only Michal's inability to read literally, allegorically or metaphorically and it points towards irrationality on the one hand and a failure of empathy on the other. And if Katurian is the rescuer of Michal from the bad fairytale parents, Katurian's heroic status is affirmed by Michal's idealisation of his writer brother on the one hand, but on the other, Michal's attempt to engage partially with the external world through the stories is deeply problematic.

In Michal's instance, despite a happy ending of sorts, relating to his rescue, there are no solutions or resolutions readily available to him, and his scrambled consciousness cannot avail of any form of clarification and there is no sense that he can be assured that he can be healed. Michal cannot succeed in overcoming his traumatic past, but can through the enactment of the stories find a way of re-staging the violations perpetrated against his own body. The actor playing Michal must initially garner empathy on first appearance and later incite revulsion towards his actions. Still the spectator must equally be enthralled by how the stories are utilised by him as templates for the ritual slaughter of innocent children, acts carried out with considerable indifference or with 'zero-empathy'.

At times, Adam Godley as Michal in the London production slurs his words, and on other occasions, seems especially lucid, and his vague, indifferent annoyance toward his brother as he overhears the torture, points to a lack of empathy, which is initially like the Kid character in his response to the public suffering of the Dooleys.[150] What Godley expresses is not only his character's love and dependence on Katurian, but also how disconnected he is from the deeds that he carries out. This ensures that his existence is not firmly grounded simply in his body, in his imagination or in any reality which he can verify, apart from the apparent logic and irregular coherence of narrative provided by his brother's stories.

Beyond fairytales, these stories are effectively templates for some of his killings and document unofficially and unconsciously the cruelty that he has suffered. Within the boundaries of this storied world, the pain and trauma suffered by Michal's victims are inconsequential. Eventually when Michal confesses his murderous deeds to Katurian, his disassociation from and the sheer perversion of his re-enactments are fully evident in his comment: '[...] The little boy was just like you (Katurian) said it'd be.' (p. 48) He claims further that he was 'just doing' Katurian's stories to test 'how far-fetched' the stories were. (p. 50)

If sanity is a capacity to distinguish between reality and fiction, then by that measure Michal is simply not sane. Psychopaths can recognise that they are causing pain, but there is no effective or emotional response to what they are doing. In contrast, Michal does not precisely see the damage he is truly causing. However, he eschews the imaginative register of the narratives.[151] Michal does claim that he knows 'it was wrong. Really. But it was very interesting.' (p.48) Thus his moral co-ordination is malfunctioning.

For Baron-Cohen, those with 'zero positive' degrees of empathy are primarily people who are on the autistic spectrum, who have capacities to be super-moral, even if their empathy levels are set very low or at zero. For instance, those with Asperger's Syndrome can have strong or super strong moral codes in their lives, as morality becomes a pattern, which they can '*systemize* to an extraordinary degree',[152] but it is a schema, Baron-Cohen argues, which is based primarily on order and fairness, without necessarily being one prompted by empathy.[153] These individuals rely heavily on orderly patterns which can be a fixation and security, and which can become toxic if anything changes, as the unexpected can incite a sense of havoc. Michal tries to order his world, 'systematise' it, based on patterns not so much of fairness but of those found in his brother's fairytales. He wants the order that such narratives can proffer.

Alongside that of his colleagues, Baron-Cohen's work on autism has proved that people with Zero-positive empathy have a 'difficulty in understanding their *own* minds,' that is called 'alexithymia', which translates as a state of mind that is 'without words for emotion.'[154] Those with this condition face particular challenges when it comes to decoding facial expressions or day-to-day emotions, and have very low functionality in their mirror neural response system, so when 'asked to imitate other people's emotional facial expressions', they tend to respond poorly.[155] For instance, 'When people with autism are asked to rate how they feel after viewing emotionally charged pictures, they show less activity during such "emotional introspection" within a number of regions in the empathy circuit', Baron-Cohen's research suggests.[156]

Those with deficits in the empathy circuit display 'atypical neural activity' along with lower sensorimotor response to others' pain, in other words, less flinching by the observer in response to another's hand being pricked by a needle for instance.'[157] (Pinker also effectively demonstrates that 'lower-level embodied processes affect empathy in autism and higher-level self-reflection processes are also impaired'.[158]) Despite Michal's deficits, the connections between the two brothers are still very powerful and in particular the gestural mimicking in the staging of *The Pillowman* in New York clearly hints at the basic mechanisms of neural mirroring, with such gestures becoming an affirmation of the bond and communicative strategies shared by both brothers.

When Michal and Katurian sit down, Crudup makes a prayer-like gesture with his hands and Stuhlbarg's Michal mirrors it back to him. Indeed, for most of the scene, both are sitting on the floor and it becomes very poignant when Stuhlbarg mimes how he has killed the children, without butchering them. Later as Crudup poignantly tells 'The Little Green Pig' story, he runs his hands over Michal's face as if to hypnotise him, as if to create a spell that brings a form of childlike sleep.[159] Stuhlbarg then repeats the same gesture back to him. Once Michal is lulled into sleep, Katurian then sits over his chest and shoulders, smothers him, till eventually the frantically struggling body gives in to death. It is a long-drawn-out moment and as close to realism as possible, leaving Katurian to face down his fate as he promises to confess all to his interrogators, with the hope that his own impending doom will not be the destiny of his stories.

Katurian regards the suffocation of Michal as a mercy killing and as a fundamental gesture of empathy.[160] However, although the goriness of 'The Little Jesus' narrative is the anticipated template for the missing girl's murder, she survives thanks to the fact that Michal instead enacts 'The Little Green Pig' story, proving that he like his brother, enjoys one final twist to a story.

Whether the character's behaviour is because he has suffered brain damage as a consequence of his parent's torture or that Michal is a character with an innate form of autism is not as important as the fact that he cannot easily respond to or make sense of another's suffering. He is cruel, but it is not prompted by the callousness and insensitivity of the Type P, Zero negatives.[161] (Many of McDonagh's characters seem to be unable to articulate who and what they think they are.) Following on from Bettelheim's ideas, Michal should be capable of taking the side of the child in Katurian's stories, but instead has no fixed focus, his mode of identification is random, a randomness that leads back partially to discussions about Maureen's motivations in *Beauty Queen*.

THE WHIPLASH EFFECT

In *Seven Psychopaths* the non-intervention of a deity is reflected on by Hans and Myra. Myra asks: 'You ever worry that we was wrong all of those years and there ain't no heaven and there ain't no nothing.' For Hans, God does not intervene: '[....] God loves us but he has a funny way of showing us sometimes [....] He's had a lot to contend with in his time. Bastards killed his kid too.' In *The Pillowman*, the Gods remain absent apart from being an omnipotent and intervening presence when coming to the rescue of the little green pig in 'The Little Green Pig' story'.[162] Kearney notes, 'From the word go, stories were invented to fill the gaping hole within us, to assuage our fear and dread, to try to give answers to the great unanswerable questions of existence: Who are we? Where do we come from? Are we animal, human or divine? Strangers, gods or monsters?'[163]

In *The Pillowman*, it is the figure of the fantastical Pillowman in the story bearing his name who is the intervening figure, and he is some combination of monster, human, animal, and the divine. Previously, when Katurian tells 'The Pillowman' story, he impersonates the Pillowman figure. Michal earlier identifies with the Pillowman, regarding him as somewhat of a hero: 'He reminds me a lot of me', as if somehow his killing of the children is a mercy killing of sorts, and is a way of avoiding pain (p. 52). And of course, Katurian slays both of his parents by covering their faces with a pillow and he does the same thing to Michal. (Ariel also killed his father with a pillow in order to stop the sexual abuse.) For the Pillowman character the mercy killings or assisted deaths that he offers are preferable to cycles of rape, trauma, violation, and suffering. (Tupolski admits that his own child drowned while fishing alone.)

Despite Katurian's innocence with regard to the murders of the children, Tupolski proceeds with his execution. In the final moments of both of Crowley's productions, the light that hangs over the interrogation table is whisked away, altering the nature of the space and now making it an unencumbered space of the imagination. There are three single spotlights on Ariel, Katurian and Michal; Ariel has started to burn the stories,[164] Katurian removes the hood and displays his bullet wound and Michal is also resurrected, so to speak, appearing in his old childhood room. In Katurian's narrative from the afterlife, Michal is visited as a child by the Pillowman figure and is told how tough his life will be.

In the earlier version of 'The Pillowman' story, the figure visited children and offered them the option of suicide as a way out of future trauma. Eventually, the Pillowman figure visits his younger self and opts out of life. Here McDonagh's recycling of the story is vital for a number of reasons, not only because this story intermeshes with most of the others, in terms of the capacity of an outside or external force to intercede, but principally because it is affirmed as the drama's overarching or governing meta-narrative.[165] Knowing that his own presence and suffering will be fundamental to Katurian's success as a writer, Michal chooses a future of trauma regardless.[166]

The focus of the London production was mainly on Katurian and his final narrative, while the New York production seems to give equal emphasis to Michal. At one poignant moment, Michal acts out his part and delivers his lines as Katurian impersonates the Pillowman figure in Katurian's final story. Tennant's final moments are perhaps less poignant and more about making connections, framing or pulling together all that has gone on before in an over-arching, all-embracing fashion, drawing an audience for one final time back into the sensation and spectacle of the story. (Crudup extracts a great poignancy from this scene, as there is a more resolute dignity on display.) In effect, instead of offering one of his usual downbeat endings, Katurian tenders one which is unfashionably optimistic. Worthen and Worthen identify, using de Man's phrase, that this 'apparent closure of the narrative is, through the "*staccato* of irony", extended in a second, nonetheless formal, peripeteia.'[167] In such a manner, 'while Katurian's stories dramatise the tension between pathos and mechanisation in modern allegory, *The Pillowman* tends to blur the distinction between allegory and *allegoresis*, or allegorical *interpretation*', the Worthens suggest.[168] Equally in the work there is a failure to read metaphorically as well as a presumption to disbelieve the insights of the writer. Ramachandran uses the term 'metaphor blindness', equally there must be allegory blindness as McDonagh offers something uniquely insightful and that is as far away from issues of representation as possible.[169]

Regardless, and also beyond an ironic frame, there is a coy sentiment that becomes more and more obvious in McDonagh's work, upon close inspection. Patrick Pacheco notes that McDonagh says that he is not averse to sentiment, as long as it is earned: 'Terrence Malick's *Badlands* and the holiday classic *It's a Wonderful Life* [Frank Capra] are among this film lover's [McDonagh's] top 10. He loves Sam Peckinpah's movies as well, not for their slow-motion violence, he says, but because the director is so good at capturing the "sadness and truth" of men going to meet their doom.'[170]

Bettelheim argues that in fairytales, instead of the happy ending being an unrealistic wish-fulfilment and dangerously delusional, the happy ever after ending is crucial for a number of reasons as the child escapes from 'the separation anxieties' from the mother and 'death anxieties' that haunt him/her, yet the optimism of the endings is not to 'fool the child that eternal life is possible.'[171] Instead, what is suggested, Bettelheim argues, is that by identifying interpersonal connections of merit and substance: 'one has reached the ultimate in emotional security of existence and permanence of relationships available to man; and this alone can dissipate the fear of death. If one has found true adult love, the fairy story also tells one that one does not need to wish for eternal life.'[172] Thus Katurian's final story from the afterlife is the fundamental affirmation of a deep bond of love between brother and brother and Ariel's actions confirm a happy ever after existence for the fate of Katurian's stories.[173]

So it is not endless game playing that wins out, it is not only a world of sinister postmodern simulacra, but there is something more than simply satisfying the temptation to find meaning and purpose in the choice to bear pain for another's purpose, or in self-sacrifice. There is a testimony to persistence. Speaking on behalf of his brother, Katurian projects his own aspiration of endurance and sacrifice. Katurian's trust in empathy is beyond dispute, as legacy rather than eternity is the outcome.

Charles McGrath gives a complex assessment of the range of audience responses to the play's New York production, suggesting that a study by a behavioural scientist would identify the 'sighs, whimpers, flinches, squirms, tears and head-shakes, along with giggles, guffaws, snorts, snickers, barely suppressed chuckles and full-blown bouts of hilarity – only some of them occurring at predictable moments.'[174] He continues: the 'torture scene involving an electric drill elicits the expected gasp, for example, but a description of severed toes, a few minutes later, makes people laugh out loud'.[175] This point is reinforced by Ben Brantley who suggests that 'one electric shock of a moment in the first act jolts comfort-food-fed Broadway audiences the way the shower scene in *Psycho* must have slapped moviegoers four decades ago'.[176] And McGrath cites Crudup, who states that he has never been 'in anything that takes such twists and turns,' in 'something that manages to have an audience go completely in one direction and completely in another'.[177] Crudup elaborates as follows: 'I've never felt an audience be so condensed in a moment like that, so routinely [....] Sometimes you're in a play and you feel it can only go one way,' but 'here it's like whiplash.'[178]

At the point when Katurian pounds the head of Michal, Ivanek tells McGrath that he can 'hear the whole place go quiet [....] It's like an explosion of exhalation. All the air goes out of the room, they're just so shocked by it.' [179] It is that sense of constant jolting or of shifting of mood, tone and perspective in this play that offers the inconclusive ambivalence of carnival, the jolted sensation of Grand-Guignol and the squeamish terror of the darker fairy tale, but in stressing this, let us not forget the optimistic sentiment of the work more generally.

In his review of the London production, Paul Taylor views the broad attempts to shock in a very different way:

> Sure, it raises profound questions. Can art (including McDonagh's own) corrupt and cause damage? Is it parasitic on suffering and does its survival count for more than human life (including the artist's own)? But it toys with those issues, playing fast and loose for the short-term gain of an outraged yelp of laughter here or a shuddering shock there. In the end, you may feel McDonagh has more in common with his pair of creepily teasing interrogators than with his author-surrogate.[180]

Taylor also queries McDonagh's moral frame, stating: 'McDonagh strikes me as a fascinating case of a dramatist with extraordinary technical talent and a disturbingly defective moral sense. I don't like this play, but I can't promise you that I won't go and see it again.'[181] I could not disagree more with Taylor's views on a 'disturbingly defective moral sense'. And I would say that the 'defective moral sense' of many of his characters is dangled before an audience, where it becomes their responsibility and not that of the playwright.

5 | Zero Degrees of Separation: *Seven Psychopaths*

CARNIVAL OF THE ANIMALS

There is a common perception of psychopaths being fixated on their animals and equally the belief that those that take delight in harming or torturing animals in childhood are more likely to go on to display pathological tendencies. There is the additional question as to why narratives about harming animals or its staging can evoke greater audience responses than the wounding or killing of dramatic characters. Such matters also raise interesting questions around performance sensibilities and the use of special effects in theatre and film.

On the one hand, there are regular acts of narrated and performed violence perpetuated on animals across the work; in *Connemara* Mairtin cooks a hamster in an oven in his school and he kills a cow with a brick; in *Lonesome* Valene's dog, Lassie, is slaughtered by Coleman;[182] in *Inishmaan*, Helen is a hit-woman of sorts, slaughtering a cat and a goose for payment; in *Inishmore*, two cats are killed, a dog chokes on a human nose and Mairead blinds cattle as an act of political protest – however confusingly motivated that happens to be. In *Six Shooter* the Kid character delights in a childhood experience of witnessing a cow exploding. When trapped wind is released from its stomach and is set alight, the methane had been freed by a character using a screwdriver to puncture the animal's hide. Also in this short film a mercy killing of sorts is performed on the rabbit, David. On the other hand, there is Padraic and Mairead's obsessive love for their cats in *Inishmore*, Mervyn's infatuated visits to the zoo to see a gibbon in *Spokane*, and Charlie's obsession with his dog in *Seven Psychopaths*. In these instances, the animal is not only the object of desire, but also is indicative of a fixation on an unconditional state of love that is almost impossible to achieve between people. A dognapping scam is central to the mayhem in *Seven Psychopaths*, which McDonagh also wrote and directed.[183]

'CHICK KILLING SHAKES'

Under the iconic sign of Hollywood set into Mt Lee, Los Angeles, the film opens on Lake Hollywood reservoir with a screwball conversation between two hitmen, Tommy (Michael Stuhlbarg) and Larry (Michael Pitt), who converse in a faux *Pulp Fiction* hoodlumese, while readying themselves to kill and then shoot the eyeballs out of Angela (Olga Kurylenko), the girlfriend of their boss, Charlie Costello. (Angela is also the name of Carmichael's mother in *Spokane*.) Their verbal exchange focuses on torture techniques in Cuba, the hits they previously carried out, and comments on the real life gangster, John Dillinger, getting shot in the eyeball. (His life is also fictionalized in numerous Hollywood films.) They also comment on the character Moe Greene from Francis Ford Coppola's *The Godfather* (1972), who dies after being shot in the eye. Distracted by their own self-indulgent arrogance, Tommy and Larry are themselves executed as they wait to carry out this hit. Thus fiction and reality are interconnected from this earliest scene, and the slippage from one to the other occurs as if there is little or no differentiation between each of them. As Philip French notes, 'This is life imitating art, soon to be followed by art attempting to imitate life in a city where the two are virtually inseparable.'[184] That blurring and inseparability of both fiction and reality is handled with supreme skill by McDonagh. The film suggests that Hollywood through its cultural significances, celebrity lifestyles and the values it endorses, functions as a sort of governing, if deceptively non-tangential, master narrative.

However, the power of Hollywood studios to determine forms of representation and to mediate aspects of violence in particular ways is of huge importance to McDonagh's work more generally. The general cultural obsession with violent representations has a sensationalist impulse, but is also indicative of complex issues such as desensitisation to cultural expressions of violence. Perhaps, even more ominously, it may well be fear and the actualities of the violence and intimidation, that is the glue which binds cultures and societies and pits individuals and communities against each other, aspects of which are cleverly highlighted in critical work of Slavoj Žižek, as previously mentioned in Part 2.

In *Seven Psychopaths*, Marty Faranan (Colin Farrell) is the alcohol dependent, Irish writer, who lives in a plush apartment, who has a different experience of Hollywood to that of Billy Claven in *Inishmaan*. Marty has a troubled relationship with Kaya (Abbie Cornish), and he cannot kick-start a screenplay that bears the same title as the film itself.[185] Farrell's character in *Seven Psychopaths* is primarily signalled as Irish, however, it is both Farrell's accent and his roles as *iconic* Dubliner in both *Intermission* (1993) and *In Bruges* which allude to his suburban Dublin background. In some respects, the Dublin accent is in part recognisable by what it is not, that is, the accent which dominates, with some variation it has to be said, Alan Parker's *The Commitments* (1991) which came to the screen with a glossary to explain the Dublin phrases. Farrell's impressive but clearly audible working-class accent for his character in *Intermission* makes way for an even smoother, almost generic dialect in *In Bruges*, and in *Seven Psychopaths*, his accent is slightly more polished again. Additionally, the significant distance between Billy's fake and intentionally bad Irish accent and Farrell's almost mid-Atlantic, internationalised Dublinese, means that the clarity of his diction frames it as both Irish and discernibly Dublin in origin. Annoyed at Kaya and Billy, Farrell says the line, 'What are yous lookin' at', with a very pronounced Dublin accent.

Late in the film, Marty reflexively blesses himself over the body of Hans, linking him with the innate Catholicism that is also hugely significant to both Dublin characters, Ray and Ken in *In Bruges*. (This re-affirms that religious belief is an aspect of Irishnesss that is easily and persistently circulated within many global narratives.) Likewise, throughout the movie Marty's alcohol dependency is a running gag, as is the way that drinking is perceived as being part of his Irish heritage. His out of work actor friend Billy Bickle (Sam Rockwell) – another Billy and another Bickle, as Robert De Niro's Travis Bickle is the central character in *Taxi Driver* – advises Marty to put the way he is feeling into his writing, to which Marty defends himself by stating that he is not inflicted by 'suicidal self-loathing and shit'. (Billy is the one that is far more self-destructive and self-loathing.) Clearly, McDonagh is addressing the affiliation of Irishness with drunkenness and a funerary negativity, sometimes to reinforce the stereotype, sometimes to deconstruct it, and on other occasions to undermine its simplistic presence within popular cultural representations. Charlie's comment: '[….] You don't believe in guns? They ain't fucking leprechauns, you dumb Mick', affirms further a generally flippant association of Irishness with leprechauns.[186]

While Farrell does not have access to the same emotional range as he has with Ray in *In Bruges*, he is convincingly the movie's central emotional platform, proving yet again that he does comic vulnerability exceptionally well, even if he is not the film's most flamboyant presence; at least four other characters compete for that tag. At the start of the film all Marty has for his screenplay are brief prompts: Exterior: LA street corner Day, an idea on a page to include the Jack of Diamonds and a Buddhist Psychopath, which is later scored out and replaced by the word 'Amish,' which is again supplanted by the word 'Quaker'. In an interview with Joe Utichi McDonagh comments that Marty is

> trying to strive against the violence in the film, as I am. I really did want it to be about Buddhism and peace and love, at the same time as making a Sam Peckinpah film – to me, his films were anti-violence, too, about the doomed nature of violent men. I don't think this is as weighty as that, because it's dealing with frivolous Hollywood tropes. But every single movie poster has a guy with a gun on it. It's so cheap and easy and thick.[187]

In one of Marty's early narrative fragments, the Vietnamese Buddhist monk (Long Nguyen) is a former Viet Cong soldier, a 'sicko, a psycho', (Psychopath 4) and is now in an American hotel room dressed as a Catholic priest, in the company of a topless prostitute (Christine Marzano).[188] He speaks in his native tongue, and promises murderous revenge on the whole of the American nation. In the first version of the tale, the hooker can only say: 'Didn't we like have a big war with you guys one time.' For him that war is not over.

During a later flashback to the war zone, he sets alight two enemy American soldiers, before shooting them dead. He returns home after the war intent on peace only to find that American soldiers have raped and butchered his entire family in the Mỹ Lai massacre, a notorious and real historic event that included many civilian casualties that did nothing for the reputation of the American army.[189] Having already slain six members of Charlie Company, beheading one, he now plans on attending the 1st Battalion of the 20th Infantry Regiment Convention in Phoenix, on the rights and wrongs of the Vietnam War, with the intention of strapping explosives to the hooker. Marty instinctively knows that such a story is going to end in carnage and horror, so does not want to commit to the writing of it.[190]

Notions of violence, justice, vengeance and revenge are followed through not only in this very public narrative of international political and military conflict, but also through the more private, familial trauma provoked by the murder of a young Quaker girl. 'The daughter of a Quaker went missing', is how Marty's narrative draft begins. A cut throat was the least of the damage done to her, and the rest is left to the imagination. A year on, the killer (James Hébert) gives himself up, spends seventeen years in jail, finds God, repents, and many years later is paroled and hopes to 'live a simple, joyous life'. He obtains a place to live and surrounds himself, like Valene in *Lonesome*, with Christian figures and images. Eleven years after his release, the Quaker girl's father is still stalking him and causes the killer to eventually go mad. Consoled by a Catholic tract that those who die by their own hand are guaranteed a place in hell, suicide is the killer's 'beautiful' solution', for at 'least in Hell the Quaker father would not be there'. But just like the dramatic twists that are evident in the narratives in *The Pillowman*, the last thing the killer ever sees is the Quaker, standing across the street and cutting his own throat, determined to follow him to hell. The Quaker is deemed to be a psychopath (Psychopath 2), not the killer of the girl who is remorseful and has made retribution for the killing. Steven Pinker notes: 'The Quakers parlayed Enlightenment arguments against slavery and war into effective movements for abolition and pacifism.'[191]

In both of these governing narratives, the Buddhist and the Quaker want justice and go about seeking it in different ways. In the former, it takes the form of retribution and violent acts, and, in the latter, the pacifist protest becomes so twisted that it is potentially pathological in its fixation. In their first incarnations, both of these actions come at the expense of everything else, as forgiveness, compassion, understanding or even empathy are not part of the emotional reflex. The motivations, actions and consequences of the Buddhist and the Quaker characters set the film's predominant dialectical tensions and can also be linked back to the motivations of Republican freedom fighters discussed in Section Two, who in the name of war, tolerate the killing of the innocent as collateral damage. How these two early narratives evolve is one of the stunning achievements of the piece.

Alongside these two extreme characters, a number of other psychopaths interconnect with Marty's life. Billy's small ad in *LA Weekly* looking for psychopaths gets a response from Tom Waits' Zachariah Rigby. (He has a white rabbit as his constant companion and it calls to mind the rabbit in *Six Shooter*.) At seventeen, while breaking into the home of a Delacroy judge, Zachariah comes across the corpses of two young black girls in his basement, plus a half alive young woman in chains. It is instant love for him, but somewhat less so for Maggie (Amanda Warren), the imprisoned and terrorized woman. The two of them hang the judge 'by the neck until he is dead'. (This carries echoes of Katurian's rescue of Michal and punishment of their parents in *The Pillowman*.) This act of retribution spring boards them into a cycle of terror, or as it is put in the film, they go 'around the country killing people going around the country killing people'. Zachariah accounts for the deaths of three real-life notorious serial killers – the Texarkana Moonlight Murderer (1947), the Butcher of Kingsbury Run (also known as Cleveland Torso Murderer) (1954), and the Zodiac Killer (1975). With the hippy Zodiac killer (Richard Wharton), the

Zodiac's hands are knifed to a table, and petrol is used to set him alight. (The red and yellow gasoline can seem as if it is straight from the set of *Spokane* or Quentin Tarantino's *Reservoir Dogs* (1992).) There are also echoes of how the Pillowboy dies in *The Pillowman*. A gasoline can will re-appear later in the film.) Burnt at the table, the Zodiac character appears very like the image of skeletal death in Jan Provoost's 'The Miser and Death', which, as already mentioned, unnerves Ray in *In Bruges* during the visit to the Groeninge Museum. (p. 24) Maggie abandons him because he did not help her kill the hippy and leaves her ring behind after Zachariah gets angry with her because she has doused a rabbit with petrol, a rabbit incidentally who is on the table drinking the Zodiac's blood. (Both are tagged as Psychopath 5 and 6.) Zachariah offers Marty the opportunity to use his story in return for a promise to have a credit in the film stating how much he misses Maggie and longs for her return.

Although fixated on psychopaths, Marty does not see the psychopath closest to hand, that is of course, Billy, who is deemed a psychopath in his own right for the calculated way that he kills Angela. Of course, Billy's alter ego is the serial killer the Jack of Diamonds, who under this persona, murders as if he is auditioning for a lead part in Marty's movie – the lengths an actor might go to get a part! (Thus Billy doubles up as Psychopath 1 and 7.) In response to an article in the paper about the Jack of Diamonds and in an attempt to prompt Marty to write about Jack, Billy interestingly frames the figure as one with a degree of integrity, one who will only kill mid- to high- ranking members of an Italian-American organised crime syndicate or perhaps the Yakuza, but Marty does not want to address the challenge of 'Jap dialogue' in the screenplay. In allowing Billy to express a measure of rational discernment, McDonagh is being provocative. Rockwell's Billy is simultaneously goofy, charismatic and maniacal, as he is someone who cannot control his impulses, a carry-over perhaps from his role as Mervyn in *Spokane*.

THE PEYOTE IN THE ROOM

So it is Billy's dognapping or 'dog borrowing' scam with Hans Kieslowski (Christopher Walken) – an appropriate name for the star of *A Behanding in Spokane* – that draws them to the attention of the wrong individual. Bonny, a snatched dog, is the 'beloved Shih Tzu' of Woody Harrelson's Charlie Costello (Psychopath 3) – a mafia figure with an Irish surname – who is a crazed character in the mould of *In Bruges*'s Harry Waters.[192] (The dog's identity disc bears the inscription 'Return to Charles Costello or you will fucking die', side by side with the requisite contact telephone number.)[193]

Billy has been sleeping with Angela, Charlie's girlfriend, whom he confides in as to how he intentionally targeted Charlie's dog, making what follows less accidental and more conscious destructive intent: 'This dog is my Pattie Hearst. Expect that I'm not going to keep it in a closet and make it rob a bank.' Discovered at Billy's and Hans's holding space for the dogs, Marty gets inadvertently drawn into the world of psychopaths as if it reflects a battle between the ego's desire for rationality, security and calm and the unconscious desire for destruction and mayhem.

Charlie's aggression towards his dog-walker Sharice (Gabourey Sidibe) is especially sinister, but also playfully deranged in its maniacal excessiveness, yet his composed killing of Hans's wife Myra (magnificently played by Linda Bright Clay), who is in hospital for the treatment of breast cancer, alters the perspective audiences may have on Harrelson's character. In this chilling scene between Harrelson and Bright Clay, Charlie slowly comes to the realisation that he is talking to the wife of Hans – that the 'Polack married a Nigger'– a moment that leaves her spitting back at him her defiance as she grasps the reality of her impending fate. Charlie is now far more than the routinely intimidating, slightly deranged bully that he was towards Sharice, but is clearly a very nasty, dispassionate psycho-killer.

However, it is Walken's character Hans that is central to how the film develops. Charlie waits in the hospital, expecting that Hans will come out of the ward 'screaming', once he discovers Myra's dead body. Thus spontaneously expressed grief will reveal the identity of his next target. Instead, a composed Hans sits opposite Charlie in a waiting area in the hospital, stares him out, aggressively offers him his cravat, which Charlie rejects and then Hans uncovers his cut throat. Through this action Hans not only provocatively demonstrates his displaced trauma, but his confrontational fearlessness signals something utterly different, as it also indicates the lengths to which he may go to retaliate and gain some measure of justice. Walken's Hans is now utterly different to the way he was earlier with Myra, in how they communicated so lovingly to each other and in how he responds initially with such compassion and intimacy on the discovery of her body.

After Marty's initial imagining of the Quaker story, Billy then overhears him tell it at Kaya's party, Marty with a glass of alcohol in hand of course. Billy is prompted to tell Kaya that he himself had told that story to Marty in a bar two months previously, and that it is a story that a friend had told to him, 'so there might be copyright issues at *the very least*'. (my italics) And later again in a bar, Marty starts the Quaker story again on the invitation of Hans. Billy interrupts and urges him to stop, but Hans insists that he continues as he wants to 'know what happens in the end'. However, Hans interjects and finishes the story, again making visible the scar on his neck. Curiously and dismissively Hans remarks: 'That's a very good story. Did you make that up... all by yourself.' Later he goes on to inform Marty that some of the details are not exactly right, in an extended conversation in the car as they drive in the Joshua Tree National Park to flee Costello's terror. 'Of course I would not necessarily call myself a psychopath' is Hans's view of himself. Instead of a flashback narrative with Harry Dean Stanton playing the Quaker Father, it is now Walken in a hospital as that figure, resisting treatment for the cut neck, while held against his will by two security guards.[194]

Hans further adds the fact that the Quaker was not alone in his stalking, but was accompanied by his African-American wife, thus in hindsight, what becomes apparent is the even more complex relationship he has with Myra, and the additional significance of their discussions about their dead daughter (Wendy) as to whether or not they will meet in heaven. Hans cites Gandhi's comment on revenge: 'an eye for an eye leaves the whole world blind' in response to Billy's justification of Hans's and Myra's pacifist revenge and years of stalking: 'Course it had to be done, he killed your kid', and adds, 'You had to fuck him over by any means necessary.' Billy proves that Gandhi's perspective is logically incorrect, because there would be one person who would escape that final fate. (The Zodiac killer also has a poster with a quotation from Gandhi on his wall.) If revenge in Pinker's taxonomy is a major driver of violence, here there is a struggle to either avoid it or re-conceptualise it. However, Marty's immersion into the criminal underworld, his discovery that Billy is a serial killer and the revelation of Myra's and Hans's back story, ensure that a very complicated ethical dimension emerges as the line between fiction and reality is increasingly blurred. (The eye for an eye cycle of crime and retribution is also a central dilemma in *In Bruges*.)

Camping in the desert and notionally on the run from Charlie, there is now ample opportunity for Marty to progress his movie. He also offers Hans and Billy the chance to be co-creators, more out of generosity rather than as an exploitation of their experiences and accumulated knowledge. Marty's rough screenplay outline is that the 'First half is set up as a revenge flick [....] the lead characters just walk away [...] drive off into the desert somewhere, pitch a tent and just talk' until the film's end. (In the film itself they do most of that.) And Marty has in mind that there will be no shoot-outs and no 'payoffs'. Hans will help with the script only if it is not too violent, but Billy knows that only one sort of ending is possible if it is a film about seven psychopaths and that it cannot possibly be 'life affirming' in the ways that Marty wants it to be. Hans speaks his impressions into a dictaphone, and Billy throws himself about as if devising a violent shoot-out.

Billy outlines his climactic, heavily ironic-laden ending, which is set at night in a cemetery (echoes of *Connemara*) and he recycles the characters at the core of Marty's narrative. By the end, Zachariah, Maggie and the Vietnamese monk are killed and Jack dies, having slain Costello and having saved Hans and Marty from death. Homosocial bonds are affirmed, as Jack goes with the angels, with an indicative promise of peace someday, but in this narrative Billy cannot resist having a final go at Kaya. Billy's fiction has more than some overlap with the reality of how the film itself ends. Costello does get lured into the desert by Billy, whose suicidal bravado only leads to one outcome. Unlike Billy, Marty survives the shoot-out to finish his script, move into Billy's home with his new canine companion, Bonny. Kaya is nowhere to be seen.

And discovered after his death is a voice recording that Hans has left to suggest how Marty might transform the Buddhist psychopath story or 'Viet Cong psychopath conundrum' as he puts it. In this version the Hooker is no longer topless, but wears a red dress. She offers to make love or to have a discussion, stating 'I have been reading a lot of Noam Chomsky lately, I think he is a marvel.' The Buddhist does not understand her. While having sex, he hears the voice of a Vietnamese colleague, translated as 'Desist, brother. You know this will not help us.' Instead of reflecting on his intended actions, he persists with imagining how he will drag her into the Convention Centre while holding a can of petrol, and she strapped into a dynamite vest. He pours the petrol on the floor, takes out a match, but in perfect Vietnamese, as she has studied the language at Yale, she re-affirms the 'Desist brother' request. He shuts his eyes and is no longer in Phoenix, but in Saigon circa 1963, and is not wearing the garments of a Catholic priest but the orange robes of a Buddhist monk. The crowd which surrounds him includes another Buddhist monk, the Hooker and an American soldier. The monk is covered in petrol. For Hans, as he 'finally manages to push the thoughts of anger and hate out of his gentle mind', and rejecting final pleas for him to 'desist', the monk believes his actions 'might' have a purpose, might have positive consequences. (Hans sees it as the first monk to protest the war.)

Thus according to Hans, Marty's Viet Cong story becomes the 'final thoughts of man who chose not the darkness but the light, the light being, you know, suicide by self-immolation'. This moment of course references an iconic moment from 11 June 1963 on a busy Saigon street, when the Vietnamese Buddhist monk Thich Quang Duc, according to James Verini,

> offered to burn himself in a Saigon intersection as 'a donation to the struggle.' The struggle was not, as is commonly thought, the American intervention in Vietnam – it was only 1963 – but rather the persecution of Buddhists by the Catholic (and US-backed) Diem

> regime. Duc has since become the most famous self-immolater in history, only partly thanks to the cover of Rage Against the Machine's début album. His fellow-monks and nuns saw to his fame, alerting the international media to the event beforehand, lying down below fire engines to prevent them from arriving at the scene, and distributing texts, translated into English, of Quang Duc's final words.[195]

Malcolm Browne's widely-circulated and Pulitzer Prize-winning photograph of the incident made this a hugely important and symbolic international incident. The fallout from Quang Duc's actions was significant. In November 1963, the Diem regime was overthrown and American support for this government was further questioned, but not enough happened to stop the Vietnam War that followed. Coincidentally, Verini adds, 'in the US, Duc's most famous echoer ("imitator" seems unequal to so fearless an act), though not his only one, was Norman Morrison, a Quaker from Pennsylvania, who doused himself in kerosene and lit a match outside Defense Secretary Robert McNamara's Pentagon office in 1965. A stamp was issued in Morrison's honor in North Vietnam.'[196] Verini draws on Émile Durkheim's categorisation of suicide into 'four types: the egoistic, the altruistic, the anomic (moral confusion) and the fatalistic. Perhaps self-immolation captivates so thoroughly because it wins on all counts. It is the ultimate act of both despair and defiance, a symbol at once of resignation and heroic self-sacrifice.'[197]

In *In Bruges*, Ray has a lengthy deliberation on the fate of 'midget' movie actors and how so many kill themselves – 'Hervé Villechaize off of *Fantasy Island* [a TV Series 1977–1984]. I think somebody off the *Time Bandits*', namely David Rappaport, who starred in Terry Gilliam's movie (1981). (p.15) Ray's comments are a reflection of his own state of mind and his suicidal tendencies. In *Lonesome*, Valene and Coleman also discuss the fate of the actor, Pete Duel, from *Alias Smith and Jones* who also allegedly killed himself. The suicides of public figures haunt the work in many ways. In *Lonesome*, Fr Welsh's actions are a mix of despair and confusion, egoistic, in terms of not belonging to his community, which he wishes to both address and re-frame as sacrificial, altruistic, virtuous, restorative and redemptive and the prompter of miracles.

In Hans's narrative in *Seven Psychopaths*, the act of self-immolation is not defeatist, it is courageous, it is not denying life, but life enhancing. It is an action of moral clarity and not confusion, more utopian than fatalistic. Desistance reconstituted becomes resistance, defiance a message loudly sent to the oppressor that what they are doing is morally corrupt. So Hans views this action as a recuperative action, driven by courage and a quest for justice, which in many ways mirrors what he and Myra had done to the killer of their daughter. Hans's actions benefit from analysis within Pinker's model, where reason and self-control are positive aspects.

Pinker praises the need for self-control as a block on impulsivity, asking 'is self-control a single faculty in charge of taming every vice, from overeating to promiscuity to procrastination to petty crime to serious aggression?'[198] It is not so much under what circumstances is self-control rational or irrational, but to focus on self-indulgence, or short-term gain, long-term cost, the discounting of 'the future *too steeply*'.[199] People with poor self-control and impulsiveness, are shaped more by their aggression than anything else·

For Pinker there are seven major ways of increasing self control, firstly, 'when the present self handicaps the future self', say by not shopping on an empty stomach, or throwing away the cigarette as one begins to crave one. Secondly, avoiding trouble by anticipating where trouble lies and staying away. Thirdly, mental self-control is vital, in terms of not responding to insults, by re-framing them cognitively. The fourth way is not to discount the future so steeply. The fifth way is for people to improve 'nutrition, sobriety, and health.' The sixth way is to increase willpower by training it, as willpower fatigues like muscle, so it must be trained up for greater endurance. The final way is to address what is fashionable in a culture or society. Culture often sets the tone, as if individuals are licensed by role models towards decency or self-indulgence.[200] Further measurements proposed by Pinker include distinctions between, short-term and long-term orientation, based on the work of Geert Hofstede, and one between restraint and indulgence.[201]

Societies that emphasise the longer time perspective and promote restraint over indulgence have lower levels of violence. In the Connor household, it is only the immediate and the indulgent that matter. The confessional scene is in part about will power, but they fatigue so easily. Evidence of the poor nutrition of characters is seen right across McDonagh's work, and in particular the absence of sobriety. Equally, creativity is partly about discipline, dedication and self-control and Marty's struggles in *Seven Psychopaths* demonstrate this. While Pinker's moral sense taxonomy does not include the imagination, I think the connection between imagination and morality is very evident in how the narratives in *Seven Psychopaths* evolve. It is just as important in *The Pillowman*.

Pinker suggests that the history of the world shows that so many of the older ideas and values were primitive and inept, and it is reason which has evolved these over time. And given a significant rise in levels of intelligence, there is a greater capacity to conceptualise and think rationally. Reason's capacity for the de-bunking of untruths and reason's link with self-control and moral sense are vital to his model of change. Reason is Pinker's most important better angel, as he sees empathy's elasticity as being 'limited by kinship, friendship, similarity and cuteness. It reaches a breaking point long before it encircles the full set of people that reason tells us should fall within our moral concern'.[202] On the other hand, reason gives us the impetus to act and reason tells us when it is time for self-control, but also to 'cut loose'. [203] 'And the one ethic that we can design to bring about the greatest good for the greatest number, the Rational-Legal mindset, is not part of the natural moral sense at all.'[204] Effectively for him, the more educated one is, the less connection one has to violent crime, the more experiences one has of cooperating, the more likely one is to move away from violence, the more liberal a society is, the less violence there is, and those that think like economists, market-driven economists are more likely to accept the theory of 'gentle commerce' and classic liberalism's positive-sum payoffs of exchange and its knock-on benefit of expansive networks of cooperation.

For Pinker, it is through the exercising of 'logic, clarity, objectivity and proportionality' that reason 'expands moral sensibilities' and not from grand intellectual 'systems'.[205] Hans is an especially good example of evolved reasoning and self-control. So rather than seeing this character as psychopathic, we have to discard the limited labelling of him and instead, see him as sympathetic, dynamic, self-controlling and imaginative.

Desistance and self-control also carry forward into the final moments of the piece as well. Initially and contentiously perhaps, a repeated shot of the half-burnt American flag of Billy's neighbours appears to be the final image of the film – a demonstration of his lack of self-control in light of his diary entry urging himself not to do it – only for the credits to be interrupted by a call to Marty from Zachariah, who is angry with Marty as his new film did not include a message to Maggie, as Marty had promised on his life in return for Zachariah's permission to use his story. But, noting that Marty sounds different as if damaged by recent experiences, Zachariah desists or at least postpones his promise to come round and kill Marty, as the Tuesday that he initially mentions does not quite suit him. Zachariah it seems breaks the cycle of revenge and retribution, through his recognition of Marty's altered mindset.

NON-RECIPROCATED ALTRUISM

There is a self-caricaturing of the self-consciousness of the writer, there is also a parodying of the gangster genre, but each is done with different agendas in mind. In a way, the deranged nature of Harrelson's Charlie cannot but remind one of his notorious role as Mickey Knox in Oliver

Stone's *Natural Born Killers* (1994), and a mix of Walken's signature iconic roles where intensity and satire, strangeness and derangement go hand in hand and thus feed into the intertextual mélange.

For some it is grist to the mill that McDonagh has his psychopathic cake and eats it. While the idea of having serial killers of serial killers taps into a postmodern frame in terms of repetition and pastiche, there is also a curious sense of justice lingering throughout as well. Zachariah and Maggie, as two vigilante killers, seem to have not just a desire to shed blood but also to punish and eradicate mass murderers. Their killing of serial killers who never got caught may partially suggest how in real life these killers stopped killing. It is not that they were simply imprisoned for other crimes, or died of natural causes, they were potentially exterminated, as part of a cycle of retributive justice. There is the further complication that the rescue of Marty and Hans by Billy, as Jack of Diamonds, saves them from death at the hands of two of Charlie's men.

Yet, if violence is commonplace in most films, what is not supported here are the usual systems of justice central to the action or detective genres. When initially trapped in a hostile situation, Marty's impulse is to go to the police. Instead Billy wants to join forces with Jack of Diamonds, but Hans is especially aggressive in his dismissal of an intervention by the forces of law, as if the police did little to respond adequately to the death of his child. The police arrive too late to put a stop to the 'final shoot-out.' Billy sees himself as an action hero and most people have grown up with a mythology around these figures, aware of the implausibility but buys into the possibilities. In their own ways male action-heroes or maverick cops are loners, in dysfunctional relationships, unreliable, over-estimate their beliefs and resources, defiant, persistent, charming, and are socially non-compliant. They tend to overly rely on intuition, self-absorbed and narcissistic, discount the future, fail to plan ahead or see the consequences of their actions, accept collateral damage and trust their capacity to make decisions under severely challenging circumstances, thus they are only slightly different to the pathological gangsters or serial killers that they are pursuing.

Their characteristics are not far from those identified through Cleckley's research on psychopathology and those identified in Baron-Cohen's Anti-Social Personality Disorders. It is the genre rather than their innate resources that set them up for victory – much like fairy tales, one knows what side to be on in the main. But the notion of resolution, closure and imaginative justice does not map on to the systemic and persistent injustices of societies more generally. The latter ones do not go away, but often the film work seems to hold out that possibility, however implausible it might be.

6 | Conclusion

In *The Pillowman*, Katurian affirms that a good writer must invent, not rely on real life. Katurian suggests in his briefly mentioned story 'The Shakespeare Room' that the Bard gets inspiration for new work by stabbing with a stick the imprisoned 'little black pygmy lady in a box'. (p.62) Both the tortured, vengeful and defiant figure of the colonised Caliban in *The Tempest* and the impact of destructive imperial or colonial practices appear implicit in McDonagh's story fragment.

However, it is Katurian's own particular inept understandings of the nature of writing which troubles the play: 'Well ... I kind of hate any kind of writing that's even vaguely autobiographical. I think people who only write about what they know only write about what they know because they're too fucking stupid to make anything up.' (p.76) However, attempts by writers in general to deny contexts and the potential of experiences even as indirect influences, or to hide behind the fiction of purely imaginatively inspired work are clearly fallacious and ultimately self-deluding as is the notion of authorial intent. For not only do Katurian's comments dismiss formative and life-changing influences or the impact of social epoch, race, gender and social class on writing practices, but also his comments illustrate an absence of recognition of the obvious relationship between his own work and the realities of how he was reared, socialised and interpellated by his society and of what the horrors suffered by his brother brought into his life. For these he killed his parents and took on the role of primary carer for Michal.

In *Seven Psychopaths*, Marty's encounters with the world around him may prompt his inspiration to flow. Of course, there is nothing new about a piece of theatre about the making of theatre or films about the making of films, writing about the act of writing, or about writers dealing with writer's block or indeed real life providing inspiration for fiction or being more strange than fiction. Joel Coen's *Barton Fink* (1991), Charlie Kaufman's *Adaptation* (2002), or John Madden's *Shakespeare in Love* (1989) all do this in various ways. *Seven Psychopaths* suggests that fiction does not evade reality for too long and equally reality does not evade fiction either. Marty's final inspiration is drawn as much from creativity as it is from real life, from the narratives and experiences of acquaintances and encounters with strangers. So Marty, defined by the stories of others and what he unconsciously borrows and what he can access by permission, is very much at odds with Katurian's duty of the storyteller. There is nothing unifying about any one story and little unique about the ability of the storyteller.

In the four pieces of work discussed here, there are continuing concerns with equality, justice and empathy, and with how to incorporate or make sense of trauma. Suicidal impulses, in the form of a death wish are very apparent in Billy Bickle's anarchic need to bring forward a chaotic ending, and in Kid's non-surrender and inevitable slaying by the police. Such actions then are distinguished from losing one's life in order to save that of others, deeds sometimes framed as tragic, sometimes comic, but fundamentally life affirming in especially complex ways. This obsession with self-sacrifice, in its various forms, draws on McDonagh's own awareness, evident in the comment: 'I guess it's a suicidal Christ figure, which is a figure I've always been interested in. Somebody who kills himself for the sake of others.'[206] If Fr Welsh's notions of self-sacrifice are astray in *Lonesome*, *In Bruges*'s Ken is the one who represents a more purposeful, if not quite clear-cut sense of redemptive possibilities, and it is his self-sacrifice that is critical to any understanding of the film. Equally, *The Pillowman* is informed by dissimilar forms of self-sacrifice. In *Seven Psychopaths* Hans chooses death in order to signal to Billy and Marty the close proximity of Charlie's gang, and the Vietnamese monk's self-immolation is imagined by Hans as not only an act of protest, but one of significant self-sacrifice, in line with perhaps how he and Myra obsessively stalked the killer of their daughter in their pursuit of justice, pacifist revenge or some combination of both. Distinctions between altruism and messiah complexes, and revenge and justice are blurred across the body of work, but less in the form of ambivalence and postponement and more in terms of complex situations, ambiguities or moral conundrums.

The distance between characters who express little or no empathy and those with medium to high levels of empathy is clearer in the films than in the plays, where there is a central figure with whom one can align oneself more easily, such as Donnelly, Ken and Marty. The Kid's dysfunctional empathy circuit is offset by Donnelly's high levels of empathy and love for his wife, in his compassion for the strangers on the train that have lost their child, and there is something oddly and curiously emotional in the mercy killing of the pet rabbit. In *In Bruges*, Ken's self-sacrifice is both noble and highly empathetic, and even Harry's killing of himself has something suspiciously moral at its twisted core. Still there is generosity, for it is the miser, as in Provoost's canvas, who will ultimately pay the price of final judgment. Marty's growing sense of awareness is affirmed by Zachariah's comments at the end of the film. If *Schadenfreude* is the 'experiencing of pleasure at someone else's pain', as Baron-Cohen suggests, then its opposite occurs here, as there is not pleasure to be found in another's pain, only the affirmation of human connections, and the rewards of noble self-sacrifice.[207]

There is great complexity dramatised in the following incidents: Mrs Dooley's grief-prompted suicide, Donnelly's response to his failed attempt of suicide, Hans and Myra's pursuit of the killer of their child, the self-immolation of the Vietnamese monk, in Ken's self-sacrifice, Ray's acceptance of his plight and in his instinctive willingness to save Harry from his own moral code by pointing out that he did not kill a child but an adult small in stature, Harry's killing of himself, Katurian's killing of his parents and then his brother and Katurian's final story that is a fundamental and elementary fantasy of absolute empathy. Discussing the work of Anton Chekhov, Michael Fryan argues that:

> The traditional function of literature in general, and of drama in particular, has always been to simplify and formalise the confused world of our experience; to isolate particular emotions and states of mind from the flux of feelings in which we live; to make our conflicts coherent; to illustrate values and to impose a moral (and therefore human) order upon a non-moral and inhuman universe; to make intention visible, to suggest the process by which it takes effect.[208]

McDonagh demonstrates the complexities of such an endeavour to give moral and psychological coherence and outlines both its desirability and inevitable failure. Endings bring great complexity from the first play discussed here in this book. *Beauty Queen*'s Maureen's murder of her mother leaves her trapped within her own delusional consciousness. *Connemara* has an ambivalent ending, where neither Mick Dowd's innocence nor guilt are confirmed, but his deep feelings of loss over his dead wife are obvious. In *Inishmaan*, the comic imperative concludes with Helen agreeing to go on a date with Billy, but his terminal illness means that a tragic sensibility dominates.

By the end of *Lonesome*, both brothers have come close to destroying each other, but Valene more then Coleman has at least made some effort to bond and forgive. The final moments of the play have Valene, despite him initially setting alight Fr Welsh's letter, quenching the flame and attaching the charred letter to the crucifix, bound by the chain Girleen had purchased for Fr Welsh as a mark of affection and later abandoned in the Connor household. The crucifix, the chain and Welsh's note symbolise a need to materialise existence which is bound by some notions of bizarre empathy or compassion. In *Inishmore*, after all the carnage, the return of the presumed dead Wee Thomas from his sexual exertions is met initially by an impulse from Donny and Davey to kill the cat, as he is the indirect cause of the carnage. Comically they cannot go through with it, with the cat's survival placing all the previous mayhem in a sort of zero-empathy vacuum, as randomness and chaos also enter the moral frame. Closure and carnage do not always go hand in hand.

The territory of empathy is complex and problematic in the instance of criminality and gangland, and even more particularly in relation to terrorism and paramilitarism, because the individuals supporting such causes believe that their freedom or identity is threatened or denied, thus their actions are not necessarily a result of a persistent 'empathy deficit', but about justice. In *Inishmore*, the attitude of Donny to the actions of his son Padraic is curious as is that of Mairead's mother towards her daughter leaving home and going up North to fight. Both parents in their relative states of indifference capture not only that deficit of empathy, but equally, the switching off of empathy for those they injure, despite Mairead's mother's concerns about the harming of innocent children, as previously articulated. However, in the act of terrorism, Baron-Cohen indicates that temporarily 'the terrorist's empathy is switched off'.[209] In some instances that is right, but for McDonagh there are others for whom paramilitarism is how they give expression to their pathologies and sadistic tendencies.

For instance, spectators also may be divided between having compassion for Michal and sympathy for his victims, between having some empathy for Ray's plight and even more for the boy. But in both instances, it is empathy for two killers of children. Yet how often in theatre or cinema might a spectator be inclined to have empathy for child killers, as I reiterate a question asked earlier?

But across all the work there are the notions of free will and determinism, good and evil, proportional and disproportional causes and effects all melding in complex ways. Baron-Cohen seems to relegate the significance of criminal intent, free will, choice and the criminal act itself in his emphasis on a 'neurological disability.'[210] Negative actions can be thus disassociated from choice, context and moral consequence. In his emphasis on 'empathy disorders,' over immorality and evil, there is a failure ultimately in his work to deal with morality in all its complexity. McDonagh's work situates morality in a more complex frame where there is increasingly in the work a sense of choice, well beyond either the instinctive prompts of children that Bettelheim recognises before maturation, or behaviours pre-determined by 'empathy disorders'.

Endnotes

1 In *Lonesome* Valene uses the term 'against god' in relation to blackmail and killing, and the melting of figurines is 'against God outright' (pp. 143, 157)
Tom Hanlon uses the term in response to Mairtin's cursing in the graveyard. (p.91)
Kid uses the same phrase in *Six Shooter* (2005). In *Inishmaan*, there is the exchange, 'Sure, pegging eggs at a priest, isn't it pure against God?' Eileen asks. Helen responds: 'Oh, maybe it is, but if God went touching me arse in choir practice I'd peg eggs at that fecker, too.' (p.12)

2 S. Pinker, *The Better Angels of Our Nature: A History of Violence and Humanity* (London: Penguin Books, 2011), p.755.

3 Ibid., p.755.

4 Ibid., p.773.

5 Ibid., p.752.

6 Ibid., p.753.

7 Ibid., p.753.

8 McDonagh notes: 'I was trying to write a character, in Ray, who had no self-censorship, who was unaware of what could be offensive.' See E. Caesar, 'Hard acts to follow,' *Sunday Times*, 6 April 2008, Culture, p. 8, http://www.lexisnexis.com/uk/nexis/results/docview/docview.do?docLinkInd=true&risb=21_T17285878182&format=GNBFI&sort=BOOLEAN&startDocNo=126&resultsUrlKey=29_T17285878186&cisb=22_T17285878185&treeMax=true&treeWidth=0&csi=332263&docNo=133 (Accessed 29/4/2013)

9 See Pinker, *The Better Angels of Our Nature*, p.753.

10 Ibid., p.754.

11 Ibid., p.756–8.

12 While each of these modes of relating can have positive outcomes, they also have potentially negative ones as well. Communal sharing has a tendency to exclude out-groups, 'legitimise tribalism and jingoism' and only serves the needs of those close to hand and affiliated. Authority Ranking justifies authority way beyond paternalism. Imperialists, slave owners and despots have their own logical application of authority to themselves. Equality Matching provides a justification for retaliation in relationships, the rationale for Rational-Legal model can be used to justify major global inequalities. Ibid., pp.766–9.

13 Ibid., p.759.

14 Ibid., p.760.

15 Ibid., p.766.

16 For instance, Mark Ravenhill claims that in hindsight the murder in February 1993 of the almost three-years-old Jamie Bulger by the young boys Robert Thompson and Jon Venables, both ten at the time, was the event that prompted him to write. He describes it as 'somehow something had shifted, that a tear in the fabric had happened […] Shop, videos, children killed by children. It wasn't a project I set out to write. But it became one.' Such a tragedy motivated Ravenhill, and he speculates as to how others of his generation, including McDonagh, were moved by the same incident and how their dramaturgical practices bore the weight of that horror.

The two boys killed by the bomb in Warrington in 1993 are not mentioned by Ravenhill, but as earlier indicated, they are central to McDonagh's *Inishmore*. See 'A Tear in the Fabric: the James Bulger Murder and New Theatre Writing in the 'Nineties', *New Theatre Quarterly*, 20.4, (2004), pp.305–314, p.310.

17 S. Baron-Cohen, *Zero Degrees of Empathy: A New Theory of Human Cruelty* (London: Allen Lane an imprint of Penguin Books, 2011), pp. 4–5.

18 Ibid., p.30.

19 Ibid., p.4.

20 Ibid., p.16.

21 For Pinker, 'The overall picture that has emerged from the study of the compassionate brain is that there is no empathy center with empathy neurons, but complex patterns of activation and modulation that depend on perceivers' interpretation of the traits of another person and the nature of their relationship with the person.' See *The Better Angels of Our Nature*, p.698. (And pages 698–9 for details of the circuit).

22 See Baron-Cohen, *Zero Degrees of Empathy* p.12.

23 Ibid., p.63.

24 Ibid., p.86.

25 While Pinker rejects the connection between mirror neurons and sympathy, as that there is no simplistic hotwiring of the brain for empathy and that mirror neurons, 'are mostly found in the brain that according to neuroimaging has little to do with empathy in the sense of sympathetic concern.' He continues: 'Empathy, in the morally relevant sense of sympathetic concern, is not an automatic reflex of our mirror neurons. It can be turned on and off and even inverted into counterempathy, namely feeling good when someone else feels bad and vice versa.' 'Sympathy is endogenous, an effect rather than a cause of how people relate to one another. Depending on how beholders conceive of a relationship, their response to another person's pain may be empathic, neutral, or even counterempathic.' See Pinker, *The Better Angels of Our Nature*, pp.696–7.

26 See Baron-Cohen, *Zero Degrees of Empathy*, p.86.

27 Ibid., p.90.

28 Further for Pinker, 'the brain tissue that is closest to empathy in the sense of compassion is neither a patch of cortex nor a subcortical organ but a system of hormonal plumbing. Oxytocin or [....] the cuddle hormone.' See Pinker, *The Better Angels of Our Nature*, p.699.

29 See Baron-Cohen, *Zero Degrees of Empathy*, pp.93–4.

30 Ibid., p.63.

31 Ibid., p.34.

32 Ibid., p.40.

33 Ibid., p.41.

34 Ibid., p.60.

35 Ibid., p.62.

36 Ibid., p.60.

37 See Pinker, *The Better Angels of Our Nature*, p.627.

38 Ibid., p.632.

39 In a revealing interview McDonagh acknowledges: 'Like Katurian in [*The Pillowman*], I stayed in and wrote and that's all I did,' said Mr. McDonagh. 'And the arrogance of Katurian, to some degree, I share with him. Or certainly I did when I was younger.' See J. McKinley, 'Suffer the Little Children,' *New York Times*, 3 April 2005, http://www.nytimes.com/2005/04/03/theater/newsandfeatures/03mcki.html?_r=1&scp=2&sq=The%20pillowman&st=cse. (Accessed 2/3/2012)

40 See Baron-Cohen, *Zero Degrees of Empathy*, p.45.

41 Ibid., p.43.
42 Ibid., pp.141–2.
43 Ibid., p.45.
44 Ibid., p.46.
45 Ibid., p.46.
46 Ibid., p.48.
47 See Pinker, *The Better Angels of Our Nature*, p 714.
48 *The Six Shooter* was an NBC weekly radio broadcast which ran in 1954 and starred James Stewart.
49 Ray is called a 'kid' in the film by Harry (p.39) and Ken calls him a 'boy' on a number of occasions. (pp.66-7)
50 See Internet Movie Database (IMDB) for list of nominations and awards. http://www.imdb.com/title/tt0780536/awards (Accessed 15/2/2103)
51 In an interview with R. Carnevale, McDonagh explains that although written for working-class Londoners, having cast Farrell and Gleeson 'it didn't make much sense to have everyone doing a London accent when the change was so minimal, from London working class to Dublin working class. So, it all fell into place after that'. See http://www.indielondon.co.uk/Film-Review/in-bruges-martin-mcdonagh-interview.(Accessed 2/3/2012)
52 J. FitzPatrick Dean, '*In Bruges*,' *Estudios Irlandeses*, 4, (2009), pp.166–9, p.167, http://www.estudiosirlandeses.org/Issue4/Film%20Reviews4/pdfTheYearinIrishFilmandTV2008.pdf (Accessed 12/3/2011)
53 Ibid., p.167.
54 See http://www.rte.ie/archives/exhibitions/1323-patrick-kavanagh/1331-on-raglan-road/ and http://www.rte.ie/archives/exhibitions/1323-patrick-kavanagh/1331-on-raglan-road/336053-benedict-keily-the-first-person-to-see-the-words-to-on-raglan-road/ (Accessed 2/8/2013)
55 According to legend, the city 'twice sheltered fugitive English kings from being murdered in 1471 and 1651'. (p.13)
56 McDonagh notes: 'Yeah, just whenever we came to travel, just to see a new place and didn't really know anything about it at all and was just struck by how stunningly cinematic and just picturesque and creepy and medieval, but cinematic ... how cinematic the place was. I always wondered why it hadn't been used in film before because it is so distinctive and just stunning really. Then I just wandered around to all the churches and museums and got bored shitless and just wanted to get drunk and get out of there, but then those two halves of my brain started chatting with each other; the culture vulture and the drunk. They just kind of became characters.' See 'Colin Farrell & Martin McDonagh Interview,' 2 May 2008, posted by Frosty, *Collider*, http://www.collider.com/entertainment/article.asp/aid/6863/cid/13/tcid/1 (Accessed 2/3/2012)
57 'The stationery of the hotel where Ken and Ray are staying has the hotel name as "De Rozenkransje - Brugge." Brugge being the Flemish name for the town of Bruges. Even a fictitious Belgian hotel would never be named like that, because the article is incorrect. "Rozenkrans", meaning Rosary, would indeed have the article "de." However, 'Rozenkransje' is the diminutive and as such would always have "Het" as the article. Even for proficient but non-native Flemish or Dutch speakers, this is a commonly made mistake.' See goofs at http://www.imdb.com/title/tt0780536/goofs (Accessed 2/3/2012)
58 McDonagh notes: 'Bruges is completely organic. If we hadn't been allowed to film there I'd have scrapped the whole script because it had to be there. It couldn't be Paris. It couldn't be Venice. It had to be a place that beautiful and strange, but kind of unknown. You know? Because there would be a reason why someone was sent

to Paris. There'd be a reason why someone was sent to Venice. There's no reason to be sent to Bruges. (*Laughter*) ... unless you're making a film.' See Colin Farrell and Martin McDonagh Interview, *Collider*.

59 C. Landesman, 'Review,' *The Sunday Times*, April 20, 2008, http://entertainment.timesonline.co.uk/tol/arts_and_entertainment/film/film_reviews/article3758013.ece (Accessed 2/3/2010)

60 C. O'Brien, 'In Bruges, Heaven or Hell?,' *Literature & Theology*, (2011), pp. 1–13, p.3.

61 G. King, 'Striking a balance between culture and fun: "quality" meets hitman genre in *In Bruges*,' *New Review of Film and Television Studies*, 9:02, (2011), pp.132–151, p.135.

62 As they check into a hotel, they have assumed the aliases of Cranham and Blakely. Ken Cranham and Colin Blakely starred in a 1985 BBC production of Harold Pinter's 1960 play *The Dumb Waiter*, which Joan Dean notes. See '*In Bruges*', p.168.

63 Irina Melnikova, notes how 'Death and the Miser sharpens the problem of the partial representation of canvases. The narrative shows two panels from a triptych which belonged to the former Dominican monastery in Bruges. The central panel was lost and the reverse sides of the two remaining parts of it (Death and the Miser) were detached from the obverse parts (Donor with St Nicholas and his Wife with St Godelieve) and are exhibited separately. What is more, when showing this, the lower area depicting the Miser's money-bag and the coins on the Table of Death is cut off. In that way Ken, together with the spectator, sees a piece of paper (perhaps a ticket from the money lender) handed from the Miser to Death [....] Ken sees the coins in the piece of painting that is hidden from us. This hidden piece also points to the events of the past (to the coins with which he tried to pay for the ticket to the Belfry) and at the same time foretells an event in the future – the throwing of coins with which he will try to warn Ray about the danger of death. Furthermore, this future throwing of coins repeats the action of the person on the invisible obverse part of Provoost's artwork – the charitable gesture of St Nicholas – one of the most popular saints of Eastern and Western churches, the patron of sailors, children, travellers, etc., traditionally associated with Christmas. See 'In(visible) Bruges by Martin McDonagh', *Journal of European Studies* (2013) 43, pp.44–59, p.50.

64 D. Ipp notes that 'According to Herodotus, Sisamnes was a royal judge in Persia under the reign of King Cambyses II. Sisamnes accepted a bribe from a party in a lawsuit and rendered an unjust judgment. Cambyses learned of the bribe and arrested him. Sisamnes was sentenced to death, but before the execution, his skin was flayed off (portrayed in graphic detail by David). Cambyses used the skin to string and cover the chair on which Sisamnes had sat when delivering his verdicts. To replace Sisamnes, Cambyses appointed Sisamnes's son, Otanes, as the new judge. Cambyses admonished Otanes to bear in mind the source of the leather of the chair upon which he would sit as a judge. Cambyses's instruction as to the need for judicial impartiality, emphasised as it was by the reupholstered chair, must have left a lingering impression on his new judge.' See 'Maintaining the Tradition of Judicial Impartiality,' http://www.lawlink.nsw.gov.au/lawlink/Supreme_Court/ll_sc.nsf/vwFiles/ipp211108.pdf/$file/ipp211108.pdf (Accessed 23/3/2011)

65 Manohla Dargis also summarises very well the moment before this picture: 'two hit men pause before a painting, awe and puzzlement and perhaps something else shading their faces. The painting ... shows a prisoner wearing a loincloth and a strangely calm expression given that he's being flayed alive. A small gathering of men (an audience, you might say) stands around the condemned, whose left calf is being peeled like a blood orange.' See 'Hit Men on Holiday Get All Medieval', *New York Times,* 8 April 2008, *http://movies.nytimes.com/2008/02/08/movies/08brug.html* (Accessed 23/3/2011)

66 M. Rouse, 'Hit Men on Holiday Get All Medieval', *European Journal of English Studies*, 15:2, (2011), pp.171–182, p.177.

67 Catherine O'Brien notes that: 'Most significantly, Ray and Ken ostensibly visit the Basilica of the Precious Blood (the Heilig-Bloedbasiliek), in which a holy relic – a vial that purportedly contains Christ's blood – has been venerated by pilgrims in Bruges since the 12th century. As filming could not take place in the real basilica, a replacement location was found in the city's 15th-century Jeruzalemkerk, a private chapel modelled on the Church of the Holy Sepulchre in Jerusalem. It is a logistical decision that adds a fresh dimension to the narrative.' See 'In Bruges, Heaven or Hell?,' *Literature & Theology*, 2011, pp.7–8.

68 For Philip French, the two main characters 'engage in philosophical conversations about life and their bizarre profession, which are even funnier and more scabrous than the exchanges between Samuel L. Jackson and John Travolta in *Pulp Fiction*.' See 'In Bruges', *The Observer*, Sunday 20 April 2008, http://www.guardian.co.uk/film/2008/apr/20/thriller.comedy/. (Accessed 2/3/2012).

69 The addition of these deleted scenes on the DVD I would contend are there more to confuse than clarify.

70 C. O'Brien, 'In Bruges, Heaven or Hell?,' p.7.

71 See 'McDonagh and Farrell Interview' in *Collider*.

72 In a deleted scene there is a flashback of a policeman called Potter, who kills Ken's wife in a brothel, and then later Harry beheads Potter in a police station.

73 In the hotel room Ken watches part of the famous almost three-minute long tracking shot from Orson Welles's *Touch of Evil* (1958), which starred Charlton Heston, Janet Leigh, Orson Welles, and Joseph Calleia. Margitta Rouse points out that as 'Ken speaks to Harry, the camera never leaves Ken. In a six-minute real-time take, the film evokes, and then outstrips, the black and white milestone of cinematic history.' See 'Hit Men on Holiday Get All Medieval,' p. 178.

74 And later there is the line describing Eirik's demeanour as 'looking as guilty as Judas,' as he informs Harry of Ray's presence in the city. (p.87)

75 See Pinker *The Better Angels of Our Nature*, p.91.

76 Ibid., p.162.

77 Ibid., p.703.

78 bid., p.703.

79 Ibid., p.712.

80 J. FitzPatrick Dean notes 'The production design of Michael Carlin, whose set design for *The Duchess*, also 2008, earned him an Academy Award nomination, fills the film-within-the film's misty, hallucinatory set with enormous animals, menacing nuns, disconcerting doubles, masked figures, and, yes, dwarves.' *In Bruges, Estudios Irlandeses*, p.167.

81 Roeg's psycho-thriller is about a couple Laura (Julie Christie) and John Baxter (Donald Sutherland) who are staying in a hotel (like Ray and Ken) in an off-season, almost deserted Venice, as they deal with loss and grief after the death of their young daughter who drowned in a domestic accident. John is an art restorer who works on churches, which allows Christian iconography to be central to the piece. The grieving father is killed by the female psycho-dwarf. Both *In Bruges* and *Don't look Now* use the found city spaces to provide telling atmosphere, and both have premonitions of further catastrophe. The paintings in *In Bruges* foretell a future of sorts, whereas in Roeg's work it is the blind female psychic seer, who warns of impending death. The unexpected figure of a mature aged, serial killing murderous female dwarf, dressed in a red coat, similar in colour to the one the couple's child died in, is the unexpected twist in Roeg's movie. While Bruges does not have the specific daylight eeriness of Venice in Roeg's work, its relationship with fairytale

and medieval religious values and dispositions really heightens the register of the piece in a very different way, especially during the night-time scenes. Roeg's film has an intimate and well commented upon lovemaking scene between the grieving couple, which holds out the possibility of pregnancy and a new start. In *In Bruges* that is never possible, Ray does go to bed with Chloë, but they are interrupted. There is no consummation. *Don't Look Now* has a strange mix of genres, *In Bruges* does likewise.

82 'McDonagh's dum-dums are ballistically inaccurate – expanding later rather than earlier – although they nonetheless serve an important function in the story's trajectory, leading to its bloody finale.' See http://www.imdb.com/title/tt0780536/trivia?tab=gf. (Accessed 2/3/2012)

83 J. Dean reports that when Colin Farrell accepted the Golden Globe award he described the movie as 'simultaneously profound and beautifully comic and wonderfully painful, filled with delightful remorse and more than anything else, the sweetest, sweetest redemptive qualities.' And from an actor's point of view, it is easy to see what he would consider 'redemptive.' See *'In Bruges,'* p.166.

84 A. Lane, 'Strangers,' *New Yorker,* 11 February 2008, http://www.newyorker.com/arts/critics/cinema/2008/02/11/080211crci_cinema_lane?currentPage=1, (Accessed 2/3/2001)

85 Ibid.

86 P. French, 'In Bruges.'

87 P. Bradshaw, Review of *In Bruges*, *The Guardian*, Friday 18 April 2008, http://www.guardian.co.uk/film/2008/apr/18/drama.thriller (Accessed 2/3/2001).

88 M. Dargis, 'Hit Men on Holiday Get All Medieval.'

89 A. Lane 'Strangers.'

90 J. Rocchi, 'Sundance Review: In Bruges,' 18 January 2008, http://www.cinematical.com/2008/01/18/sundance-review-in-bruges/. (Accessed 2/3/2012).

91 Totalitarianism is often regarded as either single-personed dictatorship or a 'dictatorship of the proletariat.' See K.D. Bracher, 'The Disputed Concept of Totalitarianism: Experience and Actuality' in *Totalitarianism Reconsidered*, ed. E.A. Menze (Kennikat Press: New York and London, 1981), pp.16–17.

92 P. Pacheco, *'Laughing Matters,'* 'Laughing Matters', *The Los Angeles Times*, 22 May 2005, http://articles.latimes.com/2005/may/22/entertainment/ca-pillowman22 (Accessed 14/9/2011)

93 C. James, 'Critic's Notebook: A Haunting Play Resounds Far Beyond the Stage,' *New York Times*, 15 April 2005, *http://theater2.nytimes.com/mem/theater/treview.html?res=9E06E1DC103EF936A25757C0A9639C8B63&fta=y* (Accessed 10 March 2009)

94 V. Segal, 'Review of *The Pillowman*', *Sunday Times,* 23 Nov 2003. Re-printed in *Theatre Record* 23 (5–18 November 2003), pp.1554–55, p.1554.

95 This Theatre's Steam Industry's new writing development scheme assisted with this script, as confirmed by the Theatre's Artistic Director Neil McPherson, in an email to me on 29/4/2013. See also http://www.finboroughtheatre.co.uk/history.php (Accessed 29/4/2013)

96 See P. Lonergan, *The Theatre and Films of Martin McDonagh* (London: Methuen, 2012), p.234.

97 For images from the Royal National Theatre production see http://www.nationaltheatre.org.uk/?lid=6096&dspl=images (Accessed 6/9/2011)

98 For images from the Broadway production see http://broadwayworld.com/article/Photo_Preview_The_Pillowman_20050330 (Accessed 6/9/2011)

99 Christine Madden, commenting on the production of *The Pillowman,* directed by Tina Lanik at the Deutsches Theater, Berlin, during the Heidelberger Stüchkemarkt

festival, notes that 'Far from being presented naturalistically, everything in the play converged on the idea of a world gone wonky, from the ingenious set – an Irish drawing room, complete with typical doors and wall mouldings, tilted 90 degrees to the left – to the cartoon-like yet sinister presence of the actors. In its sharp absurdity the production felt like Flann O'Brien on cocaine.' *The Irish Times, 24 May 2004, http://www.irishtimes.com/newspaper/features/2004/0524/index.html* (Accessed 3/8/2012)

100 See http://www.japantimes.co.jp/text/ft20041117a1.html (Assessed 3/8 2012) and Hiroko Mikami's '"Not Lost in Translation": Martin McDonagh in Japan,' http://dspace.wul.waseda.ac.jp/dspace/bitstream/2065/26868/1/003.pdf (Accessed 3 August 2012)

101 See also Rufus Didwiszus's scenography for the production at the Elverket Theatre Stockholm in 2004, directed by Stefan Larsson, http://3.bp.blogspot.com/_qOTDjx8Aj58/Sgflkqtf4nI/AAAAAAAAAtM/8wii-PrJAPM/s1600-h/pillow1.jpg (Accessed 3 August 2012)

102 Note also Steppenwolf Theatre company's production in September 2006 Seehttp://www.steppenwolf.org/Plays-Events/productions/index.aspx?id=371 (Accessed 29/4/2013)

103 Paul Kerryson's production of the play at the Curve Theatre Leicester in 2009 as reviewed by Lyn Gardner, *The Guardian*, 18 February 2009, http://www.guardian.co.uk/stage/2009/feb/18/the-pillowman-review (Accessed 15 November 2012)

104 I saw the play's premiere in London, and have on two occasions viewed a video recording of the production held at the National archive in November 2005 and May 2011. (Recording made 6/12/2003). I have also viewed a recording of the Booth Theatre New York performance (Recording made 22/6/2005) held by the New York Public Library in April 2010.

105 See P. Rego's, *The Pillowman Triptych*, which are inspired by the sensibility of the *mise-en-scène*. *http://www.tate.org.uk/britain/exhibitions/rego/pillowman.shtm* (Accessed 10 March 2009)

106 C. James adds, 'It was here in the conversation that Mr. Crowley cited Bruno Bettelheim, who observed that imposing an interpretation on a fairy tale diminishes its enchantment.' See 'Critic's Notebook.'

107 See M. Bakhtin's concept of Carnival in *Rabelais and his world*, Helene Iswolsky, (trans.) (Bloomington: Indiana University Press, 1984) and *Problems of Dostoevsky's Poetics*, C. Emerson, (ed. and trans.) (Minneapolis: University of Minnesota Press, 1984).

108 S. Vice, *Introducing Bakhtin* (Manchester: Manchester University Press, 1997), p.152.

109 Ibid., p.174.

110 See Pinker, *The Better Angels of Our Nature*, p.671.

111 Ibid., p.671.

112 Ibid., p.672.

113 Ibid., pp.673–88.

114 O. Pilný, 'Grotesque Entertainment: *The Pillowman* as Puppet Theatre' in L. Chambers and E. Jordan, (eds), *The Theatre of Martin McDonagh: A World of Savage Stories*, (Dublin: Carysfort, 2006), pp.214–223, p.215.

115 Ibid., p.215.

116 H. and W.B. Worthen '*The Pillowman* and the Ethics of Allegory,' *Modern Drama*, 49.2, (2006), pp. 155–173, p.172, http://muse.jhu.edu/journals/modern_drama/v049/49.2worthen.html (Accessed 14/9/2011)

117 See Pilný, 'Grotesque Entertainment,' p.214.

118 S. Žižek, *Violence,* (London: Profile Books, 2009), p.135.

119 Ibid., p.135.

120 P. Müller, 'Body Politics in a Fictitious Eastern European Dictatorship: Martin McDonagh's The Pillowman,' in M. Kurdi, (ed.), *Literary and Cultural Relations: Ireland, Hungary and Central and Eastern Europe* (Dublin: Carysfort, 2009), p.49.

121 Ibid., pp.49–50.

122 Surprisingly, when the play was produced in New York in 2005, some critics saw no need to draw any parallels to the torture and violation of human rights by American forces during the Iraq War, incidents such as those that had occurred at Abu Ghraib prison. Part of the intention of the 'War on Terror' was to spread democracy and to protect its own citizens, whose conferred rights are very different to what was sometimes dished out in Iraqi prisons. Equally, the reality of black operations and rogue prison sites must not be forgotten, as they nominally afforded a freedom to torture detainees on non-US soil. The complicity of many other countries to aid and abet such practices must not be ignored, including Ireland and Britain.

123 M. Reizbaum raises a substantial point about the boy's Jewish background: 'The police ask Katurian has he been trolling the Jewish quarter? – as if to wonder whether, Frankenstein-like, he will find his ideal subject for child murder there.' She adds: 'Initially, this detail seems inexplicable, an inversion of the blood-libel myth. But the resonances are clear: the tip cutting/ castration, rats/disease, the lure, the proxy child. It is also key that this is an *urban legend* in which the children are taken away beyond the city's festering borders and the worries about public hygiene that are centred there. The spectre of urban contagion in particular was often personified in the figure of the "dirty Jew," who becomes the stand-in for the city itself in these terms.' See 'Urban Legends,' *Éire-Ireland*, 45:1&2, (Spring/ Summer 2010), pp.242-265, pp.260-1. http://muse.jhu.edu/journals/eire-ireland/v045/45.1.reizbaum.html#f37-text (Accessed 21/3/2011)

Such details become further complicated by the fact that when asked to describe the little Jewish boy, Katurian states that he had 'browny-black' hair. However, the boy was half-Irish: – 'It's a shame his mum was fucking Irish, and her son closely resembled a red fucking setter,' according to Tupolski. (p.97) Such a revelation complicates ideas of ethnicity and nationality and foregrounds a diasporic imaginary, where migrants were often seen in terms of contamination and contagion. The belief that members of the Jewish community sacrificed their children to get blood for religious ceremonies, also ties in with how the Irish as a disaporic group were regarded as having barbaric practices, including living with pigs as the likes of some Victorian magazines would have it, but not quite on the scale of blood-sacrifice.

124 As an actor, Jeff Goldblum has great physical presence, but his Tupolski in the New York production is a little too driven, almost too polished and corporate in his tone, leaving less space for the nuances and subtextual subtleties that Broadbent brought to his performance. It is as if Goldblum has internalised more easily and with less suspicion the ideology of state, remaining easily on a strict party line and is confidently on solid ground, whereas Broadbent creates enough hesitation and ambivalence to suggest a more manipulative, maniacal state that is constantly shifting perspective and that confuses even him.

125 Željko Ivanek's Ariel is not only pale and slight of frame in contrast to Goldblum's much taller physical presence, he also contrasts nicely with the more burly and aggressive, Ariel of Lindsay's. (Ivanek also played a Canadian character in *In Bruges* and Paulo in *Seven Psychopaths.*) Ivanek gives the impression that his Ariel is under orders to perform with aggression, but that it is less an innate disposition, whereas it is as if interrogating detainees and putting them under duress is the natural disposition of Lindsay's Ariel. For Ben Brantley, Goldblum and Ivanek

'turn the classic good cop-bad cop formula into a coruscating vaudeville routine. Mr. Goldblum's trademark deadpan wryness has rarely been put to better use, as his Tupolski toys with Katurian like a jaded latter day version of the police inspector in Dostoyevsky's *Crime and Punishment*.' See 'A Storytelling Instinct Revels in Horror's Fun', *New York Times*, 11 April 2005. http://theater.nytimes.com/2005/04/11/theater/reviews/11pill.html (Accessed 6/9/2011)

126 Billy Crudup's Katurian for the New York production is very different to Tennant's. Crudup is far more physical and gestural in his characterisation. He is more unnerved by and passive aggressive towards his interrogators. From the start, the composure and suspicion of Tennant contrasts with the frantic, over-eager, over-enthusiasm of Crudup's Katurian to impress and to placate his interrogators. Crudup resorts to hand gestures and twitches and rubs his tie reverentially, giving the impression of a really, intense creative type, who has had far too much caffeine, and who has dedicated far too much time to his own thoughts and to reflections on his talents. Brantley notes that Crudup's 'finely chiselled features turn out to be ideal for registering the seductiveness, defensiveness and pure vanity of an artist for whom writing means even more than the brother he has protected for many years. Katurian's self-enchanted satisfaction when he tells a story is that of a young magician, pulling off a tricky sleight of hand. And Mr. Crudup makes it clear that the flame of anger burns brightest in Katurian when his stories are criticised or threatened with extinction.' See Brantley, 'A Storytelling Instinct'.

127 R. Kearney, *On Stories* (London and New York, Routledge, 2002), p.3.

128 Ibid. p.129.

129 P. Pacheco in his article notes that 'At one point, when the conversation with McDonagh turns to Bruno Bettelheim, McDonagh is genuinely moved to hear that the writer, a Holocaust survivor, committed suicide [....] Asked whether the Pillowman should have visited Bettelheim, McDonagh shudders. "Oh, that's too creepy," he says. "That kind of horror, that kind of sadness, is just too specific. I find it much harder to think about that than any kind of make-believe having to do with *The Pillowman*."' See 'Laughing Matters.'

130 B. Bettelheim, *The Uses of Enchantment: The Meaning and Importance of Fairy Tales* (London: Penguin Books, 1976, reprinted 1991), p.7.

131 Ibid., p.3.

132 Ibid., pp.3–4.

133 Ibid., p.5.

134 Ibid., p.7.

135 Ibid., p.7.

136 Ibid., p.8.

137 Ibid., p.9.

138 Ibid., p.9.

139 Ibid., p.10.

140 Ibid., p.9.

141 Ibid., p.10.

142 Ibid., p.10.

143 The second story considered is 'The Three Gibbet Crossroads' and it is Tupolski who paraphrases it, and examines it for hidden meanings. For Katurian it is 'puzzle without a solution'. What might be the unmentionable crime of the prisoner held in his cell?

144 For instance, Marilyn Reizbaum suggests that the Pied Piper myth can be traced back to thirteenth-century Germany: '[I]ts German title, translated as "The Ratcatcher", suggests its medieval role as an allegory of disease. It has been understood as a way to mythologise the deaths of the children of the town from the plague, an allegory

of the devil's conniving work. And sometimes it is explained as a fable about the children's enlistment in the Crusades, a glorified accounting of their eventual death [....]' See 'Urban Legends,' p.260.

145 M. Haughton's work looks at the play in relation to space and Michel Foucault's work on power and discipline. See 'Merging Worlds: Place, Politics, and Play in Martin McDonagh's *The Pillowman', Focus: Papers in English Literary and Cultural Studies*, (2012), pp.77-92.

146 In the New York production, as Katurian burns his story in the interrogation space, the boy in the room goes to do the same and pulls a bit of red paper from the story to suggest that it is burning.

147 See images of the room in Heidi Schumann's photographs for *The New York Times,* http://www.nytimes.com/imagepages/2005/04/26/arts/26whip.ready.html (Accessed 14/10/2013)

148 Crudup responds as if he is surprised by such readings, Tennant's comments have an element of bravado in his denials. Both actors appear strategic in the face of their interrogators.

149 See Worthen and Worthen, '*The Pillowman* and the Ethics of Allegory', p. 161.

150 In the New York production, Michael Stuhlbarg as Michal wears a pink shirt closed at the collar, a wine-coloured cardigan and braces. His voice suggests the damage from the screaming that the torture has prompted. The hair on the lower part of his head is shaved to give a clichéd institutionalised sort of look.

151 Pacheco asks McDonagh about the responsibilities of writers: 'In terms of the larger issues he raises about creativity and the writer's moral responsibilities,' he says, there are no easy answers. 'I think it does say that creativity is beautiful and worthwhile for its own sake,' he says, 'But in terms of responsibility? I don't think that Martin Scorsese can be held responsible because John Hinckley saw *Taxi Driver* many times and became obsessed with Jodie Foster. If something happened to a child after a person saw *Pillowman*, I'd definitely feel guilty about it, but I wouldn't be culpable.' See 'Laughing Matters'.

152 S. Baron-Cohen, *Zero Degrees*, p.71.

153 Ibid., p.84.

154 Ibid., p.69.

155 Ibid., p.69.

156 Ibid., pp.69–70.

157 Ibid., p.70.

158 Ibid., p.70.

159 Of Katurian's 400 stories 'The Little Green Pig' is the most optimistic. It really captures sentiments of individuality and uniqueness in the face of collective interference, and the redemptive figure is that of a God-like power overhead, watching out for the little pig or vulnerable citizen. The narrative conclusion suggests that individuality cannot be obscured, despite the broad strokes of an ideologically repressive society, bent on the insistent affirmation of sameness and non-differentiation. The colour green has also a fundamental association with Irishness, and, secondly, classical British stereotypes have long associated the Irish with pigs. Victorian representations of Ireland used illustrations of the Irish families sharing living spaces with pigs, as indications of the lack of civilisation amongst the Irish, rather than reading the fact of shared accommodation as having more to do with grave economic lack. (The little green pig 'really liked being green...liked being a little bit different, a little bit peculiar', (p.65) and is 'peculiar' whether it is green or pink.

160 See M. Carr's *By the Bog of Cats...* in *Plays 1* (London: Faber and Faber, 1999) and J. Steinbeck's *Of Mice and Men* (London: Penguin, 2000, originally published in 1937) both texts include mercy killings of sorts.

161 As Pinker notes, in some people, signs of psychopathy develop after damage to these regions [the amygdale and orbital cortex] from disease or an accident, but the condition is also partly heritable. See *The Better Angels of Our Nature*, p.615, based on research by A. Raine, 'From Genes to Grain to Antisocial Behaviour', *Current Directions in Psychological Science*, 17, pp.323–8.

162 On his early writing of fairytales McDonagh notes:
'I'd write a whole list of titles which I hoped would spark up story ideas like The Chair and The Wolfboy. You know just looking around this place it'd be: The Short Fellow and The Strange Frog; The Violin and The Drunken Angel – twin ideas that might go somewhere. I'd sit down and write 50 titles. And then the next week or whatever, I would try to write them almost like fairy-tale stories [....] In re-reading the Grimm's, they're pretty bloody dark. It was interesting to compare my memory, what I remembered about the fairy tales, and then to see the actual text. To be not quite sure if you were told a cleaned up version of it or if your child's memory cleaned it up yourself. I think more often than not it was that you were told a cleaned up version.'
See Martin McDonagh in interview with Fintan O'Toole, *BOMB 63*, (Spring 1998), http://bombsite.com/issues/63/articles/2146
(Accessed 20/11/11)

163 See Kearney, *On Stories*, pp. 6–7.

164 There is a fixation on fire and burning across the work, whether it is Valene setting Fr Welsh's letter on fire, Mick Dowd burning his confession, Ariel's initial burning of Katurian's stories, The Pillowboy setting himself alight, Carmichael's failed attempt to set the room alight, or the Buddhist monk self-immolating.

165 Pilný notes that *The Pillowman* invites – not merely by its title – an interesting analogy with the famous story by E.T.A. Hoffmann, 'The Sandman'. ('The Sandman' in *Tales of Hoffmann*, trans. R.J. Hollingdale (Harmondsworth: Penguin, 1982)). See 'Grotesque Entertainment', p.217.

166 For the first two previews of the play's premiere, as Caryl James reports, Crowley had 'an actor in a pink Pillowman costume onstage', initially thinking that 'it would be quite spooky and scary,' but it was not. He adds, 'For one thing, that Pillowman too closely resembled an English cartoon character called Mr. Blobby. For another, people said it looked nothing like *The Pillowman* of their imaginations, even though the costume had faithfully reproduced Katurian's description.' This was a crucial discovery for the director, but his realization that the imagination of an audience needs to be unencumbered by representation as the literal is an inappropriate response to the symbolic, the allegorical and metaphoric. See 'Critic's Notebook: A Haunting Play Resounds Far Beyond the Stage'.

167 See Worthen and Worthen, '*The Pillowman* and the Ethics of Allegory', p162, citing P. de Man, 'The Rhetoric of Temporality.' *Blindness and Insight: Essays in the Rhetoric of Contemporary Criticism* (Minneapolis: U of Minnesota Press, 1983, 2nd ed.) pp.187–228, p.228.

168 Ibid., p.165.

169 See V.S. Ramachandran, *The Tell-Tale Brain: Unlocking the Mystery of Human Nature* (London: William Heinemann, 2011), p.7.

170 P. Pacheco, 'Laughing Matters.'

171 See Bettelheim, *The Uses of Enchantment*, p.11.

172 Ibid., pp.10–1.

173 In *In Bruges* Ken is reading a book, not visible on screen, but named in screen play as *The Death of Capone* by K. K. Katurian who died from neurosyphilis. This is a playful extension of the play's ending.

174 C. McGrath, '*The Pillowman* Audience: Shocked and a Bit Amused' 26 April 2005, *New York Times* http://www.nytimes.com/2005/04/26/theater/newsandfeatures/26whip.html (Accessed 10 March 2009)
175 Ibid.
176 B. Brantley, 'A Storytelling Instinct'.
177 C. McGrath, '*The Pillowman* Audience'
178 Ibid.
179 Ibid.
180 P. Taylor, 'Review,' *Independent,* 17 November 2003, http://www.independent.co.uk/arts-entertainment/theatre-dance/reviews/the-pillowman-cottesloe-theatre-nt-london-736037.html (Accessed 6/9/2011)
181 Ibid.
182 Coleman's father kicked Girleen's cat, Eamonn. She notes: '.... But there'd be a lot less cats kicked in Ireland, I'll tell ya, if the fella could reassured he'd be shot in the head after.' (162)
183 In the promotional materials McDonagh is listed as 'The Marty behind the Marty', and the seven main characters are listed as Marty – The Seemingly Normal One, Hans – The non-violent one, Billy – The Best Friend, Angela – The Hot Girlfriend, Zac –The one with the Bunny, Kaya – The passive-aggressive girlfriend, Charlie – The One with Issues. In the film the numbering of the psychopaths is different.
184 P. French, 'Review- *Seven Psychopaths*', *The Observer*, 9 December 2012, http://www.guardian.co.uk/film/2012/dec/09/seven-psychopaths-review-french-mcdonagh (Accessed 19/12/2012)
185 On the issue of creativity and writer's block issue, McDonagh notes, 'It's a comment on the comment. It's exposing that cliché and playing with it. I actually think that writer's block is a myth. I am lazy. But I don't have writer's block.' See D. Clarke, 'Psycho thriller', *The Irish Times*, 7 December 2012, http://www.irishtimes.com/newspaper/theticket/2012/1207/1224327589235.html (Accessed 7/12/2012)
186 In a deleted scene, at the funerals of two hitmen, Costello promises both grieving mothers to crucify the killer of their son, and he calls the Priest a 'potato head Irish fuck'.
187 J. Utichi, 'It's a mad, mad world,' *The Sunday Times*, 9 December 2012, pp 16–17.
188 In an interview, Samuel Wigley reminds McDonagh that it is very close to Ingmar Bergman's *Persona* (1966) – 'as you have both a Vietnamese monk setting light to himself' and that 'Bergman has the film grind to a halt momentarily about 30 minutes in, as the film appears to melt in the projector.' McDonagh admits to the influence, but he had forgotten about it, even though he had seen it recently, conceding it as a 'rip-off'. See 'Seven Psychopaths: Martin McDonagh interview,' *British Film Institute News*, 7 December 2012, http://www.bfi.org.uk/news-opinion/bfi-news/seven-psychopaths-martin-mcdonagh-interview (Accessed 19/12/2012)
189 BBC report notes 'The My Lai massacre, which took place on the morning of March 16, 1968, was a watershed in the history of modern American combat and a turning point in the public perception of the Vietnam War. In the course of three hours more than 500 Vietnamese civilians were killed in cold blood at the hands of US troops.' See BBC News Monday, 20 July, 1998, 'Murder in the name of war – My Lai', http://news.bbc.co.uk/2/hi/asia-pacific/64344.stm (Accessed 230/3/2113)
190 Philip French notes that 'The stories are enacted on screen in the minds of Marty, Billy and Hans, recalling such films of the 1960s as Alain Robbe-Grillet's *Trans-Europ-Express* and Agnès Varda's *Les créatures*, where what we see are the books the central characters are writing, rewriting and tinkering with.' See 'Review- *Seven Psychopaths*.'
191 See Pinker, *The Better Angels of Our Nature*, p.819.

192 Harrelson was a late replacement for Mickey Rourke.

193 Cosmo Landesman asserts: 'Harrelson, who has played a few psychos in his time, brings to the screen an authentic and energetic mix of murderous madman and sentimental dog-lover.' See 'A perfect derangement; Martin McDonagh's *Seven Psychopaths* turns genre clichés on their head with a racking cast', *The Sunday Times*, 9 December 2012, p.14.

194 Donald Clarke notes that 'Walken has rarely been better (and that's saying something). His carefully spoken sage has a mild hint of madness about him, but – decked out in a smashing cravat – he is also allowed moments of genuine poignancy.' See 'Seven Psychopaths.'

195 J. Verini, 'A Terrible act of Reason: When Did Self-Immolation Become the Paramount Form of Protest,' *New Yorker*, 16 May 2012, http://www.newyorker.com/online/blogs/culture/2012/05/history-of-self-immolation.html (Accessed 29/1/2013)

196 Ibid.

197 Ibid.

198 See Pinker, *The Better Angels of Our Nature*, p.715.

199 Ibid., p.717.

200 Ibid., pp.734–5.

201 Ibid., pp.737–8.

202 Ibid., p.808.

203 Ibid., p.808.

204 Ibid., p.808.

205 Ibid., p.798.

206 F. O'Toole, 'Martin McDonagh Interview', *Bomb*.

207 See Baron-Cohen, *Zero Degrees*, p.48.

208 M. Fryan, 'Introduction', *The Seagull*, by A. Chekhov, translated by Fryan (London: Methuen, 1986), p.xiv.

209 See Baron-Cohen, *Zero Degrees*, p.114.

210 Ibid., p.109.

Conclusion

While Druid Theatre Company was instrumental in premiering McDonagh's plays, this book suggests that to focus only on that initial breakthrough would form an inaccurate impression.[1] Around that time he also came to the attention of the London theatre community, including the Bush, Finborough and National Theatres, and with the latter he received significant support, including the two residencies mentioned in my introduction. As already stated, *The Leenane Trilogy* was a co-production between Druid Theatre Company and the Royal Court, London. The National Theatre's premiering of *Inishmaan* and *The Pillowman* in 1997 and 2003 respectively, and the Royal Shakespeare Company's production of *Inishmore* in 2001 are of great significance; these decisions to produce the work served as endorsements of McDonagh's dramaturgy, which when aligned with positive reviews and any of either the many award nominations or successes that followed, these particulars then gave others both impetus and confidence to produce the work elsewhere. The considerable Anglo-Irish involvement into the premiering of McDonagh's work equates in part with his status as a complex, cosmopolitan, post-colonial, diasporic and Anglo-Irish subject. The many productions of his work around the globe are also of huge importance and much research needs to be done in this area.[2]

In her work on British culture, Jen Harvie argues that national identities are always 'staged, culturally produced, dynamic, and [...] inherently troubled',[3] and that these identities 'are equally multiple, mutually contingent and mutually embedded – simultaneously holding in tension multiple determinants, from affinities with locale, region and nation to affinities with Europe, global subjectivity and diasporic communities'.[4] McDonagh's writing for both theatre and film demonstrate aspects of British, American and Irish identities, which are equally culturally produced and received, just as dynamic and 'inherently troubled', and veer away from notions of authenticity. They highlight both the effortlessly consumable and less easily digestible forms of Britishness and Americanness, with the dominant emphasis placed on Irishness.

From the point of view of reception, and, by default or otherwise, simply by locating many of the plays and films in Ireland or in the instance of *In Bruges* or of *Seven Psychopaths*, with the inclusion of Irish characters central to these films, McDonagh's work will almost always invite audiences to conceive and supplement an imaginary Ireland and to fictionalise some forms of Irishness.[5] (Furthermore, that engagement does not necessarily make the plays, as Patrick Lonergan validly suggests; 'tell us something about Ireland'.[6])

From the 1990s onwards public narratives were self-consciously positioning Ireland in new ways, especially during the 'Celtic Tiger' period of economic boom and the tendency was to see Ireland not in terms of lack but in terms of abundance, and not in terms of its isolation or peripheral position, but in terms of its connectedness to the world and its central significance to the European Union, as well as culture and politics on global stages. Its towns and cities had increasingly more in common with the UK or America than with a traditional, rural, and conservative Ireland.[7]

If this outlook was contemporary, cosmopolitan and global in focus, in contrast the more successful 'Irish' plays internationally, as I have outlined earlier in my introduction, which seemed in general terms to be historic in perspective, rural in location and pastoral in sensibility, with a few notable exceptions. McDonagh's early work seems to have been regularly associated with these works by critics, scholars and theatre producers, but, in many respects McDonagh's dramaturgical template was rather atypical of this trend, apart from the appearance of notional Irish characters in not quite superficial west of Ireland settings.

In plays like *Dancing at Lughnasa* the ennobled tropes were the defiant responses to subsistence living, the emphasis on collegiality and family, the wish to calibrate or cross-check moralities, and above all else the ability to relate with empathy, thus potentially signalling in performance forms of reassuring authenticity. In contrast, the markers of Irishness deployed by McDonagh's work are less about authenticity and more about artifice and the relative lack of empathy, and are less about traditional sensibilities, values and Christian moralities and more about keeping aspects such as provisionality, irony and kitsch in telling focus. Also resisted is any sense of merit or nostalgia associated with victimisation and grand narratives of colonial oppression. (Many writers from other cultures have similar methods to contest nostalgically, symbolically and/or mythologically rural and marginal environments.)

Colin Graham cites Fintan O'Toole, who talks about the disappearance of 'Ireland': 'while the place itself persists, the map, the visual and the ideological convention that allows us to call that place "Ireland" has been slipping away. Its coordinates, its longitudes and latitudes, refuse to hold their shape.'[8] On that basis, Graham adds that 'Ireland becomes a plenitude of images, replicating itself for continual consumption and at times achieving an over satiation. It is here that the "Ireland" which is excessive topples into an Ireland of ceaseless reproduction and commodification.'[9] So the 'Ireland' that is potentially staged in McDonagh's work must be dealt with as part of a complex, if provisional signifying process, that includes excessiveness, absence, depletedness, supplementation and commodification. While there is a privileging of Irishness in the work, there is no exceptionalism and neither is there an essence of Irishness.

Additionally, it is vital to keep in mind what scholars like Diane Negra have pointed out; it is the more transactionary, porous and performative qualities of Irishness that make it fluid and commercially exploitative, but also subversive and substantial, and that it is not a concept that can be simply reduced by narrowly obsessive identity politics. Yet, that said, one cannot easily sidestep the fact that the lapsed Catholicism of the two Irish hitmen in *In Bruges* allows the characters the chance to engage with, respond more to and be affected by the surrounding Christian iconography of punishment and judgment found in the city. (It is not simply that their Irishness determines their Catholicism, or their Catholicism their Irishness, as the characters could easily be from British or American Catholic backgrounds, but probably would not have the same cultural resonance.)

However much they are steeped in the values of gangland and capitalism, the religious instruction of Ken's and Ray's rearing in Dublin determines much of their engagements and thoughts. The rendition of 'Raglan Road', adds to the sensibility of the moments leading up to Ken's self-sacrifice, especially, as already argued, the music is radically different to the style of Carter Burwell's musical score. Equally, given that *Inishmore* has the tangential context of Irish Republican paramilitarism, reflections on the play must somewhat account for a legacy of colonisation, Republican bombing campaigns in Ireland and Britain, the issue of collateral damage and the connections between paramilitarism, criminality and terrorism. The play also speaks to the rhetorical justifications and the actions of paramilitarism and terrorism more broadly as well. That said, how context is framed within a performance is important, but genre is an even more crucial aspect of this play than any contextual referencing of real historical moments or any framing of Irishness.

The contrasts between Garry Hynes's and Joe Hill-Gibbins's productions of *Beauty Queen* account for how differences in terms of performance sensibility might impact on spectators' responses. Part 2 also emphasises that genre framing is central to a performance sensibility, so I spend a good deal of time reflecting on the importance of the anti-mimetic dramaturgies of Farce and Grand-Guignol, and on how these overlap with the excessive and shocking representational strategies of fairytale and a range of Hollywood films set in gangland that make so much of gore, violation, torture and murder. There are also the implications of *In-Yer-Face Theatre* practices and the collapse of the binaries that Aleks Sierz has noted and which are cited in Part 2. On the basis of the challenges to such a breakdown of binaries, McDonagh is not just positioned within this style of theatre, but also alongside a broader engagement with a postmodern performance framework, a term which of course has no single focus or meaning.

McDonagh has admitted that in his film work, male and female relationships often end up on the cutting floor.[10] If we look at patterns to the work where there are four characters in plays like *Connemara*, *Lonesome*, or *Spokane*, it is a 3:1 ratio of male to female, with *Beauty Queen* an exception. My discussions have shown that issues of gender are a very complex component in McDonagh's work, even as masculinity is persistently and sometimes exclusively prioritised. In Part 2 I outlined the complexity of not just farcical and subservient masculinities, but also femininities, and I also address these issues in relation to whiteness and marginality and the general character fixation on violence.

Part 1 includes reflections on the competitive mother and daughter game-playing and the inevitability of murder in *Beauty Queen*. In terms of murder, Maureen is little different to the likes of Coleman and Kid. Both male and female parents are dangerous to be around. Billy's mother and father in *Inishmaan* have a role in trying to kill him. In *The Pillowman*, the mother and father partake in the sadistic torturing of their child and Carmichael's mother, Angela, incites racism and violence in *Spokane*. These facts prompt Joan FitzPatrick Dean to note that 'rather than give us the stereotypes of nurturing, self-sacrificing mothers, he confronts us with the consummately selfish Mag, the alcoholic Mammy O'Dougal and the vindictive and avaricious Maryjohnny Rafferty.'[11] (Of course, there are other elderly characters that are different: against the perceived conventions of their time, Eileen and Kate run their own grocery business in *Inishmaan*, and while this is a positive attribute, they are also very scattered, confused and prone to mindlessness.)[12]

To different degrees, the young female characters Girleen, Helen, Mairead and Chloë are complex characters, but they share aggressive, abusive, assertive and defiant behaviour. Helen gets paid to kill a cat and a goose, Girleen sells poteen and intervenes aggressively in a brawl between the two brothers. Chloë sells drugs to film crews and scams tourists and she is more than able for Ray, but does seem to have a strong affectionate side to her. And Marilyn is a scam artist, with a capacity for toxic thinking. Girleen has civilising, earthy and empathetic qualities that Helen seems to possess in part as well, even if they are hidden behind a multitude of confrontational and self-protective strategies.

However, FitzPatrick Dean claims that unlike the male characters, Ray in *Beauty Queen*, Bartley in *Inishmaan*, and Mairtin in *Connemara,* 'who seem gormless and dim-witted, their female counterparts are characteristically ruthless and determined', and are also 'witty, ambitious and clever.' Additionally, 'no less shocking are the vanity and promiscuity that Girleen and Helen claim for themselves,' while they also possess a 'level of mobility and a measure of independence'.[13] Girleen comically invokes the possibility of her selling sex, Helen seems to get into a number of compromising sexual liaisons, including one suspects, an affair with the eggman, and Mairead's fixation on Padraic is based on fantastically unreal notions, somewhat like Gwendolen's and Cecily's in Oscar Wilde's *The Importance of Being Earnest* (1895).

Of the young women characters, in temperament and attire, Mairead is by far the more traditionally masculine and this disposition contrasts with her very effeminate appearing brother, Davey. Mairead is by far the most psychopathological of all of the female characters. However, just as Brendan is about to die he views Mairead as 'a boy with lipstick' and Joey regards her as 'a girl with no boobs'. And Brendan believes he 'will never live it down' that he was shot by a 'girl'. (p.51) In this instance, there is not only the incongruous blurring of gender, but some superb comedy in the inappropriateness and irrelevance of their final words. Absurdity and illogically win out in the flagrant foregrounding of the performativity of gender and heteronormativity, alongside a purposefully unsettling misogyny. (When Harry abuses his wife Natalie (Elizabeth Berrington) in their home, he calls her an 'inanimate fucking object'. (p.61) He does later apologise for making that comment.)

In general, repression and dysfunctionality only partly explain what McDonagh does with sex, as there are additional confusions, ambiguities, fears of intimacy and anxieties about pleasure that are generally evident in the behaviours of many of the characters. Maureen and Pato manage to share a bed, but no sexual intimacy transacts between them. Valene and Coleman's obsessions with sex and virginity are a bit like the characters in the TV series *Bottom* (1991–95), which starred Adrian Edmondson and Rik Mayall. Celibacy seems to be the destiny of the Connor brothers. The fledgling romance between Helen and Billy is marked by doom.[14] Katurian will not produce any offspring, but writing is his legacy.

In the Garrick production of *Inishmore* Mairead's and Padraic's impassioned kissing and almost frantic if clothed and interrupted sex, in front of her brother and his father, is as close as any of the characters get to sexual conjugation. And Ray's and Chloë's sexual encounter is interrupted long before consummation. Billy Bickle cannot have sex with Angela, as he is unable to maintain an erection. The only characters with living offspring in all the plays are Mag Folan and Mammy O'Dougal, and in *In Bruges* the hotel owner, Marie, is about to give birth and Harry and Natalie have three children. In Nicholas Roeg's *Don't Look Now* there is the infamous love scene which seems to suggest the possibility of pregnancy and the idea that there can be some level of compensation or consolation for a couple who have lost a child, but in *In Bruges* the murdered child cannot be resurrected. Han's and Myra's daughter, Linda, has been murdered in *Seven Psychopaths*. And in the plays there is not the presence of dead babies to suggest a previous fundamental loss or the possibility of a child in the future; these are tropes that regularly appear in Anglophone dramaturgy in particular.

As Richard Dyer claims, 'Whites must reproduce themselves, yet they must also control and transcend their bodies. Only by (impossibly) doing both can they be white. Thus are produced some of the great narrative dilemmas of whiteness, notably romance, adultery, rape and pornography.'[15] Equally, for Dyer, in science fiction, the vampire or the zombie genres, death and reproduction are particularly exposed, as an inability of whites to reproduce contrasts 'with the hyper-reproductivity and engulfment of alien figures'.[16] McDonagh's 'liminally white' characters, are less the vampires of horror, the living dead of zombie movies, the automatons or androids of science fiction or the replicants of say Ridley Scott's *Blade Runner* (1982), but they almost invariably fail to reproduce.

The plays and films demonstrate casual and hostile homophobia, xenophobia, prejudices against people with disabilities and racism. In *Connemara*, Babbybobby will not bring Billy in the boat, 'Since Poteen-Larry took a cripple fella in his boat and it sank.' Billy rejects the superstition, and of course Babbybobby's retort implies that he is without prejudice, '[....] I did kiss a cripple girl one time. Not only crippled but disfigured too. I was drunk, I didn't mind. You're not spoilt for pretty girls in Antrim' (pp. 24–5.) There are also some crude reflections on disability and race in this work:

> Bobby: [....] I did see a film there one time with a fella who not only had he no arms and no legs but he was a coloured fella too.[17]
> Billy: A coloured fella? I've never seen a coloured fella, let alone a crippled coloured fella. I didn't know you could get them. (p.25)

As already outlined the negative attitudes of most of the community to Billy's disability is substantial, and across the plays lines like Mervyn's in *Spokane* 'Don't talk to me like I'm a mongoloid man', (p.26) capture innate and disdainful character prejudices and modes of expression. Billy calls Charlie a 'mongoloid' in *Seven Psychopaths*.

In *In Bruges*, Jimmy is treated aggressively and insensitively by Ray because of his stature. At one point Ray karate chops Jimmy and calls him 'Shortarse', (p.52) and tactlessly discusses the suicide of actors short in stature. Equally, Ray's comment that 'Ken, I grew up in Dublin. I love Dublin [...] If I'd grown up on a farm, and was retarded, Bruges might impress me, but I didn't, so it doesn't.' (p.7) In one context such a statement is about insensitivity and a poor choice of words; in another context it leaves so much to be desired.

In terms of homophobic thinking, it is systemic in many of the exchanges between characters. In *Beauty Queen* Ray will not buy Fr Welsh's car for it will make him look like a 'poof'. In my discussions of *Lonesome*, I have already raised the equation of virginity with a latent homosexuality by the characters. In *Inishmore*, Sir Roger Casement is referred to as 'that oul poof', (p.65) and there is a recurrent anxiety about homosexuality in Padraic's reflections on armed struggle. Kid in *Six Shooter* attempts to insult Mrs Donnelly by identifying her dead baby with a member of the gay pop group, Bronksy Beat. Charlie takes offence at Billy's slight when he suggests that Bonny has a gay head in *Seven Psychopaths*.

Ray is blatantly homophobic in *In Bruges*. He has the line: '[....] One gay beer for my gay friend, one normal beer for me, because I am normal.' (p.10) After Eirik tries to rob Ray, Ray disarms him and wounds him by firing blank bullets into his face, and in the aftermath of this incident, Ray exclaims: 'Exactly at what point was it that all skinheads suddenly became poofs? It used to be, if you were a skinhead, you just went around beating up Pakistani twelve-year-olds. Now it seems a prerequisite to be a fucking bum-boy.' (p.42) He also tells Eirik to stop whingeing like a 'big gay baby'. (p.43) Ray is not alone in his prejudices. Harry remarks to Eirik: '[...] he [Ray] stitched you up like a blind little gayboy.' (p.66) In *Connemara*, Mairtin's following comment needs little glossing other than to signal his naivety and provocativeness more than his aggression: 'hospitals are for poofs, sure [....] For poofs and for Lesbos who can't take a middling dig.' (p.123) Moments later in the play the hospital is his next destination.

In terms of nationality, *In Bruges*'s Ray initially casually discourages an overweight American from climbing the Bell Tower. The warning soon turns to insult, as he calls a family a 'bunch of fucking elephants'. (p.9) When Harry turns up first at Yuri's to get a normal gun for 'a normal person', and not an Uzi machine gun, he retorts: 'I didn't come here to shoot 20 black ten-year olds in a fucking drive-by', as they do in Los

Angeles. (p.64) Ray's attack on the Canadian couple in the restaurant, played by Stephanie Carey and Željko Ivanek, who have initially taken offence from Chloë's smoking, is based on Ray's assumption that they are American. Ray frames his physical assault in terms of retributive justice for the killing of John Lennon by an American citizen, Mark David Chapman, and for the victimisation of the Vietnamese during the Vietnam War. Ray's comments are utterly inappropriate and emptied of significance as this child and priest killing Irishman is unsettlingly self-assured in doling out restorative, summary and inappropriate justice.

In *Connemara* Mairtin tells of Ray Dooley losing his job having insulted American tourists by cracking 'Vietnam jokes'. (p.113) This anti-America streak is also evident in Billy Bickle's part burning of the American flag in *Seven Psychopaths*. The disability prejudices and anti-American sentiments are frequently reversed. The overweight American family's encounter with Ken, just after theirs with Ray, is a good example. While Ken, from a different mental place and out of a different sense of responsibility tries to warn them that the stairwell to the top is very narrow, it results in a female member of the family replying: go 'screw yourself, motherfucker'. (p.10) Her rage is justifiable in that Ken appears to be adding insult to injury, but that was never his intent. McDonagh sets up the joke, makes it and then recycles it in order to milk it further. Later still in the movie the Bell Tower is closed off because an American tourist has suffered a heart attack. Then there is also McDonagh's laudable framing of Billy's disability in *Inishmaan*, in its complexity and in its challenges to the negative attitudes that the other characters have to his physicality.

In terms of race, in *Six Shooter*, when challenged about his lack of respect, the Kid's response is, 'hasn't a black fella stole mine', and is thus repetitive of the association of blackness with evil. *Lonesome* has the Connor brothers use inappropriate terms like 'darkies', and 'Pakies'. (p.142) Further, Ray's language in *In Bruges* is sometimes racist: 'Somehow I believe, Ken, that the balance shall tip in the favour of culture. Like a big fat fucking retarded fucking black girl on a see-saw, opposite... a dwarf.' (p.19) At one point, Ray makes a comment about being bullied by a black girl in a playground as a child, and in response, Ken wonders what has her race got to do with it. 'Well she was black' (pp 19–20) is Ray's reply; this obviously does not answer the question posed.

Furthermore, *In Bruges*' Jimmy turns out to be the most racist of all of the characters, but he puts that down to the taking of illegal drugs. However, particular complications around racism occur during the party scene, involving alcohol, drugs and prostitution in a five-star hotel. Jimmy initiates a conversation about an impending race war, black versus white, with no uniforms. He faces questions as to which cohort the Vietnamese would join. Jimmy will be on the side of the blacks, as they will be the victors, despite his own skin colour. Ken also wonders which side is for him, given that his black wife (played by Susan Ateh in a deleted scene) was killed by a white man. Jimmy's response is 'I think you need to weigh up all your options and let your conscience decide.' (p.51) Although all of this talk is shaped by alcohol and cocaine, the assumptions that there can be a choice in a battle that is defined by skin tone is incongruous, but the conversation signifies something more complicated than an easy racism.

Regardless, Anthony Lane argues that 'No one wants a movie that tiptoes in step with political correctness, yet the wilful opposite can be equally noxious, and, as *In Bruges* barges and blusters its way through dwarf jokes, child-abuse jokes, jokes about fat black women and mouldy old jokes about Americans, it runs the risk of pleasing itself more than its paying viewers.'[18] However, McDonagh has his own take on issues of political correctness:

> For me it's just about creating the character and letting them speak. I mean I wouldn't share any of Ray's character's points of view in the film, from the possible racist stuff to the homophobic stuff to the anti-midget stuff. It's not my cup of tea. But I don't like shooting kids in the head, either. I hope the film doesn't share those sensibilities. For me, that was the main thing – not to censor the dialogue or the traits of the characters.[19]

As Josè Lanters correctly notes, it is 'precisely because McDonagh's characters are lost in a choppy ocean of signification' that 'they tend to latch on to linguistic markers of (racial, sexual, national, physical) difference – coloured, gay, Norwegian, crippled – that appear to serve as solid signifying anchors in an irrational world'.[20] For me, the work is not the 'wilful opposite' of political correctness. The inadequacy of McDonagh's character's thoughtless words and wilful thinking are available for audiences to interrogate. Further, my earlier reflections on Christopher Walken's performance as Carmichael in *Spokane* registers the play's opposition to racism. This argument places my views in opposition to those of Hilton Als.[21]

Some of the racist and homophobic comments in *Seven Psychopaths* are not only blatantly intended, but sometimes a little too forced and unnecessary.[22] That said, the inter-race relationship between Toby and Marilyn is one of the few that hints of a functioning sexual relationship. Indeed, inter-race relationships seem like the more complex, if not quite perverse ones, in the form of Ken and his wife, Maggie and Zachariah, and of course Hans and Myra and are, in part, an answer to some of the questions posed about racism.

Probably one of the most important dramaturgical strategies of McDonagh's work is to deny a fixed, coherent subjectivity for his characters and not to provide them with anything close to absolute motivation for or validation of anything they do. (And from a performance point of view, the implication is that there is no sense of the actors having a means of anchoring their characters in any 'Super Objective' or there being any sense of true line.) In *Inishmaan*, McDonagh affirms that character identities are dependent on narratives that are also never affirmed by another, and that these identities are mediated by various forms of fiction from gossip to film scripts, and obscured and rehashed by perverse or subsequent performances evident in the game of Ireland-England devised by Helen, for which Bartley is her dupe.

Beauty Queen's Maureen seems to have more motivation to do a dastardly deed than most of the other characters in the plays. In *Lonesome*, Coleman's expressed motivation for killing his father is insignificant and there is no other evidence to the contrary provided. *Connemara*'s Mick Dowd seems to have no real cause to kill his wife, as the only negative things he has to say about her are of her failures in preparing scrambled eggs and in not wrapping cheese and bread with due diligence after use. Mick Dowd is not proven either guilty or innocent of his wife's death in a dramatic world of hearsay, aspersions, circumstantial evidence, where there can be no absolute confirmation beyond reasonable doubt. In his review of Decadent Theatre Company's production of *Connemara* in 2013, Peter Crawley claims '[W]hether or not Mick killed his wife some years earlier' is 'a question on which almost nothing depends.'[23] My perspective could not be further from Crawley's, as to my mind, almost everything seems to depend on that question as to whether or not Mick has a role in her death: one of the play's strengths is its refusal to offer such confirmation.

The existential questions faced by McDonagh's characters are not packaged through anxieties, self-questioning or self-recognition. The characters share the compulsions of those untutored in the art of compromise, mature reflection or civilised negotiation. The inability to let go of past incidents, the refusal to forfeit a position in the face of evidence, the desire to see problems when they are not there, and not to see them when they are, a general unwillingness to see through on compassion and empathy, and most importantly, an inability to contextualise seem to be the challenges that the characters face.

The unenthusiastic disposition of McDonagh's characters towards change can be regarded as an indirect querying of the fundamental positivism of Liberal capitalism, of the American Dream or the 'can do' or cruelly and crudely perhaps, and not to diminish the gains, the 'can borrow' mentality of the Irish Dream during the so-called Celtic Tiger period. In McDonagh's world there is a disbelief in sustained hard work and the inevitability of ensuing rewards. McDonagh's characters are not skilled up for jobs in the pharmaceutical, banking, engineering or technology sectors – his are not characters readied for globalisation by education, cultural exposure, technology and the embracement of transnational best business practices. To different degrees, the characters do not so much live or participate in an ideology, as perform it. They are un-free, are somewhat aware of that fact, but often do not care enough to even attempt to quest for any form of freedom. In some respects, it is less the power of now, but the power of never.

Yet there is also a distinctive *jouissance* in the negative resoluteness of the characters and the tenuousness of their hold over situations. If characters do not behave conventionally or appropriately, audiences can reflect on the instinctive, unfiltered behaviours, and the tokenistic narratives by which these characters justify or legitimise their behaviours. Four umbrella concepts have to be integrated here, self-awareness, deception, exaggerated stimuli and comic failure as I work towards my final remarks.

McDonagh finds ways for his characters either to disassociate from their behaviours or to stand firmly behind what to most would seem to be inappropriate actions, thus capturing complex and contradictory compulsions. However, as Robert Trivers puts it for people generally, the 'conscious mind seems more like a post-hoc evaluator and commentator upon – including rationalising – our behaviour, rather than the initiator of the behaviour'.[24] That distinction is affirmed by McDonagh's characters. David Eagleman's work views brain functioning not from the perspective of a single mind, but from a 'team-of-rivals framework', so that 'we can often interpret the rivalrous elements in the brain as analogous to *engine* and *brakes*: some elements are driving you towards a behaviour, while others are trying to stop you'.[25] Again, McDonagh's work seems to expose persistently the braking and the drives of the engine, temptations, cravings, the decision-making, the impulse controls and an understanding and disregard of consequences.

Indeed, for Eagleman most behaviour is not shaped by consciousness or free will, instead 'human behaviour largely operates without regard to volition's invisible hand'.[26] Instead of the notion of free will he proposes the '*principle of sufficient automatism.*' Automatism is a legal plea made against behaviour that is beyond a person's rational control.[27] Eagleman admits that while there may be some veto power, a sense of 'free won't' or a chance for consciousness to halt, stall, divert what is being processed in the mechanisms of the brain, in the alien and 'hidden subroutines' or 'conflicting zombie systems'[28] beyond consciousness, but more often than not or as he puts it succinctly, most of the brain's operations 'are above the security clearance of the conscious mind. The *I* simply has no right of entry. Your consciousness is like a tiny stowaway on a transatlantic steamship, taking credit for the journey without acknowledging the massive engineering underfoot.'[29] Through his characters McDonagh captures in language, impulse and action the absence of a veto. 'Conflicting zombie systems' remain beyond awareness or acknowledgement, and actions are unerring in their unpredictability.

Robert Trivers's work on deceit and self-deception is also useful to apply: he notes, 'Our sensory systems are organised to give us a detailed and accurate view of reality, exactly as we would expect if truth about the outside world helps us to navigate it more effectively. But once that information arrives in our brains, it is often distorted and biased to our conscious minds. We deny the truth to ourselves. We project onto others traits that are in fact true of ourselves – and then we attack them! We repress painful memories, create completely false ones, rationalise immoral behaviour, act repeatedly to boost positive self-opinion, show a suite of ego-defence mechanisms.'[30]

So, why do we have wonderful 'organs of perception', only to 'systematically distort the information gathered', he asks? And his answer, put simply is that 'self-deception is offensive – measured as the ability to fool others', so we fool ourselves unconsciously to better deceive others, with the conscious mind kept in the dark.[31] (And for him, 'a defensive view of self-deception is congenial to an inflated moral self-image – I am not lying to myself the better to deceive you, but rather I lie to myself to defend against your attacks on myself and my happiness'.[32]) When Trivers connects deception and humour his work speaks even more to McDonagh's overall style. For Trivers, an important function of humour is to 'to expose and deflate hidden deceit and self-deception'.[33]

As Trivers notes: 'those who are low in self-deception' have a greater capacity to appreciate humour over 'those high in self-deception'. But 'at the same time, those with greater implicit biases toward black people or toward traditional sex roles laugh more in response to racially and sexually charged humor than do those with less implicit biases'.[34] Performances of McDonagh's work purposefully incite such responses, by being exceptionally reliant on exaggeration, stereotype and broad stroke characterisations, triggering audience self-awareness and biases. But it has comedic and performative 'layers'.

Eric Weitz's work further discusses a clowning disposition in terms of 'carriage, gesture and facial expression', and how these expressions align with failure and persistence. Weitz notes: 'Anyone of a certain age in Western culture knows in their bones Wolfgang Iser's characterisation of clown metaphysics: "Everything he does goes wrong, but he persists, as if the repetition denotes constant success."'[35] The comedic impulse of *Beauty Queen, Lonesome* or *In Bruges*, for example, is not just dark; it has a fundamentally strong clowning component that keeps the darker side of things not so much at bay, but at a tangent.

Weitz adds: 'the clown's sleight-of-frame game plan allows for repeated changes of tack in a variety of comedy-friendly directions', including the following list, 'incompetence', 'misfortune', 'blithe disregard' for things like hygiene, 'violation of social frames and of the protected status usually accorded to the spectator', 'random incongruity and reversal', 'snowballing momentum', 'puncturing of theatre convention', 'set up of the identifiable stock gags and a crowning reversal'.[36] McDonagh is strong in terms of comic exaggeration and reversals, and in particular in establishing almost faux or forced intensities; dramaturgical situations where there is either too much or too little at stake. Weitz concludes that 'perhaps the soul of clowning', serves as a 'psychic buffer for life's wilful vacillation between elation and despair, fortune and disaster, success and failure'.[37] The same might be said of McDonagh's dark clowns.

Finally, there is a particular perspective on aesthetics put forward by V.S. Ramachandran that offers a very useful elucidation. He outlines nine universal laws of art, including a fascinating one called 'the Law of Peak Shift'. This Law considers how the brain responds to 'exaggerated stimuli' and is based on studies in animal behaviour, 'especially the behaviour of rats and pigeons that are taught to respond to certain visual images'.[38] Ramachandran explains that in studies on herring gulls, the Nobel Prize winning biologist, Nikolaas Tinbergen, notes how after birth the baby birds peck vigorously on the red spot on the mother's beak when it wants food. Tinbergen observes that he got the same spirited response when he 'waved a disembodied beak in front of the chick'.

Further Tinbergen found that he got even a similar reaction when he had a 'rectangular strip of cardboard with a red dot on the end', but even more unpredictability, the chick responded with even more enthusiasm to a 'very long stick with three red stripes', in fact the chick 'goes berserk'. Bizarrely, it 'prefers this strange pattern, which bears almost no resemblance to the original'. This occurs thanks to 'evolutionary wisdom', whereby the bird takes short-cuts 'to minimise computational load'.[39] For Ramachandran then, this effect is often very evident in caricatures and portraits of internationally renowned or notorious figures and that this is an 'ultra-normal' stimulus. He suggests that by 'trial and error, intuition or genius, artists like Picasso or Henry Moore have discovered the human brain's equivalent' of the seagull brain's response to the stick with three stripes. 'They are tapping into the figural primitives of our perceptual grammar and creating ultranormal stimuli that more powerfully excite certain visual neurons in our brains as opposed to realist-looking objects', he observes.[40]

This particular component offers an insight into how McDonagh distorts patterns of character interactions and creates work that potentially stimulates responses in spectators in ways that are highly sophisticated, alert to the 'short cuts' and propensity for 'ultra-normal stimuli'. In his review of the Atlantic Theatre Company's 2006 production of *Inishmore*, John Lahr regards the text as 'a sort of cautionary fairytale for our toxic times. In its horror and hilarity, it works as an act of both revenge and repair, turning the tables on grief and goonery, and forcing the audience to think about the unthinkable.'[41] For him, 'The louts and lunatics who inhabit the play are just such gruesome and unforgettable figures; as all gargoyles do, they inspire an almost childish terror and elation in the audience.'[42] Lahr's response links in with the argument I have been just making.

By articulating the above and by complexly combining Grand-Guignol and farcical sensibilities with fairytale narratives and metatheatrical re-enactments as in *The Pillowman* or with the gory and highly stylised meta-fictional flashbacks or scenarios of creative revision in *Seven Psychopaths*, McDonagh regularly generates, through depletion and exaggeration, transgression and subversion, these sorts of 'ultra' or extra-normal stimuli, thus effectively 'tapping into the figural primitives of our perceptual grammar'. There are the embellished environments in which the plays are set, and there is this slapstick, anarchy and randomness of the violence, the downplaying or almost eroding of empathy in almost all character transactions and in the midst of all of the carnage, an emphasis on un-reciprocated altruistic self-sacrifice that is disproportionate to most of the previous transactions.

Thus gross excesses or glaring lacks, blind spots, deceptions and deficits feed into the motivations, desires and behaviour of the characters and into the overall dramaturgy of the plays and potential performances. McDonagh's meshing of a capacity to exaggerate, to focus on 'free won't' rather than free will, to distort empathy and altruism, and a high-end concentration on self-deception in terms of survival, are clearly distinguishing features of the work for characters that are stereotypes, clowns, gargoyles and archetypes. How McDonagh evolved such a methodology I cannot say, other than to acknowledge it has become increasingly more sophisticated over time.

To date, this outstanding body of work is reinforced more and more by critical reflection and an increasingly global interest that any internet search will confirm. Those that remain hostile to the work are perhaps less vocal than they were originally, given that the grounds for their initial antagonisms have been in many instances challenged and opposed. There is a growing pattern of increasing admiration and respect for the body of work, and with the dramas being performed across the world there are numerous opportunities for other critics to map out the territory very differently to me. What makes McDonagh's work so compelling is clearly not to be determined by successes alone. In my estimation, his best work *The Beauty Queen of Leenane*, *The Lonesome West*, *The Lieutenant of Inishmore*, *The Pillowman* and *In Bruges* will stand the tests of time.

For Martin McDonagh it has been a long journey from the initial rejections of the stories and radio plays to the great mainstream successes in the world of theatre and to film. It is vital to see how the creative spell between 1994 and 1996, which McDonagh accredits as the period when much of his work was drafted or at least conceived, has led to him not only being one of the most accomplished, renowned and widely produced playwrights in the world today, but he is also a writer who has in a relatively short period of time in the film industry amassed three critically acclaimed, and outstanding films.[43]

Finally, as playwright, screenwriter, film director and producer, his work is less about making clear-cut distinctions between protagonist and antagonism, between good and bad, punishment and revenge, but more about the collapse of determinism, carnivalesque reversals and highlighted absurdities, as McDonagh offers exceptionally accomplished insights into creativity, non-conformity, endurance, freedom, compassion, self-sacrifice, altruism and empathy. And, as I hope I have proved, this body of work has a great deal to say about the fundamental issues of justice and inequality for people of different beliefs, sexualities, races, genders, classes, backgrounds and abilities.

McDonagh makes clear how his disenfranchised, marginalised and subordinate communities while alert to and absorbed by the circulation of prevailing ideologies – in many instances influenced by methods of socialisation, rituals, myths, belief systems, relational models, media and popular culture expressions – do not benefit adequately from and do not have access to the dividends of global, liberal capitalism. Cumulatively, the violence and the carnage of the characters, their refusal to play by the rules, their going against the grain, their unnatural selections and their illegitimate performances are the fundamental hallmarks of anarchic empathy, punk altruism and disaporic resistance.

Endnotes

1 As Fintan O'Toole somewhat humorously proposes, 'If Martin McDonagh had not existed, Garry Hynes would have invented him, for all of this is uncannily in line with what she and Druid have been about over the last 21 years.' See F. O'Toole, 'Murderous Laughter' – 'The Leenane Trilogy,' *The Irish Times*, 24 June 1997.

2 See K.T. Powell's accounts of productions in Estonia in '"Life Just Is Like That": Martin McDonagh's Estonian Enigma', *New Hibernia Review*, 15.1, (Earrach/ Spring 2011), pp. 138–150. http://muse.jhu.edu/journals/new_hibernia_review/ v015/15.1.powell.html (Accessed 29/4/2103)

3 J. Harvie, *Staging the UK*, (Manchester: Manchester University Press, 2005), p.3.

4 Ibid., p.7.

5 See C. Leeney's review of Marina Carr's *Portia Coughlan* and *By the Bog of Cats...* 'of the RO Theater double bill production which was produced without any "performance references to "Irishness"', in *Irish Theatre Magazine*, 3 (14) (Spring 2003), pp.82–6, cited in 'Introduction', in C. Leeney and A. McMullan (eds), *The Theatre of Marina Carr: Before Rules Was Made* (Dublin: Carysfort Press, 2003), p.xiii.

6 P. Lonergan, *The Theatre and Films of Martin McDonagh* (London: Methuen, 2012), p.229.

7 The growth and demise of the 'Celtic Tiger' period has been well documented by now, as have the collapse of the property market, and catastrophic losses in Ireland's banking sector, which prompted state guarantees and massive state borrowing to save the banking system. Without the intervention of the European Union, the European Central Bank and the International Monetary Fund the country faced sovereign default in late 2010. The country went from almost full employment in the early to mid-2000s to a figure of about 15% unemployment in 2012, just short of the dismal 18% level reached in the early to late 1980s.

8 C. Graham, *Deconstructing Ireland: Ireland, Theory, Culture* (Edinburgh University Press, 2001), p.2, citing F. O'Toole; *The Lie of the Land: Irish Identities* (Dublin: New Island, 1988), p.2.

9 Ibid., p.2.

10 McDonagh suggests that 'There's a jigsaw-puzzle nature about screenplays, and you can still make a smaller jigsaw if you take things out. Even this film was 2½ hours long up until three months ago. It was always a bit too unwieldy, but there's another 40 minutes of material that just wasn't as truthful to the story that I ended up finding, which was the friendship between Colin and Sam Rockwell's character. That's the thing that runs through the film, as it did with Colin and Brendan Gleeson's character in *In Bruges*. Colin had more scenes with Clémence Poésy in the other one, too, and more with Abbie Cornish in this one. They both became more about the love between the guys.' See J. Utichi, 'It's a mad, mad world', *The Sunday Times*, 9 December 2012, pp. 16–17.

11 J. FitzPatrick Dean, 'McDonagh's gender troubles', in P. Lonergan, *The Theatre and Films of Martin McDonagh* (London: Methuen, 2012), pp.209–222, p.214.

12 Notable also in terms of gender, is how frequent the middle-aged male characters have wives, who are no longer living, namely Babbybobby in *Inishmaan*, Ken in *In Bruges*, Mick in *Connemara*, Donnelly in *Six Shooter* and Donny in *Inishmore*.
13 See J. FitzPatrick Dean, 'McDonagh's gender troubles', pp. 211–12.
14 As M. Kurdi notes of *Inishmaan*, 'Eggs are symbolic of fertility, therefore a young female's destruction of them in 1930s Ireland could qualify as a symbolic feminist protest against the conservative ideology of gender exploitation. Helen, however, does not employ the gesture as a form of meaningful resistance: her serial pegging of eggs expresses merely her barren rage against the whole world without distinction.' See, 'Gender, Sexuality and Violence in the Work of Martin McDonagh', in L. Chambers and E. Jordan (eds), *The Theatre of Martin McDonagh: A World of Savage Stories* (Dublin: Carysfort Press, 2006), pp.96–129, p.112.
15 R. Dyer, *White* (London and New York: Routledge, 1997), p.30.
16 Ibid., p. 218.
17 Laura Eldred, suggests that is in reference to Tod Browning's 'widely banned' film *Freaks* (1932). See. 'Martin McDonagh and Contemporary Gothic', in R. Rankin Russell, (ed.), *Martin McDonagh, A Casebook*, (London: Routledge, 2007), pp.111–130, pp.114–15.
18 A. Lane, 'Strangers,' *New Yorker,* 11 February 2008, http://www.newyorker.com/arts/critics/cinema/2008/02/11/080211crci_cinema_lane?currentPage=1, (Accessed 2/3/2001)
19 M. McDonagh interview with R. Carnevale. See http://www.indielondon.co.uk/Film-Review/in-bruges-martin-mcdonagh-interview.(Accessed 2/3/2012)
20 J. Lanters, '"Like Tottenham": Martin McDonagh's postmodern morality tales', in P. Lonergan, *The Theatre and Films of Martin McDonagh* (London: Methuen, 2012), (pp.165–178), p.168.
21 On Als, McDonagh states: 'He's missed the point. Toby is the smartest character in the whole play; all the others are psychos. Christopher Walken's character is a racist and a bigot and I don't know what other language he would be using. If I worried for a second that I had any of those thoughts in me, then maybe I might get angry about a review like that.' See A. Goldman, 'Martin McDonagh Is Glad He Swore at Sean Connery,' *New York Times*, 12 October 2012. http://www.nytimes.com/2012/10/14/magazine/martin-mcdonagh-is-glad-he-swore-at-sean-connery.html?ref=martinmcdonagh (Accessed 8/4/2013)
22 For instance, Billy disparagingly and provocatively suggests changing Marty's film title 'from *The Seven Psychopaths* to *The Seven Lesbians*, who are all disabled and who have overcome this spazzy shit, and who are really nice to everybody and two of them are black – how about that?'
23 P. Crawley's review, '*A Skull in Connemara*', *The Irish Times*, 7 March 2013, http://www.irishtimes.com/newspaper/features/2013/0307/1224330860943.html (Accessed 8/3/2013)
24 R. Trivers, *Deceit and Self-Deception: Fooling Yourself the Better to Fool Others* (London: Allen Lane, 2011),p.56
25 D. Eagleman, *Incognito: The Secret Lives of the Brain* (Canongate: Edinburgh, 2011), p.197.
26 Ibid., p.171.
27 Ibid., p.170.
28 Ibid., pp.142–4.
29 Ibid., p.4.
30 To that end, Trivers identifies nine categories of self deception: self-inflation, derogation of others, in-group-out-group associations, moral superiority-moral hypocrisy, the illusion of control, the construction of biased social theories

'regarding our immediate social realities', false personal narratives 'that hide true intention and causality' and unconscious modules devoted to deception. See, *Deceit and Self-Deception: Fooling Yourself the Better to Fool Others* (London: Allen Lane, 2011), pp.15–27

31 Ibid., p.3

32 Ibid., p.70

33 Ibid., p.25. (There is also 'imposed self-deception, when the subject works against itself for the benefit of others,' (Ibid., p.28)

34 Ibid., p.173.

35 E. Weitz, 'Failure as Success: On Clowns and Laughing Bodies', *Performance Research*, 17.1, (2102), pp.79–87, pp.79–80, citing Wolfgang Iser 'Counter-sensical comedy and audience response in Beckett's *Waiting for Godot*', in Steven Conner (ed.), *New Casebooks: Waiting for Godot and Endgame* (Houndmills: Macmillan), pp. 55–70, p.56.

36 Ibid., pp.83–4.

37 Ibid., p.86.

38 V.S. Ramachandran, *The Tell-Tale Brain: Unlocking the Mystery of Human Nature* (London: William Heinemann, 2011), p.206.

39 Ibid., p.210.

40 Ibid., p.212.

41 J. Lahr, 'Blood Simple', *New Yorker*, 13 March 2006: pp. 92–4, p.92.

42 Ibid., p.92.

43 It is more likely to be a film than a play. In an interview with Donald Clarke McDonagh states 'I have written a film script and I am very happy with it. It's called *Three Billboards outside of Ebbing, Missouri* and it has a strong female lead. It's a bit sad, like *Bruges* without quite so many laughs.' See 'Psycho thriller', *The Irish Times*, 7 December 2012, http://www.irishtimes.com/newspaper/theticket/2012/1207/1224327589235.html (Accessed 7/12/2012)

Bibliography

PLAYS:

The Beauty Queen of Leenane, A Skull in Connemara, and The Lonesome West in *Plays 1* (London: Methuen, 1999)
The Cripple of Inishmaan (London: Methuen, 1997)
The Lieutenant of Inishmore (London: Methuen, 2001)
The Pillowman (London: Faber and Faber, 2003)
A Behanding in Spokane (New York, Dramatists Play Services Inc, 2011)

FILMS:

Six Shooter (2005) (A missing in Action and Funny Farm Films Production in association with Fantastic Films, financed jointly by Film Four Lab (UK) and the Irish Film Board.)
In Bruges (2008) (Blueprint Pictures, Film4, Focus Features and Scion Films).
Seven Psychopaths (2012) (Film4, Blueprint Pictures, British Film Institute (BFI))

UNPERFORMED PLAYS:

The Banshees of Inisheer
The Retard is Out in the Cold
Dead Day at Coney
The Maamturk Rifleman

UNPRODUCED SCREENPLAYS:

Barney Nenagh's Shotgun Circus
Suicide on Sixth Street
Three Billboards Outside of Ebbing Missouri

SELECT BIBLIOGRAPHY

Augé, M., *Non-Places: An Introduction to Supermodernity* (London: New York: Verso, 2008, Second English-language edition).

Baron-Cohen, S., *Zero Degrees of Empathy: A New Theory of Human Cruelty* (London: Allen Lane an imprint of Penguin Books, 2011).

Barry, K., 'An end to representation', *Irish Review* 27, (Summer 2001), pp. 183–6.

Bayne, T. and N. Levy, 'Amputees By Choice: Body Integrity Identity Disorder and the Ethics of Amputation', *Journal of Applied Philosophy*, (2005), 22.1, pp.75–88. http://onlinelibrary.wiley.com/doi/10.1111/j.1468-5930.2005.00293.x/pdf (Accessed 10/3/2011)

Benson, C., *The Cultural Psychology of Self: Place Morality and Art in Human Worlds* (London: Routledge, 2001).

Bentley, E., *The Life of the Drama* (London: Methuen, 1965).

Bettelheim, B., *The Uses of Enchantment: The Meaning and Importance of Fairy Tales* (London: Penguin Books, 1976, reprinted 1991).

Bigsby, C.W.E., *Joe Orton* (London, Methuen, 1982).

Bolger, D., (ed.), *Druids, Dudes and Beauty Queens: The Changing Face of Irish Theatre* (Dublin: New Island, 2001).

Brophy, P., 'Horrality-The Textuality of Contemporary Horror Films' in Ken Gelder, (ed.), *A Horror Reader* (London: Routledge, 2000), pp.276-84.

Brown, K. and E. Viggiani, 'Performing Provisionalism: Republican Commemorative Practice as Political Performance' in Lisa Fitzpatrick (ed.), *Performing Violence in Contemporary Ireland* (Dublin: Carysfort Press 2009), pp.225–248.

Cain website Services, http://cain.ulst.ac.uk/othelem/organ/iorgan.htm#inla (Accessed 19/9/09)

Cave, R., 'The Abbey Tours in England' in N. Grene & C. Morash (eds), *Irish Theatre on Tour* (Dublin: Carysfort Press, 2005), pp.9–34.

Chambers, L. and E. Jordan (eds), *The Theatre of Martin McDonagh: A World of Savage Stories* (Dublin. Carysfort Press, 2006).

Chaudhuri, U., *Staging Place: The Geography of Modern Drama* (Ann Arbor: The University of Michigan Press, 1995).

Cole, M., *Critical Race Theory and Education: A Marxist Response* (Basingstoke: Palgrave, 2009).

Connell, R.W., 'The Social Organisation of Masculinity', in S.M. Whitehead and F. Barrett (eds), *The Masculinities Reader* (Cambridge: Polity Press, 2001), pp.30–50.

Deane, S., *Civilians and Barbarians: Field Day Pamphlet No.3*. Rpt. in *Ireland's Field Day* (Derry: Field Day Theatre, 1985), pp.33–44.

Demastes, W.W., (ed.), *Realism and the American Dramatic Tradition*, (Tuscaloosa, University of Alabama Press, 1996).

Beyond Naturalism: A New Realism in American Theatre (New York: Greenwood Press, 1988).

Demastes, W.W., and Michael Vanden Heuvel, 'The Hurlyburly Lies of the Causalist Mind: Chaos and Realism of Rabe and Shepard' in W.W. Demastes, (ed.), *Realism and the American Dramatic Tradition* (Tuscaloosa, University of Alabama Press, 1996), pp.255–274.

Di Benedetto, S., *The Provocation of the Senses in Contemporary Theatre* (London: Routledge, 2012).

Diehl, H.A., 'Classic Realism, Irish Nationalism, and a New Breed of Angry Young Man in Martin McDonagh's *The Beauty Queen of Leenane*', *The Journal of the Midwest Modern Language Association* , 34. 2 (Spring, 2001), pp. 98-117. http://www.jstor.org/stable/1315142 (Accessed 10/6/2012)

Doyle, M., 'Breaking bodies: The presence of violence on Martin McDonagh's stage', in R. Rankin Russell (ed.), *Martin McDonagh, A Casebook*, (London: Routledge, 2007), pp.92–110.

Dromgoole, D., *The Full Room: An A-Z of Contemporary Playwriting* (London: Methuen, 2000).

Dyer, R., *White* (London and New York: Routledge, 1997).

Eagleman, D., *Incognito: The Secret Lives of the Brain* (Canongate: Edinburgh, 2011).

Eldred, L., 'Martin McDonagh and Contemporary Gothic', in *Martin McDonagh, A Casebook*, R. Rankin Russell, (ed.) (London: Routledge, 2007), pp.111–130.

English, R. *Armed Struggle: The History of the IRA* (Basingstoke: Macmillan, 2003).

Eyre R. & N. Wright, *Changing Stages: A View of British Theatre in the Twentieth Century* (London: Bloomsbury, 2000).

Fanon, F., *The Wretched of the Earth* (Harmondsworth: Penguin, 1967).

FitzPatrick Dean, J., 'Joe Orton and the Redefinition of Farce', *Theatre Journal,* 34.4, (1982), pp.481–92.

------'Martin McDonagh's Stagecraft' in Richard Rankin Russell (ed.), *Martin McDonagh, A Casebook*, (London: Routledge, 2007), pp.25–40., 38.

------*'In Bruges', Estudios Irlandeses*, 4, 2009, pp.166–9, p.167, http://www.estudiosirlandeses.org/Issue4/Film%20Reviews4/pdfTheYearinIrishFilmandTV2008.pdf (Accessed 12/3/2011)

------'McDonagh's gender troubles', in P. Lonergan, *The Theatre and Films of Martin McDonagh* (London: Methuen, 2012), pp.209–222.

Fitzpatrick, L., 'Language Games: *The Pillowman, A Skull in Connemara, and Martin* McDonagh's Irish-English', in *A World of Savage Stories: The Theatre of Martin McDonagh* (Dublin: Carysfort Press, 2006), pp. 141–154.

------ (ed.), *Performing Violence in Contemporary Ireland* (Dublin: Carysfort Press 2009).

Flannery, E., 'Outside in the Theory Machine: Ireland in the World of Post-Colonial Studies', *Studies: An Irish Quarterly Review*, 92.368, (Winter 2003), pp. 359–69.

Fly, R, 'Accommodating Death: The Ending of Hamlet', *Studies in English Literature, 1500–1900*, 24.2, (Spring, 1984), pp. 257–274. http://www.jstor.org/stable/450527 (Accessed: 13/04/2011)

Fogarty. A., 'Other spaces: Postcolonialism and the politics of truth in Kate O'Brien's *That Lady*', *European Journal of English Studies*, 3:3, (1999), pp.342–353.

Foucault, M., 'Of other Spaces', Jay Miskowiec, (trans.), *Diacritics*, 16.1, (Spring 1986), pp.22–7. (Accessed 13/4/2011)

Freshwater, H., *Theatre and Audience* (Basingstoke: Palgrave, 2009).

Fryan, M., 'Introduction', in *The Seagull*, by Anton Chekhov, trans. M. Fryan (London: Methuen, 1986).

Frye, R.M., 'Ladies, Gentlemen, and Skulls: Hamlet and the Iconographic Traditions', *Shakespeare Quarterly*, 30.1 (Winter 1979), pp. 15–28. http://www.jstor.org/stable/2869658 (Accessed 13/4/2011)

Fuchs, E., *Death of Character: Perspectives on Theater After Modernism* (Bloomington: Indiana University Press, 1996).

Gibbons, L., *Transformations in Irish Culture* (Cork: Cork University Press, 1996).

Gifford, T., *Pastoral* (London: Routledge, 1999).

Gilbert, H. and J. Tompkins, *Post-colonial Drama: Theory, Practice, Politics* (London: Routledge, 1996).

Gordon, R. *The Purpose of Playing: Modern Acting Theories in Perspective* (Ann Arbor, University of Michigan Press, 2006).

Graham, C., *Deconstructing Ireland: Ireland, Theory, Culture* (Edinburgh University Press, 2001).

Grene, N., 'Ireland in Two Minds: Martin McDonagh and Conor McPherson', *The Yearbook of English Studies*, 35.1, (2005), pp. 298–311.

Gula, M., M. Kurdi & I. D. Rácz, (eds), *The Binding Strength of Irish Studies. Festschrift in Honour of Csilla Bertha and Donald. E. Morse* (Debrecen: Debrecen UP, 2011).

Hand, R.J. and M. Wilson, *Grand-Guignol: The French Theatre of Horror* (Exeter: University of Exeter Press, 2002).

Harte, L., *The Literature of the Irish in Britain: Autobiography and Memoir, 1725–2001* (London: Palgrave Macmillan 2009).

Harvie, J., *Staging the UK* (Manchester: Manchester University Press, 2005).

Haughton, M., 'Merging Worlds: Place, Politics and Play in Martin McDonagh's *The Pillowman*', *Focus: Papers in English Literary and Cultural Studies*, (2012), pp.77–92.

Hughes, D., 'Reflections on Irish Theatre and Identity', in E. Jordan, (ed.), *Theatre Stuff: Critical Essays on Contemporary Irish Theatre* (Dublin: Carysfort Press, 2000), pp.10–15.

Hynes, G., 'An interview with C. Leeney', in L. Chambers et al. (eds), *Theatre Talk: Voices of Irish Theatre Practitioners*, (Dublin: Carysfort Press, 2001), pp.195–212.

Innes, C., (ed.), 'Introduction' in *A Sourcebook on Naturalist Theatre* (London: Routledge, 2000).

Ipp, D., 'Maintaining the Tradition of Judicial Impartiality', http://www.lawlink.nsw.gov.au/lawlink/Supreme_Court/ll_sc.nsf/vwFiles/ipp211108.pdf/$file/ipp211108.pdf (Accessed 23/3/2011)

Jordan, E., 'The Fallacies of Cultural Narratives, Re-enactment, Legacy and Agency in Arthur Miller's *Death of a Salesman* and Martin McDonagh's *The Pillowman*', *Hungarian Journal of English and American Studies*, 11.2, 2005, pp.269–296.

------'Martin McDonagh's *The Lieutenant of Inishmore*: Commemoration and Dismemberment through Farce', *Hungarian Journal of English and American Studies*, 15.2, 2009, pp. 32–50.

------ *Dissident Dramaturgies: Contemporary Irish Theatre* (Dublin and Portland: Irish Academic Press, 2010).

------ 'The Native Quarter: The Hyphenated-Real: The Drama of Martin McDonagh,' in *Ciaran Ross (ed.), Sub-Versions, Trans-National Readings of Modern Irish Literature,* (Amsterdam: Rodopi, 2010).

------ 'Heterotopic and Funerary Spaces: Martin McDonagh's *A Skull in Connemara*', in *Focus: Papers in English Literary and Cultural Studies*, (2012), pp.63–76.

------ 'Performing Postmodern Whiteness in the West of Ireland Plays of Martin McDonagh,' in M. Gula, M. Kurdi, I. D. Racz (eds), *The Binding Strength of Irish Studies: Festschrift in Honour of Csilla Bertha and Donald E. Morse*. Debrecen: Debrecen University Press, 2011).

------'Martin McDonagh and postcolonial theory: practices, perpetuations, divisions and legacies', in P. Lonergan, *The Theatre and Films of Martin McDonagh* (London: Methuen, 2012), pp.193–208.

------'A Grand Guignol Legacy: Martin McDonagh's *A Behanding in Spokane*', *Irish Studies Review*, 24, (Winter 2012), pp. 447–461.

------'"The Kings of Odd": Farce and Depleted Masculinities in Martin McDonagh's *The Lonesome West*', in Catherine Rees (ed.) *Changes in Contemporary Ireland: Texts and Contexts* (Newcastle: Cambridge Scholars Publishing, 2013), pp.218–34.

Katz Clarke, B., *The Emergence of the Irish Peasant Play at the Abbey Theatre* (Ann Arbor: UMI Research Press, 1982).

Kiberd, D., *Inventing Ireland: The Literature of the Modern Nation* (London: Vintage, 1996).

King, G., 'Striking a balance between culture and fun: "quality" meets hitman genre in *In Bruges*', *New Review of Film and Television Studies*, 9:02, (2011), pp.132–151.

Kuhling, C., '"Liquid Modernity" and Irish Identity: Irishness in Guinness, Jameson and Ballygowan Advertisements', *Advertising & Society Review,* 9.3, 2008.

Kurdi, M. 'American and Other International Impulses on the Contemporary Irish Stage: A Talk with Playwright Declan Hughes', *Hungarian Journal of English and American Studies*, 8.2, 2002, pp.76–7.

------'The Helen of Inishmaan Pegging Eggs: Gender, Sexuality and Violence', in L. Chambers and E. Jordan (eds), *The Theatre of Martin McDonagh: A World of Savage Stories* (Dublin: Carysfort Press, 2006), pp.96–129.

Lachman, M., '"From Both Sides of the Irish Sea": The Grotesque, Parody, and Satire in Martin McDonagh's *The Leenane Trilogy*', *Hungarian Journal of English and American Studies* 10:1–2 (2004), pp. 61–73.

Lanters, J., 'The Identity Politics of Martin McDonagh', in R. Rankin Russell (ed.), *Martin McDonagh: A Casebook* (London: Routledge, 2007), pp.9–24.

----- '"Like Tottenham": Martin McDonagh's postmodern morality tales', in P. Lonergan, *The Theatre and Films of Martin McDonagh* (London: Methuen, 2012), pp.165–178.

Lehmann, H-T., *Postdramatic Theatre*, translated and introduced by Karen Jürs-Munby (London: Routledge, 2006).

Leeney, C., 'Ireland's "Exiled" Women Playwrights: Teresa Deevy and Marina Carr', in *The Cambridge Companion to Twentieth-Century Irish Drama*, ed. S. Richards (Cambridge: Cambridge University Press, 2004), pp.150–63.

Letzler Cole, S., *The Absent One: Mourning Ritual, Traged, and the Performance of Ambivalence*, (Pennsylvania: Pennsylvania University Press, 1885) http://books.google.com (Accessed 4 May 2011).

Lonergan, P., 'Druid Theatre's *Leenane Trilogy* on Tour: 1996–2001', in N. Grene and C. Morash (eds), *Irish Theatre on Tour* (Dublin: Carysfort Press, 2005).

----- *Theatre and Globalization: Irish Drama in the Celtic Tiger Era* (Basingstoke: Palgrave, 2008).

------ 'Commentary and Notes to Student Edition' to *The Lieutenant of Inishmore* (London: Methuen, 2009).

----- 'Commentary and Notes to Student Edition' of *The Lonesome West* (London: Methuen, 2010).

----- *The Theatre and Films of Martin McDonagh* (London: Methuen, 2012).

Loomba, A., *Colonialism/ Postcolonialism* (London and New York: Routledge, 1998).

Luckhurst, M., 'Martin McDonagh's *Lieutenant of Inishmore*: Selling (-Out) to the English', *Contemporary Theatre Review*, 14.4, 2004, pp. 34–41.

Magee, P., *Gangsters or Guerillas? Representations of Irish Republicans in Troubles Fiction* (Belfast: Beyond the Pale, 2001).

Magennis, C. and R. Mullen, (eds), *Irish Masculinities: Reflections on Literature and Culture* (Dublin: Irish Academic Press, 2011).

Maguire, T., *Making Theatre in Northern Ireland: Through and Beyond the Troubles* (Exeter: University of Exeter Press, 2006).

Maloney, E., *The Secret History of the IRA* (London: Lane, 2002).

Mathews. P.J., 'In Praise of "Hibernocentricism": Republicanism, Globalisation and Irish Culture', http://www.republicjournal.com/04/pdf/mathews004.pdf (Accessed 1/6/2010)

McAuley, G., *Space in Performance: Making Meaning in the Theatre* (Michigan: University of Michigan, 1999).

Meaney, G., 'Dead, White, Male: Irishness in *Buffy the Vampire Slayer* and *Angel*' in *The Irish in Us: Irishness, Performativity, and Popular Culture,* editor Negra, Diane (Duke University Press, Durham and London, 2006), pp.254–281.

Melnikova, I., 'In(visible) Bruges by Martin McDonagh', *Journal of European Studies*, 43. 1 (2013), pp. 44–59.

Merriman, V, 'Decolonization Postponed: Theatre of Tiger Trash', *Irish University Review*, 29.2, 1999, pp.305–17.

-----'Heartsickness and Hopes Deferred' in *Twentieth Century Irish Drama*, ed. Shaun Richards (Cambridge: Cambridge University Press 2004), pp. 244–57.

Meszaros, M.B., 'Enlightened by Our Afflictions: Portrayals of Disability in the Comic Theatre of Beth Henley and Martin McDonagh', *Disability Studies Quarterly,* Summer/Fall 2003, 23. 3/4, http://dsq-sds.org/article/view/433/610 (Accessed 3/2/2013)

Middeke, M., 'Martin McDonagh', in M. Middeke & P. P. Schnierer (eds), *The Methuen Drama Guide to Contemporary Irish Playwrights* (London: Methuen, 2010), pp. 213–233.

Mikami, H., 'Not "Lost in Translation": Martin McDonagh in Japan', http://dspace.wul.waseda.ac.jp/dspace/bitstream/2065/26868/1/003.pdf (Accessed 3 August 2012)

Milner Davis, J., *Farce*, (New Brunswick & London: Transaction Publishers, 2003).

Morash, C., *A History of Irish Theatre 1601–2000* (Cambridge: Cambridge University Press, 2002).

Müller, P.P., 'Body Politics in a Fictitious Eastern European Dictatorship: Martin McDonagh's The Pillowman', in M. Kurdi (ed.), *Literary and Cultural Relations: Ireland, Hungary, and Central and Eastern Europe,* (Dublin: Carysfort, 2009),pp.49–61.

Murphy, M., 'Martin McDonagh: Prodigy of the Western World' http://www.roundabouttheatre.org/fc/spring01/martin.htm (Accessed 13/4/2011)

Murphy, P. 'The Stage Irish Are Dead, Long Live the Stage Irish: *The Lonesome West* and *A Skull in Connemara*', in L. Chambers and E. Jordan (eds), *The Theatre of Martin McDonagh: A World of Savage Stories* (Dublin: Carysfort Press, 2006), pp. 60–78.

----- *Hegemony and Fantasy in Irish Drama, 1899–1949* (Basingstoke: Palgrave, 2008).

Murray, C., '*The Cripple of Inishmaan* Meets Lady Gregory', in L. Chambers and E. Jordan (eds), *The Theatre of Martin McDonagh: A World of Savage Stories* (Dublin: Carysfort Press, 2006), pp.79–95.

Negra, D., (ed.), *The Irish in Us: Irishness, Performativity, and Popular Culture* (Duke University Press, Durham and London, 2006).

O'Brien, C., 'In Bruges, Heaven or Hell?', *Literature & Theology*, 2011, pp. 1–13.

O'Brien, K., '"Ireland mustn't be such a bad place so": Mapping the "Real" Terrain of the Aran Islands', *Journal of Dramatic Theory and Criticism*, (Spring 2006), pp. 169–183. https://journals.ku.edu/index.php/jdtc/article/viewFile/3554/3430 (Accessed 1 March 2011)

O'Connor, F., 'In Conversation with Charlie McBride'. 26 August 2004, http://www.druidsynge.com/inconversation/in-conversation-francis-oconnor (Accessed 12/6/2010)

O'Doherty, M., *The Trouble with Guns: Republican Strategy and the Provisional IRA* (Belfast: Blackstaff Press, 1998).

O'Sullivan, M., 'Raising the Veil: Mystery, Myth and Melancholia in Irish Studies', in P. Coughlan & T. O'Toole (eds), *Irish Literature Feminist Perspectives*, (Dublin: Carysfort Press, 2008,), pp. 245–278.

O'Toole, F., 'Introduction' in *Martin McDonagh, Plays One* (London: Methuen, 1999).

-----*The Lie of the Land: Irish Identities* (New York: Verso, 1997).

Pavis, P., *Analyzing Performance: Theatre, Dance, and Film*, David Williams (trans.) (Ann Arbor: University of Michigan Press, 2004)

Phelan, M., '"Authentic Reproductions" Staging the "Wild West" in Modern Irish Drama', *Theatre Journal*, 61. 2, (May 2009), pp.235–248.

Pilkington, L., *Theatre and the State in Twentieth-Century Ireland, Cultivating the People* (London and New York: Routledge, 2001).

Pilný, O, 'Martin McDonagh: Parody? Satire? Complacency?', *Irish Studies Review* 12.2, 2004, pp.225–32.

------ 'Grotesque Entertainment: *The Pillowman* as Puppet Theatre' in L. Chambers and E. Jordan (eds), *The Theatre of Martin McDonagh: A World of Savage Stories* (Dublin: Carysfort Press, 2006), pp.214–223.

------ *Irony and Identity in Modern Irish Drama* (Prague: Litteraria Pragensia, 2006).

Pinker, S., *The Better Angels of Our Nature: A History of Violence and Humanity* (London: Penguin Books, 2011).

Pitcher. B., *The Politics of Multiculturalism: Race and Racism in Contemporary Britain* (Basingstoke: Palgrave, 2009).

Powell, K.T., '"Life Just Is Like That": Martin McDonagh's Estonian Enigma', *New Hibernia Review*, 15.1, (Earrach/ Spring 2011), pp. 138–150. http://muse.jhu.edu/journals/new_hibernia_review/v015/15.1.powell.html (Accessed 29/4/2103)

Rafter, K., *Sinn Féin 1905–2005: In the Shadow of Gunmen* (Dublin Gill and Macmillan, 2005).

Ramachandran, V.S., *The Tell-Tale Brain: Unlocking the Mystery of Human Nature* (London: William Heinemann, 2011).

Rankin Russell, R., (ed.), *Martin McDonagh, A Casebook*, (London: Routledge, 2007).

Ravenhill, M., 'A Tear in the Fabric: the James Bulger Murder and New Theatre Writing in the 'Nineties', *New Theatre Quarterly*, 20.4, 2004, pp. 305–314.

Rees, C., 'The Politics of Morality: *The Lieutenant of Inishmore*', *New Theatre Quarterly* 21.1, (2005),pp. 28–33.

------ 'Narratives of power' [Unpublished Phd Thesis on Martin McDonagh's work, Aberystwyth University, 2007]

------ 'Representing Acceptability: Power, Violence and Satire in Martin McDonagh's '*The Lieutenant of Inishmore*', in Lisa Fitzpatrick (ed.), *Performing Violence in Contemporary Ireland*, (Dublin: Carysfort Press 2009), pp.85–103.

------(ed.), *Changes in Contemporary Ireland: Texts and Contexts* (Newcastle: Cambridge Scholars Publishing, 2013).

Reizbaum, M. 'Urban Legends', *Éire-Ireland*, 45:1&2, Spring/Summer 2010, pp.242–265. http://muse.jhu.edu/journals/eire-ireland/v045/45.1.reizbaum.html#f37-text (Accessed 21/3/2011)

Richards, S. '"The Outpouring of a Morbid, Unhealthy Mind": The Critical Condition of Synge and McDonagh', *Irish University Review*, 33–1, (Spring – Summer 2003), pp. 201–14.

------ *The Cambridge Companion to Twentieth-Century Irish Drama*, (Cambridge: Cambridge University Press, 2004)

Richardson, B., 'Introduction: The Struggle for the Real-Interpretative Conflict, Dramatic Method and the Paradox of Realism' in W.W. Demastes, (ed.), *Realism and the American Dramatic Tradition*, (Tuscaloosa, University of Alabama Press, 1996), pp.1–17.

Roche, A., 'Re-Working *The Workhouse Ward*: McDonagh, Beckett and Gregory' *Irish University Review*, 34.1 Special Issue: Lady Gregory (Spring – Summer, 2004), pp.171-184. http://www.jstor.org/stable/25504965 (Accessed: 13/4/ 2011)

------ *Contemporary Irish Drama* (Basingstoke: Palgrave 2009).

Rouse, M., 'Hit Men on Holiday Get All Medieval', *European Journal of English Studies*, 15:2, (2011), pp.171–182.

Ryan, C.J., 'Out on a Limb: The Ethical Management of Body Integrity Identity Disorder', *Neuroethics* 2, (2009), pp.21–33. http://www.springerlink.com/content/nw13778v8m220693/fulltext.pdf (Accessed 10/3/2011)

Scolnicov, H., *Woman's Theatrical Space* (Cambridge: Cambridge University Press, 1994).

Singleton, B., *Masculinities and Contemporary Irish Theatre* (Basingstoke: Palgrave, 2011).

Sorene, E.D., C. Heras-Palou, & F.D. Burke, 'Self-Amputation of a Healthy Hand: A Case of Body Integrity Identity Disorder', *Journal of Hand Surgery*, 31.6, (December 2006), pp. 593–5, http://jhs-euro.com/content/31/6/593.abstract (Accessed 10/3/2011)

Styan, J.L. *Drama, Stage and Audience* (Cambridge: Cambridge University Press, 1975).

Taggart, A., 'An Economy of Pity: McDonagh's Monstrous Regiment' in L. Chambers and E. Jordan (eds), *The Theatre of Martin McDonagh: A World of Savage Stories* (Dublin: Carysfort Press, 2006), pp.162–173.

Third, A. '"Does the Rug Match the Carpet?" Race, Gender and the Readheaded Woman', in D. Negra (ed.), *The Irish in Us: Irishness, Performativity, and Popular Culture* (Duke University Press, Durham and London 2006), pp.220–253.

Trivers, R., *Deceit and Self-Deception: Fooling Yourself the Better to Fool Others* (London: Allen Lane, 2011).

Ubersfeld, A, *Reading Theatre*, Frank Collins, (trans.) (Toronto: University of Toronto, 1999).

Van Gennep, A., *The Rites of Passage*, M.B. Vizedom and G. L. Coffee, (trans.), (Chicago: Chicago University Press, 1960).

Verini, J., 'A Terrible act of Reason: When Did Self-Immolation Become the Paramount Form of Protest', *New Yorker*, 16 May 2012, http://www.newyorker.com/online/blogs/culture/2012/05/history-of-self-immolation.html (Accessed 29/1/2013)

Wallace, C., (ed.), *Monologues: Theatre, Performance, Subjectivity*, ed. Clare Wallace (Prague: Litteraria Pragensia, 2006).

------*Suspect Cultures: Narrative, Identity and Citation in 1990s New Drama* (Prague: Litteraria Pragensia, 2006).

Waters, J., 'The Irish Mummy: The Plays and Purpose of Martin McDonagh' in D. Bolger (ed.), *Druids, Dudes and Beauty Queens: The Changing Face of Irish Theatre* (Dublin: New Island, 2001), pp. 30–54.

Weitz, E., 'Failure as Success: On Clowns and Laughing Bodies', *Performance Research*, 17.1, (2012), pp.79–87.

Whybrow, G., 'Introduction' to *The Methuen Book of Modern Drama* (London: Methuen, 2001).

Wilcock, M., '"Put to Silence": Murder, Madness and "Moral Neutrality" in Shakespeare's *Titus Andronicus* and Martin McDonagh's *The Lieutenant of Inishmore*', *Irish University Review*, 38.2, (Autumn Winter 2008), pp.325–369.

Williams, R., *Modern Tragedy* (London: Chatto and Windus, 1966).

Wilson, R., 'Macabre Merriment in *The Beauty Queen of Leenane*', in E. Weitz (ed.), *The Power of Laughter: Comedy and Contemporary Irish Theatre*, (Dublin: Carysfort Press, 2004), pp.129–144.

Wise, T.N., and R.C. Kalyanam, 'Amputee fetishism and genital mutilation: Case report and literature review', *Journal of Sex and Marital Therapy*, 26, (2000), pp.339–344.

Witoszek, N., and P. Sheeran, *Talking to the Dead: A Study of the Irish Funerary Traditions* (Amsterdam-Atlanta, GA: Rodopi, 1998).

Worthen, H. and W.B. Worthen, '*The Pillowman* and the Ethics of Allegory', *Modern Drama* 49.2, (2006), pp. 155–173, http://muse.jhu.edu/journals/modern_drama/v049/49.2worthen.html (Accessed 20/10/2012)

Worthen, W.B., *Modern Drama and the Rhetoric of Theatre* (Berkeley: University of California, 1992).

------'Drama, Performativity, and Performance', *PMLA*, 113.5, Oct 1998, 1093–1107, p.110. http://www.jstor.org/stable/10.2307/463244 (Accessed 8/4/2013)

Žižek, S., *Violence* (London: Profile Books, 2009).

SELECTED INTERVIEWS, FEATURE ARTICLES AND REVIEWS

The Beauty Queen of Leenane

Billington, M., 'New Themes in Synge-song Land: *The Beauty Queen of Leenane*', *The Guardian*, 8 March 1996.

Brantley, B. 'A Gasp for Breath Inside an Airless Life', *New York Times*, February 27, 1998, http://theater.nytimes.com/mem/theater/treview.html?html_title=&tols_title=BEAUTY%20QUEEN%20OF%20LEENANE,%20THE%20(PLAY)&pdate=19980227&byline=By%20BEN%20BRANTLEY&id=1077011432270 (Accessed 29/4/2013)

Coveney, M. 'The Week in Reviews: Backstage: He Compares Himself With the Young Orson Welles. Oh Dear', *The Observer*, 1 December 1996, p13. http://www.lexisnexis.com/uk/nexis/results/docview/docview.do?docLinkInd=true&risb=21_T12577053696&format=GNBFI&sort=BOOLEAN&startDocNo=1&resultsUrlKey=29_T12577092600&cisb=22_T12577053699&treeMax=true&treeWidth=0&csi=143296&docNo=6 (Accessed 22/8/2011)

Coveney, M. Review, *Whats on Stage*, 22 July 2010, http://www.whatsonstage.com/reviews/theatre/london/E8831279790437/The+Beauty+Queen+of+Leenane.html (Accessed 10/8/2010)

Lyman, R. 'Most Promising (and Grating) Playwright', *New York Times*, 25 January 1998, http://www.nytimes.com/1998/01/25/magazine/most-promising-and-grating-playwright.html?pagewanted=all&src=pm (Accessed 20/11/11)

Keating, S., 'Review', 22 May 2011, *Sunday Business Post*, http://www.sbpost.ie/the-guide/theatre-56347.html (Accessed 31/5/2011)

Marks, P., 'Depicting the Hurt of Love Curdling Into Hate', *New York Times*, 21 April 1998. http://theater.nytimes.com/mem/theater/treview.html?res=9C05E4D6113CF932A15757C0A96E958260 (Accessed 12/6/2010)

O'Toole, F., '*The Beauty Queen of Leenane*' *The Irish Times* 6 February 1996

------ 'Murderous Laughter – The Leenane Trilogy', *The Irish Times* 24 June 1997, *Art Section,* p.12.

Spenser, C., '*The Beauty Queen of Leenane*, Young Vic, Review', *Daily Telegraph*, 22 Jul 2010, http://www.telegraph.co.uk/culture/theatre/theatre-reviews/7904562/The-Beauty-Queen-of-Leenane-Young-Vic-review.html (Accessed 31/5/2011)

Taylor, P., 'The Leenane Trilogy Royal Court, London', *The Independent*, 28 July 1997, http://www.independent.co.uk/life-style/theatre-the-leenane-trilogy-royal-court-london-1253000.html# (Accessed 20/11/11)

A Skull in Connemara

Brantley, B., 'Leenane III, Bones Flying', *New York Times*, February 23, 2001. http://theater.nytimes.com/mem/theater/treview.html?html_title=&tols_title=SKULL%20IN%20CONNEMARA,%20A%20(PLAY)&pdate=20010223&byline=By%20BEN%20BRANTLEY&id=1077011432186 (Accessed 4/4/2011)

Crawley, P., 'Review', *The Irish Times*, 7 March 2013, http://www.irishtimes.com/newspaper/features/2013/0307/1224330860943.html (Accessed 8/3/2013)

Edelstein, G., and D. Gallo 'In Discussion: Grave Matters', *http://www.roundabouttheatre.org/fc/spring01/grave.htm (Accessed 13/4/2011)*

Gritten, D., 'The Enigma of South London,' *Los Angeles Times*, 25 October, 1998, http://articles.latimes.com/1998/oct/25/entertainment/ca-35842 (Accessed 22/8/2011)

The Lonesome West

Brantley, B., 'Another Tempestuous Night in Leenane (Sure, It's Not a Morn in Spring)', *New York Times*, April 28, 1999.

Fitzpatrick, L., 'Review', *Irish Theatre Magazine*, 25.5, Winter 2005, pp.81–2.

Harrison, M., 'Review', *Irish Theatre Magazine*, June 2009, http://www.irishtheatremagazine.ie/Reviews/Current/The-Lonesome-West.aspx#, (Accessed 10/6 2010).

Lonergan, P., 'Review', *The Lonesome West, The Irish Times*, 21 September 2009, http://www.irishtimes.com/newspaper/features/2009/0921/1224254908459.html (Accessed 10/6/ 2010)

O'Toole, F., 'Martin McDonagh Interview' *BOMB* 63/Spring 1998. http://bombsite.com/issues/63/articles/2146, (Accessed 28/7/2011)

The Cripple of Inishmaan

Brantley, B., 'Twisted Lives in a Provincial Irish Setting', *New York Times*, 8 April 1998, http://theater.nytimes.com/mem/theater/treview.html?html_title=&tols_title=CRIPPLE%20OF%20INISHMAAN,%20THE%20(PLAY)&pdate=19980408&byline=By%20BEN%20BRANTLEY&id=1077011432368 (Accessed 1/ 3/2011)

------'On a Barren Isle, Gift of the Gab and Subversive Charm', *New York Times*, December 22, 2008, http://theater.nytimes.com/2008/12/22/theater/reviews/22bran.html (Accessed 1/ 3/2011)

Crawley, P., 'Review', *The Irish Times*, 25 February 2011.

Gardner, L. 'Review', *The Guardian,* Friday 10 October 2008.

Keating, S. 'Review', *Sunday Business Post,* 27 February 2011.

Lonergan, P., 'Review', *The Irish Times*, 18 September, 2008,

http://www.irishtimes.com/newspaper/features/2008/0918/1221599462349_pf.html

Meany, H., 'Review', *Variety*, 19 September 2008, http://www.variety.com/story.asp?l=story&r=VE1117938440&c=33

O'Neill, M. C., 'Performance Review', *Theatre Journal*, pp.259–60. *use.jhu.edu/journals/theatre_journal/.../50.2pr_mcdonagh.html* (Accessed 1/3/2011)

The Lieutenant of Inishmore

Brantley, B., 'Terrorism Meets Absurdism in a Rural Village in Ireland', *New York Times*, 28 February 2006, http://theater.nytimes.com/2006/02/28/theater/reviews/28inis.html?pagewanted=all (Accessed 18/11/11)

Curtis, N., 'Brit's short rise to fame', *Evening Standard*, 7 March 2006, http://www.thisislondon.co.uk/arts/film/brits-short-rise-to-fame-7241660.html (Accessed 23/2/2013)

Lahr, J, 'Blood Simple', *New Yorker,* 13 March 2006, pp. 92–4.

McDonald, H., 'The Guardian profile: Martin McDonagh', *The Guardian*, Friday 25 April 2008. http://www.guardian.co.uk/film/2008/apr/25/theatre.northernireland (Accessed 13/11/11)

O'Hagan, S. 'The Wild West', *Guardian* 24 March 2001, p. 32. <http://www.guardian.co.uk/books/2001/apr/28/northernireland.stage> (Accessed 10 October 2009)

O'Toole, F., 'A Mind in Connemara: The Savage World of Martin McDonagh', *New Yorker,* 6 March 2006, http://www.newyorker.com/archive/2006/03/06/060306fa_fact_otoole (Accessed 10/10/2009)

Peter, J., 'Review', *Sunday Times*, 20 May 2001.

Rosenthal, D., 'How to slay 'em in the Isles', *Independent*, April 11, 2001, http://www.independent.co.uk/arts-entertainment/theatre-dance/features/how-to-slay-em-in-the-isles-681030.html (Accessed 10 October 2009)

Segal, D., 'Buckets of Blood Means It's Curtains: Stage Crew Concocts Gallons of Fake Gore For Theatrical Spatter Fest', *Washington Post,* 13 April 2006, http://www.washingtonpost.com/wp-dyn/content/article/2006/04/12/AR2006041202233.html (Accessed 7/3/2013)

Spencer, C, 'Devastating Masterpiece of Black Comedy', *Daily Telegraph*, 28 June 2002, <http://www.telegraph.co.uk/culture/film/3579406/Devastating-masterpiece-of-black-comedy.html#> (Accessed 10 October 2009)

The Pillowman

Billington, M., 'Review', *The Guardian*, 14 November 2003, http://www.guardian.co.uk/stage/2003/nov/14/theatre (Accessed 6/9/2011)

Brantley, B., 'A Storytelling Instinct Revels in Horror's Fun', *New York Times*, 11 April 2005, http://theater.nytimes.com/2005/04/11/theater/reviews/11pill.html (Accessed 6/9/2011)

James, C, 'Critic's Notebook: A Haunting Play Resounds Far Beyond the Stage', *New York Times*, 15 April 2005. *http://theater2.nytimes.com/mem/theater/treview.html?res=9E06E1DC103EF936A25757C0A9639C8B63&fta=y* (Accessed 10 March 2009)

McGrath, C., '*The Pillowman* Audience: Shocked and a Bit Amused', 26 April 2005, *New York Times,* http://www.nytimes.com/2005/04/26/theater/newsandfeatures/26whip.html (Accessed 10 March 2009)

McKinley, J., 'Suffer the Little Children', *New York Times*, 3 April 2005, http://www.nytimes.com/2005/04/03/theater/newsandfeatures/03mcki.html?_r=1&scp=2&sq=The%20pillowman&st=cse, (Accessed 14/9/2011)

Pacheco, P., 'Laughing Matters', *The Los Angeles Times*, 22 May 2005, http://articles.latimes.com/2005/may/22/entertainment/ca-pillowman22 (Accessed 14/9/2011)

Segal, V., 'Review', *Sunday Times*, 23 Nov 2003. Re-printed in *Theatre Record* 23 (5–18 November 2003), pp.1554–55.

Simon, J. *'Exquisite Corpses',* New York Magazine, *21 May 2005,*http://nymag.com/nymetro/arts/theater/reviews/11755/ (Accessed 2/3/2012)

Taylor, P., 'Review', *Independent*, 17 November 2003 http://www.independent.co.uk/arts-entertainment/theatre-dance/reviews/the-pillowman-cottesloe-theatre-nt-london-736037.html (Accessed 6/9/2011)

A Behanding in Spokane

Als, H., 'Underhanded: Martin McDonagh's slap in the face', *The New Yorker,* 5 March 2010, http://www.newyorker.com/arts/critics/theatre/2010/03/15/100315crth_theatre_als?currentPage=2 (Accessed 103/2011)

Brantley, B., 'Packing Heat, and a Grudge', *New York Times*, 5 March 2010, http://theater.nytimes.com/2010/03/05/theater/reviews/05behanding.html (Accessed 15/8/2011)

Haun, H., '*A Behanding in Spokane* — Watch Where You're Walken', *Playbill*, 5 March 2010, http://www.playbill.com/features/article/137585-PLAYBILL-ON-OPENING-NIGHT-A-Behanding-in-Spokane-Watch-Where-Youre-Walken/pg2 (Accessed 15/8/2011)

Healy, P., 'Please, No More Mr. Bad Guy Roles! (But Creepy Is Fine)', *New York Times* February 21, 2010, *http://www.nytimes.com/2010/02/21/theater/21walken.html?ref=theater* (Accessed 15/8/2011)

O'Toole, F., 'Arch McDonagh takes a wrong turn to dead-end Americana', 20 March 2010, *Irish Times*, http://www.irishtimes.com/newspaper/weekend/2010/0320/1224266695345.html (Accessed 20/2/2010)

Shone, T., 'The loopy oeuvre of Sam Rockwell, America's sweetest badass', *New York Magazine*, 28 February 2010,http://nymag.com/arts/theater/features/64269/ (Accessed 18/8/2011)

Zinoman, J., 'Is He Mellower? Ask the Guy Missing a Hand', *New York Times*, 7 March 2010, http://www.nytimes.com/2010/03/07/theater/07mcdonagh.html?partner=rss&emc=rss (Accessed 16/04/2012)

Six Shooter

James, C., 'Martin McDonagh Finds His Inner Thug as Film Director', *New York Times*, 4 April 2006, http://www.nytimes.com/2006/04/04/movies/04jame.html. (Accessed 16/10/2009)

Lane, A., 'Strangers', *New Yorker,* 11 February 2008, http://www.newyorker.com/arts/critics/cinema/2008/02/11/080211crci_cinema_lane?currentPage=1, (Accessed 2/3/2010).

In Bruges

Bradshaw, P., 'Review', *The Guardian*, Friday 18 April 2008, http://www.guardian.co.uk/film/2008/apr/18/drama.thriller (Accessed 2/3/2001).

Caesar. E., 'Hard acts to follow', *Sunday Times*, 6 April 2008, Culture, http://www.lexisnexis.com/uk/nexis/results/docview/docview.do?docLinkInd=true&risb=21_T17285878182&format=GNBFI&sort=BOOLEAN&startDocNo=126&resultsUrlKey=29_T17285878186&cisb=22_T17285878185&treeMax=true&treeWidth=0&csi=332263&docNo=133 (Accessed 29/4/2013)

Carnevale, R., In an interview with Martin McDonagh, http://www.indielondon.co.uk/Film-Review/in-bruges-martin-mcdonagh-interview (Accessed 2/3/2012)

Dargis, M., 'Hit Men on Holiday Get All Medieval', *New York Times,* 8 April 2008, *http://movies.nytimes.com/2008/02/08/movies/08brug.html* (Accessed 23/3/2011)

French, P., 'In Bruges,' *The Observer*, Sunday 20 April 2008, http://www.guardian.co.uk/film/2008/apr/20/thriller.comedy/(Accessed 23/3/2011)

Landesman, C., 'Review', *The Sunday Times,* April 20, 2008, http://entertainment.timesonline.co.uk/tol/arts_and_entertainment/film/film_reviews/article3758013.ece (Accessed 2/3/2010)

Rocchi, J., 'Sundance Review: *In Bruges*', 18 Jan 2008, http://www.cinematical.com/2008/01/18/sundance-review-in-bruges/ (Accessed 2/3/2010).

Seven Psychopaths

Bradshaw, P., 'Review', *The Guardian*, 6 December 2012, http://www.guardian.co.uk/film/2012/dec/06/seven-psychopaths-review (Accessed 19/12/2012

Clarke, D, 'Psycho thriller', *The Irish Times*, December 2012, http://www.irishtimes.com/newspaper/theticket/2012/1207/1224327589235.html (Accessed 7/12/2012)

------ 'Review', *The Irish Times*, 7 December 2012, http://www.irishtimes.com/newspaper/theticket/2012/1207/1224327585343.html (Accessed 7/12/2012)

French, P., 'Review', *The Observer*, 9 December 2012, http://www.guardian.co.uk/film/2012/dec/09/seven-psychopaths-review-french-mcdonagh (Accessed 19/12/2012)

Godfrey, A., 'Seven Psychopaths: "You can't kill dogs in Hollywood"', *The Guardian*, 1/12/2012, http://www.guardian.co.uk/film/2012/dec/01/seven-psychopaths-martin-mcdonagh?intcmp=239 (Accessed 19/12/2012)

Landesman, C., 'A perfect derangement; Martin McDonagh's Seven Psychopaths turns genre clichés on their head with a cracking cast', *The Sunday Times*, 9 December 2012, p.14.

Utichi, J., 'It's a mad, mad world', *The Sunday Times*, 9 December 2012, pp. 16–17.

Wigley, S. 'Seven Psychopaths: Martin McDonagh interview', *British Film Institute News*, Friday, 7 December 2012 http://www.bfi.org.uk/news-opinion/bfi-news/seven-psychopaths-martin-mcdonagh-interview (Accessed 19/12/2012)

Index